THE TIMES

Guide to

THE NEW BRITISH
STATE

THE GOVERNMENT
MACHINE IN THE 1990s

BY MICHAEL DYNES & DAVID WALKER

TIMES BOOKS
London

First Published by Times Books
77-85 Fulham Palace Road
London W6 8JB

British Library Cataloguing in Publication Data.
A catalogue record for this book is available from
the British Library.

ISBN 0·7230 0687 3

Typeset by Times Books

Printed and bound in Great Britain by
HarperCollins Book Manufacturing, Glasgow

UNITED KINGDOM AREA CODES:
All UK area telephone codes will change from 16th April 1995. Most codes starting
with an 0 will start with 01 instead. An 081 number in London will therefore
change to 0181, and an 0223 Belfast number will start with 01223. There will be
entirely new codes for five cities: Leeds (0532) becomes 01132; Sheffield (0742)
becomes 01142; Nottingham (0602) becomes 01159; Leicester (0533) becomes
01162; Bristol (0272) becomes 01179. The code for making international calls from
the UK will also change on 16th April 1995. The current 010 code prefixing all
international numbers will become 00.

CONTENTS

PREFACE

If it seems astonishing that no comprehensive directory of government exists in the United Kingdom, having spent one year compiling one it is not hard for us to see why. The machinery of state is so vast and so varied that no one has ever properly attempted to track it. Even the Central Office of Information, the executive agency which runs the government's publicity and information machine, does not keep a list of government and non-government organisations. Partial directories are available, such as the *Civil Service Year Book*, the Cabinet Office's *List of Ministerial Responsibilities*, and the annual publication, *Public Bodies*. But these provide only a limited route map for anyone trying to navigate their way around the ship of state. Indeed, basic information such as the names, addresses and telephone numbers of the various organisations and bodies that exercise power over us are often not made available. Moreover, those in central government do not feel it is their responsibility to publish details of the new organisations that have sprung up since the mid-1980s, such as NHS Trusts and grant-maintained schools, which affect us all.

We have attempted to provide such a directory. But we have sought to do much more than that. In addition to listing Whitehall departments, executive agencies, non-ministerial government departments, and non-departmental public bodies or 'quangos', we have also identified the individuals who run those bodies, providing where possible biographical details. Europe, the regions, and the new organisations which have assumed responsibility for many of the key functions traditionally carried out by local government, are subjected to a similar spotlight. Finally, we have attempted to combine the detailed geography of government with an explanation of its origins and its possible destination in the light of the government's public sector reform programme.

We owe thanks to Peter Stothard, the Editor of *The Times*, who has consistently given prominence to the subjects discussed in the pages that follow, and who sanctioned this project; Peter Roberts, Managing Editor, who gave us his encouragement and put *The Times*'s telephones, fax machines, library and data bases at our disposal. Michael Dynes thanks James MacManus, Assistant Editor (Home), who granted time away from daily office duties. David Walker would like to note the positive attitude of Chris Cramer, head of newsgathering, BBC News and Current Affairs, and Peter Mayne, home editor. Our thanks go also to Sir Robin Butler, the Cabinet Secretary, and Head of the Home Civil Service, who, when notified of our proposal to compile a map of the government machine, in the spirit of open government, took a deep breath, and gave us his blessing. Particular mention must be made of the assistance given to us by dozens of press and information officials in 'state' offices in England, Scotland, Wales and Northern Ireland, who helped us track down details of a bewildering variety of government bodies, agencies and organisations, and the people who run them. A similar debt is owed to the staff of the European Commission's offices in London. Without their patience in the face of our incessant requests for more and more information, this book could not have been written.

Michael Dynes and David Walker

5

1
INTRODUCTION

'State' remains an unusual word to use to describe the way Britain is governed. The word still has a foreign ring to it. States are what the French and Germans have. The British, preferring the particular to the general, the concrete to the abstract, simply possess a variety of governing institutions. Conventional wisdom identifies Parliament as the basis of government, and, while acknowledging that many other public bodies are far removed from Westminster and Whitehall, is generally happy to leave definitions and links imprecise.

But valuable though that British tradition of empirical government is, there is a danger that important changes in the way we govern ourselves may be missed or hidden. It seems to us that, increasingly, we need some concept such as 'state' not just to embrace the variety of institutions through which public power is exercised in modern Britain but to try to understand connections and correspondences between them.

Our first purpose, however, is practical. Here is a map. Government has recently expanded, albeit at a time when ministers have been talking about rolling back its frontiers and cutting its spending. While the Conservative government elected in 1979 seems to have stemmed what at the outset appeared an inexorable increase in the share of the national product spent by the government, it has proved extraordinarily difficult to slim the state.

Civil service manpower has undoubtedly been cut, notably in defence, trade and industry and tax assessment and collection. Large-scale transfers of functions from the public to the private sector have taken place, above all in the large-scale privatisation of the nationalised industries. But beyond these areas, how far has government retreated? The Government itself may, for example, have ceased to provide training programmes for young people through the Manpower Services Commission, but it has set up a network of Training and Enterprise Councils which, though they involve private firms and business people in large numbers, depend on public money and exercise a kind of public authority.

Instead of a steady withdrawal, the state has taken new forms. Here new islands have risen from the waves; there the sea has receded leaving unexplored land; elsewhere the waters have covered over some old territory. This book is a chart. Yet even as it is published, the waters are moving, rapidly in the case of the National Health

Service where a new structure of purchasers and providers of health care is being formed. But this is the first public description of the new geography.

It is not an academic treatise. Who the chairman of the Birmingham Training and Enterprise Council is and what he does may not be a constitutional issue, but it matters a great deal to young people and their parents who are anxious about jobs and skills just as it matters to all who might be affected by faster or slower movement in Birmingham's economy, which the Tec is – in theory at least – supposed to affect.

In much the same way, knowing who the Permanent Secretary of the Department of Social Security is, what he has done and where he has come from, matters for those who receive welfare benefits and pensions. It surely ought also to interest all those on whose behalf Sir Michael Partridge accounts for the expenditure of upwards of £80 billion a year. And if we learn about Sir Michael then certainly we need to know a little about the man appointed under him to execute welfare policy, Michael Bichard, chief executive of the Benefits Agency, which is charged with the effective and efficient delivery to millions of people of the Income Support on which they depend.

It is no longer enough to describe the core of government – conventionally termed Whitehall – and leave it there. Despite initial efforts in the Thatcher years to prune the effulgent growth of 'quasi-autonomous' or 'non-departmental' government, they have proved remarkably hardy, and lately indeed have expanded significantly. The number and variety of appointed bodies have grown. Meanwhile, as the result of deliberate government policy, new organisations have been formed at more local level, in housing and education, utilising public money but not directly elected. In health, the Government enacted a major reform which has entailed the creation of a new generation of not-for-profit trusts 'providing' health care which is 'purchased' by a new generation of appointed health authorities at district and regional level.

A question for anyone who reads these pages is: has government been brought closer to the people as a result of recent changes (which include some radical steps in the direction of greater openness at the centre)? Our aim is that all who have dealings with government – most of us at one time or another – will find the information and analysis contained here of some use both in answering the question and acting upon the answer.

Don Cruickshank is an agent of the 'new state'. He is neither a civil servant as conventionally understood, nor does he resemble a private-sector business executive. He is a regulator, the director-general of the Office of Telecommunications. This is the body established at arm's length from the Department of Trade and Industry (which none the less oversees its budget and the appointment of its staff) to supervise phone services after the privatisation of British Telecom. In a recent annual report – the means by which he accounts to public and Parliament for his supervisory work – he stated that for Oftel, 'the focus must be on the customer...customers should get the best possible deal in terms of quality, choice and value for money. The interests of customers as the first priority is closely followed by the national economic interest – although that is consumers again in the end'.

That is rhetoric, and somewhat misleading for Oftel knows there are other interests than those of the producers, including the shareholders of BT and Mercury. Still, the proposition is clear. Much talk in the new state is about giving people who rely on government or government agencies better service, superior treatment as consumers.

A recent survey published by the Benefits Agency – the 'arm's length' organisation established by the Department of Social Security to dispense cash and cheques to successful claimants of Income Support – showed an increase in the 'satisfaction' of customers. The chief executive, Michael Bichard, said the majority of customers (as benefits claimants are now officially designated) have a 'positive experience'. He cited the shorter time taken to provide advice and to answer the telephone.

There is no reason to doubt that the Benefits Agency's pollsters got it right. Since becoming an executive agency of the Department of Social Security it has been making an effort to smarten up its offices and treat its customers/claimants with more respect. In a speech in the autumn of 1993, the head of the Civil Service and putative head of the public service at large, Sir Robin Butler, identified a number of trends in public service management in the United Kingdom and linked them with movements in the United States as well as New Zealand and Australia that amounted – he coined the title of a recent book – 'to reinventing government'.

'The pressures which political forces bring to bear on democratic governments to find ways of delivering better public services at no greater cost to the taxpayer are too obvious to require elaboration. Those forces are at work in every country of the developed world. They will apply whichever political party is in power.'

In Britain, too, it is 'steer not row' that the cox is crying: public authorities (ministers, civil servants, councillors) should no longer themselves be providing services but should delegate provision to, or purchase services from, agencies or contractors. This inevitably has meant the delegation of a good deal of management control to those agencies and greater use of the private sector to provide public services. Yet we need to retain some sense that both the purchasers and the providers are working within the public interest, and that is where the notion of a 'state' may be useful.

One of the principal war cries of Prime Minister John Major on the domestic front has been the Citizen's Charter, unveiled in 1993. This, the Government hopes, is more than a document listing ways in which people can complain about poor performance in public services. It was, at least at first, intended to rally public servants and encourage them to reinvent themselves. The goal is more effective (and economical) response to the demands of the public.

One of the principal tools for this, as envisaged by the Conservative government, has been to subject public provision to a test: could the private sector do better and cheaper? In local government this process is known as compulsory (because the Government insists on it) competitive tendering; in central government and its agencies the catchword is market testing.

In his speech Sir Robin Butler – a master craftsman of nuance and political subtlety – was being a little disingenuous in lauding the American book, *Reinventing*

Government. Yes, it did extol entrepreneurial government and urged extensive use of the private sector to carry out functions stipulated by local authorities and other tiers of government. It also foresaw the birth of a new class of enterprising public servants adopting the methods and style of successful private business, trying to offer greater choice. But, being American, it also argued for greater freedom for local (and 'sub-national') authorities to do things differently both one from another and differently from the central or federal government. It urged the central government to keep its hands off local experiments and argued strongly for local diversity.

That, however, is not the British way. In Britain the Government has sought to keep control, especially control of spending. The power of the Treasury, as the controller of spending, has reached new peaks. The official auditors of spending have grown in number and influence and that has tended, necessarily, to suggest there is always one right way of doing things. Strains and stresses have shown as the centre has apparently encouraged managers of public services to be more creative but at the same time sought to corral their spending.

There is no point in pretending that reform of the machinery of the government will prevent bad or controversial policy being made. In April 1994, celebration of the first year of the Child Support Agency (CSA) was all but drowned in criticism from left and right about its purposes and operations. Was this a question of the wrong machinery? Could the Government have saved itself from the political flak it has taken over the Agency if it had thought harder about how it was going to be managed?

The CSA is an executive agency of the Department of Social Security. Most such agencies do relatively uncontentious tasks, such as dispensing drivers' licences. Some people have argued there is very little that is controversial about the CSA's main goals, for example, 'to deliver on behalf of children a fair and effective service for the assessment of payment of maintenance and ensure that parents maintain their children whenever they can afford to do so'.

What seemed to have gone wrong at the CSA's birth was the rigidity of the formula devised to collect money. To meet managerial targets the formula allowed no room to recognise the multitude of personal circumstances of men, women and children moving apart. The targets gave the CSA no incentive to take a more balanced approach. How far were those very harsh targets the product of an excessive desire on the part of the Treasury to keep controls tight, to squeeze while at the same time apparently encouraging managerial freedoms?

Ros Hepplewhite, the CSA's first chief executive, who resigned in September 1994, following a barrage of criticism, was one of the new breed of agency chiefs who have come into government service from the outside. She lacked the political antennae which civil servants grow as they advise ministers on policy. An irony is that failure to liaise with ministers earlier on – because of an over-rigid adoption of Next Steps theory – resulted in ministers becoming involved in detail in subsequent decisions by the agency.

While managerial reform has been enthusiastically pursued in the health service, on the periphery of the state, the application of managerial disciplines at the very heart of the government has been resisted. It is an old observation in Whitehall that the Treasury itself is the one department where doorkeepers have not been contracted out. And as government has become more diverse, the centre has failed to keep up and, for example, acquire new means of co-ordinating policies across different departments. At the very heart of the centre, in the private offices belonging to ministers, problems have emerged. How can a minister know what is happening among these new bodies, staffed by active managers, let alone account for it to Parliament?

And yet what is there except Parliamentary accountability to ensure the public interest is maintained: the British Constitution, that great unwritten document, allows nobody other than a minister standing at the dispatch box in the House of Commons (only rarely these days the Lords) and answering questions lobbed at him or her by Members.

Some observers of the core have started to ask whether there is a constitutional crisis in the making. Look, they say, at the ambiguities in the minister's role uncovered by Lord Justice Scott's inquiry into the sale of defence and 'dual-use' equipment to Iraq. At the time of writing the judge's conclusions have yet to be published. But the evidence taken seems to show that no one is convincingly clear any more just what it is ministers are supposed to do, and how they are meant to relate to the great machinery of state they are nominally in charge of. Do they take the advice of their officials without demur?

Whom do they ask in order to check officials' advice? What responsibility can they possibly take for agencies and bodies not just at arm's length but at a stone's throw distance? Professor Peter Hennessy quotes a remark of the Victorian Prime Minister William Gladstone, to the effect that the British Constitution presumes 'more boldly than any other the good faith of those who work it'. But what if that good faith is in decreasing supply? Has the time come to start writing down in black and white what civil servants' jobs are – for no such document yet exists?

Other countries, notably New Zealand, have travelled an interesting distance down the road of attempting to specify in much more detail than ever before what government employs people to do, including top people. There, ministers establish the outcome they desire, then buy outputs from their departments on the basis of written contracts.

This *Times Guide* is offered as a reminder of what government personnel do – who they are, where they are to be found, and telephoned. We start, as we must, with the core of the state, the collection of departments colloquially called Whitehall, after the famous London thoroughfare on which still stand the 'core of the core' – the Treasury, the Cabinet Office and Number 10 Downing Street. Although the modern British state is ostensibly very powerful, one of its paradoxes is how weak these innermost departments can sometimes appear. They may control purse-strings and broad-gauge policy but it is the substantive departments which carry the policy into effect, or not. A minister in the Cabinet Office can ordain a full-blooded programme of market testing in departments but departmental ministers may be luke-warm, their permanent

11

secretaries may drag their feet and the programme shrinks and slows. The Treasury may end the Public Expenditure round in triumph having secured great reductions in estimated spending, but a political drama (sometimes carefully rehearsed) saves the department's bacon, and the threatened expenditure remains in the budget.

The British state is weakly co-ordinated. There is, it is true, a network of committees spanning the departments which carry recommendations to the Cabinet but there exists little by way of machinery to ensure that once a decision affecting more than one department is taken at the centre it is followed through. One of Whitehall's most striking attributes is how civil servants can at one and the same time share a common culture and – sometimes – move between departments on promotions and transfers while fighting like cats over a policy which goes against departmental tradition or interest.

But departments have lately been subdividing. We describe the way in which since the late 1980s they have been encouraged to identify blocks of work which could be 'hived off' to new agencies. These remain part of the Civil Service yet, if they look plump and juicy, may become candidates for privatisation. Each has its chief executive, and some of these reformed civil servants (such as Mike Fogden, chief executive of the large Employment Service Agency) have acquired a public persona, at odds with the traditional image of Civil Service reticence. The accountability of these agencies has been exercising Members of Parliament. Some MPs resist the efforts of ministers to have agencies respond directly to inquiries and complaints, apparently cherishing the myth that ministers are personally responsible for (and so know about) what goes on in their administrative departments.

Departments have also been creative in their use of non-departmental public bodies. This is a common yet exotic species in the zoology of public administration in Britain. Common because there are hundreds upon hundreds of such bodies, advising, reporting, monitoring and executing; exotic because even finding a single term to describe them is extremely difficult, so protean are their legal and administrative personalities. After advertising her intention to cull the creatures, and succeeding in cutting the population, Mrs Thatcher began from the mid-1980s on to find jobs which, apparently, only new non-departmental public bodies could do, and their numbers started to grow again.

In the public's mind 'quango' is a useful catch-all, which has come to encompass a new generation of public body, created in recent years on the express instructions of the Government, often as a way of circumventing or even altogether replacing elected local authorities. Grant-maintained schools, self-governing colleges of further education, housing action trusts are examples of what we are here calling the 'new state'. Ministers strive to make a distinction between them and quangos, emphasising that they are rooted in local communities, even if their membership is often selected by central government and may only include local people if it suits those officials and ministers in the core departments who make the appointments.

But 'quango' is a poor description of yet another new class of public bodies which needs to be noted, bodies that together form the 'regulatory' or the 'audit' state. New bodies were created specially to oversee the prices charged by the privatised gas, electricity and water utilities, because they are monopolies; but the departments which set them up seem to have been taken by surprise by the imaginative use of regulatory powers by those appointed, for example Sir Bryan Carsberg, the former director-general of the Office of Telecommunications. Another regulating and auditing body, the Audit Commission for Local Government and the Health Service, created a role for itself perhaps larger than the Department of the Environment, its progenitor, had envisaged.

In addition to the 'new state', there exists outside the core departments, umbilically linked to them, an extensive regional apparatus of government. Outside the sphere of the elected local authorities in several of the larger cities there are small civil service empires. The arms of the Department of Trade and Industry stretch from Penzance to Newcastle-upon-Tyne, in the form of offices offering advice under the Enterprise Initiative and other programmes; the Department of Employment is also strongly represented in the regions. Outside the core in a physical sense are the three great 'national' departments of state, the Scottish, Welsh and Northern Irish Offices, each commanding a host of non-departmental public bodies.

No account of the state in the 1990s would be complete without reference to the presence within the United Kingdom of, and the United Kingdom's presence in, the European Union. And no account of the state can perhaps ever be complete. Should it include the state church, for much to do with the Anglican Church in England obeys rules and procedures remarkably similar to those which govern Civil Service and other secular bureaucracies? Is the Bank of England not equivalent to an executive agency of the Treasury, despite its long and separate history? Where do we place those genuine agencies of the Treasury, the Inland Revenue and Customs and Excise which none the less possess legal duties and responsibilities that set them apart from the mainstream Civil Service? Certain other functions – the collection of statistics, the registration of births and deaths – are vital to the functioning of this or any other state and deserve to be noted separately from the core departments to which they technically belong.

This, then, cannot be a complete guide to the modern British state. It cannot take in, for example, the remarkable use made by the state in recent years of management consultants. No one can plausibly suggest that, say, Price Waterhouse or Coopers Lybrand has as a result become a branch of the state, yet a substantial slice of their revenues comes from state work; their consultants possess intimate knowledge of how aspects of the state work; some of them are de facto civil servants. So much do they resemble civil servants that a scrutiny of their contributions to Whitehall in the summer of 1994 said that £130 million could be saved over three years if the contracts awarded to them were tightened up.

This is necessarily a snapshot taken from a moving vehicle. As mentioned before, further, substantial changes in the organisation of the health service are in

13

train as we go to press, as the health authorities and the family health service authorities merge into 'unitary' purchasing bodies, contracting with hospital trusts and fund-holding general practitioners for care plans. The reorganisation of schooling into large numbers of grant-maintained schools allocated grants by a central Funding Agency while many schools are still maintained by local education authorities is incomplete. The reorganisation of social rented housing with the transfer of stock from local authority control into the hands of not-for-profit housing associations has barely begun.

2
THE CORE OF THE STATE

Searching for the core of the British state is, like the pursuit of the British Constitution, an exercise in the hunting of the snark. One moment it is visible – in 'Whitehall', that convenient expression for the mainstream Civil Service, functioning in such departments as the Home Office and Treasury. The next it is gone, lost in that Sargasso Sea between the executive and the legislature, in Parliament. Even within Whitehall, there is no single 'centre'. To describe, say, Number 10 Downing Street as the top of the pyramid of power from which orders go out to departments would be to miss, for example, the peculiar power of the Treasury not just over spending but over Civil Service appointments.

Various metaphors can be applied. British government is like a dance, a quadrille in which the participating groups exercise figures in the middle of the floor but never entirely give up their independent identities. British government is a competition in which, one side never finally gaining complete mastery, the contending forces advance and retreat. More cosily, the American academics Hugh Heclo and Aaron Wildavsky called Whitehall a village in which post is delivered and everyone is on first name terms while underneath, as in Ambridge, there is backbiting and name-calling.

Here we identify the partners in the dance and give some examples of how they come together, acknowledging all the while that describing one part or even several parts may still not amount to a fully satisfactory description of the whole.

There are some obvious markers of the central territory of the modern British state. One is the department, both very old such as the Home Office and new, such as Trade and Industry. Departments exist independently of the politicians who come, from time to time, to occupy their ministerial suites. It is striking how, for all the changes made in the state in recent years, the basic geography of departmental government remains recognisably what it was in 1979, or indeed 1969.

A second dancing partner is the minister of the Crown, a role undefined in law and subject to the widest differences in interpretation by its occupants. During recent years, the formal power – discretion – of ministers seems to have grown. In two famous statements of Civil Service duties in the 1980s, Sir Robert Armstrong and his successor as head of the Civil Service, Sir Robin Butler, said more or less that civil servants existed to do the bidding of their ministers: when asked to jump only to respond 'how high?'. The unfolding evidence presented to Lord Justice Scott's inquiring into the sale of defence equipment to Iraq has convinced many observers this doctrine is a dangerous one if it prevents civil servants ever raising objections to ministers' actions, even if they include misleading Parliament.

But there are checks and balances of a kind. A third element in the core is the Civil Service itself, or rather the existence at the top of that institution of a cross-departmental network of job openings, training and 'common culture'. This is the so-called Open Structure, through which in principle top jobs in departments are open to civil servants from other departments – but rarely to people from outside the Civil Service. The 1994 White Paper on the future of the Civil Service – supposedly representing the fruit of the Major government's reflections – hesitated over this question. Some jobs, but it is not clear how many, are to be opened to external appointments, but the Civil Service's 'fast stream' is to be retained and the high flyers will still be offered a pathway to the top.

A fourth element in the core is those institutions in the state that consciously look across the whole and seek to co-ordinate. The Treasury is responsible for the totality of public expenditure and snoops. The Cabinet Office has formal responsibility for those committees of ministers and officials set up under the auspices of the Cabinet to deliver policies which cross-cut between departments. In addition we need to note a variety of organisations, some more formal than others, that range across the centre of the state: the semi-formal network of government press officers in the Government Information Service, the National Audit Office which technically services the Public Accounts Committee of the House of Commons. Then there are the various parts of the secret state, notably the Security Service and the Secret Intelligence Service. Although MI5 answers to the Home Office and MI6 to the Foreign Office, by history and convention their senior officers have access to Prime Minister and the Cabinet both in their own names and through such central bodies as the Cabinet's Joint Intelligence Committee.

THE SENIOR OPEN STRUCTURE

In terms of its people, the core of the British state is the 600 posts above the rank of 'principal', or Grade 7 and, even more tightly defined, the 'Senior Open Structure', the civil servants ranked at Grade 3 (Under-Secretary) and above. The chieftains are the Permanent Secretaries who maintain the machine and the Deputy Secretaries who provide the bulk of detailed policy advice to ministers; the workhorses of the British system of political administration are the Under-Secretaries or Grade 3s.

These jobs are distributed among the departments which are listed in this chapter. In 1994 the Government announced its conclusions on what should happen to Whitehall's common spine – it is to stay, though more effort is to be devoted to recruitment from outside Whitehall into top positions. It looks as though most of the next generation's top people are to be recruited, as now, through the Civil Service Selection Board and its legendary procedures for testing their social and political as well as intellectual mettle. Though Civil Service training is not formal, officials will tend to come together on courses at the Civil Service College, and on two programmes for those deemed to be high-flying, the Node and the Top Management Programme.

Recruitment to the upper ranks of the Civil Service is regulated by Civil Service Commissioners, created in the mid-nineteenth century by the Northcote-Trevelyan reforms to stop Palmerston and his colleagues appointing their nephews to clerk for the Foreign Office. The need for this kind of supervision of recruitment is nowadays in some doubt. Palmerston's descendant as Foreign Secretary, Douglas Hurd –who did in fact begin his own career as a Foreign Office clerk – is extremely unlikely to harbour the ambition of appointing his nephew; he and his Cabinet colleagues might well think he would be better off doing something more lucrative in the City.

In 1991 the Government reorganised recruitment – allowing departments and their agencies to recruit more of their own executive as well as clerical staff instead of having to use the old Civil Service Commission. The old Commission was broken up into a semi-autonomous Recruitment and Assessment Services Agency (anyone who has ever applied for a Civil Service job will remember their address in Alençon Link, Basingstoke) and – based in the Cabinet Office – a small group of 20 staff. This is centred around the First Commissioner, graded at Deputy Secretary level, Ann Bowtell, plus a team of part-time monitoring staff, one full-time and four part-time commissioners.

Procedure is guaranteed according to a set of ministerial rules laid down in 1991 to replace the volume of detailed instructions under the Civil Service Order in Council (the nearest thing we have in Britain to a set of rules for how the Civil Service should behave). The rules state that all prospective applicants for Civil Service jobs should be given a reasonable opportunity to 'become aware of the vacancies and terms'; all eligible applicants 'must be considered equally on merit'; all selection criteria 'must be reliable, valid and relevant to the jobs concerned'.

In Whitehall these days there are some 3,000 separate points at which people are recruited into the Civil Service. Ann Bowtell says that as such delegation of decision-making goes on, so the need for external monitoring of standards has grown, and that is where the Commissioners come in. But nobody is standing over the shoulder of managers in a private-sector company such as Marks and Spencer – which like every one else has to obey the law of the land on equality and fairness for ethnic groups and women, and rules of natural justice in appointments. It is assumed that organisations anxious to succeed can generally be relied upon to seek out the best candidates.

Basing recruitment on the principle of merit, the Civil Service has striven in recent years to present itself as a modern employer concerned for equal opportunities. Special effort has been put into recruitment from Britain's ethnic minorities, and women's conditions of employment in Whitehall, for example concerning child-bearing and returning to work, are relatively generous. However the senior ranks remain predominantly male and white. The sociology and gender of the core of the state has not changed a great deal in recent years. In the Open Structure women are sparse, forming around 9 per cent – though the Cabinet Office is committed to raising this to 15 per cent by the turn of the century. There are few females at the head of substantial Civil Service departments – among them Valerie Strachan at HM Customs and Excise, Barbara Mills at the Director of Public Prosecutions and Stella Rimington at the Security Service. The over-representation of the Clarendon public schools and the Universities of Oxford and Cambridge, let alone the smarter colleges there, was and remains legendary.

Some people have associated the relative failure of women to penetrate the top ranks with the persistence of a 'courtier' culture in which 'club' and 'social' skills are as important as any expertise or formal knowledge. It is more these social skills than rational, intellectual skills that young civil servants exhibit as they participate in the (male) network. Sue Richards of the Public Management Foundation has argued that women, as outsiders, are regarded as unclubbable.

Training, recruitment and promotions are in the province of the Cabinet Office which can fairly claim to be the conscience and the mainstay of the idea of a unified Civil Service. It is the Cabinet Office's Senior Appointments Selection Committee (SASC) which keeps up lists of eligible candidates for promotion, up to and including Permanent Secretary jobs which are allocated according to a Byzantine procedure overseen by the Head of the Home Civil Service and Cabinet Secretary, Sir Robin Butler. The Permanent Secretary is the head of the department, usually the person who formally accounts for its expenditure to the Public Accounts Committee, that crucial yet curiously impotent body connecting the will of the people expressed in Parliament and policy outcomes, expressed in the quantity and quality of public money spent.

Permanent Secretaries come in two different types. One is the expert, who may have been promoted through a department and knows its policies and clients in a lifetime's detail. The other type is the Permanent Secretary who has been drafted in, either when a minister changes or because the 'centre' considers it time for a promotion or a change of scene. For centre, read Sir Robin Butler and the Senior Appointments Selection Committee.

The Open Structure exists, constitutionally speaking, to provide a service to government ministers most of whom have departmental portfolios. Civil servants can apparently both answer a minister directly and without hesitation while at the same time keeping an eye on wider Whitehall and Civil Service issues, like for example his or her promotion prospects. It is rare for civil servants to climb to the top of the tree having remained throughout their careers in a single department. That means they need to garner experience in other departments and especially in the two central departments of Whitehall, the Treasury and the Cabinet Office. But these have a vested interest in the mainstream departments and their ministers not being too autonomous: their officials need to play two ends against the middle.

THE MINISTER

There is a puzzle underneath the changes in management and structure in the state described here. If much government work is being handed over to semi-autonomous agencies, to quangos and appointed bodies; if the Civil Service is being cut back; if much former government work is being contracted out to the private sector or privatised altogether, one conclusion ought to be inescapable. There ought to be less work to be done at the centre. Ministers, in other words, should have an easier life. If, as every appearance indicates, ministers are as busy now as they ever were, if their every waking moment is filled with engagements political and administrative, what does that say about the nature of recent changes in the state?

It would be odd if all those changes did not entail some reduction in the minister's workload. Hard evidence, for example an estimate of the hours ministers put in, does not exist for the simple reason that this key role is one of the least studied and understood. Sir Peter Kemp, the civil servant formerly in charge of the Next Steps programme, says 'We've not had enough debate about the role of the Permanent Secretary or about the role of the minister. What has happened is that in empowering the Chief Executive of agencies we have forgotten if you like to disempower the Permanent Secretary and we've forgotten to look at where that leaves the minister'.

This is curious. On the one side are managers and executives whose outputs (so the theory of new management says) are now measurable and whose jobs can be minutely specified. On the other, the ministers. When was the last time a minister was promoted or sacked because he or she was an effective or ineffective manager of the administration, or even an imaginative deviser of policy? Ministers come and go, usually at the whim of the Prime Minister, sometimes because the media will it, regardless of their managerial competence. Management, in other words, has not superseded politics.

This means that at the heart of the management reform process in Whitehall there is a black hole. William Waldegrave, the former Chancellor of the Duchy of Lancaster and minister responsible for public services, says 'the freeing of ministers from some of the administrative tasks which they're not very well suited for gives them more time'. But more time for what?

Since most government activity is carried out in the name of a minister, the core of each department is the Private Office which organises the minister's life. Whitehall's holy of holies, the axis on which the career Civil Service turns, is presenting and packaging advice to ministers. Ministers can have a few special advisers; private contractors can take on some of the executive work; but even in the heat of the Thatcher years it was the core Civil Service, the top administrators alone, who specified the policy to be executed in detail and ensured it was legislated and implemented. But they have access to the minister only through the Private Office.

It is little wonder that Private Office jobs are regarded as the pathway to promotion. Indeed, one of the most intense rivalries in some departments has been between the Private Office and the Permanent Secretary who him or herself must join the queue of supplicants to see the minister. And the queue itself is regulated or even instigated by the Private Office.

A misleadingly simple way of seeing how the core department is organised is to think of the minister – and some do indeed picture themselves in this way – as le Roi Soleil. Around him (Sun Queens are rare) civil servants and advisers spread out in Olympic rings. Closest to the minister are special advisers, usually recruited as temporary civil servants, albeit at low grades. The most prominent special advisers are those in the Number 10 Policy Unit headed by the former journalist Sarah Hogg and those individuals, such as Tessa Keswick adviser to the Chancellor of the Exchequer, Kenneth Clarke, who have moved with their minister through a succession of departments acquiring on their way considerable knowledge of the machine.

NUMBER 10 AND NUMBER 11

Whitehall has three centres at the centre. These are the departments of state which function as co-ordinators of policy and expenditure. Physically, the centre is the group of offices around the Prime Minister's official residence at Number 10 Downing Street, and the official address of the minister who is usually, in Cabinet terms, his nearest rival or strongest supporter, the Chancellor of the Exchequer. At the back of Number 10 – in locational terms – and a perennial rival of the Treasury is the Cabinet Office, nowadays expanded into a substantive department in its own right, including responsibilities for government computing and science. The heart of the Cabinet Office is the secretariat, little changed in function or in style since it was created by Lloyd George in response to the massive expansion of state activity during the First World War.

The Treasury and Number 10 are enigmatic departments. Visitors to Number 10 are often shocked by its tiny size, and the domestic nature of arrangements there. It divides, sometimes ambiguously, between providing a political service to an incumbent Prime Minister and serving as the ultimate source of administrative decision-making, delivering to the system the wit and wisdom of the Prime Minister.

The Chancellor's department is the Treasury, which in a number of subtle and overt ways exercises command and control functions throughout Whitehall. Through its control of public expenditure, through the network of economic advisers, through its role in monitoring and enforcing value for money and efficiency measures within departments, Treasury civil servants do appear on paper to possess, position for position, more power than their departmental colleagues. That, of course, is too simple a way of describing what turns out to be a war of skirmishes and attrition in which the Treasury, for all its vaunted reputation for intelligence, often has to rely on the departments for information.

The clever chaps of the Treasury – women are few and far between in Great George Street – had a good decade under Mrs Thatcher. They have not, it is true, got all their forecasts right and macroeconomic policy advice has had its ups and downs, but on the central terrain of public expenditure control, the Prime Minister's instincts and the Treasury's ethos knitted nicely together. A cynic might even say that a good deal of new management-mindedness in the Civil Service these days is no more or less than the product of years of tight Treasury controls on departmental manpower and spending. But for all that, it seems the Treasury worships only two of the three household gods enshrined at Number 10 Downing Street – economy, efficiency and effectiveness. Economy means cutting down. Efficiency means minimising what you put in for a given output. But effectiveness can mean asking whether enough is being spent, and that can give the Treasury indigestion.

Assessing effectiveness could lead one into deep waters. From the right one could argue that much of government is ineffective, just as from the left there is an argument that the effectiveness of much the state does is reduced by inadequate spending. In principle the Treasury does not flinch at such judgements: it is all in favour of 'policy evaluation'. And yet the radical ideas on revamping policy during the past ten years have tended not to come from the Treasury. It has been rather passive in its thinking about the shape of Whitehall and the functions of government, contenting itself with ensuring the existing machine is made cheaper. That is no inconsiderable task but focusing on it has perhaps left the Treasury curiously unprepared for the decade ahead. Government is not ceasing to take an interest in private business, either: the growth of the regulatory state (in the shape of offices monitoring telecommunications, gas, electricity and water and boards overseeing activity from financial services to aviation) has been rapid, and yet the Treasury's role in it oddly marginal. The Treasury's song is the need for continuous – unending – review of what the Whitehall departments, their quangos and their agencies think they are doing, and whether what they do could be done better and more cheaply. That has come, in recent years, to mean done outside government either by contractors or by privatisation. Similar inquiries are undertaken, sometimes in parallel, sometimes overlapping, by the Cabinet Office and by the Efficiency Unit, a small group currently headed by the former industrialist Sir Peter Levene, which while located in the Cabinet Office has a reporting line to the Prime Minister.

The Cabinet Office is a peculiar department, simultaneously weak and strong. Locked in old rivalry with the Treasury over who manages the Civil Service itself, the Cabinet Office sometimes appears to be less of a nerve-centre in Whitehall than a post office. The Cabinet Office, for example, holds responsibility for the Chessington computer centre (now an executive agency) which prepares civil servants' pay slips. But how much they get paid is decided by the Treasury; meanwhile the qualities they bring to their jobs are under the purview of the Office of Public Services and Science (part of the Cabinet Office). The Cabinet Office is responsible, in a broad sense, for Civil Service training, especially at the Civil Service College. The College is one of the few institutions which is, more or less formally, charged with instilling in civil servants a sense that they do belong to a single 'culture' rather than separate, often competing departments. The Cabinet Office, in other words, holds the key to one of Whitehall's higher mysteries: how civil servants can simultaneously serve departments and ministers yet retain some conception of a wider entity, called variously the Crown, or the state, or Whitehall which may require from them different loyalties.

The Cabinet Office is home to the Efficiency Unit, theoretically an important source of co-ordination across Whitehall. Established in Mrs Thatcher's glory days, the Unit was initially a rather glamorous place where bright young men and women, led by the Marks and Spencer's chief Lord (Derek) Rayner, swooped on departments examining their costs and efficiency. Quieter times have succeeded. The 'catalysing' effect of the Unit on Whitehall seems, in retrospect, to have been less than the expenditure savings of more than a billion a year that were being claimed in the mid-1980s. The Rayner model was that the thirst for efficiency savings would establish itself within departments and the unit would act as an internal Whitehall consultancy. Perhaps in retrospect the forces of inertia have proved to be stronger than the radical scrutineers of the early 1980s could have imagined.

THE SECRET CENTRE

In theory the various intelligence agencies report up a line to the Cabinet through what are coyly called 'central mechanisms', based in the Cabinet Office. Political control of the intelligence community is exercised partly by the Prime Minister directly, partly through a Ministerial Committee on the Intelligence Services (coded IS) whose brief is 'to keep under review policy on the security and intelligence services'. The clean lines of the organisation chart are thrown into disarray by the traditional access that the respective heads of the Security Service MI5 and the Secret Intelligence Service MI6 have to Number 10 and the Prime Minister via the Cabinet Secretary. Matters of security involving Members of Parliament, or the Royal Family may be directly referred to the Prime Minister. The Home Secretary (MI5) and the Foreign Secretary (MI6 and the Government Communications Headquarters) also have bilateral relationships with the intelligence agencies. The IS Committee is chaired by the Prime Minister; other members are the Home Secretary, Foreign Secretary, Chancellor of the Exchequer and the 'Minister for Open Government', the Chancellor of the Duchy of Lancaster.

The central intelligence mechanisms consist primarily of the Joint Intelligence Committee, supervised by the Permanent Secretaries' Committee on the Intelligence Services (PSIS). The Permanent Secretaries scrutinise expenditure. The JIC meets weekly and comprises civil servants from the Foreign and Commonwealth Office, the Ministry of Defence, and the Treasury; other Whitehall departments attend as appropriate. The heads of the three intelligence-gathering outfits also attend along with the Chief of the Assessments Staff, whose job is to draft inter-departmental reports on situations of specific concern (such as the former Yugoslavia). Formerly reporting to the Chiefs of Staff of the Armed Forces, and still empowered to provide special assessments solely for military use, the JIC was brought into the Cabinet Office in the 1950s. Since the late 1960s there has also existed – in parallel – an Intelligence Co-ordinator based in the Cabinet Office and acting as adviser to the PSIS.

The chairman of the JIC is a key player. The position belonged until the Falklands War to the Foreign Office since when it has been a Cabinet Office fiefdom. Until the end of 1993 the position was held by Sir Rodric Braithwaite, who was succeeded briefly by Pauline Neville-Jones and then Paul Lever in 1994 The JIC is the purchaser of intelligence, collated in its weekly survey, the Red Book. It lets ministers know what is happening 'at agreed intervals' and liaises 'as appropriate' with the Central Intelligence Agency and other foreign but friendly intelligence operations.

The providers of intelligence are what are called by Whitehall the Agencies. These employ some 10,700 people at an annual cost (in 1994-5) of £881 million.

There are four:

1 THE SECURITY SERVICE, MI5

PO Box 3255

London SW1P 1AE

Director-General: Stella Rimington

Since 1989 the Security Service has operated on the basis of public law, the Security Service Act which, paradoxically, makes it more visible in a legal sense than much of the home Civil Service, which operates on a rag-bag of statute and administrative law, codification of which is long overdue.

Having begun life as a counter-espionage agency (directed against the Germans), MI5's raison d'etre became the monitoring and countering of Communist subversion. MI5 is the domestic security and intelligence agency. Its official purpose 'is to protect the State against substantial, covertly organized threats, primarily from terrorism, espionage and subversion'.

At home its job is to investigate threats by gathering and analysing intelligence; to counter threats; and to advise the Government on threats and protective measures. MI5 has no police powers; its operational arm for the purposes of arrest and prosecution is usually the Special Branch of the Metropolitan Police.

Stella Rimington, the Director of the Security Service, was appointed in Feburary 1991 in what was an unprecedented fanfare of publicity. In her foreword to the booklet *The Security Service* (HMSO 1993, £4.95), Mrs Rimington said she wanted to put the facts of its work before the public 'in order to dispose of some of the more fanciful allegations surrounding its work'. MI5 is moving to new headquarters at Thames House on Millbank, being constructed at a cost of £265 million.

MI5 is under the authority of the Home Secretary. MI5 employs some 2,200 people of whom just over half are female. Much work is clerical. MI5's General Intelligence Group, with 340 people, does the investigating, assessment and policy work.

2 THE SECRET INTELLIGENCE SERVICE, MI6

PO Box 1300

London SE1 1BD

Chief: Sir Colin McColl

A prisoner of history in more ways than one, the head of MI6 signs himself 'C' for no better reason than that the bureaucratic infighter under whom SIS was carved out of the Edwardian Secret Service Bureau did so – he was Sir Mansfield Cumming, a reserve naval commander. During the Second World War, SIS grew an operational arm in the Special Operations Executive. Among its famed exploits was the plan to degrade the fighting spirit of the Japanese by firing hollow shells behind their lines containing photographs of nude Home Office librarians.

SIS has been headed since 1988 by Sir Colin McColl though that has only been a matter of public knowledge since 1992, when Prime Minister John Major avowed the agency's existence. Under the Secret Intelligence Bill published in November 1993, SIS is placed on a statutory footing parallel to that of the Security Service. The Bill provides for a Commissioner to oversee its activities and a tribunal to investigate complaints.

The main function of SIS is 'the production of secret intelligence in support of Her Majesty's security, defence, foreign and economic policies'. Officially it does this through 'a variety of sources, human and technical, and by liaison with a wide range of foreign intelligence and security services'. SIS employs around 2,300 staff. The Chief of SIS is responsible to the Foreign Secretary. For a secret service, SIS has very visible, very new and grandiose headquarters at Vauxhall, which cost some £93 million to build.

3 GOVERNMENT COMMUNICATIONS HEADQUARTERS (GCHQ)

Priors Road
Cheltenham
Gloucs GL52 5AJ
0242-221491

Director: Sir John Adye

GCHQ began life as the Government Code and Cipher School, which covered itself in glory during the Second World War for its work in breaking German signalling codes. It is a 'signals intelligence' (sigint) organisation – concerned with tracking and analysing communications of all kinds but using mechanical rather than human means to listen in. For this purpose it controls the Composite Signals Organisation, which operates from a number of locations throughout the UK and overseas. GCHQ also advises the Government and the Armed Forces on the security of communications and information technology. Its Communications Electronics Security Group – keeping in close contact with private industry – seeks to ensure official information is protected. GCHQ moved in 1953 to a complex of buildings in the suburbs of Cheltenham. It currently employs 6,200 staff.

Thanks in part to a prolonged struggle over the recognition of trade unions there, the existence of GCHQ has long been officially acknowledged.

4 DEFENCE INTELLIGENCE STAFF

Main Building
Ministry of Defence
London SW1 2HB
071-218 3137

Chief of Defence Intelligence: Sir John Walker

The DIS is part of the Ministry of Defence, created in the early 1960s from the three service intelligence staffs and the civilian Joint Intelligence Bureau. Its task is to analyse information from a variety of sources, non military as well as military.

Under both Margaret Thatcher and John Major, significant steps have been taken to open out the intelligence community to greater public and parliamentary inspection. Until the Security Service Act of 1989, MI5 operated on a flimsy Directive issued to the Director General by the Home Secretary Sir David Maxwell Fyfe in 1952. That Act and the Intelligence Services Bill, which covers GCHQ as well as MI6, give the agencies legal personalities for the first time and put the intelligence community on a formal footing allowing Parliamentary scrutiny. The Intelligence Services Bill proposes oversight of all three agencies by a committee of Parliamentarians drawn from the House of Commons and the House of Lords; they would examine spending and policy and report annually to the Prime Minister. 'Sensitive material' would be censored from this report.

HOLDING IT TOGETHER

The centre of the state is held together by a network of committees and cross-departmental bodies, ranging from the professional groupings of statisticians and information officers to the financial regulators of the National Audit Office. One way in which Whitehall holds together is through the committees and sub-committees of the Cabinet on which senior ministers sit to draft legislation and deal with government's on-going problems. The principal committees are those on economic and domestic policy and on defence and overseas, which are chaired by the Prime Minister. The committee on the intelligence services, also chaired by the Prime Minister, brings together the Foreign Secretary, Home Secretary, Chancellor of the Exchequer and Chancellor of the Duchy of Lancaster, with the Lord President of the Council and Attorney General attending 'as appropriate'. The Chancellor heads the important Committee on Public Expenditure coded EDX. The Environment Secretary chairs the sub-committee on London, while the Employment Secretary – a man, at time of writing – chairs the sub-comittees on Women's issues. The full list of these central organisations is disparate. Some cross-cut departmental responsibility; others seem to exist in a sort of administrative limbo, co-ordinating only within their sphere of interest rather than within a general scheme for co-ordinating government work. For example, the Department of the Environment, inheritor of the functions undertaken by the old Ministry of Work and the Property Services Agency (much of which has now been privatised), still manages and leases property on behalf of other departments according to complicated arrangements for notional repayments to and from the Treasury depending on the length and age of the lease.

Just as the Chief Executive of the Central Office of Information is also head of the Government Information Officers' professional group (which is managed by a unit based in the Cabinet Office) so the Director of the Central Statistical Office is head of the Government Statistical Service, responsible for example for the reliability of official numbers across all departments. The Government's Chief Accountancy Adviser is based in the Treasury but is also head of the Government Accountancy Service, responsible for the conduct of accountants throughout Whitehall. Her Majesty's Stationery Office, now an executive agency, operates centrally as the supplier of office services and publishing to many departments; in addition, as the Hansard Press, it prints much of the paperwork of Parliament.

Once a week, in a room somewhere in that labyrinth of offices behind the right angle formed by Whitehall and Downing Street, the Prime Minister's Press Secretary convenes a regular meeting of Government press officers. By all accounts a businesslike affair, it notes ministers' movements and departmental diaries and attempts to spot banana skins on the road ahead. Under Mrs Thatcher's Press Secretary, Sir Bernard Ingham, efforts were made to lay down a firm press and PR line across the departments. Sir Bernard was not a man to spare press officers' blushes in criticising this or that department's failure to get the message across.

Yet Sir Bernard's personal dominance was only a temporary solution to the

question of how to keep some central co-ordination in a system that is inherently fissiparous. Ministers want the best press possible for them; whether their headlines and
television appearances are good for the government as a whole is not self-evident.
These ambiguities in the management of government public relations are not new.
Since Sir Bernard Ingham's time, they have become more obvious. Does the
Government Information Service (GIS) constitute a definable block of Civil Service
work which could be better and cheaper managed as a free-standing executive
agency or – the thought is a mere whisper in Whitehall corridors – privatised.

Government press officers are individually employed by Whitehall departments
but they have uniform Whitehall-wide grading and promotions masterminded from
within the Cabinet Office. Government Information Service managers pat themselves on the back over the fact that they were able to offer ministers good candidates
to head up the press function in the two new departments created after the election
and then successfully reshuffle the press officer portfolios.

The sense of esprit de corps among Whitehall press officers is embodied in the post
of 'head of profession', who for example adjudicates the occasional decision on
whether a press release ought more appropriately to come from Conservative Central
Office than this or that ministry. When Sir Bernard Ingham assumed the title, eyebrows
were raised, for whatever his other qualities Sir Bernard is not generally reckoned to be
judicial in temperament. The post is now occupied by the altogether different figure of
Mike Devereau, Chief Executive of the Central Office of Information (COI). The COI
is an executive agency. Its work in commissioning advertising agencies and producing
campaign and publicity material is budgeted and paid for by departments item by item–
the COI's success in winning contracts and tenders and maintaining its £150 million a
year turnover could well mean ministers will soon start thinking about its privatization.
Terry Perks, head of the Government Information Service Management Unit, says it is
worth remembering that though press officers have a centralised grading system they
remain departmental civil servants.

Could the Government Information Service become an executive agency? Making
the GIS an agency would involve transferring some 1,300 civil servants out of their own
departments. Much press work, says Mike Devereau, involves detailed and even intimate contact between press officers and ministers and it is not at all clear how executive
agency status would affect that. A more likely fate for at least some government press
work is privatisation. Much publicity material is already purchased direct from the private sector (85 per cent of the Central Office of Information's work is commissioning
private-sector projects). There is – from Saatchi and Saatchi down – a flourishing private
public relations market. The Audit Commission for Local Government and the Health
Service has never had in-house public relations: its press liaison work has always been
done by a private PR firm. Within the government press corps there is a view that says
press liaison work tends to be so delicate, so bound up with the political fate of individual politicians that it needs to be kept within the Civil Service. But ministers' press officers are only a part of the machine. It could be that the Government Information Service

will inevitably fragment as the new executive agencies seek to manage their own publicity and public relations work.

THE CHANGING CENTRE

Mrs Thatcher arrived in power in 1979, strongly critical of Britain's economic failure. But she – publicly at least – never applied that criticism to the advice tendered successive generations of politicians by the Civil Service. She interested herself in questions of how the state was managed, but left intact the enclosed area in which civil servants interact with ministers, and map public policies. The advice tendered by individual officials or departmental processes to ministers remains well guarded; only after the passage of years do clues emerge – as when Sir Alec Cairncross recently fingered Sir Edward Bridges, former Treasury Permanent Secretary, as the author of disastrous macroeconomic policy advice. The point is that, compared with management, the central Whitehall activity of policy advice has escaped the attention of ministers and their reforming zeal.

A conspiracy-minded surveyor of recent years might be tempted to ask whether Whitehall had not directed attention away from the question of policy advice: does the education and training of senior officials properly equip them to give to ministers, who of course have their own agendas, the fullest range of options for policy and its implementation?

There has been a debate of sorts about the duties and responsibilities of senior officials. Prompted by the celebrated case of Clive Ponting, a Ministry of Defence official who communicated information to a Member of Parliament, the then head of the Civil Service, Sir Robert Armstrong, laid down a memo. His successor felt he needed, with minor amendments, to repeat the message which was that civil servants have no separate duty to Parliament, except in so far as their ministers have Parliamentary responsibilities. The prime obligation of a civil servant is to his or her minister, with the exception of certain duties specified in for example the Income Tax and Census Acts. Sir Robin Butler has, in testimony to House of Commons committees, emphasised that the law binds ministers in what they can do, and so civil servants operate within a statutory context. Both Civil Service Chiefs have resisted the idea that civil servants with problems of conscience or unsure whether there is a statutory basis to what they are being asked to do either by ministers or their superiors should have recourse to an 'independent' arbitrator. However, anxieties about the operations of the Security Service, MI5, did lead the Home Office to appoint a 'father figure' who, very much behind closed doors, would listen to officers' problems.

Under the Major premiership some hard questions about how the centre of Whitehall operates have been asked. William Waldegrave, former Minister for the Civil Service, even wondered aloud whether the process of giving policy advice might be contracted out, just as other functions of government can be offered for tender to alternative, perhaps private-sector suppliers. There is nothing new in the idea of farming out policy advice. In one sense, all governments have been prepared to subcontract advice by establishing royal commissions (though Mrs Thatcher preferred smaller committees to large-scale commissions under royal warrant). Lord Runciman's inquiry into the criminal justice system was in a sense the Government giving over to outsiders (in this case unpaid outsiders) detailed and highly sensitive policy advice. Government is more open, since the authorship of the advice is clearly labelled.

Some academics, for example Patrick Dunleavy at the London School of Economics, have argued that Whitehall's centre has become stronger in recent years as managerial and executive work has been pushed out to Next Steps agencies or been privatised. What is going to be left as the 'core' of Civil Service work if the number of executive agencies at arm's length from Whitehall expand in number, and other functions are contracted out to the private sector? Sir Robin Butler answers: 'The whole of government is having to think about this question, but we are not looking for defining characteristics of what must be inside government. We cannot tell what the core is a priori, in some absolute way'.

Defence, Britain's diplomatic representation, ministers' Private Offices, some types of policy advice – these appear to Sir Robin inalienable government functions. But he adds that particular operations are being examined all the time, and nobody has successfully produced a definition of what the 'core' state is. 'The idea of a career Civil Service is unravelling', according to William Plowden, former director-general of the Royal Institute of Public Administration, and 'There is an urgent need to codify what is expected of civil servants as there is more movement in and out, as we move to a new relationship between public and private sector, and short-term contracts. Some kind of common ethical culture has got to be preserved in these new circumstances'.

Traditionally top civil servants have been 'lifers' – getting to the top of the Whitehall tree has taken a lifetime in the administration business. Of the present cadre of Permanent Secretaries, only three out of 17 heads of domestic departments have less than 24 years inside the machine; only four have more than a year's full-time experience outside it. But is this pattern now obsolete? How well does it serve the government of modern Britain? Should Whitehall cease trying to 'grow its own'?

It is not that outside appointments to Civil Service jobs are new. Sir Terry Burns, the Treasury's Permanent Secretary, came into Whitehall on a five-year contract as chief economic adviser in 1980. Other senior 'specialist' posts are also held by outsiders. What is new is the proposition that mainstream management posts in the Civil Service need people with skills that are more likely to be found outside than inside government.

If agency Chief Executives concerned with 'implementation' can and ought to be found outside, why not senior officials concerned with 'policy'? If the permanent head of the Treasury can safely be an outsider, why not his opposite numbers at Trade and Industry or Education or the Home Office? If it were too radical to fill Permanent Secretary jobs directly from outside, promising outsiders might be brought in a grade lower and groomed for the post, even for a decade, as Sir Terry Burns was.

The government of the United Kingdom has more executive power and is subject to less effective external scrutiny than any other in the western world. Within our government senior civil servants have enormous influence in advising ministers and in carrying out policies, and are in post for much, much longer than the individual ministers they are advising.

In such circumstances are the best possible people being appointed? The pool is tiny, filled by those recruited to the Civil Service 25 or 30 years ago. Do these people know enough about the society, in all its aspects, that they are seeking to govern? If senior civil servants are as good as they claim to be – and many are very good indeed – they have nothing to fear from opening out senior appointments to competition from outside the machine. It is likely many of the top jobs will continue to go to those nurtured within Whitehall. There would still be a professional Civil Service, with its own ethic, but it would be one leavened and strengthened by the presence at the top of people with a new diversity of background and skill. The 1994 Civil Service White Paper seemed to note the questions while proposing no radical change to existing procedures. It dismissed the American pattern, where Civil Service jobs at senior levels are reallocated each time a new President is elected. There is to be a gradual move to opening up senior jobs to competitive recruitment, but it seems that most ministers are sufficiently satisfied with the Civil Service they get and have no wish for radical change.

THE HOLE AT THE CENTRE?

The personal ascendancy in Parliament and politics of Mrs Margaret Thatcher seems, in retrospect, to have led to an illusory sense of co-ordination at the centre. On subsequent examination, it seems that the British state has a hole at its heart – machinery to co-ordinate 'difficult' policy seems weak. To take a recent example, policy on the family, cutting across half a dozen departments, the system seems to lack a means of holding ministers and their departments in line, of thinking ahead, to plan.

The Central Policy Review Staff, created in 1970, was intended to assist then Prime Minister Ted Heath precisely to hold his government to a set of policies. Its abolition by Mrs Thatcher perhaps reflected her sense of personal mission, but has left – in the view of many commentators – a renewed sense of a 'hole at the centre'.

It is not that Mrs Thatcher needed no advice. She built up the Number 10 Policy Unit and drew in policy proposals from the right-of-centre research organisations. Yet what she seemed to want from the Civil Service machine was not ideas on what to do, but concrete proposals for implementation, 'solutions not problems'. This touches on a deeper, constitutional question, which is the relative strength of the Prime Minister, ministers individually and the Cabinet. Under a somewhat weaker Prime Minister, Cabinet discussions appear to be more important. But do ministers make sufficient a contribution? Sir Peter Kemp, former project manager for Next Steps, says 'I think the minister needs to acquire new skill of a rather negative sort. He needs to stop being worried about the details of management. He has to re-learn how to make policy, to re-learn how to be a member of the government, how to sit in a Cabinet, and have a view on the general things instead of the current situation in which if it's not your subject you don't put up your hand'.

Wouldn't that require a strengthening of Cabinet and the Cabinet Office relative to Whitehall departments? William Waldegrave says there is a question of whether 'strengthening the vertical delivery mechanisms' (setting up executive agencies) exposes a gap in the 'lateral connections' – co-ordination between departments. 'I actually think the Cabinet Office machinery is rather good at ensuring collective lateral communication but I think it essential that we keep that in good repair. Freeing ministers from some of the administrative tasks which they're not well suited for should give them more time to sit on the Cabinet committees properly'.

Referring to his experience earlier in his career as a member of the original Think-tank, the Central Policy Review Staff, he added 'That is where I came in in 1971 – the purpose being to try to reinforce that lateral coherence by providing a staff available to all Cabinet ministers to brief on all matters of importance'. If he is right – and privately many senior officials in Whitehall and not a few ministers agree with him – the abolition of the Think-tank by Mrs Thatcher and the consequent weakening of 'lateral communication' begins to look like a mistake.

THE DEPARTMENTS

Edward Bridges, a former head of the Civil Service, believed in the 'departmental view'. It is the civil servant's duty, he said, 'to give his minister the fullest benefit of the storehouse of departmental experience, and to let the waves of the practical philosophy wash against ideas put forward by his ministerial master'.

Departments are the baronies of British government, each with a distinctive culture and internal network of officials, interest groups and Parliamentary contacts. In Washington DC the connection between departments, interest groups and legislators is referred to as the iron triangle; the British connection is perhaps not quite so tight, strong none the less. Departmental officials feel free to lobby against colleagues in other departments, not least the Treasury; some rivalries – for example that between the Departments of the Environment and Social Security on who pays for housing poorer people – run deep. The custodians of policy in most departments are the Deputy Secretaries, who tend to have spent long years in a single department, have mastered areas of policy and serve as custodians of departmental memory.

This list of the principal positions at the top of Whitehall starts with the 'core of the core', the departments at the very centre of the machinery of state. The mainstream departments follow. A key phrase in the annotated biographies for officials is 'Private Office'. By Whitehall tradition it is high-flying younger officials who are selected by their elders for a period of service in junior positions in the outer offices of ministers and Secretaries of State; those still on track to the top are often drafted back in later in their careers as Private Secretaries. The role is pivotal. The official has to 'get on' with a minister in a personal sense; channel and condense papers and messages from the department to the minister; diplomatically refer ministerial messages back to colleagues. All the while the Private Office has to keep an eye on the Permanent Secretary who, depending on minister and circumstances, may have separate lines of communication with the minister. At the least, Private Office knows a lot.

Another ingredient of the successful Whitehall career is a spell out of the mainstream department in either the Cabinet Office or the Treasury. Such sojourns are intended to indoctrinate the rising official in the culture of the centre, to plug him or her into networks of contacts. The Treasury – though this is always denied by its senior officials – takes a leaf out of the Jesuits' book: give me an official for a two-years' secondment and he/she is ours for life. What this means is that the Treasury hopes a departmental official will become accultured, or sensitised, to the difficulties of the Treasury's task of expenditure control and play the game when, in future, it comes to the annual round of spending negotiations between departments and itself. Some officials find these periods at the centre intensely frustrating: no longer are they running policies, instead they are, as in the case of the Cabinet Office, struggling to impose minimum coherence on a fissiparous structure.

The civil servants whose names follow are all members of the Senior Open Structure, that is Grade 3 (Under-Secretary) and above; the annotations assume they are at Grade 3 unless otherwise indicated. Where only a name is shown, biographical data has not been forthcoming – some public servants wish to keep themselves private.

PRIME MINISTER'S OFFICE
No 10 Downing Street
London SW1A 2AA
Telephone: 071-270 3000

The group of civil servants and unofficial and political advisers clustered around the Prime Minister at the heart of Whitehall can appear, if the current occupant of Number 10 is strong, like a praetorian guard; but if the Premier is weak, Number 10 can seem like a bunker, its staff dangerously exposed. For civil servants, service in Number 10 is usually a passport to promotion; Sir Robin Butler, the current head of the Civil Service, was Mrs Thatcher's Principal Private Secretary, and senior positions in Whitehall are filled by veterans of Downing Street. Both the Prime Minister's Office and the Cabinet Secretariat contain more than the usual proportion of Etonians, Harrovians and Wykehamists, partly because these schools do produce some of the brightest and best; partly because the pupils they do produce are supremely well versed in the arts of Court, and offer ministers that Rolls-Royce service of memo-drafting and administrative bag-carrying which is one of the British Civil Service's proudest boasts.

Principal Private Secretary to the Prime Minister: Alex Allan. Born: 1951. Educated Harrow; Clare College, Cambridge, University College London. Joined HM Customs and Excise 1973. Moved to HM Treasury 1976 and served in the Chancellor's Private Office 1986 before promotion to Under-Secretary (international finance) 1989.

Private Secretaries (Overseas Affairs): Roderic Lyne. Born: 1948. Educated: Eton; Leeds University. Joined Foreign and Commonwealth Office 1970, serving abroad, in Moscow 1972, and Dakar 1974. Returned to London to the FCO's Soviet Department. Experience in the Foreign Secretary's Private Office, 1979. Further service overseas, in Moscow 1987.

(Economic Affairs): Mary Francis

(Parliamentary Affairs): William Chapman

(Home Affairs and Diary): Mark Adams

Secretary for Appointments: John Holroyd. Born: 1935. Educated: Kingswood School, Bath; Worcester College, Oxford. Joined the Ministry of Agriculture in 1959, gained Private Office experience 1961, promoted to Under-Secretary 1978. Transferred to the European Secretariat in the Cabinet Office, 1985. Appointed as First Civil Service Commissioner 1989.

PRIME MINISTER'S POLICY UNIT

Head: Sarah Hogg. Born: 1946. Educated: St Mary's Convent, Ascot; Lady Margaret Hall, Oxford. Mrs Hogg, daughter of the former Conservative minister Lord Boyd-Carpenter, worked as a journalist for most of her career, as Britain and economics editor of *The Economist*; as economics editor of *The Times*; as a presenter for Channel Four News then as economics editor of the *Daily Telegraph*. She is married to the Conservative MP and minister, Douglas Hogg.

Other members: Nicholas True; Alan Rosling; Damian Green; Lord Poole; Jill Rutter; Katharine Ramsey; Dominic Morris;

Political Secretary: Jonathan Hill. Born: 1960. Educated: Trinity College, Cambridge. Before joining Lowe Bell Communications, Mr Hill was special adviser at the Department of Health to Kenneth Clarker. He joined the Prime Minister's Policy Unit in 1991.

Chief Press Secretary: Christopher Meyer (Grade 2). Born: 1944. Educated: Lancing; Peterhouse, Cambridge. Joined the Foreign and Commonwealth Office 1966, serving abroad, in Moscow 1968 and Madrid 1970. Further overseas service included UK Permanent Representative, European Communities 1978, then Moscow again 1982. He became Head of News at the FCO 1984, was a Fellow, Center for International Affairs, Harvard 1988 and Minister (commercial) at the UK's Washington Embassy in 1989.

CABINET OFFICE
70 Whitehall
London SW1A 2AS
Telephone: 071-270 3000

The Cabinet Office began life as no more than the Cabinet Secretary and his assistants but has recently burgeoned to become a substantial mini-department, with a specific administrative remit covering science as well as the administration of the Civil Service. Its work in managing the flow of paper to the Cabinet and carrying back Cabinet decisions to the machine is now only part of an array of responsibilities. Yet if the British state is anywhere 'co-ordinated' it is in the Cabinet Office, as it daily tends the ministerial and official committees which ensure the various departments sing from the same song sheet, to coin the usual phrase. The Cabinet Office has a substantial secret side, providing central co-ordination and analysis of the intelligence gathered by the several security services. Even its domestic responsibilities used to be veiled. Not long ago Cabinet Office officials were still being instructed if asked at a party where they worked to answer mysteriously 'for the government'. The Cabinet Office in principle runs the Civil Service. It contains the service's titular head and its conscience, for officials with problems have the opportunity if their Permanent Secretary cannot offer satisfaction, of sharing their thoughts with the head of the service. Since the early 1980s the jobs of Civil Service head and Cabinet Secretary have been combined though the functions are different. The Cabinet Office has around 615 staff, numbers having increased somewhat in recent years.

The Cabinet Office is the fulcrum of the patronage state. Sir Robin Butler keeps lists of his colleagues and oversees senior appointments; his colleagues keep long lists of members of the public and others who may be eligible for appointment to the plethora of public bodies listed elsewhere in this book.

Secretary of the Cabinet and Head of the Home Civil Service: Sir Robin Butler. Sir Robin Butler has been the 'head prefect' since 1988, taking over from Sir Robert now Lord Armstrong, of whom he is a fair clone. Born: 1938. Educated: Harrow; University College, Oxford. Joined HM Treasury 1961, serving in the Private Office of the Financial Secretary to the Treasury 1964. Sir Robin was a member of the original 'Think-tank', the Central Policy Review Staff under Lord Rothschild 1971 before joining the Prime Minister's Private Office in 1972 and serving both the Conservative Edward Heath and his Labour successor Harold Wilson. After further Treasury work on spending, he again served at Number 10, this time with Mrs Thatcher. The next leg of his smooth journey to the top placed him as second Permanent Secretary in charge of public expenditure at the Treasury from 1985.

CABINET SECRETARIAT

Home and Social Affairs: Richard Bird. Born: 1932. Educated: Winchester; Clare College, Cambridge. Joined Ministry of Transport 1955, serving in Private Office 1966. His subsequent career carried him to the Department of the Environment 1971 then to the Department of Education and Science 1973, where he became an Under-Secretary 1975.

Defence and Overseas: Paul Lever. Born: 1944. Educated: St Paul's; The Queen's College, Oxford. Joined the Foreign Office in 1966, serving in Helsinki and at NATO. Went to Brussels as Chef de Cabinet to Christopher Tugendhat, Vice-President of the EC in 1982 before a series of Foreign Office defence and security appointments.

David Gould. Born: 1949. Educated: West Buckland School, Barnstaple; University of Sussex. Joined the Ministry of Defence 1973 and subsequent appointments in the defence area included a period at the NATO Defence College and head of resources (air).

Joint Intelligence Organisation: Gerald Warner (Grade 2). Born: 1931; Educated: University of Oxford. Joined HM Diplomatic Service 1954 and served abroad in Peking, Rangoon and Warsaw as well as in the Foreign Office itself in the 1970s.

Anthony Galsworthy. Born: 1944. Educated: St Paul's School; Corpus Christi College, Cambridge. Joined the Foreign Office 1966 and served abroad, in Hong Kong, Rome and Peking and, in 1986, in Private Office.

Economic Secretariat: Rachel Lomax (Grade 2). Born: 1945. Educated: Cheltenham Ladies' College; Girton College, Cambridge; London School of Economics. Joined HM Treasury 1968, working as an economic adviser and in Private Office 1985 before promotion to Deputy Secretary (financial institutions) 1992.

European Secretariat: Richard Carden. Born: 1943. Educated: Merchant Taylors' School; St John's College, Oxford (DPhil 1970). Did research before joining Ministry of Agriculture. Moved to Treasury in 1977 then, at MAFF, specialised in European policy and later fisheries.

OFFICE OF PUBLIC SERVICE AND SCIENCE

(headed by the Chancellor of the Duchy of Lancaster and Minister of Public Service and Science)

Permanent Secretary: (until March 1995) Richard Mottram (Grade 1a). Born: 1946; Educated: King Edward VI Camp Hill School, Birmingham; Keele University. Joined the Ministry of Defence 1968 where he subsequently made his name both as a defence thinker and a proponent of the new managerialism. His career took in Private Office in MoD 1971; a transfer to the Cabinet Office 1975 then work in the MoD on manpower control and policy.

Principal Establishment and Finance Officer: Robert Venning. Born: 1946; Educated: Midhurst School; University of Birmingham. Began an academic career moving to Lancaster Polytechnic before joining Department of Health and Social Security in 1971 where he worked in Private Office, later as Under-Secretary (personnel).

CITIZEN'S CHARTER UNIT

This small unit in the Cabinet Office was set up to mastermind the implementation of Prime Minister John Major's enthusiasm for a charter encoding the rights and expectations of people to specified standards in the delivery of public services; specific charters for patients, rail travellers and others were subsequently devised.

Director: Genie Turton (Grade 2). Born: 1946. Educated: Nottingham Girls' High School; Girton College, Cambridge. Joined the Ministry of Transport in 1970. Her subsequent career took in two spells in Private Office in 1973 and 1978, a secondment to the private sector, to Midland Bank and to the Cabinet Office in 1982.

EFFICIENCY UNIT

This sits poised between the Cabinet Office and Number 10, a child of Mrs Thatcher's time. Devised by Prime Minister Thatcher's business adviser Derek (Lord) Rayner, efficiency scrutinies were a means of bringing fresh thought to bear on established departmental practices. The Unit – originally composed of young turks, leavened by some old Whitehall salts – was , in essence, to take a clear-eyed look at their senior colleagues' work patterns. The Unit has a titular head in the Prime Minister's Adviser on Efficiency, an external appointment.

The Prime Minister's Adviser on Efficiency: Sir Peter Levene. Born: 1941; Educated: City of London School; University of Manchester. Business career included working for United Scientific Holdings. Official career included becoming Chief of Defence Procurement at the Ministry of Defence in 1985. Sir Peter has been special adviser to several ministers. He is currently deputy chairman of financiers, Wasserstein Perella and Co and Chairman of Canary Wharf.

Head of Unit: John Oughton. Born: 1952; Educated: Reading School; University College, Oxford. Joined the Ministry of Defence 1974, served in Private Office, had a period abroad working for the Canadian government and subsequently specialised in defence procurement policy.

Head of Management Development Group: Hugh Taylor. Born: 1950. Educated: Brentwood School; Emmanuel College, Cambridge. Joined Civil Service 1972. Served in Home Office, as Principal Private Secretary to Home Secretaries Sir Leon Brittan and Douglas Hurd, later dealing with life prisoners and parole and head of personnel, Prison Service with a spell as head of security division in the Cabinet Office.

Head of Senior and Public Appointments Group: Brian Fox. Born: 1944; Educated: East Ham Grammar School. Joined HM Treasury 1963, working in Private Office 1967. After a secondment to the 3i Group – investment specialists – in 1981, he became the Treasury head of defence policy in 1987.

Machinery of Government Division: Andrew Whetnall. Born: 1948. Educated: Kings Norton Grammar; University of Sussex. Joined Civil Service in 1975 later serving in the Department of the Environment on inner cities and water. Joined the Cabinet Office, machinery of government division in 1989.

OFFICE OF THE CIVIL SERVICE COMMISSIONERS

The Commissioners are meant to be independent checks on the procedures by which civil servants at principal (Grade 7) and above are first appointed; they do not oversee subsequent appointments within Whitehall. They are the modern custodians of the Northcote-Trevelyan principles of fair and open competition to jobs in the public service though their work is – it seems to some – increasingly compromised by the delegation of authority and recruitment responsibilities down the line.

First Commissioner Ann Bowtell (Grade 2). Born: 1938. Educated: Kendrick Girls' School, Reading; Girton College, Cambridge. Joined the National Assistance Board (its work now absorbed into the Department of Social Security) in 1960, then the Department of Health and Social Security becoming deputy secretary in the Department of Social Security and principal establishments and finance officer in the Department of Health.

First Commissioner David Clark. Born: 1947. Educated: University of Kent. His career in the Department of Health and Social Security and its successor departments led to promotion to Under-Secretary in 1990.

Commissioners are lay, part-time appointments. They include the Tootal group executive, Geoffrey Maddrell; the former director of the National Council for Voluntary Organizations, Usha Prashar (Mrs V. K. Sharma); Mrs J C Rubin; and Eric Sorensen, the former Department of the Environment official who moved to become Chief Executive of the London Docklands Development Corporation.

CCTA: THE GOVERNMENT CENTRE FOR INFORMATION SYSTEMS

CCTA is an 'internal' consultancy, responsible for promoting the use of IT within Whitehall.

Director: Roy Dibble. Born: 1940. Educated: Maidstone Technical School and Medway College of Technology. Mr Dibble is a chartered engineer who worked on the design of airborne navigational systems while employed in the private sector by GEC, Decca and Motorola. He joined one of the units that was eventually to form CCTA in 1971 and became director in 1993.

OFFICE OF SCIENCE AND TECHNOLOGY

Formerly a responsibility of the Department of Education and Science, the research councils' budget has been passed, together with an overall responsibility for civilian science to the Cabinet Office.

Chief Scientific Adviser and Head of the OST: Professor Sir William Stewart (Grade 1a). Born: 1935; Educated: Dunoon Grammar; Glasgow University (PhD). Sir William pursued an academic career at Nottingham, London, becoming head of the department of biological sciences at the University of Dundee where he was Vice-Principal 1985. His career in government began as secretary and Chief Executive of the Agriculture and Food Research Council 1988. He was elected a Fellow of the Royal Society for his work in biology in 1977.

OST Research Policy. Director-General of the Research Councils. (This new appointment sweeps up some of the work previously done by the Advisory Board for the Research Councils): Sir John Cadogan (Grade 2). Born: 1930. Educated: Grammar School, Swansea; King's College, London. After a career in academic chemistry including university appointments at St Andrew's and Edinburgh, Sir John became chief scientist at the BP research centre and later the company's director of research. He became a Fellow of the Royal Society in 1976.

Transdepartmental Science and Technology Group: Helen Williams. Born: 1950. Educated: Allerton High School, Leeds; St Hilda's College, Oxford. She joined the Civil Service in 1972, working for the Department of Education as secretary for the Advisory Board for the Research Councils, later on curriculum policy and local government spending.

Science and Engineering Base Group: David Wilkinson. Born: 1947. Educated: Boteler Grammar School, Warrington; Bedford College, University of London; London School of Economics; Moscow State University. He joined the Department of Education and Science in 1974 and became an Under-Secretary there 1989 as head of its science branch.

PARLIAMENTARY COUNSEL OFFICE

The Office houses the Parliamentary draftsmen – the technical authors of legislation and statutory instruments placed before the Houses of Parliament for approval.

James Jenkins (Grade 2). Born: 1939. Educated: Lewes County Grammar; Magdalen College, Oxford. A solicitor, he joined the Office of Parliamentary Counsel in 1967 and has remained there since, with two periods at the Law Commission in 1970 and 1983.

Sir Peter Graham. Born: 1934. Educated at St Bees School; St John's College Cambridge. A barrister, he joined the Office of Parliamentary Counsel in 1959 and worked at the Law Commission in 1979.

PRIVY COUNCIL OFFICE
Whitehall
London SW1A 2AT
Telephone: 071-270 0472

The Office is one of the more genteel engine rooms of the executive state. It is responsible for the arrangements – formalities in most cases – for making Royal Proclamations and Orders in Council, the announcements following changes in ministerial positions. It looks after bodies which are chartered, including universities. Its remit covers the appointment of High Sheriffs and many other appointments in the name of the Crown to the governing bodies of institutions.

The Privy Council mixes the partisan and the non-partisan in baffling measure. The political head of the Office is the Lord President of the Council who is usually Leader of the House of Commons and as such principal manager of the Government's legislative business and – usually – a trusted colleague of the Prime Minister. Yet he is also in some sense a token head of the whole house. Officially 'he upholds the rights and privileges of the House as a whole and in this capacity it falls to him to move motions relating to the procedures of the House'. The Council's membership is diverse. Nowadays membership has become an honorific accorded to members of the Cabinet, senior backbenchers, top people in the Opposition parties and senior judges. Some commentators have recently argued the Privy Council should have more muscle as an expert scrutineer of proposed legislation, endeavouring to head off potential failures in policy and implementation.

The Judicial Committee of the Privy Council is a residual appeal court for certain Commonwealth countries. It has limited jurisdiction within Britain itself, for example in certain ecclesiastical cases and the hearing of appeals by doctors and other professionals against decisions of their disciplinary bodies.

Clerk of the Privy Council: Nigel Nicholls. Born: 1938. Educated King's School, Canterbury; St John's College, Oxford. Joined Admiralty 1962 and the Ministry of Defence in 1964, serving in the Navy Minister's Private Office and, later, the Defence Secretary's. His career has included the Royal College of Defence Studies, and the arms talks at Vienna in 1977 (defence counsellor). After a Cabinet Office secondment in 1986 he became Assistant Under-Secretary of state (systems) at MoD.

HM TREASURY
Parliament Street
London SW1P 3AG
Telephone: 071-270 3000

The Treasury's declared strategic objective is to orchestrate the monetary and fiscal conditions required to promote sustained economic growth, to maintain the stability, integrity and efficiency of the nation's financial system, and to promote Britain's economic interests abroad.

Its antecedents are Norman when an official was given responsibility for 'regulating the King's accounts'. The wholesale expansion of the state, particularly in the economy during the third quarter of the twentieth century, created the modern Treasury, marked by the influence it now has over all the other Whitehall departments. Its tentacles are said to be everywhere, and its civil servants are genuinely feared and disliked. Indeed, post-war history is littered with attempts by politicians to curb that power by laying siege to the Treasury machine and its 'abominable no men' which have constrained their ambitious spending plans. No such attempt has ever succeeded. However, the Treasury, which has always seen itself as Whitehall's housekeeper, has rarely emerged from such conflicts unscathed. Consequently, the relationship between the Treasury and other Whitehall departments is more accurately seen as a state of armed truce rather than that of victor and vanquished.

Though infinitely proud and – recently – the subject of much discussion about making it 'independent', the Bank of England remains the Treasury's principal instrument for day-to-day negotiations with the possessors of capital, the issuing of money and control of the banking system.

Delivering permanently low inflation, maintaining sound public finances, pursuing tax policies which do the least damage to economic efficiency, restricting public spending to a level which the nation can afford, and improving the efficiency of the public sector, are listed as key objectives in the Treasury's 1994 annual report. It is in pursuit of these that tax increases, public expenditure cuts, and a fundamental review of spending programmes have been set in motion. As a result, Treasury officials are now confident that the 1993-4 £45.9 billion public-sector borrowing requirement (the gap between what the government raises in taxes and what it spends) will be progressively eliminated. Critics have insisted, however, that much of this painful medicine is being administered in an effort to rectify a series of political mistakes, and the policy advice upon which they were based, dating from the late 1980s, including the excessive relaxation of monetary policy in 1988 (the so-called Lawson boom), the failure to rein in public expenditure in the run-up to the 1992 general election, and the Poll Tax débâcle.

Observers have been surprised by the Treasury's apparent failure to exploit the Next Steps executive agency initiative to gain a tighter grip of policy in other Whitehall departments. It has been suggested that this oversight was due in part to the appointment of Sir Peter Kemp, a former Treasury mandarin, who believed passionately in breaking up the monolithic Civil Service, and who was simply allowed to put Whitehall's new contract culture in place as he saw fit. The Treasury has, however, in partnership with the Office of Public Service and Science, taken a much keener interest in the market testing initiative, designed to expose Whitehall's protected markets to the cut and thrust of outside competition, although its own market testing programme remains one of the most modest in Whitehall. Like most other Whitehall departments, the Treasury has had a recent history marked by what has been described as the drift towards open government. There is now more openness about the background to policy decisions, in an effort to stimulate informed public debate. Moreover, the creation in December 1992 of the Treasury Panel of Economic Forecasters has been welcomed as a means of exposing ministers to a wider range of views on key economic issues, thereby increasing the prospects of the Chancellor being able to challenge the prevailing Treasury orthodoxy.

The Treasury itself is relatively cheap to run – in 1994-5 its net spending on itself was some £67 million. Within its sphere fall several other major departments of state, notably the two on which the state depends for the bulk of its revenues, the Inland Revenue and HM Customs and Excise. There are around 2,000 Treasury civil servants.

Permanent Secretary: Sir Terry Burns (Grade 1). Born: 1944. Educated: Houghton-Le-Spring Grammar School; Manchester University. After research and teaching posts, including Director of the London Business Centre for Economic Forecasting, Sir Terry became Chief Economic Adviser to the Treasury and Head of the Government Economic Service in 1980, and was appointed Permanent Secretary in 1991.

Second Permanent Secretary: Sir Nigel Wicks (Grade 1a). Born: 1940. Educated: Beckenham and Penge Grammar School; Portsmouth College of Technology; Cambridge and London Universities. After working for BP, Sir Nigel joined the Treasury in 1968, held a variety of posts, including Private Secretary to James Callaghan and Principal Private Secretary to Margaret Thatcher, before becoming Second Permanent Secretary (Overseas Finance) in 1989.

Aid and Export Finance: Jamie Mortimer. Born: 1947. Educated: Latymer Upper School, Hammersmith; Wadham College, Oxford. Joined HM Treasury in 1971, and worked in the Home Office, Transport Department and Foreign Office, before becoming Head of Aid and Export Finance in 1991.

European Community: David Bostock. Born: 1948. Educated: Cheltenham Grammar School; Balliol College, Oxford; University College, London. Joined HM Treasury 1971, and served in the UK Representation in Brussels and the Cabinet Office before becoming responsible for European Community there, 1990.

International Finance: David Peretz. Born: 1943. Educated: The Leys School, Cambridge; Exeter College, Oxford. Joined HM Treasury 1973. Worked on housing policy, international energy issues, and external finance. Promoted to Head of International Finance in 1990.

Second Permanent Secretary: Alan Budd (Grade 1a). Born: 1937. Educated: Oundle School; London School of Economics; Churchill College, Cambridge. He held a variety of teaching posts at home and abroad, served as economic adviser to the government and private-sector interests, before becoming Head of the Government Economic Service and Chief Economic Adviser to the Treasury in 1991.

Chief Economic Forecaster: Colin Mowl. Born: 1947. Educated: Lawrence Sheriff School, Rugby; London School of Economics. Joined HM Treasury as an economic adviser in 1972, before becoming Chief Economic Forecaster in 1990.

Medium Term Policy Analysis: Chris Riley. Born: 1947. Educated: Ratcliffe College, Leicester; Wadham College, Oxford; Leicester and East Anglia Universities. He joined HM Treasury as an economic adviser in 1969, and later spent a year as a research fellow at Nuffield College, Oxford, before becoming Head of Medium Term Policy Analysis in 1988.

Second Permanent Secretary (Public Expenditure): Robert Culpin (Grade 1a). Born: 1948. Educated: Christ's College, Cambridge; Universities of Harvard and California. Joined HM Treasury in 1968, and served as Head of the Treasury Information Division and Press Secretary to the Chancellor. Appointed Director Fiscal and Monetary Policy in 1993, before being promoted to Second Permanent Secretary in 1994.

General Expenditure Policy: John Gieve. Born: 1950. Educated: Charterhouse; New College, Oxford. After four years in the Employment Department, joined HM Treasury in 1979, and worked on industrial, energy and investment issues, before becoming Head of Banking in 1991, and then Head of General Expenditure Policy in 1994.

Defence Policy and Materiel: Alice Perkins. Born: 1949. Educated: North London Collegiate School; St Anne's College, Oxford. Joined Department of Health and Social Security in 1971, Personnel Director in 1990. [The integrated nature of British central government is shown by the fact she is the wife of Labour Environment spokesman Jack Straw and that fact has not apparently damaged her career prospects.] In 1993 she became Head of Treasury Defence Policy, on loan from the DSS.

Public Sector Economics: Michael Spackman. Born: 1936. Educated: Malvern; Clare College, Cambridge; Queen Mary College, London. Previous posts included economic adviser to the Energy Department, the Treasury, and Transport Department, before becoming Head of Public Sector Economics in 1993.

Principal Establishment and Finance Officer: Paul Grey. Born: 1948. Educated: Wyggeston Boys' School, Leicester; London School of Economics. He worked for the Department of Economic Affairs in 1969, before joining HM Treasury the same year. Principal Establishment and Finance Officer in 1994.

Deputy Secretary: Chris Kelly. Born: 1946. Educated: Beaumont School, Windsor; Trinity College, Cambridge; Manchester University. Joined HM Treasury 1970, served as secretary to the Wilson Committee of Inquiry into Financial Institutions, and became Head of General Expenditure Policy in 1992 before being promoted to Deputy Secretary in 1994.

Banking Policy:(awaiting announcement)

Fiscal Policy: Anthea Case. Born: 1945. Educated: Christ's Hospital, Hertford; St Anne's College, Oxford. Joined the Treasury 1966, and held a variety of posts dealing with aid and exports, education and transport, before becoming Head of Fiscal Policy in 1993.

Monetary Policy: Gus O'Donnell. Born: 1952. Educated: Warwick University; Nuffield College, Oxford. He taught economics at Glasgow University, and joined HM Treasury as an economist in 1979. He served as an economic adviser at the British Embassy in Washington. Was Press Secretary to John Major at Number 10 during the first 18 months of his premiership before returning to the Treasury as Head of Monetary Policy in 1994.

Deputy Secretary: Steve Robson (Grade 2). Born: 1943. Educated: Pocklington School; St John's College, Cambridge; Stanford University. Joined HM Treasury in 1969 as an economist, and served as Private Secretary to the Chancellor 1974-6, before being appointed Director of Industry and Financial Institutions in 1993.

Securities and Investment Services: Alan Whiting. Born: 1946. Educated: Acklam Hall Grammar School, Middlesborough; East Anglia University; University College, London. Joined HM Treasury as an economist in 1968, and worked for EFTA, the CBI, and the DTI before becoming Head of Securities and Investment Services in 1992.

Industry: Mike Williams. Born: 1948. Educated: Wycliffe College; Trinity Hall, Cambridge; Nuffield College, Oxford. He worked in the Ministry of Finance in Zambia, joined HM Treasury in 1973, before becoming Head of Industry in 1992.

Public Enterprises: Ivan Wilson. Educated: Royal School, Dungannon; The Academy, Omagh; Queen's University Belfast. Previous Treasury posts include Head of the Treasury Defence Budget and the Treasury Information Division. He was appointed Head of Public Enterprises and Privatisation in 1993.

Education Training and Employment: Peter Sedgwick. Born: 1943. Educated: Downside; Lincoln College, Oxford. Joined HM Treasury in 1969, and worked on short- and medium-term forecasting, and public expenditure issues, before becoming Head of Education Training and Employment in 1994.

Deputy Secretary: Andrew Edwards (Grade 2). Born: 1940. Educated: Fettes; St John's College, Oxford; Harvard University. Joined HM Treasury in 1963 as an Assistant Principal, and served in the Department of Education and Under-Secretary at the Treasury before becoming Director Public Services in 1990.

Social Services and Territorial: Gillian Noble. Born: 1947. Educated: Aberdeen University; University College, London. Joined the Civil Service in 1969, and has held various posts in the Treasury before becoming Head of Health, Social Security and Spending in Scotland, Wales and Northern Ireland in 1993.

Local Government: John Beastall. Born: 1941. Educated: St Paul's School, London; Balliol College, Oxford. Joined the Treasury as an Assistant Principal in 1963, and worked in the Civil Service and Education departments before becoming Head of Local Government in 1993.

Procurement: Peter Forshaw. Born: 1936. Educated: Queen Elizabeth's Grammar School, Dorset; Royal Military College of Science; the Naval Postgraduate College, Monterey, USA. After a lifelong career in the army, he joined the Treasury as Head of Public Sector Procurement in 1990.

Deputy Secretary: Andrew Likierman (special appointment). Born: 1943. Educated: Stowe, Vienna University, and Balliol College, Oxford. He has held a wide variety of teaching posts and advisory positions in both the public and private sectors, before being seconded from the London Business School as Head of the Government Accountancy Service and Chief Accountancy Adviser to the Treasury in 1993.

Treasury Officer of Accounts: (awaiting announcement)

Deputy Secretary: Robin Mountfield (Grade 2). Born: 1939. Educated: Merchant Taylors' School, Crosby; Magdalen College, Oxford. He became an Assistant Principal in the Ministry of Power in 1961, and served in the Department of Industry before becoming responsible for Civil Service Management and Pay in 1992.

Management Policy Group: Richard Allen. Born: 1944. Educated: Edinburgh Academy; Edinburgh and York Universities. He worked as a consultant for the UN Economic Commission for Europe, and an economic adviser at the Energy Department. Joined the Treasury in 1978, and was appointed Head of Management Policy in 1993.

Civil Service Pay: Stephen Boys Smith. Born: 1946. Educated: St John's College, Cambridge; the University of British Columbia. He worked in the Cabinet Office, the Home Office, and the Northern Ireland Office before joining the Treasury as Head of Civil Service Pay in 1992.

Personnel: Brian Taylor. Born: 1942. Educated: St Benedict's School, Ealing; Corpus Christi College, Oxford. He worked in the Defence Ministry and the Cabinet Office, before joining the Treasury as Head of Personnel Policy in 1992.

DEPARTMENT FOR EDUCATION

Sanctuary Buildings
Great Smith Street
London SW1P 3BT
Telephone: 071-925 5000

The culture of the Department for Education – renamed at the 1992 election when the administration of science was transferred to the new Office of Public Service and Science – has two elements. One is its administrative impotence: the department has never itself run the schools and colleges which provide education. It has over the years had to rely on intermediaries (such as the educational inspectorate) and a combination of persuasion and bludgeoning; for many of them negotiation with, for example, the National Union of Teachers seemed the only way of securing even small changes in educational practice. Yet another element in the educational culture has been, at least until recently, the existence within the department of officials who were clearly policy-makers in their own right. From the great Edwardian makers of policy such as Edgar Morant and to such post-war giants as Gilbert Fleming or John Maud, the education establishment has, in Civil Service terms, been remarkably unashamed of its prowess. The 'discovery' of education as a problem area in public policy in the later 1970s has tarnished the lustre of this tradition.

The changes in educational policy enacted under the Conservatives in recent years have given the Department a much more 'hands on' role though chalk face teaching is still done at several removes from its administrative base. To manage payments to the grant-maintained schools, which have been growing in number, a new funding agency has recently been created.

For much of the 20th century, the educational remit did not include the universities which were supported by an arm's length committee, the University Grants Committee, which until the early 1960s answered direct to the Treasury. This fact helps explain the creation of a 'dual' higher education sector in the shape of the polytechnics and colleges of higher education, which were only recognised as universities in the 1990s. Similarly the education remit has not always covered the education and training of young people for work, a field recently fought over between the Education and Employment departments. Suggestions are regularly made to the effect that the overlap between the two departments merits a merger or amalgamation.

The top of the department has in recent years been in some considerable turmoil. When Sir David Hancock was appointed as Permanent Secretary in 1983, it was said this Treasury man had caught the Mrs Thatcher's eye as someone able to 'sort out' a department about which she (a former Secretary of State) had misgivings and which her efficiency scrutineers suspected, too. A notable number of subsequent appointments within the upper ranks of Education have been made from outside. When Sir Geoffrey Holland was transferred from the Employment Department in January 1993, the expectation was that he would build up the direct administrative capacity that the DfE would need as Conservative policy on the schools unfolded – removing the local education authorities, and establishing direct grants for many schools. However, his tenure lasted only months and he departed having apparently fallen out with Secretary of State John Patten. Mr Patten's tenure ended summarily in summer 1994. The department numbers some 2,500 civil servants in total.

Permanent Secretary: Tim Lankester. Educated: Monkton Combe School; St John's College, Cambridge. Teacher and academic before joining the World Bank as an economist. Then to HM Treasury, serving in the Chancellor's Private Office, 1978. City experience with S G Warburg then overseas as Economic Minister Washington 1985 before becoming Permanent Secretary at the Overseas Development Administration in 1989.

Schools 1 Branch (local authority schools): Michael Richardson. Born: 1946. Educated: Eton; St Edmund Hall, Oxford. Joined the Diplomatic Service and served overseas in China before a stint in the FCO Private Office and further overseas service in Rome. He joined the Department of Education and Science in 1987.

Schools 2 Branch (education of ethnic minorities, special needs, preparation for work): Brian Norbury. Born: 1938. Educated: Churcher's College, Petersfield; King's College, London. Joined the War Office in 1961; gained experience in the Cabinet Office in the late 1960s before moving to the Ministry of Defence and working in Private Office, 1979. Joined the Department of Education and Science in 1984.

Schools 3 Branch (curriculum): Clive Saville. Born: 1943. Educated: Bishop Gore Grammar, Swansea; University College, Swansea. Joined DES in 1965, experience in Private Office of the Minister for the Arts in 1968. Worked for the University Grants Committee, 1973 and transferred to the Cabinet Office 1975. He gained North American experience as a Harkness Fellow.

School 4 Branch (self-governing schools, City Technology Colleges): David Forrester. Born: 1944. Educated: St Paul's; King's College, Cambridge. Joined the DES in 1967, gained extra-departmental experience at HM Treasury, 1976 and in the 1980s at the Department of Trade.

Further and Higher Education 1 Branch (higher education): Tony Clark. Born: 1940. Educated: King's College School, Wimbledon; Pembroke College, Oxford. Took a series of jobs in commerce before joining the DES in 1965 where he became Head of Finance in 1987.

Further and Higher Education 2 Branch (post-16 further education): Roger Morgan. Born: 1945. Educated: Whitgift School, Croydon; Battersea College of Advanced Technology. Subsequent career in the Civil Service has been within the Department.

Further and Higher Education 3 Branch (student support): Nicholas Summers. Born: 1939. Educated: Tonbridge School; Corpus Christi College, Oxford. Joined the predecessor of the DES, the Ministry of Education, in 1961. Private Office experience working for the Minister for the Arts in the mid-1960s. Extra-departmental experience at the Cabinet Office in 1974.

International Relations, Youth and General Branch: Stephen Jones. Born: 1944. Educated: Brentwood School, Essex; University of Southampton. Joined the Ministry of Defence in 1968, moving to the DES in 1973. After experience in Private Office in the mid-1970s, he subsequently saw something of the education institutions dependent on DES for grants, as assistant director of the City of London Polytechnic. He joined HM (educational) Inspectorate in 1986.

Legal Branch – on the staff of the Treasury Solicitor's Department but located at DfE: Robert Ricks. Born: 1942; Educated: Highgate School; Worcester College, Oxford. He qualified as a Solicitor in 1967 before joining the Treasury Solicitor's Department.

Finance Branch – Accountant General: Robert Horne. Born: 1945. Educated: Mill Hill School; Oriel College, Oxford. Mr Horne was an Assistant Master at Eton in 1967, though his biography does not say whether he was required to emulate Eton's controversial head Anthony Chevenix-Trench in wielding the cane, and joined the DES in 1968. He gained experience outside the Department at the Cabinet Office in 1979.

Director of Establishments and Organisation: Peter Shaw. Born: 1949. Educated: Bridlington School; Durham University. Joined DES 1972 and worked in Private Office in 1979. A varied career in Civil Service terms saw him at HM Treasury in the mid-1980s before moving to become Northern Regional Director, a joint appointment of the Departments of Environment and Transport in 1991.

DEPARTMENT OF EMPLOYMENT
Caxton House
Tothill Street
London SW1H 9NF
Telephone: 071-273 3000

Like most of those departments broadly concerned with welfare, the Employment Department took on its administrative sinews during the First World War. The Ministry of Labour concerned itself with the deployment of manpower, and necessarily with trade unions. After 1945, if the Department could not secure the unions' assent, its officials decamped to Number 10 to help lay out the proverbial beer and sandwiches. The Ministry of Labour was the principal department for 'tripartism' – bringing unions and employers together formally in the oversight of public bodies. The tradition has taken a battering and such major tripartite bodies as the Manpower Services Commission, created in 1973, have now been abolished, to be replaced by solely employer led organisations (the Training and Enterprise Councils) but tripartism lingers on, most obviously in the Health and Safety Commission which monitors the Health and Safety Executive.

Of course, the decline of unions has altered the character of the department in recent years making it more managerial but also making its purposes less obvious. Officially this is the Employment Department Group, a small headquarters overseeing the Employment Service, which is now an executive agency, the Health and Safety Commission, with the Health and Safety Executive and the Advisory, Conciliation and Arbitration Service. Further details on these bodies are given in other chapters. The Group's stated aim is to 'support economic growth by promoting a competitive, efficient and flexible labour market'. Its principal targets are the unemployed and those lacking job skills. It seeks to 'encourage employment patterns and practices which promote individual choice and enterprise'.

The Employment Department has a busy frontier with the European Union, though recently this has seen skirmishing by UK ministers anxious to prevent the application in the United Kingdom of work practices and agreements common in other members states of the EU and now ensconced in the Social Chapter of the Maastricht Treaty, from which Britain sought exemption. The Department carries a brief for equal opportunities at work and its Secretary of State has come to speak in Cabinet on women's issues. Employment has some 52,000 civil servants in total, including its agencies.

Permanent Secretary: Nicholas Monck (Grade 1). Born: 1935. Educated: Eton; King's College, Cambridge. Joined the Ministry of Power in 1959 before moving to the National Economic Development Office – now abolished. He worked in Tanzania on government service before joining HM Treasury in 1969. A Treasury high-flyer he served in Denis Healey's Private Office before becoming Second Permanent Secretary (public expenditure) in 1990.

Director, Industrial Relations and International Directorate: Graham Reid (Grade 2). Born: 1937; Educated: University of St Andrews. After academic life at the University of Glasgow, became Senior Economic Adviser at the Scottish office in 1973. He was with the Manpower Services Commission during its glory years between the mid 1970s and 1980s before coming to the Department of Employment in 1984.

Director of Industrial Relations Divison I: Clive Tucker. Born: 1944. Educated: Cheltenham Grammar; Balliol College, Oxford. Joined the Ministry of Labour in 1965 and has since occupied positions in the Department of Employment.

Director of Industrial Relations Division II: Richard Hillier.

Director of International Division: Leigh Lewis. Born: 1951. Educated: Harrow County Grammar; Liverpool University. Joined the Department of Employment in 1973 and – progressing upwards with speed – worked in Private Office as a junior in 1975 and again, at more senior level, in 1984. He became director of operations for Unemployment Benefit and was seconded to Cable and Wireless in 1988.

Director of Statistical Services Division: Peter Stibard. Born: 1936. Educated: City of Norwich Grammar; Hull University. Worked for Kodak Ltd in the late 1950s before moving into public service with the Greater London Council, then the Central Statistical office. He joined HM Treasury in the early 1980s before transferring to the Department of Trade and in Industry in 1985.

Director of Resources and Strategy Directorate: Nick Stuart (Grade 2). Born: 1942. Educated: Harrow; Christ Church College, Oxford. Joined the Department of Education and Science in 1964 and had Private Office experience working for the Minister for the Arts. His subsequent Private Office career embraced a spell working for the head of the Civil Service as Private Secretary in 1973 and ditto for Prime Minister Edward Heath. He was an adviser in the Cabinet of the President of the EEC – Roy Jenkins – in 1978 before resuming his DES career, becoming an Under-Secretary in 1981.

Director of Finance and Resource Management Division: Mark Addison. Born: 1951. Educated: Marlborough; St John's College, Cambridge and Imperial College, London where he took a PhD. Joined the Department of Employment in 1978 and worked in Private Office there before acting as Private Secretary to Prime Minister Margaret Thatcher in 1985.

Director of Personnel and Development Division: David Normington. Born: 1951. Educated: Bradford Grammar; Corpus Christi College, Oxford. Joined the Department of Employment in 1973 – a time when the Department was at the centre of policy development and exuded a certain glamour. His Private Office experience came in 1984.

Director of Strategy and Employment Policy Division: Peter Makeham. Born: 1948. Educated: Chichester High School for Boys; Nottingham University. Joined the Department of Employment in 1971. In the 1980s he transferred to HM Treasury and worked at the Enterprise Unit, then located in the Cabinet office, before moving on to the Department of Trade and Industry.

Director-General Training, Enterprise and Education Directorate: Ian Johnston (Grade 2). Born: 1944. Educated: Royal Grammar, High Wycombe; Birmingham University where he took a PhD. Joined the Department of Employment in 1969, subsequently serving abroad at the British Embassy in Brussels 1976. He joined the Manpower Services Commission in 1984.

Director of Adult Learning: Brian Heatley. Born: 1947. Educated: Sheen Grammar; St John's College, Cambridge; Warwick University. After teaching, he joined the Department of Trade and Industry in 1974. His career at the Department of Employment began only in 1989.

Director of Quality Assurance Division: Neill Schofield. Born: 1946. Educated: University of Leeds. Joined the Department of Employment in 1970. His extra-departmental experience came at the Department of Energy in the late 1970s.

Director of Training Strategy and Infrastructure Division: Derek Grover. Born: 1949. Educated: Hove County Grammar; Clare College, Cambridge. Joined the Department of Employment in 1971, possibly its period of highest reputation. He served outside the Department at the Cabinet Office in the late 1970s and worked inside with the Manpower Services Commission in the 1980s.

Director of Youth Education Policy Division: Valerie Bayliss. Born: 1944. Educated: Wallington County Grammar; University of Wales. Joined the Department of Employment in 1968 and has since specialised in policies for youth employment and training, notably as Head of Youth Training Scheme policy at the Manpower Services Commission in the 1980s.

DEPARTMENT OF THE ENVIRONMENT

2 Marsham Street,
London SWIP 3EB.
Telephone: 071-276 3000

The physical headquarters of the one department supposedly concerned with the quality of the built environment are unfortunate: at least until 1995, they are three ugly and jutting towers in Marsham Street, designed by the disgraced architect John Poulson. The Department of the Environment was a creation of the – relatively brief – concern of the early 1970s, later revisited, with 'environment', to which was bolted on more substantial policy concerns and the perennially difficult business of managing the elected local authorities of England and their penchant for spending out of line with Treasury edicts. Throughout much of its history the DoE has been closely linked with its neighbour the Department of Transport, sharing certain officials at headquarters and in the regions and – in principle – swapping notes about planning and developments arising from new roads.

The Department of Environment was a creation of the Heath era, carved out of the old Ministry of Housing and Local Government and the Ministry of Works, the Government's in-house manager of property and development. In principle more is known about what the DoE actually does since Michael Heseltine who took over as Environment Secretary in 1979 was a great enthusiast for new, managerially advanced techniques of listing functions and DoE officials sweated hard over the preparation of MINIS – a new system of information flows designed to show exactly who did what. Since Mr Heseltine moved on, DoE seems to have reverted to Whitehall type.

The Department's substantive policy concerns are with housing, except where interest rates and mortgages are concerned, for there the Treasury and the Bank of England lead; town and country planning; control of pollution; inner cities and management of the government's 'estate', though much of that has now been devolved to individual departments.

DoE does function as the 'sponsor' of the construction industry within Whitehall, collecting data on property market trends. It is a 'baggy' department, some of its functions hanging only loosely together, some conflicting – for example its regulation through the planning system of mineral extraction, a vital interest of the construction industry.

The old MHLG used to be the advocate at court of local authorities; the DoE has become much more the regulator of council activities, especially their spending. The DoE is responsible for allocating support grants to local authorities. This makes it one of the biggest spending departments, responsible in 1994-5 for some £39 billion of public spending. Of this some £198 million is likely to be spent on running the department which contains some 7,500 civil servants.

Permanent Secretary: Andrew Turnbull (Grade 1). Born: 1945. Educated: Enfield Grammar School; Christ's College Cambridge. Worked as an economist in Zambia before joining HM Treasury 1970. After serving on secondment to the IMF, Private Secretary and Principal Private Secretary to Margaret Thatcher, he became Second Permanent Secretary (Grade 1a) at Treasury before moving to Environment in May 1994.

Principal Establishments Officer: David Burr (Grade 2). Born: 1935. Educated: University of Oxford. Joined the Department of the Environment in 1971, becoming an under-secretary later in that decade and Principal Establishment Officer in 1991.

Director (Personnel Management): John Owen. Born: 1945. Educated: City of London School; St Catharine's College, Cambridge. Joined the Ministry of Transport 1969, working in Private Office 1972 before moving to the Department of the Environment 1973. Experience outside London has included secondment to Cambridgeshire County Council in the late 1970s; he was Regional Director, Northern in 1987.

Head of Central Management and Analysis Unit and Chief Economist: Norman Glass. Born: 1946. Educated: Trinity College, Dublin; University of Amsterdam. Worked for Shell Mex in 1969 and Economic Models Ltd before taking up an academic career. He became Economic Adviser at the Department of Health and Social Security in 1975, transferring to HM Treasury in 1977. In 1989 he became head of Analytical Services at the Department of Social Security.

Director of Administration Resources: David Peel. Born: 1940. Educated: St Edmund's College, Ware; University College Oxford. Joined the Ministry of Transport 1964, gaining experience in Private Office there 1967 and in DoE in 1975. He gained experience in Brussels as First Secretary with the UK Permanent Representation at the EC.

Director of Finance (Central): William Rickett. Born: 1953. Educated: Eton; Trinity College, Cambridge. Joined the Department of Energy in 1975. At the centre, he was Private Secretary to Prime Minister Margaret Thatcher in the early 1980s. After a secondment to Kleinwort Benson he headed the Oil Division (Department of Energy).

Local Government, Finance and Planning: Chris Brearley (Grade 2). Born: 1943. Educated: King Edward VII School, Sheffield; Trinity College Oxford. Joined the Ministry of Transport in 1966 transferring to DoE in 1970. He was Private Secretary to the Cabinet Secretary 1974 and went back to the Cabinet Office in 1983.

Director Planning: John Ballard. Born: 1943. Educated: Roundhay Grammar, Leeds; Ifield Grammar, West Sussex; Southampton and Exeter Universities. After working in the

Academic Registrar's Department at the (new) University of Surrey in 1965 he joined the Ministry of Transport transferring to the DoE in 1972. After a spell in HM Treasury, he became Regional Director, Yorkshire and Humberside 1986. Before returning to his present job he was director of the Maxwell Pensions Unit in the Department of Social Security.

Director Rural Affairs: R. J. A. Sharp. Born: 1935. Educated: Brentwood School; Brasenose College, Oxford. After training for the Methodist ministry at Wesley House, Cambridge he was ordained. Joined the Ministry of Housing and Local Government in 1966. Later he served as a special adviser in the Cabinet Office before doing road safety and local government at DoE.

Director Water: Neil Summerton. Born: 1942. Educated: Wellington Grammar, Shropshire; King's College, London, where he took a Phd (war studies) in 1970. Joined the Ministry of Transport in 1966. In 1971, out of government, he became Assistant Secretary of King's College. At DoE from 1974 he specialised in local government finance.

Property and Construction and Housing with Energy Efficiency: Dinah Nichols (Grade 2). Born: 1943. Educated: Wyggeston Grammar; Bedford College, London. Joined Ministry of Transport, 1965, gaining Private Office experience. After secondment to the Cabinet Office 1974 she rose through the ranks at DoE becoming an Under-Secretary in 1985.

Principal Finance Officer and Agency Sponsorship: Diane Phillips. Born: 1942. Educated: University of Wales. Joined the National Economic Development Office in 1967, moving on to DoE in 1972. Her subsequent experience takes in the Cabinet Office and the Department of Transport.

Director Property Holdings: Neil Borrett. Born: 1940. Educated: College of Estate Management. Mr Borrett's career was in the private sector, as the director of property companies from 1963 until he joined government service in 1990.

Director Construction Sponsorship: Philip Ward.

Environment Protection Group and Water: Derek Osborn (Grade 2). Born: 1941; Educated: Leys School, Cambridge; Balliol College, Oxford. Joined the Ministry of Housing and Local Government in 1965, moving into Private Office two years later. He worked for the Royal Commission on Standards of Conduct in Public Life 1974 before moving up the ranks in Transport and, after 1977, DoE.

Director and Chief Inspector, HM Inspectorate of Pollution: Dr David Slater. Born: 1940. Educated: University College of Wales, Aberyswyth where he took a PhD; University of Southampton 1969. As a research scientist in the private sector, he worked for Cremer and Warner before founding Technica in 1981. He joined the government service in 1991.

Director, Air, Climate and Toxic Substances and Chief Scientist: Dr David Fisk. Born: 1947. Educated: Stationer's Company School, Hornsey; St John's College, Cambridge; University of Manchester where he took a PhD. Joined the Building Research Establishment in 1972 before moving to DoE, becoming an Assistant Secretary in 1984.

Director, Pollution Control and Wastes: Richard Dudding. Born: 1950. Educated: Cheltenham College; Jesus College, Cambridge. Joined the DoE in 1972, appointed to Private Office four years later. Served as Secretary to the Committee of Inquiry into the Conduct of Local Government Business, the Widdicombe Committee.

Director, Environmental Policy and Analysis: Gavin Watson. Born: 1944. Educated: Carlisle Grammar; Merton College, Oxford. Joined DoE in 1971, where, four years later he worked in Private Office. He subsequently specialised in housing.

Director, Energy Efficiency Office: John Hobson. Born: 1946. Educated: Northampton Grammar; Manchester Grammar; King's College, Cambridge. Joined the Ministry of Transport in 1967. He was Private Secretary to the Head of the Civil Service in 1974 before moving to DoE in 1980.

Housing and Urban Group, Deputy Secretary: Philip Fletcher (Grade 2). Born: 1946. Educated: Marlborough; Trinity College, Oxford. Joined the Ministry of Public Buildings and Works in 1968. At DoE in 1986 he was promoted to Under-Secretary, becoming responsible for housing and water.

Director, Housing and Urban Monitoring and Analysis: Dr C P Evans.

Director, Inner Cities: Michael Gahagan. Born: 1943. Educated: St Mary's College, Southampton; University of Manchester. Qualified as a chartered surveyor in 1964, joining the Department of Economic Affairs (which did not survive the Labour Government 1964-70) in 1966. He joined the DoE in 1971.

Urban Development and Relocation: David McDonald. Born: 1940. Educated: Campbell College, Belfast; Trinity College, Dublin. After teaching he joined government service at the Ministry of Education (NI) in 1967 moving to London to the Ministry of Housing and Local Government three years later. Since then he has had a number of jobs close to ministers, in Private Office in 1974 then as Director of Information DoE first in 1982 and then in 1990, on both occasions when Michael Heseltine was Environment Secretary.

Local Government Finance Policy: Paul Britton. Born: 1949. Educated: Clifton College; Magdalene College, Cambridge. Joined the DoE in 1971 and had his spell in Private Office there in 1983.

Local Government: Mavis McDonald. Born: 1944. Educated: Chadderton Grammar for Girls; London School of Economics. Joined the Ministry of Housing and Local Government in 1966, serving in Private Office in 1969. She became DoE Head of personnel in 1983; her husband (see above) also works in DoE as an Under-Secretary.

Solicitor and Legal Adviser: Marilynne Morgan (Grade 2). Born: 1946. Educated: Gads Hill Place, Higham-by-Rochester; Bedford College, London. Called to Bar 1972 she joined DHSS as a legal adviser in 1973 moving to DoE in the early 1990s. She became a Member of the General Council of the Bar in 1987.

Deputy Solicitor – Environment, International and Housing: J A. Catlin. Born: 1947. Educated: University of Birmingham (law degree). Joined the Treasury Solicitors in 1975, moving in 1984 to DoE becoming deputy solicitor for local government finance and planning in 1989.

Deputy Solicitor – Local Government Finance and Town and Country Planning: Sandra Unerman. Born: 1950. Educated: Gartlett School; Orange Hill Grammar; Bristol University. She was called to the Bar in 1973, joining the DOE a year later.

PSA SERVICES, FORMERLY THE PROPERTY SERVICES AGENCY.

Chief Executive: Anthony Lane (Grade 2). Born: 1939. Educated: Caterham School, and Balliol College, Oxford. Joined the Civil Service from the private sector in 1965, and worked in the Ministries of Technology, Aersospace and Shipping, Prices and Consumer Protection, the Departments of Trade and Transport, before becoming Deputy Secretary for Laboratories in 1987. He moved to DoE in 1994.

Principal Establishment and Finance Officer: Peter Draper. Born: 1935; Educated: Haberdashers' Aske's; Regent Poly. Joined Government Communications HQ in 1953 moving subsequently to the Ministry of Transport 1956 and joining DoE at its inception in 1970.

DEPARTMENT OF HEALTH
Richmond House
79 Whitehall
London SW1A 2NS
Telephone: 071-210 3000

The Department of Health has lately been returning to its governmental roots. Instead of the department merely responsible for the running of the health services, with the launch of its 'healthy nation' initiative, it has begun to consider health in the round – harking back to the 1920s when the Ministry of Health gave grants to local authorities to build housing as a follow on to the late Victorian 'sanitary' effort founded on the belief that environmental conditions and health were closely connected. During the years from the mid-1960s until the mid-1980s when the Departments of Health and Social Security were bound together, there was little sign of a further connection being made between the health of the nation and its income or, more controversially, the distribution of its income.

The Department of Health has the characteristics of a 'shadow' department. The National Health Service runs itself in a formal sense – that is, it has a management structure. But the Department, its ministers and its officials, seem continuously to be picking away at NHS decisions, whether specific or general. This is not surprising. A dropped bed pan in Warrington (this was a famous image from Aneurin Bevan, who thought the minister should not be responsible for it) can sometimes be heard in the House of Commons and the Health Ministers willy-nilly get involved in detail, even though the NHS reforms of recent years have been intended to allow managers more discretion and room for manoeuvre.

As well as the NHS, the Department oversees services provided by local authorities for the old and handicapped – 'community care' is a recent initiative – and social work involving children and families. The Department of Health is the principal government department concerned with children and tends to take a 'softer' line than, say, the Home Office on questions of care and incarceration. It has some 4,800 civil servants on its complement.

Under the latest reorganisation of NHS management, an NHS Policy Board was established chaired by the Secretary of State ostensibly to lay down strategy. It includes other health ministers, civil servants and external appointees. Under the board the National Health Service Management Executive is responsible on a day-to-day basis for decision-taking. But lines of accountability are not altogether clear since NHS regions and districts have some discretionary powers and the new generation of NHS trusts actually delivering services are meant to be locally accountable, too.

Permanent Secretary: Graham Hart. Born: 1940. Educated: Brentwood School; Pembroke College, Cambridge. Joined the Ministry of Health in 1962, where his upwardly mobile career took in Private Office in 1972 then a spell at the Central Policy Review Staff – albeit in 1982, shortly before Mrs Thatcher abolished it. Mr Hart moved northwards on promotion, becoming Secretary of the Home and Health Department at the Scottish Office in 1990.

Departmental Resources and Services (Principal Establishments): Joe (Joseph) Pilling, (Grade 2). Born: 1945. Educated: Rochdale Grammar; King's College, London. Joined the

Home office in 1966 where, as a rising star, he served in Private Office 1970. Like a number of Home Office officials has served periods of secondment to the Northern Ireland Office, including Northern Ireland Private Office in 1978. After a Harkness Fellowship taking him to the United States, Mr Pilling administered prisons, becoming Director-General of the Prison Service in 1991 after which it became an Executive Agency.

Principal Establishment Officer: Mike Lillywhite. Born: 1937. Educated: University of London. A BBC accountant, Mr Lillywhite entered the Civil Service as a direct-entry principal. He served in David Owen's private office in the 1970s, then took a position in finance before moving five years ago to become principal establishment officer.

Chief Economic Adviser: Clive Smee. Born: 1942. Educated: Royal Grammar, Guildford. London School of Economics. Mr Smee worked initially for the British Council in Nigeria and later as an Economic Adviser for the Overseas Development Ministry (now the ODA). His subsequent career in the mainstream Civil Service has been punctuated by secondments, to the Central Policy Review Staff in 1982 and the New Zealand Department of Health in 1991.

Director of Statistics: Rosemary Butler. Born: 1946. Educated: Maynard School, Exeter; London School of Economics. Joined the Central Statistical Office in 1967 and – moving along a professional network similar to that of the government's economists – switched to statistical work in the Department of Employment in 1977, becoming Chief statistician HM Treasury 1985.

Director Finance Division: Alan Barton.

Health and Social Services Group: Strachan Heppell (Grade 2). Born: 1935. Educated: Acklam Hall Grammar, Middlesborough; The Queen's College, Oxford. Joined the National Assistance Board (its functions now part of DSS) in 1958. Punctuation points in his subsequent DHSS career were a period at the Cabinet Office in the late 1960s and in Hong Kong on government service in 1971.

Deputy Chief Medical Officer: Dr Jeremy Metters (Grade 2). Born: 1939. Educated: Eton; Magdalene College, Cambridge; trained as a doctor at St Thomas' Hospital, London. Joined the Department of Health and Social Security in 1972.

Health Promotion: Geoffrey Podger.

Senior Principal Medical Officer: Dr Eileen Rubery. Born: 1943. Educated: Westcliff High School of Girls; Sheffield University; Cambridge University where she took a research degree. After a succession of hospital appointments she joined the DHSS in 1983.

Health Aspects of the Environment and Food: Brian Bridges. Born: 1937. Educated: Harrow Weald County Grammar; University of Keele. Joined the Civil Service in the early 1960s, rising to become an Under-Secretary at the DHSS in the mid-1980s.

Senior Principal Medical Officer: Dr Gerald Jones. Born: 1939. Educated: Swansea Grammar; Merton College, Oxford; trained at London Hospital Medical College. After a career in hospital medicine he joined the DHSS in 1975.

Health Care: Dora Pease. Born: 1935. Educated: Perse School, Cambridge; Mount School, York; Newnham College, Cambridge. Joined the Ministry of Health 1958 but her subsequent career includes periods of service outside, at the Pay Board and the Cabinet Office in the 1970s and at the Office of Population Censuses and Surveys (a subordinate department of DHSS) in 1983.

Senior Principal Medical Officer: Dr Peter Bourdillon. Born: 1941. Educated: Rugby; trained as a doctor at Middlesex Hospital Medical School. After a hospital career he joined the DHSS in 1991.

Community Services: Thomas Luce. Born: 1939. Educated: Clifton College; Christ's College, Cambridge. Joined the Inland Revenue and became HM Inspector of Taxes before moving to the Civil Service Department in 1969 (its functions now performed by the Cabinet Office's Office of Public Services). Joined the DHSS in 1972; seconded to HM Treasury, 1987.

P Division (dental, pharmaceutical): Melvyn Jeremiah. Born: 1939. Educated: Abertillery County School. Joined the Home Office in the late 1950s before moving to HM Customs and Excise. With a diverse career in departmental terms, Mr Jeremiah worked in the Cabinet Office in the mid-1970s and later in that decade in the Welsh Office.

Chief Dental Officer: Brian Mouatt. Born: 1936. Educated: Blundell's School, Edinburgh University. Joined the Royal Air Force; served in public health jobs, in Bournemouth and in Zambia. Practised as a dentist before joining the Department of Health and Social Security in 1984.

NHS MANAGEMENT EXECUTIVE
(for further details of the National Health Service see Chapter Five)

Director of Research and Development: Professor Michael Peckham. Born: 1935. Educated: St Catharine's College, Cambridge; University College Hospital Medical School. His career in research was spent, in part, at the Institute of Cancer Research after which he held Consultant positions in hospital medicine before becoming Director of the British Postgraduate Medical Federation, part of London University's medical education research in 1986.

Senior Principal Medical Officer (Medical Education): Dr J R W Hangartner.

Executive Director, Information Management Group: Raymond Rogers. Born: 1940. Educated: Gunnersbury Grammar; Birmingham University. Trained to become a medical physicist at the London Hospital before joining the DHSS in 1970.

Chief Inspector, Social Services: Herbert Laming. Born: 1936. Educated: University of Durham. Trained as a Probation Officer at the London School of Economics and worked in the field before moving into local authority social services, becoming Director of Social Services for Hertfordshire in 1975.

Department of Health Solicitor: Peter Thompson (Grade 2). Born: 1937. Educated: Worksop College, Christ's College, Cambridge. Called to the Bar. Mr Thompson's career in government service included work with the Law Commission and, from 1978, the Lord Chancellor's Department.

Principal Assistant Solicitor: Allan Roberts. Born: 1950. Educated: Eton; Magdalen College, Oxford. After qualifying as a Solicitor Mr Roberts worked in private practice and joined the DHSS in 1976.

DEPARTMENT OF NATIONAL HERITAGE
2-4 Cockspur Street
London SW1Y 5DH
Telephone: 071-211 6000

This new department is a creation of the Major era. To the arts portfolio formerly located within the Cabinet Office has been added responsibilities for tourism, previously with the Employment Department, plus the Home Office's broadcasting brief. Perhaps there is a kind of rationality about grouping those subjects; perhaps the Department was created in order to give a job to Prime Minister John Major's friend, David Mellor, for whom the arts brief alone would have been too small to justify a seat in the Cabinet.

But in obedience to some deep-seated law of bureaucracies, once such a department exists, functions will be found for it. Thus DNH has become responsible for another bright idea of the 1990s, the National Lottery, and preparation for the Millenium, together with its more obvious portfolio of museums, libraries, the regulation of the newspaper press, sport and the 'heritage'. About a fifth of its spending goes on the arts, a further fifth on museums and galleries, just under a fifth each on libraries and the heritage, the rest is divided between royal parks and palaces, film and supporting the tourist industry. Among the Department's own inheritance is the British Library being built, controversially, adjacent to St Pancras Station. DNH costs about £29 million a year to run plus about £10 million for the Historic Royal Palaces Agency. Its overall spending in 1993-4 was about £991 million, nine out of every ten pounds passing through its hands being allocated to a variety of public bodies, among them the British Tourist Authority and the Historic Royal Palaces Agency. National Heritage has some 960 civil servants on its strength.

Though small in Whitehall terms, the DNH has a high profile because its decisions touch on the interests of the chattering classes, for example in issuing export licences for works of art, and making policy for the BBC. The official mission of the Department is to preserve the heritage of the past while creating the culture of today and adding to the heritage for future generations and 'broadening opportunities for people to enjoy the benefits of their heritage and culture'. Considerable emphasis is put on the DNH's role in improving the quality of life of British people.

Permanent Secretary: Hayden Phillips (Grade 1a). Born: 1943. Educated: Cambridgeshire High School; Clare College, Cambridge. Joined the Home Office in 1967, graduating seven years later to Private Office. Mr Phillips joined Roy Jenkins – president of the EC – in Brussels in 1976 as a member of his cabinet. At home he returned to the Home Office where his responsibilities included police before moving on to the Cabinet Office in 1986 and HM Treasury in 1988.

Head of Arts and Lottery Group: A Ramsay.

Head of Broadcasting, Film and Sport Group: Lester Wright. Born: 1946. Educated: Bedford School; Caius College, Cambridge. Began an academic career before joining the Home Office in 1971. A Harkness Fellowship took him to the United States before, in 1983, he became an Assistant Secretary in the Home Office.

Head of Heritage of Tourism Group: David Chesterton. Born: 1939. Educated: Reading School; St Catherine's College, Oxford. Worked as a journalist before joining the Northern Ireland Office in 1974 and becoming an Under-Secretary there in 1985.

DEPARTMENT OF SOCIAL SECURITY

Richmond House
79 Whitehall
London SW1A 2NS
Telephone: 071-210 3000

Though old age pensions were created in the Edwardian era and workmen's compensation dated from even earlier, specialist administration of what later came to be called social security dates from after the Second World War, and the creation of the welfare state. Benefits administration became big business, operated by the Ministry of Pensions, the National Assistance Board and the Ministry of Labour. The modern DSS is a smaller department, its executive work performed by large executive agencies. It is responsible through its Contributions Agency for the collection of contributions under National Insurance, though much of the actual collection work is done on its behalf by the Inland Revenue.

It pays out – through the Benefits Agency – a variety of benefits, from child benefit to Income Support. Through the Social Fund it makes discretionary payments to those in special need. The Department is also responsible for means-testing applicants for legal aid. Spending on social security accounts for 28 per cent of all planned public spending in 1994-5. Spending on benefits accounts for 95 per cent of the Department's outlays, the rest being for administration.

Recently the Department created a new agency to attempt to force parents not living with their children to pay towards the cost of their maintenance. But the Child Support Agency has been controversial, and some have questioned whether such sensitive administrative work – with all its political ramifications – should have been inserted into the tight framework of an executive agency.

In the political era when ministers thought, albeit privately, that the poor needed to be bought off, in order to forestall malcontents, social security administration perhaps had a greater urgency about it than now, when (with the exception of pensions) payments to the poor are rarely a subject of political controversy and reductions in benefits have been made without too much protest.

The DSS budget for 1994-5 was £83 billion, making it the largest gross spender in Whitehall. That worked out at about a million pounds per head of staff, who number some 85,000, a figure that has been increasing during the recession.

Permanent Secretary: Sir Michael Partridge (Grade 1). Born: 1935. Educated: Merchant Taylors'; St John's College, Oxford. Joined the Ministry of Pensions 1960 and pursued a career within social security and health administration, moving to the Home Office in 1983 before becoming second Permanent Secretary at the DHSS in 1987.

Resource Management and Planning Group: Brian Gilmore (Grade 2). Born: 1937. Educated: Wolverhampton Grammar; Christ Church, Oxford. Joined the Foreign Office and served at the British Embassy in Washington in 1965. On returning to the UK joined the Ministry of Technology (later absorbed into the Department of Industry). His subsequent jobs included the Lord Privy Seal's Private Office then the principalship of the Civil Service College. He joined HM Treasury in 1981 and the Cabinet Office in 1988 and DSS in 1992.

Director of Personnel: Stephen Hewitt. Born: 1950. Educated: Weymouth Grammar; Dulwich College; Sussex University. Joined the Northern Ireland Office in 1975 and the DSS in 1990.

Director, Analytical Services Division: David Stanton. Born: 1942. Educated: Bishops Stortford College; Worcester College, Oxford. Abroad in Uganda on government service, he went on to lecture at Brunel University before joining HM Treasury in 1974. Later he was Director of the Employment Market Research Unit and then Chief Economist in the Department of Employment.

Planning and Finance Division: Jonathan Tross. Born: 1949. Educated: Chislehurst and Sidcup Grammar; University College, Oxford. Joined DHSS in 1972 where he has remained, except for a secondment to Barclays Bank in 1987.

Social Security Policy Group: Robin Birch (Grade 2). Born: 1939. Educated: King Henry VIII School, Coventry; Christ Church Oxford. Joined the Ministry of Health in 1961.

Associated with the Home Office community development projects from 1970. He worked on personal social services policy and, after working in the Private Office of the Leader of the House of Commons in 1980 moved to social security work. He worked at the National Audit Office from 1984 to 1986.

Social Security Division A (war pensions, disabled benefits, invalid care allowance, industrial injuries): Brian Walmsley. Born: 1936. Educated: Prescot Grammar; National Service. Joined the Ministry of Pensions in 1957 and worked subsequently in several areas of social security administration, heading the North West Regional Office of DHSS in 1970. He was at the Cabinet Office as a Civil Service Commissioner on secondment from 1988 to 1990.

Social Security Division B (benefits for unemployed people and families, child support): Michael Whippman. Born: 1938. Educated: King Edward VII School, Johannesburg; University of Witwatersrand; Clare College, Cambridge. After holding academic posts, joined DHSS in 1973. His subsequent responsibilities included benefits for the disabled, and doctors' pay. He was seconded to HM Treasury 1990-3, responsible for spending on law and order, education and science.

Social Security Division C (occupational and personal pensions): Margaret Peirson. Born: 1942. Educated: North London Collegiate; Somerville College, Oxford. Joined the Treasury in 1965; seconded to the Bank of England 1982; joined the DSS in 1990.

Social Security Division D (income support, housing benefit): Robert Brown. Born: 1942. Educated: Kirkcaldy High School; Edinburgh University. Joined the Ministry of Social Security in 1967 and served a term in the Cabinet Office from 1983.

Social Security Division E (national insurance, unemployment benefit, social fund): Don Brereton. Born: 1945; Educated: Plymouth College; University of Newcastle upon Tyne. Joined the Ministry of Health in 1968, serving in Private Office eleven years later. He became the official leader of the Prime Minister's Efficiency Unit in 1989.

DSS Solicitor: P K J Thompson (see entry under Department of Health)

Principal Assistant Solicitor: Greer Kerrigan. Born: 1948. Educated: Bishop Anstey High School, Trinidad; College of Law, Inns of Court. Called to the Bar before joining the DHSS in 1974 moving up the legal ranks there to become Assistant solicitor in 1985.

DEPARTMENT OF TRADE AND INDUSTRY

Ashdown House
123 Victoria Street
London SW1E 6RB
Telephone: 071-215 5000

Established in 1621 in an effort to identify 'the true causes of the decay of trade and scarcity of coyne,' the Board of Trade or Department of Trade and Industry has been subject to perpetual restructuring. In its modern form, which dates from 1974, its central role has been to foster the international competitiveness of British industry and commerce, to help British companies meet the competitive challenge arising out of Britain's membership of the European Community, and to execute a myriad other functions ranging from the regulation of de-nationalised industries, maintaining public confidence in markets through consumer protection, encouraging innovation and technology transfer, cutting red tape, and winding up insolvent companies. The continuity and fierceness of debate over the purposes, indeed the very existence of a 'department of trade' was shown once again, in the summer of 1994, when there was a leak of a letter from the then Chief Secretary to the Treasury, Michael Portillo, to the President of the Board of Trade, Michael Heseltine. Mr Portillo ran through a number of DTI functions before concluding that they were not justified because there was not identifiable 'market failure' to make government intervention necessary.

Because Britain is a trading nation which exports 25 per cent of what it produces – considerably more than most other industrial states – encouraging industrial and commercial competitiveness, and promoting exports, are seen by trade and industry officials as the raison d'etre of their department. In an attempt to further these objectives, a new Competitiveness Division was created in 1992 to examine how Britain compared with the rest of the industrialised world, gather information on what the rest of the world thinks of Britain, analyse how different aspects of government policy affect competitiveness, and apply any lessons learnt as part of the drive to boost the overall competitiveness of British industry and commerce.

Fifteen Sponsoring Divisions, ranging from Aerospace to Atomic Energy, and from Textiles to Telecommunications, are responsible for identifying the particular needs of their sector, ensuring that these factors are taken into account when new national or European Union legislation is drafted, and encouraging businesses to enter and develop new markets. Under the Prime Minister's Deregulation Initiative, the Sponsoring Divisions are also responsible for ensuring that new or existing regulations do not work to the disadvantage of British business, and for helping to provide effective redress when they do. The Sponsoring Divisions work closely with the Export Divisions to alert each sector of economic activity to any opportunities and threats arising in their overseas markets. Through the DTI and FCO's Joint Export Promotion Directorate, companies can avail themselves of advice, information and financial support, to help them secure overseas contracts. Much of this effort is targeted at Britain's 2.7 million small and medium enterprises, although special support is also provided for larger companies exporting capital goods.

Along with its commitment to a liberal international trading system, the DTI is also committed to maintaining a liberal domestic economy in order to continue attracting inward investment. Britain now attracts the highest share of US, Japanese, and German external investment, which has helped to boost employment, and sharpen the competitive instincts of indigenous businesses. The DTI's regulatory functions have expanded significantly as the state has progressively withdrawn from direct participation in key areas of economic activity, such as the telecommunications, gas and electricity industries. New regulatory bodies, including Oftel, Ofgas, and Offer, now work alongside the Office of Fair Trading, the Monopolies and Mergers Commission, and other regulatory bodies, to provide consumer protection and maintain confidence in markets. Plans are well advanced for the privatisation of British Coal into five regional businesses, and the future of the Post Office is also under review. More than half of the DTI's staff now work in the department's nine executive agencies, and almost 2,000 DTI staff have been subject to the DTI's £80 million market testing programme. The total strength of the DTI, including its agencies, is some 12,000, a figure that has been falling in recent years.

Permanent Secretary: Sir Peter Gregson (Grade 1). Born: 1936. Educated: Nottingham High School; Balliol College, Oxford. Joined the Board of Trade in 1961, and held a variety of posts including Private Secretary to Harold Wilson and Edward Heath, and Under-Secretary at the Trade Department and Cabinet Office before becoming Permanent Secretary in 1988.

Competitiveness: Robert Dobbie. Born: 1942. Educated: Edinburgh and Cambridge Universities. After an academic career which included positions at Alberta, Bristol,

Newcastle upon Tyne, California State Universities and the Open University, he joined the DTI in 1976, and became Head of Industrial Competitiveness in 1992.

Deputy Secretary: Christopher Roberts (Grade 2). Born: 1937. Educated: Rugby; Magdalen College, Oxford. Joined Board of Trade in 1960, served in the British High Commission in New Delhi, and held a variety of posts in the Cabinet Office and Department of Trade before becoming Deputy Secretary responsible for Trade Policy and Export Promotion in 1986.

International Trade Policy: John Cooke. Born: 1943. Educated: Dragon School; Magdalen College School; Heidelberg University; King's College, Cambridge. Joined Civil Service 1966, and held posts in the UK Representation to the EC and the Trade Department before becoming Head of International Trade Policy in 1992.

European Community and Trade Relations: Bill Stowe. Educated: Cambridge University. Joined Civil Service in 1971, and held posts at the OECD in Paris, the UK Representation in Brussels, and the Internal European Policy Division before taking up his current post in 1994.

Export Control and Non-Proliferation: John Meadway. Born: 1944. Educated: Collyer's School, Horsham; Peterhouse, Cambridge; Edinburgh and Oxford Universities. Joined the Civil Service as an Assistant Principal in the Ministry of Technology in 1970, and worked on trade and consumer issues before becoming head of Export Control and Non-Proliferation Policy.

Joint Export Promotion Directorate: Ray Mingay. Born: 1938. Educated: Tottenham Grammar School; St Catharine's College, Cambridge; and London University. Joined Ministry of Transport in 1962, and held Consular positions in Milan, Washington and Chicago, before becoming Director General Export Promotion DTI-FCO.

Projects Export Promotion: David Hall. Born: 1952. Educated: Glenalmond; Pembroke College, Oxford. Joined the Foreign Office in 1964, and served in Bahrain, Dubai and Bonn. He joined the DTI in 1967, and became Head of Projects Export Promotion in 1991.

Oil and Gas Projects and Supplies Office: David Watson.

Exports to Asia, Africa and Australasia: Martyn Baker. Born: 1944. Educated: Dulwich College, Pembroke College, Cambridge. Joined Ministry of Aviation in 1965 and then the DTI, into which it was absorbed, in 1969. He represented British aviation interests at the Washington Embassy from 1978 to 1982, later becoming DTI North West regional director and director of the enterprise and deregulation unit in 1988.

Exports to Europe and the Americas: Neil Thornton. Born: 1950. Educated: Sedburgh School; Pembroke College, Cambridge. Joined Ministry of Posts and Telecommunications 1971, moving later that decade to HM Treasury. In DTI from 1984 he became head of Europe division – trade policy and export promotion in 1990.

Deputy Secretary: Alastair MacDonald (Grade 2). Born: 1940. Educated: Wimbledon College; Trinity College, Oxford. He worked as a journalist before joining the Civil Service in 1968, and held positions in DTI and the Ministry of Defence before becoming Deputy Secretary responsible for Industry in 1992.

Technology and Innovation: Dr David Evans. Born: 1949. Educated: Oxford University. Joined the Energy Department in 1974, and held posts in the Energy Technology, Petroleum Production, and Atomic Energy Divisions before serving in the British Embassy in Bonn. He also worked on gas privatisation, the Piper Alpha enquiry, before taking up his current position in 1994.

Chemicals and Biotechnology: Dr Elliot Finer. Born: 1944. Educated: St Catharine's College, Cambridge; the University of East Anglia. Joined the Department of Energy in 1975, working on industry, commercial, and energy issues. After the Cabinet Office Management Development Group, he joined the DTI as Head of Chemicals and Biotechnology in 1992.

Steel Metals Minerals and Vehicles: Martin Stanley. Born: 1948. Educated: Royal Grammar School, Newcastle upon Tyne; and Magdalen College, Oxford. Joined the Inland Revenue in 1971, transferred to the DTI in 1980, and was appointed Head of Steel Metals Minerals and Vehicles in 1992.

Aerospace: Robert Foster. Born: 1943. Educated: Oundle School; Corpus Christi College, Cambridge. He joined the Civil Service in 1971, and held posts in the Post Office and the DTI before becoming Head of Aerospace in 1993.

British National Space Centre: Derek Davis. Born: 1945. Educated: Clifton College, Bristol; Balliol College, Oxford. Joined the Civil Service in 1967, and held positions in the Board of Trade, the DTI, the Energy Department, and the National Coal Board, before becoming Head of the BNSC.

Electronics and Electrical and Mechanical Engineering: Martin Rumbelow. Born: 1937. Educated: Cardiff High School; Bristol University; Cranfield Institute of Technology. He worked on Concorde before joining the Civil Service in 1974, and held various posts before becoming Head of EEME in 1992.

Textiles and Retailing: Ian Jones. Born: 1949. Educated: Cambridge. Joined DTI in 1983, transferred to the Employment Department to work on small firms policy in 1985, returned to the DTI in 1989 as Head of Export Promotion, and was Head of the South East regional Office before being appointed to his current position in 1994.

Telecommunications and Posts: Paul Salvidge. Born: 1946. Educated: Cardiff High School; Birmingham University. Joined the Civil Service in 1967, and held various positions in the Ministry of Power and the DTI before becoming Head of Telecommunications and Posts in 1989.

Deputy Secretary: Charles Henderson (Grade 2). Born: 1939. Educated: Charterhouse; Pembroke College, Cambridge. Joined the Civil Service from the private sector in 1971, and served in the Export Credits Guarantee Department, Trade and Industry, and the Department of Energy, before becoming Deputy Secretary responsible for Energy in 1992.

Atomic Energy: Timothy Walker. Born: 1945. Educated: Tonbridge School; Brasenose College, Oxford; Virginia and Northwestern Universities. Joined the Greater London Council in 1974, and transferred to the Trade Department in 1977. Previous posts include Director of the Alvey Programme on fifth-generation computers, and various private-sector appointments, before becoming Head of AE in 1989.

Environment and Energy Technologies: Dr Colin Hicks. Born: 1946. Educated: Rutlish Grammar School, Merton; Bristol University. Joined the Civil Service in 1975, and held positions in the Laboratory of the Government Chemist and the DTI's R&D Division before being appointed Head of EET.

Coal: Bill Macintyre. Born: 1943. Educated: Merchiston Castle School, Edinburgh; St Andrews University. After working for BP, he joined the Export Credit Guarantee Department in 1972, subsequently working in the Department of Energy on gas, energy efficiency and electricity.

Coal Privatisation Unit: Peter Loughead. Born: 1950. Educated: Lincoln College, Oxford.

Joined the Civil Service in 1975, held positions in the Department of Prices and Consumer Protection, the UK Representation in Brussels, DTI, and the Treasury before being appointed Head of CPU in 1993.

Electricity and Nuclear Fuels: Christopher Wilcock. Born: 1939. Educated: Berkhamsted and Ipswich Schools, and Trinity Hall, Cambridge. Joined Foreign Office in 1962, and held posts in the DHSS, the Energy Department, before becoming Head of ENF in 1991.

Oil and Gas: John Michell. Born: 1942. Educated: Marlborough; Corpus Christi College, Cambridge. Joined the Civil Service in 1964, held positions in the Ministry of Aviation, the Industry Department, the Treasury and DTI.

Deputy Secretary: Brian Hilton (Grade 2). Born: 1940. Educated: St Marylebone Grammar. Joined the Export Credit Guarantee Department in 1958, moving to the Foreign and Commonwealth Office in 1971. His varied experience subsequently took in the Organisation for Economic Co-operation and Development, the Department of Industry and its successor DTI, the Ministry of Agriculture and the Citizen's Charter Unit.

Deputy Secretary: Roy Williams (Grade 2). Born: 1934. Educated: Liverpool University. Joined the Ministry of Power as an Assistant Principal in 1956, and held various positions in the Department of Trade and Industry before becoming Deputy Secretary responsible for Regional Policy and Small Firms in 1984.

Regional Development: Brian Bender. Born: 1949. Educated: Greenford County Grammar School; Imperial College (PhD 1973). Worked for the UK Permanent Representative at the EC, specialising in industry and energy. Joined DTI minerals division in 1982; secondment to the Cabinet Office in 1990.

Invest in Britain Bureau: Andrew Fraser (Chief Executive). Born: 1951. Educated: Denstone College, Staffordshire; Harvard School, California, and the Universities of Sussex and California. He worked for three of the world's top advertising agencies, Saatchi & Saatchi, McCann Erickson and Young and Rubicam, and became managing director of Dentsu before becoming chief executive of the Invest in Britain Bureau in 1994.

Small Firms and Business Link: Sarah Brown. Born: 1943. Educated: St Paul's Girls' School; Newnham College, Cambridge. She joined the Civil Service in 1965, and held various positions before becoming Head of SFBL in 1992.

Management and Technology Services: Keith Shotton. Born: 1943. Educated: Trinity College, Cambridge. He became Director of the DTI's Radio and Technology Division in 1987, and was appointed Head of Information technology in 1990 before becoming Head of MTS in 1993.

Deputy Secretary: Robert Priddle (Grade 2). Born: 1938. Educated: King's College, Wimbledon; Peterhouse, Cambridge. Joined the Ministry of Aviation in 1960, and held various positions in the Departments of Trade and Energy, before becoming Deputy Secretary responsible for Corporate and Consumer Affairs in 1992.

Deregulation Unit: Vivian Brown. Born: 1945. Educated: Leeds Grammar School; St John's College, Oxford, and St Cross College, Oxford. Joined the Civil Service in 1970, and held positions in the DTI, the Foreign Office, and the Cabinet Office before becoming Head of DU in 1992.

Companies: Arthur Russell.

Insurance: Jonathan Spencer. Born: 1949. Educated: Bournemouth School; Downing College, Cambridge; Oxford University. Joined the Civil Service in 1974, and held positions in the DTI and the Cabinet Office before becoming Head of Insurance in 1991.

Competition Policy: Arthur Pryor. Born: 1939. Educated: Downing College, Cambridge (PhD). Joined Board of Trade 1966. West Midlands Regional Director for DTI in 1985, becoming director-general British NationalSpace Centre three years later.

Consumer Affairs: John Dorken. Born: 1944. Educated: Cambridge and SOAS. Joined the DTI in 1967, and held posts in the Civil Aviation, Shipping, and Electricity Divisions, the Cabinet Office, and Deputy Director of Gas, before being appointed to his current position in 1993.

Deputy Secretary: Anthony Hammond (Grade 2). Born: 1940. Educated: Malvern; Emmanuel College, Cambridge. His previous positions include solicitor for the Greater London Council, legal assistant at the Home Office and the Northern Ireland Office, before becoming Solicitor and Deputy Secretary at the DTI in 1992.

Investigations: Martin Roberts. Born: 1946. Educated: Oxford University. Joined the Ministry of Technology in 1970, transferred to the DTI in 1971, and held posts in the Industrial Policy and Electronics Divisions, the Energy Department, the Foreign Office, the Environment Department, before being appointed to his current post in 1993.

Solicitors B: Chris Kerse. Born: 1946. Educated: University of Hull. Qualified as solicitor. Joined Office of Fair Trading 1976. Joined DTI 1981 becoming head of consumer affairs division in 1991.

Solicitors C: John Stanley. Born: 1941. Educated: Welwyn Garden City Grammar School; Clare College, Cambridge. After a legal career in the private sector joined the Industry Department in 1975, before being appointed Under-Secretary (Legal) in 1989.

Solicitors D: Philip Bovey. Born: 1948. Educated: Rugby; Peterhouse, Cambridge. Joined the Civil Service in 1970, and held legal positions in the Foreign Office, DTI, and the Cabinet Office, before becoming Under-Secretary (Legal) in 1985.

Solicitors E: Kathryn Morton. Born: 1946. Educated: Ealing Grammar School, and Sussex University. Qualified as a solicitor and after private practice held legal posts in the Office of Fair Trading and the DTI before becoming Under-Secretary (Legal) in 1992.

Deputy Secretary: Tony Hutton (Grade 2). Born: 1941. Educated: Brentwood School, and Trinity College, Oxford. Joined Inland Revenue, HM Inspector of Taxes and subsequent positions at the Board of Trade before becoming Deputy Secretary and Principal Establishment and Finance Officer in 1991.

Personnel: Penny Boys. Born: 1947. Educated: Guildford County School. After various postings in the former Ministries of Power and Energy, including a secondment to the British National Oil Corporation, in 1989 Miss Boys became deputy director general of the Office of Electricity Regulation. She became head of personnel at DTI in 1993.

Services Management: Roger Heathcote. Born: 1944. Educated: Birmingham University. Joined DTI in 1970, and held posts in the offshore technology, Petroleum Engineering, Gas, Electricity and Finance Divisions, before taking up his current post in 1992.

Finance and Resources Management: Mike O'Shea. Born: 1951. Educated: Bristol Grammar School; Corpus Christi College, Cambridge. Joined the DTI in 1973, and was appointed Head of FRM in 1992.

Internal Audit: Tony Elkington.

Economics and Statistics: David Coates. Born: 1942. Educated: Leeds Grammar; Queen's College, Oxford, and the London School of Economics. He became an economic adviser to the Ministry of Technology in 1968, and senior economic adviser at the DTI in 1974, before becoming Head of ES.

DEPARTMENT OF TRANSPORT

2 Marsham Street

London SW1

Telephone: 071-276 0888

The Transport Department, which has been subject to many amalgamations with other Whitehall departments since its formation in 1919, until its current incarnation in 1976, is responsible for the delivery of effective and efficient transport by road, rail, sea and air. But the exponential increase in mobility, including commuting, tourism and leisure, has put the existing transport networks under tremendous pressure. In the 30 years between 1952 and 1992, the number of passenger kilometres travelled each year increased from 219 billion to 681 billion. In addition, the number of tonne kilometres clocked up by the freight industry increased from 88 billion to 208 billion over the same period. The chronic congestion and transport bottlenecks caused by the demand for increased mobility has generated a highly charged public debate over the relative costs and benefits of public and private transport.

As a result of the government's public-sector reform programme, the 2,000 staff at the Transport Department's new London headquarters and eight regional Offices are responsible for the formulation of transport policy, and setting the framework within which its executive agencies operate. This policy core, known as the Central Transport Group, has been set the strategic objective of recruiting private-sector initiative and finance, through privatisation and public-private-sector partnerships, to help refurbish and develop the nation's transport infrastructure and transport networks. Although still in its infancy, the policy has had a number of notable successes, including the privately financed Queen Elizabeth II Bridge at Dartford in London, the Second Severn Crossing, the Heathrow Express and the Jubilee Line extension. But the real test for the private sector will be whether it is willing to take on large-scale infrastructure projects such as the construction of the Channel Tunnel rail link between London and Folkestone (four private-sector consortia have been chosen to tender for the design and construction of the new £2.7 billion link), and the design, construction, financing and operation of new roads.

The same strategic policy objective is also being applied to the national rail system. The government intends to transfer the entire national rail network into private-sector hands as rail services are progressively franchised to independent operators. Under the new structure, a Franchising Director will be responsible for letting the 25 passenger franchises created out of the old British Rail network, and distributing subsidies for loss-making but socially necessary services. Railtrack, a government-owned company, will manage the railway infrastructure, including timetabling, signalling, maintenance and investment, and is destined for privatisation along with a myriad of rail businesses such as freight and engineering services. A Rail Regulator will be responsible for licensing train operators, track access and charging, and fair competition. Critics insist, however, that the number of private-sector companies willing to take on the new rail franchises will be minimal, and that the effect will simply be to break British Rail up into its component parts.

The Transport Department is responsible for Britain's 2,700 km of motorways and 7,800 km of trunk roads. Strategy, including the introduction of motorway tolls and urban road pricing schemes, and priorities for road building, are decided by the policy core, while construction and maintenance are the responsibility of the new Highways Agency. The Department is also responsible for overseeing London Transport's Underground and bus networks (although all the London bus companies will be sold off), and for setting the framework, through international agreements, within which the air transport and shipping industries operate. Almost 85 per cent of the Department's staff now work in its eight executive agencies, and £50 million of departmental work has been subjected to market testing. Civil Service numbers in transport are just over 14,000, a figure which has been declining in recent years.

Permanent Secretary: Patrick Brown (Grade 1). Born: 1940. Educated: Royal Grammar School, Newcastle; the School of Slavonic and East European Studies, University of London. Previous posts include management consultant, Urwick Orr and Partners. Joined the Environment Department in 1972, transferred to the Transport Department, was appointed to Under-Secretary in 1983, returned to DoE as Deputy Secretary in 1988, and held the posts of Second Permanent Secretary and Chief Executive PSA. He became Permanent Secretary at Transport in 1991.

Deputy Secretary (Infrastructure): Nicholas Montagu (Grade 2). Born: 1944. Educated: Rugby; New College, Oxford. Joined the DHSS as a Principal in 1974, and became Deputy Secretary at the DSS before being transferred to Deputy Secretary, Transport in 1992.

Railways 1 (Infrastructure): Colin Grimsey. Born: 1943. Educated: Dartford Grammar School; King's College, London. Previous posts include Director of Finance, Transport Department, Under-Secretary, on secondment to London Transport, Head of Finance Transport Industries Division, Head of Personnel Policy Division, and Head of Ports Division, before becoming responsible for Railways.

Railways 2 (Privatisation, policy, legislation and franchising): Philip Wood. Born: 1936. Educated: Queen Elizabeth's Grammar School, Wakefield; Queen's College, Oxford. Joined the Civil Service in 1967, and held posts in the Ministry of Transport, the Environment Department, the Prime Minister's Office, and was seconded to British Rail before becoming Under-Secretary in 1986.

Railways 3 (Implementation and co-ordination of privatisation): Jenny Williams. Born: 1948. Educated: Cambridge University. Currently responsible for the speedy and effective privatisation of the national rail network.

Channel Tunnel Safety Unit: Peter Moss.

Civil Aviation (Infrastructure): Hugh Wenban-Smith. Born: 1941. Educated: King's College, Cambridge. Joined Civil Service as an economist in 1968, and held posts in the British High Commission in New Delhi, the DTI, the Price Commission, the Environment Department, and the Transport Department before being appointed Head of Civil Aviation in 1993.

Freight and Ports International: John Henes. Born: 1937. Educated: Christ's Hospital; Caius College, Cambridge. He held posts in the Ministry of Aviation and the DTI before moving to the Transport Department in 1992.

Deputy Secretary (Central Services): David Rowlands (Grade 2). Born: 1947. Educated: St Mary's College, Crosby; St Edmund Hall, Oxford. Previous posts include Assistant Secretary, Civil Aviation; Finance and Management; Central Finance; Shipping Policy, Emergencies and Security; and Railways 1, becoming Deputy Secretary in 1993.

Personnel: Richard Allen. Born: 1948. Educated: Bolton School; Balliol College, Oxford. He held a variety of posts in the DTI, the British Embassy in Washington, and the Transport Department, including Principal Private Secretary, and Under-Secretary, seconded to British Rail, before becoming responsible for personnel in 1990.

Finance: Elizabeth Hopkins. Born: 1941. Educated: Lady Margaret Hall, Oxford; Ibaden and

Sussex Universities. Previous posts include lecturing and research at Sussex University, Research Officer, Government of Zambia; various positions in the Transport and Environment Departments, and Regional Director South West, Environment and Transport, before becoming Finance Director in 1993.

Executive Agencies: Jonathon Phillips. Born: 1952. Educated: Queen Mary's Grammar School, Walsall; St John's College, Cambridge. Joined the Transport Department in 1977, and held various positions before becoming Head of Executive Agencies in 1993.

Director of Statistics: David Flaxen. Born: 1941. Educated: Manchester Grammar School; Brasenose College, Oxford; University College, London. He held posts in the Inland Revenue, the Employment Department, the Central Statistical Office, before becoming director of statistics in 1989.

Economics and Transport Policy: Dr John Rickard. Born: 1940. Educated: Ilford County High School; St John's College, Oxford; Aston University. Previous posts include Under-Secretary, HM Treasury, Senior Economic Adviser, HM Treasury, the Central Policy Review Staff, Cabinet Office, and economic adviser to Bahrain before being appointed chief economic adviser.

Legal Adviser: Mike Thomas. Born: 1949. Educated: Oxford and Sussex University. Joined the Civil Service in 1980 from private practice, and moved to the Transport Department as Head of the Legal Unit in 1993 where he is responsible for legal advice on all transport issues.

Deputy Secretary (Operations): John Dempster (Grade 2). Born: 1938. Educated: Plymouth College; Oriel College, Oxford. Joined the Transport Ministry in 1965, and held posts in the Property Services Agency, the Environment Department, the Transport Department, the Lord Chancellor's Department, Head of the Marine Directorate, and Principal Establishment and Finance Officer.

Public Transport London: Handley Stevens. Born: 1941. Educated: The Leys School, Cambridge; King's College, Cambridge. Joined the Foreign Office in 1964, and served as Second Secretary, Kuala Lumpur. He also held posts in the Civil Service Department, and the DTI, before moving to transport in 1991.

National Roads Policy: Henry Derwent. Born: 1951. Educated: Berkhamsted School; Worcester College, Oxford. Joined the Environment Department in 1974, and the Transport Department in 1986, where he held positions in local finance, vehicle licensing, and central finance before being appointed to his current post.

Urban and Local Roads: Jim Coates. Born: 1935. Educated: Nottingham High School; Clare College, Cambridge. Joined the Transport Ministry in 1959, and held a variety of positions, including Head of Highways and Railways Directorates, before being appointed to his current post.

Road and Vehicle Safety: Sophia Lambert. Born: 1943. Educated: London School of Economics. She held posts in the Foreign Office, the Cabinet Office, and the Transport Department, including Head of International Transport, Head of Public Transport (Met. Division), and Head of International Railways, before being appointed to her current position in 1992.

Shipping and Freight: Roger Clarke. Born: 1939. Educated: University College School; Corpus Christi College, Cambridge. Previous posts include Head of the Public Transport Directorate and Head of Civil Aviation Policy, before becoming Under-Secretary in 1991.

International Aviation: Tony Goldman. Born: 1940. Educated: Marlborough; Peterhouse, Cambridge. Joined Civil Service in 1973, and held positions as Private Secretary to the Secretary of State for Transport, HM Treasury, and the Public Transport Directorate before becoming responsible for aviation policy.

Civil Aviation (Operations): Hugh Wenban-Smith (see Civil Aviation Infrastructure above)

Director and Co-ordinator of Transport Security: Harry Ditmas. Born: 1930. Educated: Cambridge University. Joined Transport Department in 1990 after retiring from the Defence Ministry.

Head of UK Delegation to the Channel Tunnel Safety Authority: Edward Ryder. Born: 1931. Educated: Cheltenham Grammar School, and Bristol University. Joined the RAF in 1953, held a series of positions in the private sector, became HM Chief Inspector of Nuclear Installations for the Health and Safety Executive before being appointed to his current post in 1992.

Chief Inspector of Air Accidents: Ken Smart. Born: 1946. Educated: Aylesford School, Maidstone. Joined the Ministry of Aviation as an aeronautical apprentice, worked on structural and non-destructive testing of aircraft for the Defence Ministry, and moved to the Air Accidents Investigation Branch in 1974, before being appointed Chief Inspector of Air Accidents.

Chief Inspector of Marine Accidents: Captain Peter Marriott. Born: 1939. Worked for BP Shipping for 33 years, 20 years at sea and 13 years specialising in safety, and joined the Transport Department as Chief Inspector of Marine Accidents in 1989.

FOREIGN AND COMMONWEALTH OFFICE
King Charles Street
London SW1
Telephone: 071-210 6094

In the two centuries since Charles James Fox became the first Foreign Secretary in 1782, the role of the diplomat has changed out of all recognition. The Machiavellians of popular folk-lore have been replaced by a highly professional Diplomatic Service which provides a Rolls-Royce service on what can only be described as a Ford Fiesta budget. *Force majeure* has left Britain little option but to withdraw from its central position on the international stage. But, ironically, many domestic critics often appear to hold the members of the Diplomatic Service responsible for the erosion of Britain's global standing. Diplomats are regularly pilloried for their arrogance and elitism. Yet, in the words of Douglas Hurd, they are in no small measure responsible for Britain's continued ability to punch above its weight.

The Foreign Office is one of the smallest government departments with some of the biggest responsibilities. Its overall aims, as specified in its 1994 annual report, are to enhance the security and prosperity of the United Kingdom and its Dependent Territories, promote and protect British interests and standing overseas, and provide consular assistance to British citizens abroad. Of the £1.4 billion of taxpayers' money spent by the Foreign Office in 1994, £781 million went on overseas representation, £365 million on subscriptions to international organisations and international peacekeeping, £164 million on the BBC World Service, and £97 million on the British Council. Diplomatic or consular relations are maintained with 183 countries. Altogether, Britain funds 215 Overseas Posts, all staffed by career members of the Diplomatic Service, including 43 High Commissions in Commonwealth countries, 97

Embassies, 9 Missions to international organisations and conferences, 61 Deputy High Commissions and Consulates, and 5 British Interest Sections and Trade Offices.

The Chancery or political and economic functions of the Foreign Office include negotiation, reporting and analysis of developments abroad, and keeping channels of communication open with overseas governments, organisations and other bodies. Most of this effort is focused on the European Union, the UN, NATO, the Commonwealth, and bi-lateral relationships conducted by British diplomats abroad. The Foreign Office's checklist of key long-term objectives include exerting its influence to ensure that the EU develops as an economically liberal trading bloc open to new members, maintaining NATO as the cornerstone of European defence while promoting the development of the Western European Union as a bridge between Europe and the Atlantic Alliance, working for a peaceful settlement in the former Yugoslavia, providing the support required for former command economies to make the transition to market economies, and preventive diplomacy, including efforts to stem the proliferation of nuclear, chemical and biological weapons.

Great emphasis is now placed on promoting British exports and attracting inward investment. Britain's Overseas Posts double up as an extension of Overseas Trade Services, an organisation which has fused the export promotion work of the FCO and the DTI through the Joint Export Control Directorate. With more than 33 million British citizens travelling abroad each year, Britain's Consular services have faced a considerable increase in workload, ranging from visiting the 4,000 British prisoners abroad, to issuing passports, providing repatriation and financial assistance, and arranging emergency evacuations. Like all government departments, the Foreign Office is caught between mounting pressures on the public purse and ever increasing demands on its resources. Subscriptions to international organisations and international peacekeeping, which are expected to mushroom to £108 million by 1996, are a particularly acute problem. The Foreign Office has one executive agency, the Wilton Park conference centre, which seeks to contribute to the resolution of international conflicts, and it has a modest market testing programme. The Foreign Office has about 9,700 civil servants, a number that has slightly grown in recent years.

Permanent Under-Secretary: Sir John Coles (Grade 1). Born: 1937. Educated: Magdalen College School, Brackley; Magdalen College, Oxford. After joining the Diplomatic Service as an Arabist in 1960, Sir John held numerous overseas positions in Khartoum, Dubai, Cairo and the UK Representation in Brussels, before becoming Ambassador to Jordan, and High Commissioner to Australia. He was appointed Head of the Diplomatic Service in 1994.

Legal Adviser: Sir Franklin Berman (Grade 2). Born: 1939. Educated: Rondebosch Boys' High School, Cape Town; Cape Town University; Wadham and Nuffield Colleges, Oxford. Joined the Diplomatic Service in 1965, and was called to the Bar in 1966. Sir Franklin has held numerous posts, including Legal Adviser to the British Military Government in Berlin, the British Embassy in Bonn, and the UK Mission to the UN before becoming legal adviser to the FCO in 1991.

Deputy Under-Secretary (Political Director): Pauline Neville-Jones (Grade 2). Born: 1939. Educated: Leeds Girls' High School, and Lady Margaret Hall, Oxford. Joined the Foreign Office in 1963, and held overseas positions in Salisbury (Rhodesia), Singapore and Washington before becoming Chef de Cabinet to Christopher Tugendhat, the EC's Budget Commissioner, 1977-82. She has also served as head of the FCO's Planning Staff, in the British Embassy in Bonn, and the Cabinet Office, before being appointed Political Director in 1994.

Western Europe: Thomas Richardson. Born: 1941. Educated: Westminster; Christ Church, Oxford. Joined the Foreign Office in 1962, and has held overseas positions in Dar-Es-Salaam, Milan, the UK Mission to the UN and Head of Chancery in Rome. He also worked in the Cabinet Office before becoming Assistant Under-Secretary responsible for Western Europe.

International Organisations: John de Fonblanque. Born: 1943. Educated: Ampleforth; King's College, Cambridge; London School of Economics. He has held various overseas posts in Jakarta, the UK Representation in Brussels and Head of Chancery New Delhi, before becoming Assistant Under-Secretary responsible for international organisations in 1994.

Deputy Under-Secretary (Economic Director): Michael Jay (Grade 2). Born: 1946. Educated: Winchester; Magdalen College, Oxford; London University (SOAS). He has held overseas posts as a member of the UK delegation to the IMF-World Bank, and First Secretary New Delhi. After being appointed Assistant Under-Secretary responsible for EC affairs in 1990, he became the FCO's Economic Director in 1994.

European Community: Stephen Wright. Born: 1946. Educated: Shrewsbury; Queen's College, Oxford. Joined the Diplomatic Service in 1968, and served overseas in Havana, New York, the UK Representation in Brussels, and as Head of Chancery New Delhi, before being appointed Assistant Under-Secretary responsible for EC affairs in 1994.

Economic Adviser: Jim Rollo. Educated: Gourock and Greenock High Schools; Glasgow University; the London School of Economics. Joined the Civil Service in 1968 as an economic adviser in the Ministry of Agriculture, he was transferred to the Overseas Development Administration in 1979, and was appointed chief economic adviser in 1994.

Deputy Under-Secretary: David Wright (Grade 2). Born: 1944. Educated: Wolverhampton Grammar School, and Peterhouse, Cambridge. He has held overseas posts in Tokyo and Paris, was Ambassador to Korea, and worked as Private Secretary to the Cabinet Secretary and Private Secretary to HRH the Prince of Wales before being appointed deputy Under-Secretary in 1994.

Americas: William Marsden. Born: 1940. Educated: Winchester; Trinity College, Cambridge; London University. Joined the Foreign Office in 1962, and held overseas posts in the UK Delegation to NATO, Rome, Moscow, and the UK Representation in Brussels. He was also Ambassador to Costa Rica and Nicaragua (non-resident), and Minister (Trade Policy) in Washington, before being appointed Assistant Under-Secretary responsible for the Americas in 1994.

Northern Asia: Christopher Hum. Born: 1946. Educated: Berkhampsted School; Pembroke College, Oxford; Hong Kong University. Joined the Foreign Office in 1967, and has held overseas posts in Hong Kong, Peking, the UK Representation in Brussels, and Paris. He has also served as Assistant Head of the Hong Kong and Falkland Islands departments, and Head of Chancery, UK Missions to the UN, before being appointed Assistant Under-Secretary in 1992.

Southern Asia-Pacific: David Dain. Born: 1940. Educated: Merchant Taylors'; St John's College, Oxford. Joined the Diplomatic Service in 1963, and has held overseas posts in Tehran, Kabul, Bonn, Athens, Nicosia and was High Commissioner, Republic of Cyprus, before being appointed Assistant Under-Secretary responsible for Southern Asia-Pacific in 1994.

Africa: Anthony Goodenough. Born: 1941. Educated: Wellington; New College, Oxford. Joined the Diplomatic Service in 1964 after one year's VSO in Sarawak, and has held overseas posts in Athens, Paris, Islamabad and Ghana, before being appointed Assistant Under-Secretary for Africa in 1992.

Overseas Trade: Ray Mingay (Joint Export Promotion). (*See* entry in Department of Trade and Industry.)

Deputy Under-Secretary (Chief Clerk): Andrew Wood (Grade 2). Born: 1940. Educated: Ardingly College; King's College, Cambridge. Joined Diplomatic Service in 1961, and held overseas posts in Moscow, Washington, and Belgrade, before becoming Ambassador to Yugoslavia and Minister, Washington. He was appointed Chief Clerk in 1992.

Public Departments: Christopher Battiscombe. Born: 1940. Educated: Wellington; New College, Oxford. Joined the Diplomatic Service as an Arabist in 1963, and has held overseas posts in Kuwait, the OECD, the UK Mission to the UN, Cairo and Paris, before becoming Ambassador to Algeria in 1990. He was appointed Assistant Under-Secretary responsible for Public Departments in 1994.

Protocol: Anthony Figgis. Born: 1940. Educated: Rugby; King's College, Cambridge. Joined the Diplomatic Service in 1962, and held overseas posts in Belgrade, Bahrain, Madrid, Geneva and Bonn, before being appointed Assistant Under-Secretary responsible for Protocol in 1993.

Personnel (Deputy Chief Clerk): Veronica Sutherland. Born: 1939. Educated: Royal School, Bath; London and Southampton Universities. Joined the Diplomatic Service in 1965, and held overseas posts in Copenhagen, New Delhi and UNESCO before becoming Ambassador to the Ivory Coast. She was appointed Assistant Under-Secretary responsible for personnel in 1990.

Resources: Kevin Tebbit. Born: 1946. Joined the Ministry of Defence in 1969, and served in the UK delegation to NATO. He served as Head of Chancery in Ankara, Directeur du Cabinet to the Secretary-General of NATO, and Political-Military Counsellor in Washington before being appointed Assistant Under-Secretary responsible for resources in 1994.

Communications and Technical Services: Jeffrey Ling. Born: 1939. Educated: Bristol University. Joined the Diplomatic Service in 1966, and held overseas posts in Washington, OECD, Brunei and Paris, before being appointed Assistant Under-Secretary responsible for Communications in 1989.

Deputy Under-Secretary: Rob Young (Grade 2). Born: 1945. Educated: King Edward VI School, Norwich; Leicester University. Joined the Diplomatic Service as an Arabist in 1967, and held overseas posts in Cairo, Paris and Damascus. He became Head of the Middle East Department in 1987, and survived Lord Justice Scott's enquiry into the arms-to-Iraq affair to become DUS in 1994.

Middle East-North Africa: Andrew Green. Born: 1941. Educated: Haileybury and ISC; Magdalene College, Cambridge. Joined the Diplomatic Service in 1965 as an Arabist, and held overseas posts in Aden, Abu Dhabi, OECD, Washington and Riyadh before becoming Ambassador to Syria in 1991. He was appointed Assistant Under-Secretary in 1994.

Central and Eastern Europe: Roger Bone. Born: 1944. Educated: William Palmer's School, Grays; St Peter's College, Oxford. Joined the Diplomatic Service in 1966, and held overseas positions in the UK Mission to the UN, Stockholm, Moscow, the UK Representation to Brussels. He became Head of Chancery, Washington, in 1987, before being appointed Assistant Under-Secretary in 1991.

Deputy Under-Secretary (Defence): Sir Timothy Daunt (Grade 2). Born: 1935. Educated: Sherborne; St Catharine's College, Cambridge. Joined the Diplomatic Service in 1959, and held overseas posts in Ankara, Nicosia, the UK Mission to the UN, the OECD and NATO, before becoming Ambassador to Turkey in 1986. He was appointed DUS in 1992.

Defence: David Logan. Born: 1943. Educated: Charterhouse; University College, Oxford. Joined the Diplomatic Service in 1965, and held overseas posts in Istanbul, Ankara, the UK Mission to the UN, Oslo, and Moscow, before becoming Assistant Under-Secretary (defence) 1993.

HOME OFFICE
50 Queen Anne's Gate
London SW1H 9AT
Telephone: 071-273 3000

The Home Office is a social sweeper-up, overseeing the police, the administration of justice and the punishment of those found guilty of offence; it controls access to Britain from abroad, and the issue of passports to citizens wishing to travel.

The Home Office was created in 1782, as the business of the British state bifurcated into home and overseas. The Home Secretary's principal task was maintaining that most British of qualities, the Queen's Peace. Under Sir Robert Peel the peace of the capital was assured by the creation of a professional police force. (The Home Secretary remains the police authority for London, overseeing its finance and senior personnel in detail; the Home Office responsibility for the Security Service and Special Branch overlap here.) Later it was natural the Home Office should take on civil defence, the control of aliens and that rag-bag of regulatory activities that included betting and gaming, liquor licensing, obscene publications and explosives. Over the years these have been dropped or reapportioned, but not without leaving the Home Office with a core role as the department practically concerned with order in its widest sense.

The Home Office has traditionally concerned itself with the lay magistracy, leaving superior courts to the Lord Chancellor. But the Home Secretary, responsible for prisons, is concerned about what the courts decide, and through legislation seeks to alter tariffs and sentencing policies. As for the police, over the years a peculiar void has opened. Nominally, outside London, chief constables answer to police authorities. But the Home Office is influential in appointments to these, which until now have also included elected councillors. And the Home Office has taken a detailed interest in chief constable appointments. Yet chief constables, exercising vast discretionary power in the state, often appear directly accountable to no one, except their consciences and their oath as constables to uphold the peace.

The upper ranks of the Home Office, notably its deputy secretaries, have traditionally been considered wise and expert. The work of its research department has commanded wide respect, not least for its findings that the volume of crime has much to do with the number and assiduity of the police officers turning in report sheets, while the public's perception and fear of crime may be something else.

The Home Office, including the Prison Service, is a substantial department with some 51,000 staff – a number that grew by over a third in the five years to 1993. This reflects the present government's anxieties over crime.

Permanent Secretary: Richard Wilson (Grade 1). Born 1942. Educated: Radley; Clare College, Cambridge. Called to the Bar. Joined the Board of Trade 1966, gaining Private Office experience there. Moved to Cabinet Office in 1971 and then to the Department of Energy 1974; became a Deputy Secretary in the Cabinet Office in the later 1980s before moving to the Treasury 1990. He was translated to the Home Office after a brief sojourn as Permanent Secretary at the Department of the Environment. Mr Wilson is often talked of as a leading contender to succeed Sir Robin Butler as Head of the Civil Service.

Legal Adviser: Michael Saunders (Grade 2). Born: 1944. Educated: Clifton College; Birmingham University; Jesus College, Cambridge. Called to Bar in 1971, he took part in the Hague Conference on Private International Law later moving into government service at the Department of Trade and Industry. After joining the Treasury Solicitors' Department in 1973 be become Solicitor to HM Customs and Excise in 1989.

Criminal Research and Statistics: John Halliday (Grade 2). Born: 1942. Educated: Whitgift School, Croydon; St John's College, Cambridge. After teaching, he joined the Home Office in 1966. After Private Office experience there in 1980 he moved later in the decade to become an Under Secrerary at the DHSS.

Head of Criminal Policy Department: Austin Wilson. Born: 1938. Educated: Leeds Grammar; St Edmund Hall, Oxford. Joined the Home Office 1961, serving in Private Office three years later. He become Head of Community Programmes and Equal Opportunities in 1982. He had a four-year stint at the Northern Ireland Office from 1988.

Director of Research and Statistics: Christopher Nuttall. Born: 1939. Educated: Queen Elizabeth Grammar, Wakefield; University of Keele; University of California. Joined the Home Office in 1963 later becoming Director of Research. During the 1980s he worked outside the UK in Canadian government service.

Head of Criminal Justice and Constitutional Department: Robert Morris. Born: 1937. Educated: Handsworth Grammar; Christ's College, Cambridge. Joined Home Office in 1961 moving to Private Office three years later; he had another Private Office job later in 1976. Outside the Home Office, he worked in the Civil Service Department in the late 1960s.

HM Chief Inspector of Probation: G W Smith. Born: 1939. Educated: Bishop Wordsworth School, Salisbury; King's College, University of Durham. Probation Office, moving to Inner London 1971, becoming chief probation officer 1981 and HM Inspector 1992.

Principal Establishment Officer (also responsible for Fire and Emergency Planning): Terence Platt (Grade 2). Born: 1936. Educated: St Olave's and St Saviour's Grammar; Jt Services School for Linguists. Joined government service as HM Immigration Officer in 1957 moving to the Home Office proper in 1962. After secondments to the Cabinet Office and the Northern Ireland Office – where he worked in Private Office in the 1970s – he became Chief Inspector in the Immigration Service in 1991.

Head of Establishment Department: Christopher Scoble. Born: 1943. Educated: Kent College, Canterbury; Corpus Christi College, Oxford. Joined the Home Office in 1965, transferring to the Welsh Office where he worked in Private Office in 1969. His subsequent Home Office experience has included the Broadcasting and miscellaneous portfolios.

Principal Finance Officer: Sydney Norris. Born: 1937. Educated: Liverpool High School for Boys. University College, Oxford; Trinity Hall and Institute of Criminology, Cambridge. Joined the Home Office in 1963. moving into Private Office three years later and again in

1973. As a Harkness Fellow he gained experience in North America. Subsequent appointments outside the Home Office include HM Treasury and the Northern Ireland Office.

Head of Fire and Emergency Planning Department: William Innes. Born: 1934; Educated: Robert Gordon's College, Aberdeen; Aberdeen University. Served in the Royal Air Force until 1970 moving to the Home Office in 1972 and became Director of Custody in the Prison Service in 1990.

Police Department: Ian Burns (Grade 2). Born: 1939. Educated: Bootham, York. Took a law degree at London and joined the Home Office in 1965. Subsequent appointments included the Northern Ireland Office where he held a deputy secretaryship in the late 1980s and the Department of Health and Social Security.

Margaret Clayton. Born: 1941. Educated: Christ's Hospital, Hertford; Birkbeck College, London. Joined the Home Office in 1960, gaining Private Office experience seven years later. She became Director of Services in the Prison Service in 1986.

Carolyn Sinclair. Born: 1944. Educated: Laurel Bank School, Glasgow; Edinburgh University. Joined the Foreign Office in 1968, gaining Private Office experience there in 1977. After service in HM Treasury she joined the Prime Minister's Policy Unit at Number 10 in 1988, working there till the end of the Thatcher premiership in 1992.

F J A Warne.

Head of Science and Technology Group: Gordon Wasserman. Born: 1938; Educated: Westmount High School, Montreal; McGill University; New College, Oxford. After academic work joined the Home Office as economic adviser in 1967 moving to head the Urban Deprivation Unit in 1973. Attached to the 'Think-tank', the Central Policy Review Staff in 1981.

HM Chief Inspector of Constabulary: Trefor Morris. Born: 1934. Educated: Ducie Technical High School, Manchester; Manchester University. Joined Manchester City Police and moved up the ranks becoming, after reorganisation, Chief Constable of Greater Manchester in 1984. He joined HM Inspector of Constabulary in 1990.

Equal Opportunities and General, Immigration and Nationality: Anthony Langdon (Grade 2). Born: 1935; Educated: Kingswood School, Bath; Christ's College, Cambridge. Joined the Home Office in 1958 moving nine years later to HM Treasury 1967, with a subsequent secondment to the Cabinet Office in 1985.

Head of Equal Opportunities and General Department: Michael Head. Born: 1936. Educated: Leeds, Kingston and Woking Grammars; University College, London, University of Michigan. Joined the Home Office in 1960 with a move to Private Office four years later. His subsequent departmental portfolios have included probation and after-care and broadcasting.

Immigration Policy and Nationality: Anthony Rawsthorne. Born: 1943. Educated: Ampleforth; Wadham College, Oxford. Joined the Home Office in 1966 working on crime policy. Served as Secretary of the Falklands Islands Review Committee set up after the conflict in 1982 and has since worked at the Home Office on equal opportunities and general.

Immigration Operations and Resources: William Jeffrey. Born: 1948. Educated: Alan Glen's, Glasgow; University of Glasgow. Joined the Home Office in 1971, working later on criminal policy, and in the Prison Service.

HM Chief Inspector of Prisons: His Honour Judge Stephen Tumim: Born: 1930. Educated: St Edward's School, Oxford; Worcester College, Oxford. Called to Bar 1955 and after a distinguished legal career became a Crown Court recorder in 1977 and a Circuit Judge a year later.

HM Chief Inspector of Fire: Sir Reginald Doyle. Born: 1929. Educated: Aston Commercial College. After service in the Royal Navy led a career in the Fire Service becoming Chief Fire Officer for Hereford and Worcester and the County of Kent. Joined the Home Office Fire Service Inspectorate in 1984.

LORD CHANCELLOR'S DEPARTMENT
House of Lords
London SW1A 0PW
Telephone: 071-210 8500

The Lord Chancellor's is a department of highly confidential lists – mainly lists of barristers, suitably annotated as to political proclivities, skills and that peculiar set of qualities which go to make up an English judge. From these lists judges are appointed. The administration of the courts is shared between the Home Office and the Lord Chancellor's Department. The Lord Chancellor takes responsibility for the judiciary, which is notionally independent of the executive. Commentators have suggested recently that its meanness in rewarding judges is responsible for a spate of decisions by senior judges which have gone against the Government. A small department, its subject is shrouded from the public gaze by the dual insulation of Civil Service confidentiality and the special mystique which surrounds the administration of justice.

It is not easy exactly to describe the relationship between the department and the judiciary. Traditionally the Lord Chancellor spoke for judges and insulated them from public criticism – as Lord Chancellor Lord Hailsham was wont to throw his bat about at anyone who might have suggested British judges were not the acme of legal wisdom. But in recent years the department has sought reforms in the law, for example, recalibrating the responsibilities of solicitors and lawyers and bringing performance measurements to bear on what judges do in their courtrooms. Indeed the LCD's current mission includes 'promoting general reforms in the civil law'. This reforming bent has caused some friction with the judges, who themselves have been changing in attitude and to some extent sociology in recent years. None the less it was said the appearance of the Lord Chancellor acting as it were on behalf of the consumers rather than the producers of the law was upsetting.

Formally, the LCD takes oversight of procedure in the civil courts and the running of the Supreme Court (Court of Appeal, High Court and Crown Courts) and the County courts of England and Wales. The Lord Chancellor advises 'the Crown' – himself for all practical purposes – on the appointment of judges and himself directly appoints masters and registrars of the High Court, and District and County Court Registrars and magistrates. The LCD has some 12,000 staff, a figure that has been increasing in recent years.

Permanent Secretary to the Lord Chancellor: Sir Thomas Legg (Grade 1). Born: 1935. Educated: Horace Mann-Lincoln School, New York; Frensham Heights School, Surrey; St John's College, Cambridge. After his call to the Bar joined the Lord Chancellor's Department in 1962, gaining his Private Office experience three years later. He became Deputy Clerk of the Crown in Chancery in 1986.

Crown Office Clerk of the Crown in Chancery (Grade 1)
Deputy Clerk of the Crown in Chancery

Court Service (management of the courts): Michael Huebner (Grade 2). Born: 1941.Educated: Rugby; St John's College, Oxford. After being called to the Bar he joined the Lord Chancellor's Department in 1966 and the Law Officers' Department in 1968.

Circuits: Midlands and Oxford Administrator: Laurence Oakes. Born: 1946. Educated: Beckenham and Penge Grammar School; University of Bristol. Called to the Bar 1968. Worked as a barrister, joining the Department of Employment in 1977. Under-secretary in Lord Chancellor's Department 1989, as head of legal and reform group.

North Eastern: Steven James. Born: 1934. Educated: Queen Elizabeth Grammar Carmarthen; London School of Economics. After qualifying as a solicitor joined HM Land Registry in 1961. Served with Glamorgan County Council, before joining the Lord Chancellor's Department in 1981.

Northern: R A Vincent

South Eastern: Brian Cooke. Born: 1935; Educated: Manchester Grammar; University College, London. After being called to Bar, joined the Director of Public Prosecutions' Office. He came to the Lord Chancellor's Department in 1971.

Judicial Appointments Group: Robin Holmes. Born: 1938. Educated: Wolverhampton Grammar; Clare College, Cambridge; Birmingham University. After qualifying as a solicitor joined the Ministry of Housing. After a secondment to the Colonial Secretariat in Hong Kong joined the Lord Chancellor's Department in 1982.

Law and Policy Groups: Michael Malone-Lee (Grade 2). Born: 1941. Educated: Stonyhurst; Campion Hall Oxford. Joined the Ministry of Health in 1968 serving in Private Office eight years later. After various posts in health administration, including personnel management, moved to the Home Office to become Principal Finance Officer.

Legal Group (law reform, rules of courts): Richard White. Born: 1939. Educated: Sutton Vallence School; Trinity College, Oxford. Qualified as a Solicitor; pursued an academic career at the University of Birmingham before joining the Lord Chancellor's Department in 1974.

Policy and Legal Services Group (lawyers' remuneration, legal aid, family law): Charles Everett. Born: 1949. Educated: Bryanston; Reading University. Joined the Lord Chancellor's Department in 1971 serving in Private Office three years later. Moved to the Department of Transport in 1982.

Establishments and Finance Group: Nicola Oppenheimer. Born: 1950. Educated: St Margaret's School, Bushey; Queen's College, London; Queen Mary College, London. After being called to the Bar joined the Lord Chancellor's Department in 1973 where she became head of personnel in 1987.

SUPREME COURT OF JUDICATURE

Central Office: Senior Master of the Supreme Court (Queen's Bench Division) and Queen's Remembrancer: Keith Topley. Born: 1936. Educated: Bryanston; Trinity College, Oxford. Called to Bar; Bencher 1990.

Crown Office: Master of the Crown Office, Queen's Coroner and Attorney; Court of Appeal Criminal Division and Courts-Martial Appeal Court; Registrar of Criminal Appeals and Registrar of the Courts-Martial Appeal Court: Michael McKenzie QC. Born: 1943. Educated: Varndean Grammar, Brighton. Worked for Brighton Council becoming senior Clerk of the Court, Brighton Quarter Sessions. After being called to the Bar in 1970; became assistant registrar Court of Criminal Appeal Division in 1986.

Official Solicitor's Department: Official Solicitor: Peter Harris. Born: 1937. Educated: Cirencester Grammar; Royal Naval College, Dartmouth. After service in the Royal Navy he was called to the Bar in 1971, joining the Lord Chancellor's Department three years later. He became head of the Civil Courts Division in 1985

MINISTRY OF AGRICULTURE, FISHERIES AND FOOD (MAFF)
Whitehall Place
London SW1A 2HH
Telephone: 071-270 3000

MAFF has dual and – some might say – conflicting responsibilities. Can it represent both the producer of food – its original purpose was to promote output – and the consumer? Officially it both oversees the interests of the agricultural, fisheries and horticultural industries and the public who eat and drink their produce. The possibility of tension between the two roles has been demonstrated in recent months as the BSE affair has unfolded – is MAFF principally concerned with the economic well-being of beef producers and cattle rearers or with the public who might suffer from eating meat infected with Bovine Spongiform Encephalopathy?

In association with the agricultural departments in Scotland, Wales and Northern Ireland on the public – and the farmers' behalf – MAFF negotiates in Brussels on payments due under the Common Agricultural and Fisheries Policies of the European Union. It is also responsible for international food negotiations, for example under the GATT.

MAFF, alongside the Environment and National Heritage Departments, also looks after the countryside and the coast. It licenses veterinary products and register pesticides. Its research activities have largely been spun off to ADAS, the executive agency which took over from the former Agricultural Development Advisory Service. MAFF and its agencies together have some 10,000 staff, their numbers having slightly fallen in recent years.

Permanent Secretary: Richard Packer (Grade 1). Born: 1944. Educated: City of London School; Manchester University. Joined Inland Revenue in 1967, moving the same year to MAFF. After secondment to the diplomatic service in Brussels in the 1970s he became, in 1987, director of regional management for MAFF. His wife, Lucy Neville-Rolfe, was a member of the Policy Unit at Number 10 Downing Street.

Director of Establishments: David Griffiths. Born: 1940. Educated: Kingswood School, Bath; St Catharine's College, Cambridge. Joined MAFF 1960. He later became Fisheries Secretary, and head of the food, drink and marketing policy group.

Principal Finance Officer: Alistair Cruickshank. Born: 1944. Educated: Aberdeen Grammar; Aberdeen University. Joined MAFF in 1966, later becoming head of potatoes, meat hygiene and milk.

Legal Adviser and MAFF Solicitor: Roger Woolman (Grade 2). Born: 1937. Educated: Perse School, Cambridge; Trinity Hall, Cambridge. After qualifying as a solicitor joined the Office of Fair Trading in 1976 becoming senior legal assistant at the Department of Trade and Under-Secretary (Legal) there in 1985.

Principal Assistant Solicitors: Barry Atwood. Born: 1940. Educated: Bristol Grammar School, Bristol University, University College, London. After working as a solicitor with Robert Smith and Co in Bristol he joined MAFF's legal department in 1966, taking charge of food legislation and later legal aspects of the Common Agricultural Policy.
D J Pearson.

Agricultural Commodities, Trade and Food Production Directorate: David Hadley (Grade 2) Born: 1936. Educated: Wyggeston Grammar School; Merton College, Oxford. Joined MAFF in 1959; becoming an Assistant Secretary some 12 years later. After a secondment to HM Treasury in the 1970s he became a MAFF Under-Secretary moving to the Cabinet Office as a Deputy Secretary in 1989.

Under-Secretary European Community: Patrick Murphy. Born: 1944. Educated: St Chad's College, Wolverhampton; Trinity Hall, Cambridge. Joined MAFF in 1966, serving in Private Office in 1970. He was later first secretary at the British Embassy in Washington before returning to MAFF as the head of land use and tenure division 1982. As an Under-Secretary he became head of pesticides in 1989.

Under-Secretary Arable Crops and Horticulture: Christopher Barnes. Born: 1944. Educated: City of London School; London School of Economics. Joined MAFF in 1962 moving through the ranks to become principal 1971 and later Secretary to the Northfield Committee on Agricultural Land Ownership and Occupancy 1977-9. He was later head of the Personnel and the R&D Requirements Divisions.

Under-Secretary Livestock Group: G A Hollis

Under-Secretary Drink, Milk and Marketing Policy: John Hepburn. Born: 1938. Educated: Hutchesons' Grammar School; Glasgow University; Brasenose College, Oxford. Joined MAFF in 1961 serving later with the UK Delegation to the European Communities, Brussels 1969-71.

Food Safety Directorate: Charles Capstick (Grade 2). Born: 1934. Educated: King's College, University of Durham; University of Kentucky. Joined MAFF as an agricultural economist in 1961 later becoming Senior economic adviser. Mr Capstick was head of the Milk Division 1976 and later became Director of economics and statistics.

Under-Secretary Food Safety: Brian Dickinson. Born: 1940. Educated: Leighton Park School, Reading, Balliol College, Oxford. Joined MAFF in 1964 moving later to the Department of Prices and Consumer Protection before becoming an Under-Secretary in MAFF and Principal Finance Officer in 1986.

Under-Secretary Agricultural Inputs, Plans, Protection and Emergencies: Elizabeth Attridge. Born: 1934. Educated: Richmond Lodge School, Belfast; St Andrews University. Joined the Ministry of Education, Northern Ireland in 1955 moving to MAFF one year later. She became head of the plant health branch and later took charge of animal health. As an Under-Secretary she headed the European Community Group.

Veterinary Officer: Keith Meldrum Born: 1937. Educated: Uppingham, Edinburgh University. After qualifying as a veterinary surgeon he worked in general practice before joining MAFF in 1963. After serving as a divisional and regional veterinary officer he became Director of the Veterinary Field Service in 1986.

Under-Secretary Animal Health : M T Haddon. Born: 1944. Educated: Beaumont College, Windsor; Worcester College, Oxford. Joined MAFF 1966 with a spell in the Cabinet Office from 1974. In 1991 he became head of animal health and veterinary division at MAFF.

Director of Veterinary Field and Investigation Services: Iain Crawford. Born: 1938. Educated: Coatbridge High School, Lanarkshire; Glasgow University. After private veterinary practice he joined MAFF in 1968 later becoming Assistant Chief Veterinary Officer in 1986.

Chief Scientist: Dr Howard Denner. Joined MAFF in 1972, becoming chief scientist (food) in 1992.

Countryside, Marine Environment and Fisheries Directorate: Charles Cann (Grade 2). Born: 1937. Educated: Merchant Taylor's School, Northwood; St John's College, Cambridge. Joined MAFF in 1960 taking a secondment to the Cabinet Office at the end of the decade and becoming an Under-Secretary at MAFF in 1981.

Fisheries Secretary: Stephen Wentworth. Born: 1943. Educated: King's College School, Wimbledon; Merton College, Oxford. Joined MAFF in 1967. He was seconded to the Foreign Office to join the UK Permanent Rep to the EEC in Brussels in 1976 and again to the Cabinet Office in 1980. At MAFF he became head of meat in 1986.

Under-Secretary Economics and Statistics: Richard Mordue. Born: 1941. Educated: Royal Grammar School, Newcastle upon Tyne; King's College, University of Durham; Michigan State University. Joined MAFF as an assistant economist in 1964; becoming senior economic adviser in 1978.

Chief Scientific Adviser: Dr Peter Bunyan (Grade 2). Born: 1936. Educated: Raynes Park County Grammar School; University College, Durham University, King's College, University of London. Did research at King's and UCL before joining MAFF in 1963. Ten years later he was head of pest control and took charge of R&D at the Agricultural Development and Assistance Service in 1987.

Chief Scientist: Dr David Shannon. Born: 1941. Educated: Wallace High School, Lisburn NI; Queen's University, Belfast. After a research career at Edinburgh and the University of Alberta he joined the Agriculture and Food Research Council, and moved to MAFF in 1986.

Director of Regional Services and Agencies: Dudley Coates. Born: 1946. Educated: Westcliff High School for Boys, University of Sussex. He joined MAFF in 1968 serving two years later with the UK Delegation to the EC. He subsequently lectured at the Civil Service College. At MAFF he became head of the financial management team in 1983.

MINISTRY OF DEFENCE
Main Building
Whitehall
London SW1A 2HB
Telephone: 071-218 9000

The origins of today's unified Defence Ministry date from as recently as 1964, when the existing Defence Ministry absorbed the War Office, the Air Ministry, the Ministry of Aviation, and the Admiralty – the oldest of all the defence departments, whose roots can be traced back to Henry VIII's creation of the Navy Board to oversee naval affairs in 1546. The process of amalgamation was completed in 1971 when the Ministry of Aviation Supply was transferred to the Defence Ministry as part of the new Procurement Executive, which assumed responsibility for all the Armed Services military procurement programmes.

Formulating a coherent defence policy, and delivering an effective and efficient defence capability, are the department's central objectives, as defined in its 1994 annual report. But while these objectives can be characterised as timeless, the environment in which they are implemented are subject to constant change. Following the end of the Cold War and the demise of the military threat from the former Soviet Union and its allies, there has been a fundamental re-evaluation of defence policy, which has led to a root and branch programme for the restructuring of the Armed Forces. The traditional emphasis on maintaining a large standing army in Germany is giving way to a greater emphasis on flexibility and mobility to meet a new range of defence commitments, as reflected in the downward trend in the defence budget, and both civilian and military personnel. Britain's commitment to large-scale collective defence through NATO remains intact, but it is now being complimented by a greater emphasis on small-scale crisis management, and the strengthening of the European pillar of the Atlantic Alliance through the development of the Western European Union.

The structure of the Defence Ministry, which is responsible for a vast range of activities, from overseeing the nuclear deterrent to buying the feed for the horses of the Household Cavalry, is extremely complex. At the apex of some 155,000 civilian and 274,000 military staff, 9 per cent of whom work in executive agencies, sits the Permanent Under-Secretary, the Chief of the Defence Staff, the Chief of the Naval Staff, the Chief of the General Staff, the Chief of the Air Staff, the Vice Chief of the Defence Staff, the Chief of Defence Procurement, the Chief Scientific Adviser, and the Second Permanent Secretary, who along with the Defence Secretary and three Defence Ministers, make up what is known as the Defence Council, the legal authority for controlling the three Armed Services.

A Defence Staff, headed jointly by the Permanent Under-Secretary and the Chief of the Defence Staff, but run on a day-to-day basis by the Vice Chiefs of the Defence Staff, is responsible for formulating policy, crisis management and planning the defence programme. The Defence Staff is then divided into four sub-groupings:

Policy: responsible for advising ministers on the military and political aspects of defence policy, Britain's defence contribution to NATO and its allies, nuclear policy, arms control and military strategy.

Commitments: responsible for crisis management, the deployment of military forces and planning for military exercise.

Systems: responsible for advising on current and future equipment priorities and requirements.

Programmes and Personnel: responsible for advising on manpower, personnel policy, pay and conditions.

The Office of Management and Budget, which is an almost wholly civilian body run by the Second Permanent Secretary, is responsible for resource planning and allocation, financial management, and civilian personnel management. The Defence Intelligence Staff, headed by the Chief of Defence Intelligence, is responsible for producing assessments of changing world developments, analysis of weapons systems used by potential opponents, and threats to British interests abroad. The Chief Scientific Adviser and his staff are responsible for advising on the scientific aspects of policy and research, while the Procurement Executive is responsible for procuring equipment for all the Armed Services. The three Chiefs of Staff are responsible for ensuring that their particular service is ready to perform its function, although they are not in operational command during a conflict. Finally, the Defence Ministry has some 16 Next Steps executive agencies by 1994, including the Meteorological Office, the Defence Research Agency, and the Chemical and Biological Defence Agency (a total of 25 are planned), and has market tested about £346 million worth of Defence Ministry work, with plans to market test £1.2 billion by 1996. MoD and its agencies have some 130,000 civil servants, a future that has been falling significantly, even allowing for the transfer to the private sector of some of its work. The Ministry has an annual budget of £23.5 billion.

Permanent Secretary: (until March 1995) Sir Christopher France (Grade 1). Born: 1934. Educated: East Ham Grammar School; New College Oxford. Joined the Treasury in 1959, and served as Principal Private Secretary to successive Chancellors, before becoming a Deputy Under-Secretary at the Defence Ministry in 1981. He transferred to the Department of Health and Social Security as a Deputy Secretary in 1984, and became Second Permanent Secretary in 1986. He was appointed Permanent Secretary at the DHSS, in 1987; Permanent Secretary, Health Department, in 1988; and Permanent Secretary, Defence Ministry, 1992.

Chief of the Defence Staff: Field Marshal Sir Peter Inge. Born: 1935. Educated: Summer Fields; Wrekin College; Sandhurst. After receiving his commission in 1956, he served in Hong Kong, Malaya, Germany and Libya, and held a variety of military posts before becoming Director General, Logistic Policy, in 1986-7. He was appointed Commander Northern Army Group and Commander in Chief British Army of the Rhine in 1989, before becoming Chief of the Defence Staff in 1992.

Chief of the Naval Staff: Admiral Sir Benjamin Bathurst. Born: 1936. Educated: Eton; Britannia Royal Naval College, Dartmouth. He joined the Royal Navy in 1953, qualified as a pilot in 1960, and a helicopter instructor in 1964. After a series of naval posts, including Director of Naval Air Warfare, Commander in Chief Fleet, Allied Commander in Chief Channel, and Commander in Chief Eastern Atlantic Area, he became Vice Chief of the Defence Staff in 1991, before being appointed Chief of the Naval Staff in 1993.

Chief of the General Staff: General Sir Charles Guthrie. Born: 1938. Educated: Harrow; Sandhurst. Joined the Welsh Guards in 1959, and served in Germany, Aden, the SAS, Northern Ireland, and Berlin, and was appointed Commander Northern Army Group and Chief of the British Army of the Rhine in 1992.

Chief of the Air Staff: Air Chief Marshal Sir Michael Graydon. Born: 1938. Educated: Wycliffe College; RAF College, Cranwell. He qualified as a flying instructor in 1960, and has held most of the key RAF appointments, including Commander in Chief UK Air Forces.

Vice Chief of the Defence Staff: Admiral Sir Jock Slater. Born: 1938. Educated: Edinburgh Academy; Dartmouth. Joined the Royal Navy in 1956, and served as the Assistant Director of Naval Warfare, Commander of the aircraft carrier HM *Illustrious*, and Commander in Chief Fleet, Allied Commander in Chief Channel and Eastern Atlantic, before being appointed Vice Chief of the Defence Staff in 1993.

Chief of Defence Intelligence: Air Marshall Sir John Walker. Born: 1936. He held a series of key RAF posts, including head of RAF Strike Command, High Wycombe, before being appointed Chief of Defence Intelligence.

Second Permanent Secretary: Moray Stewart (Grade 2). Born: 1938. Educated: Marlborough; Keele University. Joined the Air Ministry as an Assistant Principal in 1957, and served in the UK Delegation to NATO, the Northern Ireland Office, the Defence Ministry's Director of Naval Manpower Requirements, Director of Defence Policy Staff, Assistant Under-Secretary for Defence Policy and Planning, Deputy Under-Secretary, Personnel and Logistics, before being appointed Second Permanent Secretary in 1992.

Chief Scientific Adviser: Professor Sir David Davies. Born: 1935. Educated: Birmingham University. While on the staff at Birmingham University, he held a part-time Senior

Principal Scientific Officer post at the Royal Radar Establishment, Malvern. He also held the positions of Assistant Director of Research for British Railways, and professor of Electrical Engineering at University College, London, and from 1988 to 1993 was vice-chancellor of the University of Loughborough, before becoming Chief Scientific Adviser.

Chief of Defence Procurement: Dr Malcolm McIntosh. Born: 1945. Educated: the Australian National University. After a career in the Australian Army, where he reached the rank of Major, he held a series of economic planning posts, before moving to the Defence Ministry in 1982. He served as Chief of Defence Production, and Deputy Secretary for Acquisition and Logistics, before being appointed Chief of Defence Procurement in 1991.

Deputy Chief of the Defence Staff: Vice Admiral The Honorable Sir Nicholas Hill-Norton. Born: 1939. Educated: Marlborough; Dartmouth; the US Naval War College, Newport. He joined the Royal Navy in 1957, and held the posts of Flag Officer, Gibraltar, and Flag Officer Surface Flotilla and Commander of the Anti-Submarine Warfare Striking Force, before being appointed the Deputy Chief of the Defence Staff in 1991.

Deputy Chief of the Defence Staff (Systems): Vice Admiral Malcolm Rutherford. Born: 1941. Educated: New College, Oxford; University of London; Royal Naval College, Greenwich. He served on HM Submarines *Thermopylae*, *Conqueror* and *Sceptre*, and held the posts of Director of Tactical Weapons System Upholder Class Submarines, and Director of Personnel, before being appointed to his current position in 1992.

Deputy Chief of the Defence Staff (Programmes and Personnel): Lt-General The Honorable Sir Thomas Boyd-Carpenter. Born: 1938. Educated: Stowe School. He received his commission in 1957, and served in Oman, Malaya, Borneo, and Germany, Commander of the 24th Infantry Brigade, and Director of Defence Policy, before being appointed Deputy Chief of the Defence Staff in 1992.

Deputy Under-Secretary (Strategic and Long Term Policy): David Omand (Grade 2). Born: 1947. Educated: Glasgow Academy; Corpus Christi College, Cambridge. Joined the Defence Ministry in 1970, and held the posts of Private Secretary to the Chief Executive of the Procurement Executive, member of the UK Delegation to NATO and Assistant Under-Secretary for Management Strategy and programmes before being appointed to his current post.

Deputy Under-Secretary (Resources programmes and Finance): Roger Jackling (Grade 2). Born: 1943. Educated: Wellington College; New York University; Jesus College, Cambridge. Joined the Defence Ministry as an Assistant Principal in 1969, and served in the Prime Minister's Office, and was Principal of the Civil Service College, before being appointed to his current position in 1991.

Deputy Under-Secretary (Personnel and Logistics): John Ledlie (Grade 2). Born: 1942. Educated: Westminster; Brasenose College, Oxford. Joined the Defence Ministry in 1967, and served in the UK Delegation to NATO, the Northern Ireland Office, the Cabinet Office, the Procurement Executive, the Defence Secretariat, Head of MoD Public Relations, and Deputy Secretary in the Northern Ireland Office before being appointed to his current position.

Deputy Under-Secretary (Civilian Management): John Howe (Grade 2). Born: 1944. Educated: Shrewsbury School; Balliol College, Oxford. Joined the Defence Ministry as an Assistant Principal in 1967, and served in the UK Delegation to NATO, Head of the Arms Control Unit, and Assistant Under-Secretary before being appointed to his current position in 1992.

Deputy Under-Secretary (Defence Procurement): Michael Bell (Grade 2). Born: 1941. Educated: Winchester; Magdalen College, Oxford. Joined the Defence Ministry in 1965, and held the posts of Assistant Under-Secretary, Resources and programmes, Director General of Management Audit, Assistant Secretary General for Defence Planning and Policy, NATO, Deputy Under-Secretary (Finance) before being appointed to his present post in 1992.

Deputy Chief Scientific Adviser: Dr Peter Ewins. Born: 1943. Educated: Imperial College, London; Cranfield Institute of Technology. Joined the Royal Aircraft Establishment, Farnborough, in 1966, to conduct research into the structural applications of composite materials, and held posts on the staff of the Chief Scientist and the Cabinet Office, followed by Director of Nuclear Projects, Managing Director of Command and Maritime Systems, and Managing Director of Operations, the Defence Research Agency, before being appointed to his present position in 1994.

Head of Defence Export Services (DESO): Sir Alan Thomas. Born: 1943. Educated: Dynevor School; Nottingham University. He held a series of positions in the private sector, including Chief Executive, Data Logic and President and Chief Executive of Raytheon Europe, before being seconded to the Defence Ministry as the Head of DESO in 1989.

Management Strategy: Colin Balmer.

General Finance: Terence Brack. Born: 1938. Educated: Bradfield College; Caius College, Cambridge. Joined the Air Ministry in 1961, and held the posts of Head of Defence Secretariat, Equipment Requirements, Assistant Under-Secretary, Naval Personnel, and vice-chairman of the management board of the Royal Hospital School, before being appointed to his present position in 1989.

Defence Planning and Policy: Anthony Cragg. Born: 1943. Educated: Hastings Grammar School; Lincoln College, Oxford. Joined the Defence Ministry in 1966, and served in the UK Delegation to NATO, Chief Officer, Sovereign Base Areas, Cyprus, Director General of the Management Audit Team and Chairman of the Defence Organisation Planning Team. He is currently on secondment to NATO.

Systems: David Fisher.

Quartermaster: Dr Alan Fox. Born: 1938. Educated: Bancroft's School; Queen Mary College, London. Joined the Civil Service in 1963, joined the Ministry of Aviation as a Private Secretary, and served in the Foreign Office in Paris, before being appointed Assistant Under-Secretary.

Policy: David Gould. Born: 1949. Educated: West Buckland School; Sussex University. Joined the Defence Ministry in 1963, and served in the UK Delegation to NATO, Assistant Secretary, Materiel Finance, Head of Resources and programmes, and Assistant Under-Secretary, Supply and Organisation. He is currently on secondment to the Cabinet Office.

Supply and Organisation-Air: Howard Griffiths. Born: 1939. Educated: London School of Economics. Joined the Defence Ministry in 1963, and held positions in the Procurement Executive, the UK Delegation to the Mutual and Balanced Force Reduction negotiations in Vienna, Head of the Defence Arms Control Unit, Assistant Under-Secretary (Policy) before being appointed to his present post in 1993.

Business Strategy: Procurement Executive: John Gulvin.

Resources: Michael Harte: Born: 1936. Educated: Charterhouse; Trinity College, Cambridge; University College, London. Joined the Defence Ministry's Micro-biological Research Establishment in 1963, and has held a number of key positions, including Assistant Secretary to the Central Policy Review Staff, member of the UK Delegation to NATO, and Assistant Under-Secretary (Dockyard Planning Team), before being appointed to his current position in 1992.

Director General of Management Audit: Richard Hatfield.

Programmes: Brian Hatwin. Born: 1946. Educated: Portsmouth Grammar School; Christ Church, Oxford. Joined the Defence Ministry in 1967, and held posts in the Foreign Office, the UK Delegation to NATO, Private Secretary to the Defence Secretary, and Assistant Under-Secretary (Material-Naval), before being appointed to his present post in 1992.

Civilian Management-Policy: David Heyhoe. Born: 1938. Educated: Beckenham and Penge Grammar School; Worcester College, Oxford. Joined the War Office in 1963, and held numerous posts including Private Secretary to the Leader of the House of Commons, and Director General of Management Audit, before being appointed to his current position.

Policy: William Hopkinson.

Director General of Supplies and Transport-Naval: David Jones. Born: 1941. Educated: High Storrs Grammar School. Joined the War Office in 1960, and held the posts of Private Secretary to the Defence Ministers, Regional Marketing Director for DESO, Deputy Director in the Al Yamamah Project Office, the Procurement Executive, and Civil Secretary, British Forces Germany, before being appointed to his current post in 1993.

John Kenworthy. Born: 1943. Educated: William Hulme's Grammar School; Manchester University. Joined the Defence Ministry in 1966, and held the posts of Assistant Secretary to the Director of Weapons Resources and programmes, Head of Resources and programmes, and Chief Executive of the DSS Information Technology Services Agency. He is currently on secondment to ICI.

Infrastructure and Logistics: Trevor Knapp. Born: 1937. Educated: Christ's Hospital; King's College, London. Joined the Ministry of Aviation in 1961, and held the posts of Secretary to the British Defence Research and Supply Staff, Canberra, Director General, Marketing, and Assistant Under-Secretary (Supply and Organisation), before being appointed to his current position in 1992.

Director General Test & Evaluation-Procurement Executive: Barry Miller. Born: 1942. Educated: Lancaster Royal Grammar School. Joined the Defence Ministry in 1965, and held posts in the Defence Policy Staff, Naval Personnel, the Equipment Secretariat, the Defence Secretariat, and the Director General of Defence Quality Assurance before being appointed to his present position in 1992.

Naval Personnel: Michael Moss. Born: 1936. Educated: Accrington Grammar School; King's College, Cambridge. Joined the Air Ministry from the RAF in 1960, and held posts in the Defence Ministry, the Cabinet Office, and the Procurement Executive before being appointed to his current post in 1989.

John Oughton. Born: 1952. Educated: Reading School; University College, Oxford. Joined the Defence Ministry in 1974, and held the posts of member of the UN Delegation to the UN Law of the Sea Conference, Private Secretary to the Armed Forces Minister, Assistant Secretary to the Director of Procurement Policy and Head of Resources and programmes (Navy) before being seconded to the Cabinet Office as Head of the Efficiency Unit in 1993.

Director General Marketing-DESO: Nigel Paren. Born: 1936. Educated: Highgate School. Joined the Transport Department in 1957, and held posts in the Trade and Industry Department, the Procurement Executive, and Assistant Under-Secretary (Fleet Support) before being appointed to his current post in 1991.

Fleet Support: Anthony Pawson.

Commitments: William Reeves. Born: 1937. Educated: Darwen Grammar School; King's College, Cambridge. Joined the Admiralty in 1961, and held posts in the Procurement Executive, the Office of Management and Budget, and the Cabinet Office, before being appointed to his present post in 1993.

Director General Defence Contracts: Geoffrey Roe. Born: 1944. Educated: Tottenham Grammar School. Joined the Ministry of Aviation in 1963, and held positions in Guided Weapons Contracts, the Rocket Motor Executive, Assistant Director Air Contracts, Director Underwater Weapons contracts, and Principal Director Navy and Nuclear Contracts before taking up his present position in 1991.

Security and Counter Terrorism: Arthur Rucker. Born: 1939. Educated: Radley; Magdalen College, Oxford. Joined the Air Ministry in 1961, and held various posts including Private Secretary to the Lord President of the Council, before taking up his current post in 1990.

Export Policy and Finance: Christopher Sandars. Born: 1942. Educated: Oundle; Corpus Christi College, Cambridge. Joined the Defence Ministry in 1964, and held posts in the Cabinet Office, the Defence Ministry's General Finance Division, and Head of Defence Secretariat, before being appointed to his current post in 1993.

Finance-Procurement Executive: Diana Seamman. Born: 1948. Educated: Sussex University. Joined the Treasury in 1969, and held posts in VAT Control, Customs & Excise, and Assistant Under-Secretary (Air) before being appointed to her current position in 1993.

Brian Taylor. Born: 1933. Educated: Emanuel School. Joined the National Insurance Ministry in 1952, and held various positions before being seconded to the Cabinet Office's Civil Service Commission in 1990.

Senior Directing Staff (Civilian): Peter Vereker.

Service Personnel: Alexa Walker.

OVERSEAS DEVELOPMENT ADMINISTRATION
94 Victoria Street
London SW1E 5JL
Telephone: 071-917 0503

The Overseas Development Administration (ODA) is the wing of the Foreign Office responsible for administering Britain's overseas aid to developing countries, the new assistance programmes for central and eastern Europe and the former Soviet Union, and global environment protection programmes. Its antecedents can be traced back to the 1929 Colonial Development Act, which first acknowledged the Government's responsibility for the development of her colonies, although it underwent a series of reorganisations before becoming a component of the Foreign Office, run by its own minister, in 1979. It is currently responsible for two external assistance programmes: the overseas aid budget, which covers developing countries and the new democracies in central and eastern Europe and the Commonwealth of Independent States, and the global environment budget, designed to assist developing countries meet their environmental protection obligations as laid down by the Earth Summit in Rio.

Under the overseas aid budget, Britain currently provides in excess of £2 billion a year in bilateral and multilateral aid. ODA is responsible for negotiating the inter-governmental agreements under which that aid is disbursed, the appointment and terms of service of British aid experts, and relations with international aid organisations including the European Community, the World Bank, the various UN aid agencies, and the Development Assistance Committee of the OECD. ODA's headquarters is jointly located in London and East Kilbride, and it has five regional Offices or Development Divisions in Kenya, Malawi, South Africa, Thailand and Barbados. It works closely with British High Commissioners and Embassies in developing countries, as well as the Non-Governmental Organisations, such as Oxfam and Save The Children, involved with development aid and humanitarian relief.

More than half of Britain's aid is disbursed through bi-lateral aid programmes, 80 per cent of which goes to the world's poorest countries, including India, Bangladesh, Zimbabwe, Ghana, Kenya, Zambia, Uganda, Tanzania, Pakistan and China, in the form of grants rather than loans. However, the proportion of bilateral aid is diminishing as the proportion of multilateral aid disbursed through the international aid agencies increases. The Government justifies the money spent on developmental assistance on both moral and utilitarian grounds. With more than two-thirds of the world's population living in poverty, Britain has a moral obligation to help the less well off achieve better standards of living. At the same time, however, aid is used to promote sustainable development and encourage political stability, in the expectation that British trade interests will benefit over time.

Under the ODA's aid policy goals, aid programmes are required to meet seven priority objectives, including the promotion of economic reform, the enhancement of productive capacity, and the fostering of good government. Consequently, aid is conditional on the recipients adhering to IMF and World Bank economic reform programmes, and can be withheld if those reforms are not properly implemented or ignored. This applies to traditional development programmes, and to the new Know How Funds set up to help eastern and central European countries and the former Soviet Union undertake the transition from command to market economies. ODA's development work is assisted by the Natural Resources Institute, the ODA's only executive agency, based at Chatham, which has established a global reputation for excellence in carrying out the practical scientific work and applied research aimed at promoting sustainable development. ODA also has a modest market testing programme. A small department, ODA has just over 1,100 staff.

Permanent Secretary: John Vereker (Grade 1a). Born: 1945. Educated: Marlborough; Keele University. Joined the ODA in 1967, and held posts in the World Bank, the ODA's Caribbean and Latin Department, the Finance Department, the European Department, the Prime Minister's Policy Unit, and the ODA's Asia and Oceans Division. He was appointed Deputy Secretary in the Education Department in 1986, and was Chairman of the Student Loans Company before being appointed to his current post in 1994.

Deputy Secretary: Robert Ainscow (Grade 2). Born: 1936. Educated: Salford Grammar School; Liverpool University. He worked as a statistician in Rhodesia and Nyasaland, and the UN Secretariat before joining the Department of Economic Affairs in 1965. Joined the ODA in 1968, and served as a Senior Economic Adviser, Head of the South Asia Department, Under-Secretary Aid Policy and Resources, Principal Finance Officer, and Chairman of the OECD Working Party on Developmental Assistance, before being appointed Deputy Secretary in 1986.

Asia and the Oceans Division: John Kerby. Born: 1942. Educated: Eton; Christ Church,

Oxford. Joined the Colonial Office in 1965, and the ODA in 1967, where he held the posts of Head of British Development Division in Southern Africa, and Principal Establishment Officer, before being appointed to his current post.

Africa Division: Barrie Ireton. Born: 1944. Educated: Alleyn's Grammar School; Trinity College, Cambridge. Joined the ODA as an Economic Adviser in 1973, after working as an economist in Zambia and The Gambia, and held the posts of Senior Economic Adviser, Assistant Secretary, and Principal Finance Officer, before being appointed to his current position.

Chief Economist (Economic and Social Division): Jon Wilmshurst. Born: 1936. Educated: Beckenham and Penge Grammar School; Manchester University. Joined the ODA in 1964, and worked for the British Development Division in the Middle East and the Monopolies and Mergers Commission, before being appointed Chief Economist in 1990.

Chief Natural Resources Adviser: Andrew Bennett. Born: 1942. Educated: St Edwards School, Oxford; University College, North Wales; West Indies and Reading Universities. He worked as an agronomist in the West Indies, Malawi, Nepal, and Sudan before joining the ODA in 1980, where he held the posts of Assistant Agricultural Adviser, Natural Resources Adviser, and Head of British Development Division in the Pacific, before being appointed to his current post in 1987.

International Division: Barrie Hudson. Born: 1937. Educated: King Henry VIII School; Sheffield University, and University College, London. He worked as an economist with the Economist Intelligence Unit, and as an adviser to the Jordanian Government before being appointed Senior Economic Adviser at the ODA in 1973. He held the posts of Head of the British Development Division in South East Asia, Head of the Economic Relations and Commodities Department, Head of Aid Policy, Principal Establishment Officer, and Head of the Africa Division before being appointed to his current post.

Principal Finance Officer: Richard Manning. Born: 1943. Educated: Kingston Grammar School; Cambridge University. Joined the ODA in 1968, and held various posts including Head of the South East Asia Division, Head of Education and Training Policy, Head of Aid Policy, Principal Establishment Officer, and Head of the Africa Division, before his current appointment.

Principal Establishment Officer: Peter Freedman. Born: 1947. Educated: Universities of Toronto and Oxford. Joined the ODA in 1970, and has held a variety of posts including Head of European Community and Food Aid Department, Head of Central and Southern Africa Department, Head of Aid Policy Department, and Head of International Division before his current post.

Eastern European Division: Tony Faint. Born: 1942. Educated: Magdalen College, Oxford; Fletcher School of Diplomacy, Massachusetts. Joined the ODA in 1965, and held the posts of Head of South East Asia Development Division, Head of Finance, and Head of International Division before being appointed to his current position in 1991.

3
THE INNER RING

The provision of public services at minimum cost to the taxpayer has always been part of the mantra of British public administration and public service reform. But the rediscovery of market economics in the 1980s infused this general principle with a dynamic which has set in motion some of the most sweeping changes in the British Civil Service since its creation in the middle of the nineteenth century. Although far from complete, Britain's public service reform programme, along with similar initiatives currently under way throughout most of the democratic world, appears to have sounded the death-knell of the hoary debate between proponents of big government and advocates of central government retrenchment. Consequently, demands for 'more' or 'less' government spending are slowly being tempered by a growing recognition from politicians of every ideological hue that government spending, at whatever level, must be more effective.

During the 19th century, public administration was largely confined to the maintenance of law and order; the introduction of basic improvements to public health such as the construction of sewers, and limited central government intervention in the economy to regulate weights and measures and the hours and conditions of factory workers. But the two world wars of the twentieth century transformed the so-called 'night-watchman state' from its humble status as little more than an observer – occasionally intervening from the sidelines – into the main economic regulator; a conciliator of competing economic interests, and a major industrial producer in its own right. As a result, the number of civil servants needed to service this hugely expanded role mushroomed from around 50,000 to in excess of 700,000. By the end of the 1970s the public sector accounted for almost half Britain's gross domestic product, and employed nearly one-third of the nation's labour force.

The Conservative party came to power in 1979 armed with what it regarded as a mandate to arrest and reverse this trend. Convinced that the philosophy of the command economy had allowed public-sector costs to spiral out of control, an ambitious privatisation programme was implemented which saw huge areas of economic activity, ranging from air transport to telecommunications, and oil production to steel-making, progressively returned to the private sector. But the Thatcher revolution left large parts of the public service unscathed. By the end of the 1980s, however, the focus of government attention began to switch from the sale of state-owned industries towards a more fundamental re-appraisal of what had hitherto been regarded as the essential core of government.

This process began with the launch in February 1988 of the so-called Next Steps executive agency initiative, designed to replace the monolithic Civil Service with a series of discrete management units, each focused on a particular objective. When Mrs Thatcher was replaced by John Major in November 1990, Next Steps was subsumed into the 1991 Citizen's Charter initiative, aimed at improving levels of service across the public sector over a ten-year period. The structure of the government's public service reform programme was completed in November the same year with the unveiling of the *Competing For Quality* White Paper. Under this ill-named 'market testing' programme, work carried out by all Civil Service departments, from the Department of Social Security to the Ministry of Defence, is to be repeatedly subject to the same process of competitive tendering from private-sector contractors which has been in operation at local government level since 1988.

The government's changing approach to public service reform was perhaps best summed up in November 1992 by Stephen Dorrell, the former Economic Secretary to the Treasury. Addressing the Centre for Policy Studies, Mr Dorrell helped himself to the rhetoric normally deployed by communist revolutionaries and announced that the government's tripartite public service reform programme had embarked upon a 'long march through Whitehall'. The government was 'no longer looking for obvious candidates for privatisation', he said. 'The conventional question was what can we sell? That question must now be turned on its head. Now we should ask what must we keep? What is the inescapable core of government?' Mr Dorrell said that the government's objective was nothing less than a complete redefinition of the mixed economy in which the old distinction between the public and the private sector 'becomes increasingly irrelevant'.

Opposition parties, Civil Service trade unions and a host of academics and other observers were quick to warn that the government's public service reform programme could ultimately lead to the break-up of the Civil Service. Most commentators accepted that the introduction of Next Steps executive agencies had led to considerable improvements in the delivery of a wide range of public services, even though there was some anxiety over whether traditional forms of ministerial accountability had been impaired. Similarly, few could argue with the aspirations of the Citizen's Charter, although most commentators tended to pour scorn on an initiative designed to improve standards of public service without any additional financial resources.

But it was the market testing initiative, together with the manner in which it was initiated, that provoked most hostility from civil servants towards the Government's public service reform programme. Indeed, fear that the Government had a hidden agenda more concerned with bringing about a 'leaner-cheaper' Civil Service than with improving the quality of public services provoked a mass walk-out of 250,000 civil servants in November 1993 – the first time pickets had been mounted outside government buildings throughout the country since 1981. The image of visitors being turned away from the Tower of London as Beefeaters joined civil servants from the courts, ports, tax and employment offices, customs posts and benefits agencies, was the first sign that the government's reform programme was facing opposition. As a result, the issue of whether the reforms were eroding the long-established British tradition of an incorrupt and politically neutral Civil Service, whose ethos should be preserved, moved higher up the political agenda.

ORIGINS AND DEVELOPMENT

The Northcote-Trevelyan reforms of 1854, and their piecemeal implementation over the next 50 years, are generally regarded as the modern origins of the British Civil Service. But the cardinal principle of those reforms, namely that recruitment and promotion should be based on merit instead of patronage and connection, was influenced in no small way in Britain's attempt to create an efficient Civil Service to manage the Indian Empire. As Governor of Bengal, Robert Clive had introduced a code of practice that prohibited state officials from accepting gifts, bribes, and trading for their own purposes. Sir Charles Trevelyan, who began official life as a civil servant in the East India Company in 1826, grew out of this tradition of probity. Trevelyan, who was the real architect of the great public service reforms, acquired a fearful reputation for stamping out corruption (including turning in a superior for bribery) while employed in the Indian Civil Service before returning to London to take up the position of Permanent Secretary to the Treasury aged 32.

Under the protective wing of William Ewart Gladstone, and with the assistance of Sir Stafford Northcote, the 20-page Northcote-Trevelyan report mapped out the contours of Britain's permanent Civil Service which are still in evidence to this day. Arguing the case for reform, the authors stated what has since become the standard constitutional position on the role of the British Civil Service:

'It cannot be necessary to enter into any lengthened argument for the purpose of showing the high importance of the Permanent Civil Service of the country in the present day. The great and increasing accumulation of public business, and the consequent pressure on the Government need only to be alluded to ... It may safely be asserted that, as matters now stand, the Government of the country could not be carried on without the aid of an efficient body of permanent officers, occupying a position duly subordinate to that of the Ministers who are directly responsible to the Crown and to Parliament, yet possessing sufficient independence, character, ability and experience to be able to advise, assist, and to some extent, influence those who are from time to time set over them.'

The following 20 pages outlined, and won, the argument for the creation of a permanent, politically neutral Civil Service based on the abolition of patronage; recruitment into the lower ranks of 'a carefully selected body of young men' by open competition; the separation of intellectual and mechanical work, and promotion based on intellectual attainment rather than the accumulation of any specialised scientific or technical knowledge.

By contrast, the United States embarked upon a different course. A deeply felt hostility to the idea of a permanent Civil Service, born largely out of fear that it would become an autonomous power in its own right, led to the development of a 'spoils system' in which public office is a reward for supporting candidates for political office. Although modified after the Civil War, and gradually extended up the federal hierarchy, the 2,000 or so key policy posts are still filled by presidential nomination. In addition, when legislating for new areas of government activity, Congress created new agencies or commissions independent of the executive branch of government such as the Interstate Commerce Commission, the Federal Communications Commission and the Tennessee Valley Authority. But the absence of a permanent Civil Service, and the existence of autonomous commissions, left the American system of public administration vulnerable to the twin charges of politicisation at the centre, accompanied by a 'headless fourth branch of government' at the periphery. Ironically, these two vices were later to become virtues in the eyes of some British public administration reformers in the 1980s who began campaigning for Whitehall to be overhauled and brought into the 21st century.

Nevertheless, the essential characteristics of the British Civil Service remained more or less unchanged for much of the 20th century as the public sector expanded dramatically to assume the new responsibilities imposed by welfare, war and peace. But the Yom Kippur war in October 1973, the consequent 400 per cent increase in oil prices and Britain's subsequent appeal to the International Monetary Fund for financial help in 1976, signalled that the age of plenty was over. Within three years Margaret Thatcher became Prime Minister, adamant that Britain was living beyond its means, and determined to redraw the boundaries of state. But what began as a mission to reverse the growth of the public sector ended in the re-evaluation of the role of its servants. As Sir Robin Butler, the Cabinet Secretary and Head of the Home Civil Service, said to the annual conference of the Political Studies Association in April 1993, the Civil Service had no option but to come to terms with the four election victories of a government resolved to reduce the role of the state and public expenditure as a proportion of GDP. Moreover, this development, Sir Robin said, coincided with increased demands and expectations on public services, along with the public's clear reluctance to finance them with additional taxes. Consequently, 'this combination of factors has imposed extraordinary pressures for increased efficiency, cutting costs, justifying activities and getting more and more out of the resources provided by the taxpayer ... It's a requirement that has far outstripped the traditional approach of simply slimming down within the overall structure.'

FIRST STEPS: THE FULTON REPORT

The Fulton Commission was established by Harold Wilson in 1966 to 'examine the structure, recruitment and management, including training, of the Home Civil Service and to make recommendations' at the outset of what later came to be known as the 'what's-wrong-with-Britain syndrome'. The 1960s witnessed the publication of a plethora of books and articles calling for the reform and modernisation of Britain's antediluvian institutions as a prerequisite for arresting the nation's relative if self-evident economic decline – echoes of which are still audible today. Not surprisingly, the Civil Service found itself facing the brunt of much of this criticism. Under Wilson's patronage, Thomas Balogh, a Hungarian-born economist and Oxford don, rampaged around Whitehall denouncing what he called the system of 'two-tier dilettantism' in which the amateur minister was dependent for policy advice on the amateur civil servant. The problem was perhaps best summed up in 1990 by Professor Peter Hennessy, the noted Whitehallologist, who asked: 'Can the crossword puzzle mind, reared on Greats at Oxford or Mathematics at Cambridge provide the kind of skills Britain needs for the 20th century?'

The Fulton Commission, which published its report in 1968, thought not. Setting out to overhaul Britain's nonchalant and self-satisfied administrative culture, the Fulton Report described the Civil Service as a product of the mid-19th century, unable to carry out the tasks confronted by government in the second half of the twentieth century. Although it made a total of 158 recommendations, including the abolition of the Civil Service's Byzantine system of classes, and the creation of a new Civil Service College, three broad areas of weakness were identified in the report. First, the cult of the amateur generalist, especially among the mandarin class at the top of the service, had to be jettisoned by introducing more scientists, engineers and other professional specialists in positions of power and influence. Second, the virtual absence of any managerial experience and expertise had to be replaced with a new management culture in which departments and individuals were held directly responsible for their performance. Finally, the cloistered isolation of senior civil servants from the rest of the community had to be replaced by a more open system of government which provided less anonymity for officials and more opportunities for Civil Service personnel to acquire front-line experience in commerce, finance and industry.

The Fulton Report is usually credited with paving the way for the Next Steps initiative. But the gestation period was to prove inordinately long – not least because Fulton's recommendations were extremely unpopular in Whitehall. Indeed, throughout the 1970s the Fulton recommendations were often ridiculed by civil servants as 'the lost reforms', in the face of growing public and press hostility towards the size, cost and inefficiency of the state bureaucracy. But the arrival of Margaret Thatcher in Downing Street, who was committed to the implementation of a stringent programme of 'cuts and savings', together with the entrepreneurial philosophy of government which gradually emerged during the 1980s, brought most of what Fulton had recommended back on to the agenda. The reform drive began in a small way with the introduction of the so-called Rayner scrutinies. Sir Derek Rayner, who had acquired his management skills at Marks & Spencer, was appointed the Prime Minister's efficiency adviser during 1979-83. A passionate critic of Whitehall's paper culture, Sir Derek initiated a programme of examining 'a specific policy, activity or function with a view to savings or increased effectiveness', a technique which is still in operation today. The Rayner scrutinies were followed in 1982 by the Financial Management Initiative (FMI), designed to ensure that Civil Service managers had a clear view of their objectives, and the resources needed to realise them.

Sir Robin Ibbs succeeded Sir Derek as the Prime Minister's efficiency adviser in 1983; another businessman, but this time from ICI. It was his report, 'Improving Management in Government: The Next Steps', born out of frustration over the limited impact of the Rayner scrutinies, and delivered to Mrs Thatcher amidst great secrecy prior to the 1987 general election, that was to launch Whitehall on the most far-reaching reform since the creation of the modern Civil Service the previous century. Sir Robin (and Kate Jenkins, a former member of the Central Policy Review Staff, who was the intellectual architect of the Next Steps initiative), had found that while almost 95 per cent of the Civil Service was employed in front-line service delivery, they were looked down upon by the 5 per cent of senior civil servants engaged in giving policy advice to ministers. The traditional distinction between 'doers and thinkers' meant that operational efficiency effectively went by the wayside. By separating the executive functions of government from the elitist policy-making role, Sir Robin hoped to provide Civil Service managers with the local autonomy they needed to revolutionise the provision of public services. In essence, Next Steps called for the monolithic Whitehall machine to be broken up into its component parts, each of which would be managed by its own Chief Executive, who would be given genuine power to implement individual pay and recruitment policies, and allowed to develop individual management styles, in exchange for improved service delivery. In February 1988, Mrs Thatcher announced in Parliament that the government had accepted the recommendations contained in the Next Steps report, and that to the greatest extent practicable: 'The executive functions of government, as distinct from policy advice, should be carried out by units clearly designated within departments ... as agencies.'

IMPLEMENTING NEXT STEPS

The prospect of the Next Steps initiative devolving power over budgets, staff, pay and conditions, to an unspecified number of executive agencies embracing up to 95 per cent of the work carried out by the Civil Service, was seen as both a promise and a curse. The proliferation of executive agencies, under the jurisdiction of accountable Civil Service managers or Chief Executives, promised to bring an end to ministerial overload, nail the fiction that ministers could actually be responsible for everything that happened in their departments, and improve the quality of services delivered to the public. But the devolution of control over budgets, manpower, and Civil Service pay bargaining, had serious implications for Treasury control over public spending. Moreover, the first list of 12 candidates to be hived off into agencies, including the Driver and Vehicle Licensing Centre in Swansea (DVLA), the Passport Office, HMSO and Companies House, was criticised for being too timid, as it left Whitehall's larger bureaucratic empires intact.

Any notion, however, that the Next Steps initiative was destined to be a non-starter was quickly laid to rest by the appointment of the indefatigable Sir Peter Kemp as project manager. An accountant by training, Sir Peter, who had joined the Treasury in 1967, went about his task with a missionary zeal that was eventually to lead to his downfall. Three months after his appointment, Sir Peter told the Treasury and Civil Service Select Committee in May 1988 that 75 per cent of the Civil Service would be hived off into semi-autonomous executive agencies within ten years. All Whitehall departments were instructed to review their activities and decide whether their functions should be abolished, privatised, contracted out, cast adrift into an executive agency, or retained as a core function – the so-called prior options list. Indeed, the Next Steps initiative, which set out to break up long-established bureaucratic empires, seemed to undermine Robert Michels' 'iron law of oligarchy' that every organisation is run according to its own interests and values.

Charters or Framework documents were drawn up to govern the relationship between each executive agency and its parent department. The Framework documents spelt out the agency's 'aims, objectives, responsibilities and duties'. Agency Chief Executives were granted managerial independence, within predetermined budgets, and given performance targets for which they are directly responsible to their departmental minister. From its humble beginnings in 1988, the Next Steps initiative rapidly gathered momentum. New executive agencies were launched every year. The creation of the Benefits Agency in April 1991, which employs 68,000 civil servants, and is widely regarded as the 'engine room' of the Welfare State, soon saw off the criticism that Next Steps was too timid to tackle the big Whitehall empires. By the autumn of 1994, no less than 98 executive agencies had been launched, including the Child Support Agency, and HM Prison Service, along with 31 Customs and Excise executive units, and 34 Inland Revenue executive offices. A further 40-odd candidates for agency status were identified, each of which would be in operation by 1995. When complete, almost 80 per cent of the Civil Service would be working in executive agencies. Next Steps had become the instrument by which a monolithic state bureaucracy had been broken down into a more federal structure, organised to reflect the diversity of its tasks.

Moreover, the initiative also appeared to be delivering the results expected of it. The success of the DVLA, whose inefficiency and incompetence had become a national joke after the government decided to centralise it in 1965, amounted to nothing short of a total transformation. The agency's 4,000 staff are responsible for the routine task of keeping the nation's driver and vehicle licensing records up to date. But the days when a member of the public would have to wait months for a new driving licence are long gone. Now, 90 per cent of driving licences have to be issued within 13 days, while 95 per cent of changes to vehicle registration documents have to be completed within 15 days. Both targets are achieved. Moreover, all staff go on customer care courses, and they are responsible for sorting out their own mistakes rather then passing them on to a complaints department.

Similarly, the Vehicle Inspectorate now offers tests on Saturday mornings, while Companies House provides a premium high-speed company creation service – although at a higher price. From the Meteorological Office to the Passport Office, and from the Civil Service College to the Chessington Computer Centre, civil servants have absorbed the language of business executives and now talk of 'customers and markets'. Not every executive agency has, however, been a success story. The Recruitment and Assessment Services Agency, the Cabinet Office agency responsible for public-sector headhunting, failed in 1992 to meet four of its six key targets. Its attempt to fill 5,000 vacancies fell short by more than 2,000, and instead of increasing output by 6.8 per cent, productivity actually fell by 9 per cent. But because performance has to be published in an agency annual report, civil servants, who have traditionally been protected by the cloak of government confidentiality, now have to face the full force of parliamentary, press and public scrutiny.

The claim that the Civil Service was now putting more effort into improving the quality of service delivery, as opposed to covering its back from ministerial complaint, was not the only change brought about by the Next Steps initiative. The devolution of managerial responsibility from the centre to the periphery was also bringing about a quite profound change in the ethos of civil servants themselves. A survey published in August 1992 by Saxton Bampfylde, the executive recruitment consultants, said that the public sector had traditionally seen the private sector as 'venal, vulgar and narrow', while the private sector saw the public sector as 'time-serving, slow, fixated with process, inefficient, naive and opposed to change'. The survey even quoted one civil servant as saying: 'It sounds appalling now, but we thought that "industry", whatever that was, was for northern chemists. People like us went for the Treasury or the BBC'. Now, however, the gulf between the two walks of life was being eroded, with the public sector adopting private-sector language and practices to a degree which would have been inconceivable only a few years earlier. Moreover, John Smith, the former Labour leader, told the now defunct Royal Institute of Public Administration in May 1991 that the Labour party no longer opposed Next Steps. Bipartisan support for the Next Steps initiative has, however, been placed in jeopardy following the government's announcement that individual agencies will be sold off to the private sector whenever possible.

Sir Peter Kemp, who had earned the dubious accolade 'Whitehall's brave new broom', was unceremoniously sacked in July 1992 after a reorganisation of the Cabinet Office. The same reorganisation led to the creation of the new Office of Public Service and Science (OPSS) under William Waldegrave, which was made responsible for the government's public service reform programme four months earlier. At the time, Giles Radice, the chairman of the Treasury and Civil Service Select Committee, and a great admirer of Sir Peter, described his removal as 'the revenge of Whitehall'. It was a thesis Sir Peter did much to propagate. Giving evidence to the committee in May 1993, Sir Peter suggested that he probably lost his job because he threatened the Whitehall empire. Waldegrave had told the committee in January that

Sir Peter did not have 'the right mix of qualities' to run OPSS. Asked what he thought Waldegrave had meant, Sir Peter said: 'I have heard it said that Mr Waldegrave was looking for a Permanent Secretary of the old school. It may be that he wanted somebody less pressing for change, although for a department devoted to change, that's rather an odd thing to want. I think maybe he felt that perhaps there was too much reforming going on'. The impression left by Sir Peter was that the reform drive had all but run out of steam.

Sir Peter spelt out his views in November 1993 with the publication of his Civil Service reform pamphlet, 'Beyond Next Steps: A Civil Service for The 21st Century'. Criticising the popular image of the Civil Service as a single unit organised around a policy-making elite at the top, Sir Peter pointed out that the average Civil Servant: 'is not white, male, in his 50s, and in and out of ministers' offices in Whitehall. Increasingly, in fact, she is likely to be non-white, about 22 years old, based in South Wales, unlikely ever to see a minister, and often doesn't think of herself as a civil servant'. There was no such thing as a monolithic Civil Service: 'just a vast variety of activities that must be carried out using different management skills and methods'. But between the two extremes of leaving the provision of certain public services to the market and the government assuming responsibility for others 'there are a whole range of options, including in-house agencies, contracted activities, joint ventures and regulated entities. The job is to get the best fit for each activity, of service to the public, maintenance of standards, efficiency and value for money, and accountability', he added.

Responding to claims that parent departments still exercised too much control over their executive agencies, Sir Peter called for them to be cut loose and made directly accountable to Parliament. But he also criticised Waldegrave for failing to extend the reform drive to the heart of Whitehall, and of protecting the powers and prerogative of the mandarin class. In fact, with the Next Steps programme well under way, including the delegation of pay and conditions to agency Chief Executives from April 1994, the public service reform programme was in the process of being extended to embrace the entire public sector through the Citizen's Charter and the extension of contracting out to Whitehall. Those who believed that the reform impulse had reached its high water mark were soon disabused of any such notion when Waldegrave announced plans in December 1993 for the privatisation of large parts of the Whitehall machine, including Next Steps executive agencies.

THE ACCOUNTABILITY DEBATE

There is a constitutional fiction in Britain that ministers are personally responsible for the actions of the civil servants working in their departments. According to this fiction, the Social Security Minister, for example, is responsible for each of the 14 million or so benefits paid out under the social security system. In practice, this fiction has always been diluted by a system of delegation down the bureaucratic chain of command. But the minister none the less remains accountable to Parliament for the actions of his or her department. The Next Steps initiative strips away this fiction by explicitly stating in each executive agency Framework document that the responsibility for a particular function has been delegated to the Chief Executive. When the Next Steps initiative was launched, ministers expected to encounter considerable difficulty over this constitutional innovation. Indeed, legislation was even contemplated to lay to rest the notion that ministers can be genuinely held responsible for everything done by officials in their name.

But fears that the proliferation of Next Step agencies would undermine the principle of ministerial responsibility were largely laid to rest when the Treasury and Civil Service Select Committee took the view that executive agencies were a modification rather than an abandonment of ministerial responsibility. 'In the last resort', the committee said: 'the minister will bear the responsibility if things go badly wrong and Parliament will expect him or her to put things right. But the process of Parliamentary accountability should allow issues to be settled at lower levels wherever possible.' The position of executive agencies was further strengthened in July 1992 when ministers agreed, under the Open Government initiative, to allow written answers from agency Chief Executives to be published in Hansard, the official daily report of the House of Commons.

But the accountability issue refused to go away. Writing in the *Guardian* in December 1992, Gerald Kaufman, Labour's former foreign affairs spokesman, complained that the letters he wrote to the Social Security Minister on behalf of a constituent were being passed on to Michael Bichard, the Chief Executive of the Benefits Agency. Describing the practice as a 'creeping abnegation of ministerial responsibility', Kaufman pointed out that: 'Members of Parliament have no power and only two rights. One is the right of privileged speech within Parliament. The other is the right of access to ministers. We exercise those rights', Kaufman added: 'not for ourselves but on behalf of our constituents. If ministers seek to eliminate one of those rights, as they are doing by delegating cases to agencies ... they are diminishing the rights of our constituents and the rights of Parliament. They are diminishing democracy'.

Kaufman's critique was followed in February 1993, presumably by coincidence, with the publication of a pamphlet by William Waldegrave, 'Public Service And The Future: Reforming Britain's Bureaucracies', which attempted to provide a comprehensive statement of the government's public service reform programme. The objective of the reforms was stated simply:

'We have not yet got the relationship between State and the citizen right in the provision and control of public services. The huge growth of these services, and the full extension of the franchise, are the great twentieth century constitutional innovations. If we do not get this area into proper balance, great damage can be done to the State, which can lose its prestige by entangling itself in tasks for which it is ill-fitted, and to the citizen, who trusts the State to help him, and should not be disappointed.'

In short, the state had overextended itself, and must now withdraw to the sidelines while ensuring that many of the functions it had previously performed are carried out by other means. The impetus for this retreat arose out of a disillusionment with what was seen as the failed Keynesian-Beveridgean consensus of the post-war decades. The belief that such an approach to economic activity and the provision of public services 'offered efficiency, via economies of scale and central planning which would end unnecessary duplication of provision; accountability, via upward reporting to Parliament, and fairness, via rational processes of central resource allocation' proved to be illusory, Waldegrave said. In reality: 'Central planning and resource allocation were far less efficient than the pluralism of the market place, and soon became insensitive and remote; accountability only upwards and not directly to the user became more and more theoretical; fairness became a levelling down', he added. 'Above all, the absence of either choice, the key to true accountability, or competition, the generator of quality and value, removed the dynamism and responsiveness necessary to drive big organisations. Saddled with their Forties-style structures, the public services all too often let standards slip and costs soar.'

The withdrawal of the state would not, and could not, be total. 'There is no doubt that the most radical campaigners for minimal government must accept that a substantial public sector goes with a modern democracy', Waldegrave said. 'That is why, after privatising all we should, we must have practical methods for preventing the remaining public sector reinfecting itself with the old ills of inefficiency, insensitivity and waste.' By breaking up the monolithic Civil Service into discrete management units, each of which is given specific functions for which it can be called to account, the reforms were designed to make a reality of the theoretical concepts of accountability in the public service. 'What we have done is to make clear the distinction between responsibility, which can be delegated, and accountability, which remains firmly with the minister', he added.

In a lecture to the Institute of Advanced Legal Studies in June 1993, Vernon Bogdanor, a Fellow of Brasenose College, Oxford, challenged this novel definition of ministerial responsibility. Arguing that while the fundamental rationale behind the government's public service reform programme was to make government 'operate along business lines', he insisted that those reforms 'have massive constitutional implications, whose consequences have been neither foreseen nor fully understood'. According to the traditional concept of ministerial responsibility, ministers are not to blame for departmental mistakes, but they are required to take the blame and ensure that any wrong was put right. This is possible only because ministers are intricately involved in departmental decision making processes. What is novel about the Next Steps initiative is that agency Chief Executives were being encouraged to take decisions which are not be referred upwards to a minister. As a result, more and more decisions will be removed from ministerial oversight and scrutiny. 'It is this conception of ministerial responsibility which is under threat from the growth of executive agencies under the Next Steps programme', Bogdanor said. It was, therefore, imperative that the public service managerial revolution be accompanied by constitutional revolution to ensure that reforms were given a sound constitutional basis.

The response was swift and to the point. Speaking to the Public Finance Foundation the following month, Waldegrave, a Fellow of All Souls, poured scorn on 'academic theories' and insisted that constitutional reforms designed to eliminate an alleged 'democratic deficit' would not 'achieve the real improvements in the day-to-day quality of service now being offered to the public'. On the contrary: 'Far from suffering a democratic deficit, we are now seeing the results of a substantial democratic gain'. The key point, Waldegrave added, 'is not whether those who run our public services are elected, but whether they are producer responsive or consumer responsive'.

For Waldegrave, accountability to the market place, to the citizens who consume the services provided by the public sector, is just as important (if not more so) as accountability to Parliament or the electorate. Market accountability is the instrument which the government is using to redress the deficiencies of the public sector. The new public management ethos has brought about many improvements. Government bureaucracies are noticeably more customer-friendly, agency Chief Executives are required to publish annual reports detailing their performance, and they are subject to cross-examination by Parliamentary select committees. What has alarmed some observers, however, is the distinction being drawn between responsibility, which is delegated to agency Chief Executives, and accountability to Parliament, which remains with the minister. Critics fear that this will result in ministers being called to account when things go wrong but not being held responsible because the decisions were made not by ministers but by Chief Executives.

THE CITIZEN'S CHARTER

The growth of the modern state has been accompanied by both the rise of bureaucracy and bureaucratic maladies, defined exhaustively by the *Encyclopedia Britannica* as an 'overdevotion of officials to precedent, remoteness from the rest of the community, inaccessibility, arrogance in dealing with the general public, ineffective organisation, waste of labour, procrastination, an excessive sense of self-importance, indifference to the feelings or convenience of citizens, an obsession with the binding authority of departmental decisions, inflexibility, abuse of power, and reluctance to admit error'. It was these bureaucratic maladies that the Citizen's Charter initiative, unveiled by John Major in November 1991, was designed to cure.

By publishing standards of performance across the public sector, measuring whether those standards had been reached, and offering redress to consumers where they had not, the Citizen's Charter seeks to provide public service consumers with a series of defined expectations and entitlements. While critics and supporters of Major's 'big idea' debated whether the Citizen's Charter was a new philosophy of government or an elaborate public relations hoax, some 38 charters were published, including British Rail's Passenger's Charter, the Inland Revenue's Taxpayer's Charter, and the NHS's Patient's Charter. Enthusiastic staff working for the Citizen's Charter Unit in the Cabinet Office said that the idea arose out of the Prime Minister's experience as chairman of the Lambeth housing committee in the 1970s.

Critics were quick to point out that any improvements in services, should they materialise, will stem largely from more efficient management. Charters will do nothing to ensure that additional resources are found to fund public-sector services. Under British Rail's plans, for example, to compensate passengers for services which fail to meet reliability and punctuality targets, which came into effect in January 1993, millions of pounds of discounted travel would be handed out without any additional investment funds from the Treasury to enable the railways to improve their annual performance. Here lies the rub. The Citizen's Charter initiative is based on the assumption that consumers want improved public services without the increased taxes needed to pay for them. Consequently, the only way out of this conundrum was a managerial revolution to improve service delivery at less cost.

Reforming Britain's 'sniff and snarl' tradition of public service would take ten years to implement. Moreover, encouraging complaints about deficient services was central to the reform process. Dismissing claims that the charters, name badges, and telephone complaint lines were a gimmick to deflect attention from the reality of public spending cuts, David Davis, the newly appointed Citizen's Charter Minister, said in June 1993: 'We do not want to create a generation of whingers, but no one should be deterred from complaining because they think public services will always be second rate'.

But it was the Charter Mark award scheme for outstanding service in the public sector which seemed to attract the most ridicule and scorn. John Beishon, the Consumers' Association's Chief Executive, denounced the scheme in October 1993 for being as relevant to consumer care 'as a Blue Peter badge'. British Gas, InterCity, Westminster City Council's 24-hour noise abatement team and the Suffolk constabulary were among the 93 public service organisations to win the Charter Mark at the second annual award ceremony in London. Beishon insisted, however, that no one 'least of all government ministers, has yet accounted for why the winners have received the accolade'. Although welcoming the idea, Beishon said that the Charter Mark 'would have to reflect consumers' experience before anyone could take it seriously'. Clearly, the dilemma for the Citizen's Charter initiative was how to reward the genuine efforts of public service employees to improve services before those improvements had manifestly worked their way through the system to consumers.

TESTING WHITEHALL'S MARKET

For much of the 1980s, ministers had exploited every opportunity to urge the virtues of private-sector disciplines like competitive tendering throughout the public sector. It had not gone unnoticed, however, that they had usually ignored their own backyard in Whitehall. But publication of the Competing For Quality White Paper in November 1991 was the first signal that a more radical approach was being adopted. Under the market testing initiative, overseen by Sir Peter Levene, the Prime Minister's efficiency adviser, Whitehall would now face the same pressures to organise competitive tenders and contract work out which the town halls had confronted the previous decade. But whereas the Next Steps programme inspired bipartisan support, and the Citizen's Charter scheme inspired ridicule, the market testing initiative inspired fear. Admittedly, many central government support services, including cleaning, catering, maintenance, and clerical work, had already been subject to competition from private-sector firms. Now, however, the heart of the Civil Service, its specialists and professionals, ranging from scientists to lawyers, accountants and inspectors, were in effect put on notice that they would henceforth have to compete for their jobs against private-sector competition.

Market testing is the extension to Whitehall of the same purchaser-provider philosophy applied to the NHS in 1983 and local government in 1988. Stated simply, its aim is to separate the roles of purchaser and provider so that those responsible for purchasing public services – from fisheries protection to the collection of statistics – are free to choose from a range of competing providers regardless of whether they are in the private or the public sector. According to Waldegrave: 'Those whose duty it is to spend public money on behalf of the citizen to buy public services must be quite free of pressure to provide work for whatever provider bureaucracy may happen historically to exist'. The state cannot escape its obligation to purchase public services, but there is nothing to say that it must provide them as well. In addition, Waldegrave said, the purchaser-provider division has three benign consequences:

(a) It ends potential conflicts of interest by allowing the purchaser to become the advocate of the consumer rather than the defender of the producer;

(b) It gives public purchasers access to private-sector resources and expertise; and

(c) It forces both sides to redefine the nature of the services and the standards of quality to be provided.

Private-sector companies were quick to appreciate the long-term implications of the third element of the government's tripartite public service reform programme. A report published in November 1992 by the business advisers Newchurch and Company, called 'Market Testing: The End Of The Public Sector?', predicted that whole areas of economic activity hitherto regarded as the exclusive preserve of the state would be opened up to private-sector competition. The report calculated that the public sector spent more than £100 billion annually on goods and services, and forecast that: 'within ten years up to £70 billion of this could be subject to market testing'. It added: 'This represents a clear shift in the role of public-sector management ... The government has made clear its preference for the [provider] model, and that its main concern is not who provides services, but that they are efficient, of high quality, and are the best available value for money'. The report concluded: 'Market testing would therefore make public services one of the major growth areas for the private sector during the 1990s'.

The initial target of £25 million worth of central government services to be marketed tested – the first step towards work being contracted out – was announced in November 1991. It was expanded to £1.5 billion in November 1992, with a further £1 billion announced in December the following year. Although these amounts fell short of initial targets, Waldegrave insisted that work which had been marketed tested had produced savings of around 25 per cent – whether the work was contract-ed out or remained in-house, thereby saving the taxpayer an estimated £100 million. In the process, however, thousands of civil servants found that they had to compete against outside contractors. Work covered by the initiative included information technology, computer services, payroll, building and estate management, and finan-cial and legal services. Moreover, entire executive agencies were now up for sale, from the Public Record Office to the Royal Palaces such as Hampton Court and the Tower of London, with civil servants encouraged to mount management buyouts. Waldegrave predicted that, under the purchaser-provider model, the Civil Service could be reduced to a core of 50,000 policy-makers buying public services from a range of competing public – and private-sector-providers within a few years, with savings of around 25 per cent for the taxpayer.

The expansion of the market testing initiative did much to appease critics who insisted that the government's reform programme was insufficiently radical. But it provoked an avalanche of criticism from the public-sector trade unions. The Institution of Professional Managers and Specialists (IPMS), half of whose 90,000 members are employed by the public sector, warned that market testing could only cut costs by reducing quality. The Sheffield-based Centre for Public Services, the trade union think-tank, insisted that the 25 per cent cost savings predicted by the govern-ment were ludicrous. 'Detailed surveys of the local authority experience of compul-sory competitive tendering, including one funded by the Environment Department, show average savings of only 7 per cent. And then only at the expense of slashing jobs, wages and conditions, and often letting service standards fall', it said.

Drawing on the American experience of contracting out, John Sheldon, the gen-eral secretary of the National Union of Civil and Public Servants, wrote to *The Times* in May 1993. He pointed out that a report by Richard Darman, the director of the US Office of Management and Budget, highlighted how the contracting out of public ser-vices 'has led to the waste of billions of dollars, mismanagement on a massive scale, corruption and fraud'. Moreover, the *New York Times* had described the report as 'among the most decisive critiques ever published by government of a central tenet of the Reagan-Bush era: the idea that private companies can do the federal government's work better for less money'. Similarly, Elizabeth Symons, the general secretary of the First Division Association, which represents senior civil servants, said that while it was not opposed in principle to 'new management methods where they can be shown to deliver better standards', it was bitterly opposed to the 'cloak and dagger methods' being used to bring them about. The reforms, she added, 'herald the full scale privati-sation of everything from defence communications to core activities like the Crown Prosecution Service. This is a time bomb ticking away under the responsible provi-sion of public services controlled by ministers accountable to Parliament'.

These anxieties were given further credence in January 1994 with the publica-tion of the House of Commons Public Accounts Select Committee report: 'The Proper Conduct of Public Business'. Robert Sheldon, the committee chairman, said that there had been a noticeable decline in levels of public probity and integrity during the past few years which, if not arrested and reversed, could threaten the traditional 'incorruptibility' of Britain's public services. The report listed 26 cases of wasted resources, money improperly spent, financial discrepancies, mismanagement, corruption and fraud across a range of government departments, agencies and quangos. Declining standards of public stewardship had been exacerbated by the government's attempt to bring private-sector expertise into public-sector management, the report said. Mr Sheldon added that it was not that the public and private sectors were incompatible, but that private-sector managers were not imbued with the 'public-sector ethos' of probity, integrity and accountability associated with public servants. Responding to the allegations, Waldegrave insisted that the committee had none the less endorsed the government's reform philosophy, and that Britain's public service remained one of the least corrupt in the world.

The public-sector trade unions initially thought that market testing could be stopped in its tracks under the provisions of the European Community's 1977 Acquired Rights Directive, implemented into UK law under the Transfer of Undertakings (Protection of Employment) Regulations 1981 – the Tupe regulations. Although originally designed to protect the jobs, pay and conditions of employees affected by company mergers and acquisitions, there was considerable confusion in Britain over whether the Tupe regulations applied to public services contracted out to private-sector companies as well. If they did, private-sector companies would be compelled to take over Civil Service staff with their existing pay and conditions intact, thereby drastically limiting the scope for cost savings through pay cuts and redundancies. In January 1993, however, Sir Nicholas Lyell, the Attorney-General, ruled that Tupe applied only where 'an entire entity' was transferred to the private sector. Tupe could not, therefore, force the government to abandon market testing. But the regulations could act as a brake on the initiative, at least until the circumstances of each contract had been established.

In addition to the accusation that the implementation of market testing was 'hamfisted', the government was also confronted by claims that the initiative would undermine the traditional characteristics of the Civil Service, particularly confidentiality and impartiality. In December 1992, the Association of HM Inspectors of Taxes and Senior Revenue Officials (AIT) wrote to the Chairman of the Board of the Inland Revenue warning that market testing would 'undermine their ability to guarantee confidentiality of taxpayers' records and lead to an unacceptable risk of corruption'. The warning was precipitated by a government proposal, effective from 1994, to contract out the computer processing of millions of confidential tax details, including the annual notification of individual and corporate tax assessments, tax codings, and the reimbursement of excess tax. Responding to fears that the transfer could undermine taxpayer privacy and confidentiality, Steve Matheson, an Inland Revenue deputy chairman, said that there could never be a 100 per cent guarantee that employees, in either the public or the private sector, would not go on 'fishing expeditions'. But anyone who illegally obtained access to personal tax information held on a computer would leave a trace that could be identified. Under the Finance Act 1989, unauthorised disclosure of tax information by public- or private-sector employees carries a maximum penalty of two years' imprisonment and an unlimited fine. In short, if banks and building societies can be trusted with confidential customer information, so too can private-sector companies handling sensitive tax information. The public sector does not have a monopoly on confidentiality and probity.

But the tax inspectors had also expressed anxiety over the ability of private-sector companies to tender for work without giving basic undertakings about their political neutrality and business practices. The inspectors insisted that no company 'should make financial contributions to any political party, none should have active politicians on their boards of directors, nor should any employ as a director persons deemed unfit to run a public company'. The risk of corruption was not lost on Sir John Bourn, the National Audit Office's Comptroller and Auditor General, who is responsible for auditing public expenditure. Writing in his annual report at the end of 1992, Sir John said that he would be looking closely at the market testing programme not least because 'the confusion arising from the pace of government reform could allow senior staff and departments to fall into temptation.'

WHAT'S LEFT?

In his lecture on the evolution of the Civil Service given to the Political Studies Association, Sir Robin Butler said: 'I am sometimes asked what the final shape of the Civil Service will be, in tones that imply that the Head of the Civil Service ought to know the answer to that question – I do not. It is not unusual, I guess, for an organism in the process of evolution not to know what its final state will be'. Nevertheless, it was essential, Sir Robin added, 'to maintain a degree of cohesion' across the Civil Service as a whole so the public service reform programme 'does not reach the point where individual departments and their agencies become simply different unconnected elements in the overall public sector'.

But while Sir Robin insisted that the defining characteristics of the Civil Service, including selection and promotion on merit, political neutrality, and accountability through ministers to Parliament, served to illustrate the essential continuity between the old and the new Civil Service, other observers saw the reforms as heralding a complete break with the past. John Garrett, a former member of the Treasury and Civil Service Committee, asked: 'If members of the Civil Service are on short-term contracts, and if 90 per cent of the Civil Service is in separate agencies – and there is no central pay arrangement – and there is massive privatisation ... then surely there is no Civil Service as we have traditionally understood it?' In a letter to *The Times* in February 1994, Lord Bancroft and Sir John Herbecq expressed similar anxieties, and warned that one unintended consequence of the break-up of the Civil Service would be to impair the tradition of unbiased advice to ministers which they insisted was not instinctive but had to be 'learnt and passed on'.

Sir Robin's evolutionary analogy is misleading. The Civil Service is evolving, but it is an evolution not subject to the blind random chance that is the lot of any biological organism. On the contrary, the objective of the government's public service reform programme is to redefine both the culture and the structure of the Civil Service. Sir Robin's claim that 'Marks & Spencer has become better known in the Civil Service than Marx and Engels', neatly encapsulates the point. The convention that British public administrators merely implement policies defined by the government of the day, while at the same time remaining neutral about values and goals, has been subtly but profoundly altered. In order to implement the 'new public management of devolved responsibility, Next Steps agencies, competitive tendering and a more consumer approach to public services', civil servants are in the process of absorbing a distinctly private-sector management ethos. This cultural change is designed to bring about greater public-sector efficiency and improved value for money. But there are widespread fears that the reforms will have the long-term effect of creating a new generation of public servants preoccupied with little more than financial balance sheets and meeting performance targets.

Changes to the structure of the Civil Service are equally far-reaching. Executive agencies, market testing, contracting out and privatisation are the instruments adopted by government to help reverse the growth of the state. According to Richard Mottram, the Permanent Secretary at the Cabinet Office responsible for implementing the government's public service reform programme, the objective is to create a much smaller core government and Civil Service by the middle of the 1990s whose functions are restricted to the bare essentials, such as resource allocation, strategic and policy issues, service procurement, and essential finance and personnel work. But the Whitehall diaspora created by the proliferation of executive agencies could undermine the 'cohesion' that Sir Robin said was necessary to prevent the Civil Service's being fragmented into a plethora of disparate and unconnected elements.

Indeed, according to Vernon Bogdanor: 'We seem to be in the process of developing a two-tier Civil Service, a small core with job security and career prospects, and a periphery, comprising positions which are to be filled by public advertisement, and with a wide range of pay and conditions'. Moreover, the more Chief Executives are encouraged to develop their own pay and management structures, 'the more difficult it will become to provide for a regular interchange between the centre and the agencies'. A few years from now, as pay differentials between the core and the periphery widen: 'It will be extremely difficult to tempt any civil servant working in an agency back to Whitehall ...' he added. Few would disagree with Sir Robin's claim that the idea of the Civil Service as 'a comfortable and secure sinecure' is no longer tenable. But the continuity Sir Robin sees between the past and the present is more difficult to discern. It may well be that the greatest challenge facing the Civil Service in the last years of the century is the 'need to combine the greater efficiency, flexibility and standards of service from the management changes of the last 20 years, with the maintenance of the integrity, probity

100

and cohesion' which has traditionally characterised public administration in Britain. The financial pressures which lie behind these management reforms will not disappear, and as Sir Robin has warned, they 'may well even intensify'. But the combined effects of executive agencies, market testing, contracting out and privatisation will ensure that Britain has a Civil Service in the 21st century quite unrecognisable from the body of public administrators bequeathed by the Northcote-Trevelyan reforms in the19th.

THE NEXT STEPS AGENCIES

Next Steps executive agencies now embrace a wide variety of government functions ranging from defence research to driver and vehicle licensing, and from employment services to the collection of child maintenance. Each agency has a designated Chief Executive, recruited either directly from within the Civil Service or externally from the private sector. Executive agencies are provided with a Framework document which defines their aims and objectives, and Chief Executives are responsible to Parliament via their appropriate departmental minister for the work they carry out.

Each agency is required to publish an annual report detailing its performance against predetermined targets. A total of 97 executive agencies were in operation by the summer of 1994, with plans to create another 90-odd by the end of 1995, including the Crown Prosecution Service Agency, the Serious Fraud Office Agency and the Treasury Solicitor's Agency. When the Next Steps programme is complete, almost 80 per cent of the Civil Service will be employed by executive agencies operating at arm's length from their sponsoring departments. Following the successful privatisation in December 1993 of DVOIT, formerly the Information Technology Directorate of the Driver and Vehicle Licensing Agency (DVLA), private-sector companies will be able to bid for entire agencies, thus taking them out of public-sector control.

ACCOUNTS SERVICES AGENCY

Function: Provision of a wide range of financial and management accounting services, including payroll and personnel services, to the Department of Trade and Industry and other government departments and executive agencies.

Launched: January 1991.

Chief Executive: Michael Hoddinott. Born: 1943. Educated: Bloxham School, Oxfordshire. Previous posts include Insurance Supervisor, DTI, Shipbuilding Policy Division, DTI, and Finance and Resource Management Division, DTI, before becoming Chief Executive as an internal candidate in 1991.

Accountable to: Trade and Industry Department.

Address: PO Box 100, Caerleon House, Cleppa Park, Newport, Gwent NP1 9YG.

Telephone: 0633-652332 Fax: 0633-652288

ADAS

Function: Food, farming, land and leisure industries consultancy for government departments and fee-paying private-sector customers.

Launched: April 1992.

Chief Executive: Dr Julia Walsh. Born: 1948. Educated: St Bartholomew's Hospital Medical Centre. She held a series of posts in industry, including Smith Kline and French, Amersham International, Glaxo Pharmaceuticals, and Fisons Instruments, before being appointed Chief Executive as an external entrant in 1991.

Accountable to: Ministry of Agriculture, Fisheries and Food.

Address: Oxford Spires Business Park, The Boulevard, Kidlington, Oxfordshire OX5 1NZ.

Telephone: 0865-845025 Fax: 0865-845090

ARMY BASE REPAIR ORGANISATION (ABRO)

Function: Maintenance, repair and refurbishment of a wide range of military equipment for the British Army, Royal Navy and Royal Air Force.

Launched: April 1993.

Chief Executive: Brigadier Jim Drew. Born: 1941. Educated: Sandhurst; Royal Military College of Science. He was commissioned in 1961, served in Germany and Cyprus, and held posts in intelligence, electronic surveillance systems procurement, and equipment management, before being appointed Chief Executive as an internal candidate in 1991.

Accountable to: Ministry of Defence.

Address: Monxton Road, Andover, Hants SP11 8HT.

Telephone: 0264-383194 Fax: 0264-383144

BENEFITS AGENCY

Function: Administration of more than 20 types of benefit, from income support to disability living allowance, and co-ordinating with voluntary bodies, local authorities and other government departments.

Launched: April 1991.

Chief Executive: Michael Bichard. Born: 1947. Educated: King Edward VI Grammar School; Manchester and Birmingham Universities. He held a series of positions in local government, including Chief Executive of the London Borough of Brent and Gloucestershire County Council before being appointed Chief Executive as an external candidate in 1990.

Accountable to: Social Security Department.

Address: Quarry House, Quarry Hill, Leeds LS2 7UA.

Telephone: 0532-324000 Fax: 0532-324288

BUILDING RESEARCH ESTABLISHMENT

Function: Research and advice on technical aspects of building and construction, fire prevention and control, and environmental protection.

Launched: April 1990.

Chief Executive: Roger Courtney. Born: 1946. Educated: Roan School; Trinity College, Cambridge; Bristol and Brunel Universities. Previous posts include Cabinet Office

Science & Technology Secretariat, Technical Director, Energy Efficiency Office, and Deputy Director and Director, Building Research Establishment, before becoming Chief Executive in 1990.
Accountable to: Environment Department.
Address: Garston, Watford WD2 7JR.
Telephone: 0923-664800 Fax: 0923-664010

CADW: WELSH HISTORIC MONUMENTS

Function: Preservation, conservation and promotion of the Welsh-built heritage.
Launched: April 1991.
Chief Executive: John Carr. Born: 1938. Educated: Christ's College, Cambridge. Previous posts include leader and deputy features editor, *Western Mail*, production editor, *The Sunday Times*, director, Neath Development Partnership, and director CADW, before being appointed Chief Executive in 1991.
Accountable to: Welsh Office.
Address: Brunel House, 2 Fitzalan Road, Cardiff CF2 1UY.
Telephone: 0222-465511 Fax: 0222-450859

CENTRAL OFFICE OF INFORMATION

Function: Publicity and information services for all press and broadcast media on behalf of all government departments and executive agencies.
Launched: April 1990.
Chief Executive: Mike Devereau. Born: 1937. He joined the Ministry of Public Buildings and Works in 1967, and held posts in the Building Research Establishment, the Environment Department, the Price Commission, the Transport Department, and the COI, before becoming Chief Executive in 1990.
Accountable to: Chancellor of the Duchy of Lancaster.
Address: Hercules Road, London SE1 7DU.
Telephone: 071-928 2345 Fax: 071-261 0942

CENTRAL SCIENCE LABORATORY

Function: Research and development, identification and control of plant pests and diseases, vertebrate and invertebrate pests, biocontaminants, pesticide safety, and the impact of agriculture on wildlife and the environment.
Launched: April 1992.
Chief Executive: Dr Peter Stanley. Born: 1946. Educated: Dursley Grammar School; University College, London. He joined the Civil Service in 1970, and held various posts in the Pest Infection Control Laboratory, and was Director of the Slough Laboratory, before becoming Chief Executive in 1992.
Accountable to: Ministry of Agriculture, Fisheries and Food.
Address: London Road, Slough, Berkshire SL3 7HJ.
Telephone: 0753-534626 Fax: 0753-824058

CENTRAL STATISTICAL OFFICE

Function: Compilation of UK government statistics for economic management, and provision of statistics on UK to European Community institutions.

Launched: November 1991.

Chief Executive: Bill McLennan. Born: 1942. Educated: the Australian National University. He joined the Australian Bureau of Statistics, and held various posts, including Deputy Australian Statistician, before being appointed Chief Executive as an external entrant in 1992.

Accountable to: Chancellor of the Duchy of Lancaster.

Address: Great George Street, London, SW1P 3AQ.

Telephone: 071-270 6363 Fax: 071-270 6019

CENTRAL VETERINARY LABORATORY

Function: Promotion of animal health and welfare, and the minimisation of hazards associated with animals on human health.

Launched: April 1990.

Chief Executive: Dr Tony Little. Born: 1940. Educated: Dame Allan's School; Edinburgh and London Universities. He joined the Central Veterinary Laboratory in 1966, and held a series of posts in the CVL before being appointed Chief Executive in 1990 as an internal candidate.

Accountable to: Ministry of Agriculture, Fisheries and Food.

Address: New Haw, Addlestone, Surrey, KT15 3NB.

Telephone: 0932-341111 Fax: 0932-347046

CHEMICAL AND BIOLOGICAL DEFENCE ESTABLISHMENT

Function: To provide British armed forces with effective protection against chemical and biological weapons, provide advice on chemical and biological warfare and defence matters, including arms control.

Launched: April 1991.

Chief Executive: Dr Graham Pearson. Born: 1935. Educated: St Andrews University; University of Rochester, USA. Previous posts include Naval weapons safety, the Polaris Chevaline programme, director general (research and development) Royal Ordnance, director of the Chemical Defence Establishment, before being appointed Chief Executive in 1991.

Accountable to: Defence Ministry.

Address: Porton Down, Salisbury, Wiltshire SP4 0JQ.

Telephone: 0980-613365 Fax: 0980-611777

CHESSINGTON COMPUTER CENTRE

Function: Provision of computerised systems for payroll, personnel, financial accounting and superannuation for central government departments, executive agencies, and the rest of the public sector.

Launched: April 1993.

Chief Executive: Bob Edwards. Born: 1942. Educated: Chorlton Grammar School, Manchester. He joined the Civil Service in 1962, and held a variety of management posts

in the Defence Ministry, the Civil Service Department, the Treasury, and director of the Chessington Computer Centre, before being appointed Chief Executive in 1992.
Accountable to: Cabinet Office.
Address: Leatherhead Road, Chessington, Surrey KT9 2LT.
Telephone: 081-391 3800 Fax: 081-391 3986

CHILD SUPPORT AGENCY

Function: Assessment, collection and payment of child maintenance to ensure that parents maintain their children wherever possible.
Launched: April 1993.
Chief Executive: Ann Chant. Born: 1945. Educated: the Blackpool Collegiate School for Girls. She joined the Civil Service in 1963, and held posts in the Health Department, the DHSS , and the DSS, before being appointed Chief Executive of the Contribution Agency in 1991. She succeeded Ros Hepplewhite as Chief Executive of the CHild Support Agency in September 1994.
Accountable to: Social Security Department.
Address: HQ, Millbank Tower, 21-24 Millbank, London SW1P 4QU.
Telephone: 071-217 3000 Fax: 071-217 4471

CIVIL SERVICE COLLEGE

Function: Development of Civil Service managerial and professional skills for all government departments, executive agencies and foreign civil servants.
Launched: June 1989.
Chief Executive: Dr Stephen Hickey. Born: 1947. Educated: St Lawrence College, Ramsgate; Corpus Christi College and St Anthony's College, Oxford. He joined the DHSS in 1973, and held various posts, including Assistant Private Secretary to David Ennals, Patrick Jenkin, and Norman Fowler, before becoming Chief Executive in 1994.
Accountable to: Cabinet Office.
Address: Sunningdale Park, Larch Avenue, Ascot, Berks SL5 0QE.
Telephone: 0344-634000 Fax: 0344-634233

COASTGUARD AGENCY

Function: Responsible for all civil maritime search and rescue operations around the UK coastline and for 1,000 miles into the North Atlantic, and counter-pollution operations in UK waters.
Launched: April 1994.
Chief Executive: Chris Harris. Born: 1937. Educated: Roundhay School, Leeds; the Royal Naval Colleges Dartmouth, Manadon and Greenwich. After serving in the Royal Navy for 20 years, he joined the Transport Department in 1974, and was appointed Chief Executive as an internal candidate in 1994.
Accountable to: Transport Department.
Address: Spring Place, 105 Commercial Road, Southampton SO15 1EG.
Telephone: 0703-329400 Fax: 0703-329404

COMPANIES HOUSE

Function: Incorporation and dissolution of companies, and the provision of information about companies to the public, including compilation of UK register of company directors and their appointments.

Launched: October 1988.

Chief Executive: David Durham. Born: 1937. Educated: Sandhurst. He has held posts throughout the world, including weapon procurement and bomb disposal. He was appointed Director of Housing, Rochester, and an administrator at St Mary's and St Charles' Hospitals, London, before becoming Chief Executive as an external entrant in 1990.

Accountable to: Trade and Industry Department.

Address: Crown Way, Maindy, Cardiff CF4 3UZ.

Telephone: 0222-380801 Fax: 0222-380900

COMPENSATION AGENCY

Function: Administration of compensation schemes criminal injuries, criminal damage, and emergency provisions legislation affecting Northern Ireland.

Launched: April 1992.

Chief Executive: John Robinson. Born: 1954. Educated: Down High School. He became managing director of a textile manufacturing company after holding a series of financial and general management posts, and was recruited from the private sector as Chief Executive in 1992.

Accountable to: Northern Ireland Office.

Address: Royston House, 34 Upper Queen Street, Belfast BT1 6FD.

Telephone: 0232-249944 Fax: 0232-246956

CONTRIBUTIONS AGENCY

Function: Administration, collection and distribution of funds for 60 million contributors to the National Insurance Scheme.

Launched: April 1991.

Chief Executive (Acting): George Bertram

Accountable to: Social Security Department.

Address: Longbenton, Newcastle Upon Tyne NE98 1YX.

Telephone: 091-225 7665 Fax: 091-225 4198

CUSTOMS & EXCISE

Function: Collection of value added tax and excise duties, preventing of drug trafficking, enforcement of import-export prohibitions such as firearms and endangered species, and the collection of customs duties and agricultural levies on behalf of the European Community. (For further details *see* Chapter seven, 'The Miscellaneous State'.)

Launched: April 1991.

Accountable to: Treasury.

Address: New King's Beam House, 22 Upper Ground, London, SW1 9PJ.

Telephone: 071-620 1313 Fax: 071-620 1313 ext. 5005

DEFENCE ACCOUNTS AGENCY

Function: Provision of financial and accounting services, including payroll, pensions, debt collection and banking services for the Ministry of Defence.

Launched: April 1991.

Chief Executive: Mike Dymond. Born: 1936. Educated: Colston's School, Bristol; Merton College, Oxford. Previous posts include chartered accountant, British Rail, financial controller, Metals Research; he joined the Defence Ministry in 1973, and held various posts before becoming Chief Executive in 1991 as an internal candidate.

Accountable to: Defence Ministry.

Address: Warminster Road, Bath BA1 5AA.

Telephone: 0225-828106 Fax: 0225-828681

DEFENCE ANALYTICAL SERVICE AGENCY

Function: Provision of statistical information and analysis for Defence Ministry's budgetary, personnel and logistics planning.

Launched: July 1990.

Chief Executive: Paul Autobell. Born: 1939. Educated: Gateway School; Central London Polytechnic (Westminster University); Webster University, USA. He held posts in the private sector an the Defence Ministry before being appointed Chief Executive in 1992.

Accountable to: Ministry of Defence.

Address: Northumberland House, Northumberland Avenue, London WC2N 5BP.

Telephone: 071-218 2188

DEFENCE ANIMAL CENTRE

Function: Training and supply of all Ministry of Defence dogs and horses throughout the world, including training and supply of personnel.

Launched: June 1993.

Chief Executive: Colonel Paul Jepson. Born: 1947. Educated: King Edward VI School, Lytham; Liverpool and Bristol Universities. Previous posts include Chief of Veterinary Services, British Forces Hong Kong, and Army Chief Veterinary Surgeon before becoming Chief Executive as an internal candidate in 1993.

Accountable to: Ministry of Defence.

Address: Melton Mowbray, Leicestershire LE13 OSL.

Telephone: 0664-63281 ext. 8624 Fax: 0664-410694 ext. 8629

DEFENCE OPERATIONAL ANALYSIS CENTRE

Function: Analysis of Defence Ministry policy formulation, military operational capabilities, resource allocation and equipment procurement.

Launched: July 1992.

Chief Executive: Dr David Leadbeater. Born: 1944. Educated: Tottenham Grammar School; Wanstead County High School; Rugby College of Engineering Technology; Bristol University. Previous posts include Head of Sonar, ARE, Head of Electronic Warfare, ARE, and Director of DOAC before becoming Chief Executive as an internal candidate in 1992.

Accountable to: Ministry of Defence.
Address: Broadoaks, Parvis Road, West Byfleet, Surrey KT14 6LY.
Telephone: 0932-341199

DEFENCE POSTAL AND COURIER SERVICE

Function: Mail and post office counter services for servicemen and women, and world-wide classified mail service for government departments.
Launched: July 1992.
Chief Executive: Brigadier Michael Browne. Born: 1941. Educated: Dartford Grammar School. He began his career as a Post Office executive, joined the Royal Engineers in 1963, and served in Hong Kong, Germany, and Northern Ireland, before becoming Chief Executive in 1992 as an internal candidate.
Accountable to: Ministry of Defence.
Address: MOD(A) BFPO 777.
Telephone: 081-346 2611 ext. 3417 Fax: 081-346 2611 ext. 3309

DEFENCE RESEARCH AGENCY

Function: Provision of scientific and technical advice in support of the Ministry of Defence's defence equipment procurement programme.
Launched: April 1991.
Chief Executive: John Chisholm. Born: 1946. Educated: Cambridge University. He held a series of private-sector positions, including Group Manager, Scicon, and Managing Director, Sema Metra, before becoming Chief Executive as an external entrant in 1991.
Accountable to: Ministry of Defence.
Address: Farnborough, Hants GU14 6TD.
Telephone: 0252-394568 Fax 0252-394571

DRIVER AND VEHICLE LICENSING AGENCY (DVLA)

Function: Registration and licensing of drivers and vehicles, collection of vehicle excise duty, and sale of personalised number plates.
Launched: April 1990.
Chief Executive: Stephen Curtis. Born: 1948. Educated: Forest School; Exeter University. Previous posts include Chief Statistician, DTI, Registrar of Companies, and Chief Executive, Companies House, before being appointed Chief Executive as an internal candidate in 1990.
Accountable to: Transport Department.
Address: Longview Road, Morriston, Swansea SA6 7JL.
Telephone: 0792-783112 Fax: 0792-783003

DRIVER AND VEHICLE LICENSING AGENCY (NI)

Function: Registration and licensing of drivers and vehicles, and collection of vehicle excise duties in Northern Ireland.
Launched: August 1993.
Chief Executive: Brendan Magee. Born: 1949. Educated: St Michaels College,

Enniskillen; the Open University. He joined the Civil Service in 1968 and held posts in the Home Office, the Price Commission, and the Health and Safety Executive before becoming Chief Executive as an internal candidate in 1993.
Accountable to: Environment Department (NI).
Address: County Hall, Castlerock Road, Coleraine BT51 3HS.
Telephone: 0265-44133 ext.246 Fax: 0265-320447

DRIVER AND VEHICLE TESTING AGENCY (NI)

Function: Testing roadworthiness of private cars, light goods vehicles and motorcycles using the roads in Northern Ireland.
Launched: April 1992.
Chief Executive: Brian Watson. Born: 1944. He held various posts in the Northern Ireland Office before becoming Chief Executive as an internal candidate in 1992.
Accountable to: Environment Department (NI).
Address: Balmoral Road, Belfast BT12 6QL.
Telephone: 0232-681831 Fax: 0232-665520

DRIVING STANDARDS AGENCY

Function: Conducting driving tests for car, lorry and motorcycle drivers, and approving driving instructors.
Launched: April 1990.
Chief Executive: Dr John Ford. Born: 1936. Educated: Bishop Gore School, Swansea, and the University of Wales. Previous posts include managing director, British Aluminium Company, deputy managing director, British Alcan, director, Williams holdings, and director, Christian Salvesen, before becoming Chief Executive as an external appointment in 1993.
Accountable to: Transport Department.
Address: Stanley House, 56 Talbot Street, Nottingham NG1 5GU.
Telephone: 0602-474222 Fax: 0602-485734

DUKE OF YORK'S ROYAL MILITARY SCHOOL

Function: Provision of education for the children of officers serving in the Armed Forces.
Launched: April 1992.
Chief Executive: Colonel Gordon Wilson BA MEd. Born: 1950. Educated: Queens University and University College, Cardiff. His previous posts include Chief Education Officer 1 Armd Div, and Senior Resettlement Officer, BAOR, before becoming Chief Executive as an internal candidate in 1992.
Accountable to: Education Department.
Address: Dover, Kent CT15 5EQ.
Telephone: 0304-245024 Fax: 0304-245019

DVOIT

Function: Formerly the Information Technology Directorate of the DVLA responsible for provision of information systems and computer services for the Transport Department and its executive agencies.

Launched: April 1992 and privatised in December 1993.

Accountable to: Transport Department.

Address: Oldway Centre, 36 Orchard Street, Swansea SA99 5AX.

Telephone: 0792-304357 Fax: 0792-304190

EMPLOYMENT SERVICE AGENCY

Function: Promotion of flexible labour force by helping the unemployed find work, and paying benefits and allowances to those entitled to them.

Launched: April 1990.

Chief Executive: Mike Fogden. Born: 1936. Educated: the High School for Boys, Worthing. He joined the Civil Service in 1958 and held various posts in the DHSS and the Employment Department, before becoming Chief Executive in 1990 as an internal candidate.

Accountable to: Employment Department.

Address: St Vincent House, 30 Orange Street, London WC2H 7HT.

Telephone: 071-389 1377 Fax: 071-389 1373

FIRE SERVICE COLLEGE

Function: Central training establishment for the UK fire service responsible for training in fire fighting, safety, finance, management and computing skills.

Launched: April 1992.

Chief Executive: Nigel Finlayson. Born: 1948. He joined the Home Office in 1966, and held positions in the Northern Ireland Office, the Gaming Board, various private-sector companies, and was Chief Executive of the Home Office Communications Business before becoming Chief Executive in 1994.

Accountable to: Home Office.

Address: Moreton-In-Marsh, Gloucestershire GL56 ORH.

Telephone: 0608-650831 Fax: 0608-651788

FORENSIC SCIENCE SERVICE

Function: Provision of scientific support in the investigation of crime, and providing scientific evidence to the Crown Prosecution Service, the courts, coroners and the defence.

Launched: April 1991.

Chief Executive: Dr Janet Thompson. Born: 1941. Educated: North London Collegiate School; Brighton College of Technology; Oxford University. She joined the Home Office in 1971, and held various posts dealing with prisoner casework and parole, magistrates courts procedures and bail, and director general of the Forensic Science Service, before becoming Chief Executive in 1991.

Accountable to: Home Office.

Address: Priory House, Gooch Street North, Birmingham B5 6QQ.

Telephone: 021-666 6606 Fax: 021-622 3536

GOVERNMENT PROPERTY LAWYERS

Function: Conveyancing services, including purchases of land and buildings for trunk roads, motorways and by-passes, property sales by auction and tender, and negotiation of commercial leases for office occupation for government departments, executive agencies and other public bodies.

Launched: April 1993.

Chief Executive: Tony Osborne. Born: 1935. Educated: Brighton College. He was appointed Chief Executive in 1993 as an internal candidate.

Accountable to: Attorney-General.

Address: Riverside Chambers, Castle Street, Taunton, Somerset TA1 4AP.

Telephone: 0823-345200 Fax: 0823-345202

HIGHWAYS AGENCY

Function: Responsible for delivering the government's road programme and for managing and maintaining the existing trunk road network in England.

Launched: April 1994.

Chief Executive: Lawrence Haynes. Born: 1952. Educated: Heriot-Watt University. Previous posts include Head of Contracts, British Aerospace, Legal and Managing Director, Microtel Communications, Managing Director, British Aerospace Communications, and Project Director, British Aerospace before being appointed Chief Executive as an external candidate in 1994.

Accountable to: Transport Department.

Address: St Christopher House, Southwark Street, London SE1 0TE.

Telephone: 071-928 3666 Fax: 071-921 3908

HISTORIC ROYAL PALACES AGENCY

Function: Responsible for the care, preservation and presentation to the public of the five Royal Palaces; the Tower of London, Hampton Court Palace, Kensington Palace State Apartments including ceremonial dress collection and orangery, the Banqueting House in Whitehall, and Kew Palace.

Launched: October 1989.

Chief Executive: David Beeton. Born: 1939. Educated: King's College, London. Previous posts include Chief Executive, Bath City Council, and Secretary of the National Trust, before becoming Chief Executive in 1989.

Accountable to: National Heritage Department.

Address: Hampton Court Palace, East Molesey, Surrey KT8 9AU.

Telephone: 081-781 9750 Fax: 081-781 9754

HISTORIC SCOTLAND

Function: Responsible for the preservation and maintenance of 330 historic properties in Scotland, ranging from Edinburgh Castle to remote rural sites, listing historic buildings and funding archaeological excavations.

Launched: April 1991.

Chief Executive: Graeme Munro. Born: 1944. Educated: St Andrews University. He

111

joined the Scottish Office in 1968, and held a variety of policy and management posts before becoming Chief Executive in 1993.

Accountable to: Scottish Office.

Address: 20 Brandon Street, Edinburgh EH3 5RA.

Telephone: 031-244 3144 Fax: 031-244 3185

HM PRISON SERVICE

Function: Provision of prison services in England and Wales, including custody of criminals convicted by the courts, maintenance of order, control and discipline, and prisoner rehabilitation and care.

Launched: April 1993.

Chief Executive: Derek Lewis. Born: 1946. Educated: Wrekin College; Queen's College, Cambridge; the London Business School. He held posts with the Ford Motor Company, Imperial Group, Granada Group, UK Gold, before becoming Chief Executive in 1993.

Accountable to: Home Office.

Address: Cleland House, Page Street, London SW1P 4LN.

Telephone: 071-217 3000 Fax: 071-217 6635

HER MAJESTY'S STATIONERY OFFICE (HMSO)

Function: Provision of office technology, stationery, furniture, print and publishing requirements for Parliament (including a new electronic version of Hansard), government departments and executive agencies.

Launched: December 1988.

Chief Executive: Dr Paul Freeman. Born: 1936. Educated: Manchester University. He joined the National Physical Laboratory in 1964, and held various posts in the Industry Department, before becoming Chief Executive in 1989.

Accountable to: Chancellor of the Duchy of Lancaster.

Address: St Crispins, Duke Street, Norwich NR3 1PD.

Telephone: 0603-695574 Fax: 0603-695045

HYDROGRAPHIC OFFICE

Function: Provision of charts and navigational publications for the Royal Navy, domestic and foreign commercial and private customers in the world shipping market.

Launched: April 1990.

Chief Executive: Rear Admiral Nigel Essenhigh. Born: 1944. He joined the Royal Navy in 1963, and held a variety of posts including First Lieutenant and Commander, HMS *Glasgow*, The Directorate of Naval Manpower, the Defence Ministry, Commander, HMS *Nottingham*, Assistant Director (Weapons and Ships), Commander, HMS *Exeter*, and served in Operations Desert Shield and Desert Storm, before becoming Chief Executive in 1994.

Accountable to: Ministry of Defence.

Address: Taunton, Somerset, TA1 2DN.

Telephone: 0823-337900 Fax: 0823-325522

INLAND REVENUE

Function: Administration of income tax, corporation tax, capital gains tax, petroleum revenue tax, inheritance tax, stamp duties for valuation services, and policy advice for ministers. (For further details *see* Chapter 7, 'The Miscellaneous State'.)
Launched: April 1992.
Accountable to: Chancellor of the Exchequer.
Address: Somerset House, London WC2R 1LB.
Telephone: 071-438 6622

INSOLVENCY SERVICE

Function: Administration of corporate and financial failure, investigation of fraud and misconduct in insolvencies, and providing support and confidence in financial markets and protecting customers.
Launched: March 1990.
Chief Executive: Peter Joyce. Born: 1942. Educated: Westwood's Grammar School, Northleach. He joined the Civil Service in 1960, and held a variety of posts including consumer affairs, chief examiner, official receiver, and deputy inspector general before being appointed Chief Executive as an internal candidate in 1989.
Accountable to: Trade and Industry Department.
Address: PO Box 203, 21 Bloomsbury Street, London WC1B 3QW.
Telephone: 071-291 6718 Fax: 071-291 6731

INTERVENTION BOARD

Function: Implementation of UK responsibilities under the European Union's Common Agricultural Policy, including market support for farm and food products such as dairy products, cereals and beef.
Launched: April 1990.
Chief Executive: Guy Stapleton. Born: 1935. Educated: Hill Place School; Malvern College. He held posts in the Ministry of Aviation, the Ministry of Agriculture and the Cabinet Office, before becoming Chief Executive as an internal candidate in 1986.
Accountable to: Ministry of Agriculture.
Address: Fountain House, 2 Queens Walk, Reading RG1 7QW.
Telephone: 0734-583626 Fax: 0734-566748

INFORMATION TECHNOLOGY SERVICES AGENCY

Function: Provision of information technology services for the Social Security Department and its executive agencies and other government departments.
Launched: April 1990.
Chief Executive: Ian Magee. Born: 1946. Educated: Leeds University. He held various posts in the DSS, the Cabinet Office, and the DHSS, before being appointed Chief Executive as an internal candidate in 1993.
Accountable to: Social Security Department.
Address: 4th Floor, Verulam Point, Station Way, St Albans, Herts AL1 5HE.
Telephone: 0727-815838 Fax: 0727-833740

113

LABORATORY OF THE GOVERNMENT CHEMIST
Function: Chemical and biological analysis in support of government policies towards commerce and industry, including law enforcement, maintenance of public health, and consumer and environmental protection.
Launched: October 1989.
Chief Executive: Dr Richard Warswick. Born: 1946. Educated: Magdalen College School; New College, Oxford. He held a series of posts at the Harwell Laboratory, United Kingdom Atomic Energy Authority, including Head of Research and Planning, Head of Environmental and Medical Sciences, and Director of Process Technology and Instrumentation, before becoming Chief Executive as an external appointment in 1991.
Accountable to: Trade and Industry Department.
Address: Queens Road, Teddington, Middlesex TW11 0LY.
Telephone: 081-943 7000 Fax: 081-943 2767

LAND REGISTRY
Function: Administration of land registration system in England and Wales in support of the property market and secured credit facilities.
Launched: July 1990.
Chief Executive: John Manthorpe. Born: 1936. Educated: Beckenham and Penge Grammar School. He was appointed Chief Executive in 1992 as an internal candidate.
Accountable to: Lord Chancellor.
Address: Room 107, Lincoln's Inn Fields, London WC2A 3PH.
Telephone: 071-917 8888 Fax: 071-955 0110

MARINE SAFETY AGENCY
Function: To develop, review and enforce marine safety standards and minimise the risk of pollution of the marine environment from ships.
Launched: April 1994.
Chief Executive: Robin Bradley. Born: 1940. Educated: Pangbourne College; Britannia Royal Naval College and the Royal Naval Engineering College. A former captain in the Royal Navy, he held a series of posts including Production Director, Portsmouth Dockyard, Superintendent Ships in the Directorate General of Ships Refitting, and Commanding Officer Royal Naval Engineering School, HMS *Sultan*, before joining the Transport Department as Surveyor General. He was appointed Chief Executive in 1994.
Accountable to: Transport Department.
Address: Spring Place, 105 Commercial Road, Southampton.
Telephone: 0703-329265 Fax: 0703-329404

MEDICINES CONTROL AGENCY
Function: Safeguard public health by ensuring that all medicines sold in Britain meet required standards of safety, quality and efficacy, and monitoring of pharmaceutical manufacturing and wholesaling.
Launched: July 1991.
Chief Executive: Dr Keith Jones. Born: 1937. Educated: Cathays High School, Cardiff;

114

Welsh National School of Medicine. He held a variety of posts, including Head of Medical Department, Fisons Agrochemical Division, and Head of Safety Assessment and Clinical Pharmacology, Beecham Pharmaceuticals, before becoming Chief Executive in 1989.

Accountable to: Health Department.

Address: Market Towers, 1 Nine Elms Lane, London SW8 5NQ.

Telephone: 071-273 3000 Fax: 071-273 0334

METEOROLOGICAL OFFICE

Function: Provision of wide range of weather monitoring and forecasting services to Armed Forces, shipping, civil aviation, the public sector, industry and commerce and daily weather bulletins.

Launched: April 1990.

Chief Executive: Professor Julian Hunt. Born: 1941. Educated: Westminster School; Trinity College, Cambridge. Previous posts include General Secretary of the European Research Community, Flow Turbulence and Combustion, and Vice President of the Institute of Mathematics, before becoming Chief Executive as an external candidate in 1992.

Accountable to: Defence Ministry.

Address: London Road, Bracknell RG12 2SZ.

Telephone: 0344-854455 Fax: 0344-856087

MILITARY SURVEY

Function: Provision of geographic support to Defence Ministry planning training and operations, including maps, air charts and terrain information.

Launched: April 1991.

Chief Executive: Major General Mike Wilson. Born: 1943. Educated: Duke of York's School, Nairobi; University College, London. Previous posts include Commander 512 Specialist Team Royal Engineers and Geographic Staff, Washington, Commander 42 Survey Engineer Group, and Director Geographic Operations, Defence Ministry, before becoming Chief Executive as an internal candidate in 1993.

Accountable to: Ministry of Defence.

Address: Elmwood Avenue, Feltham, Middlesex TW13 7AH.

Telephone: 081-818 2400 Fax: 081-818 2148

NATIONAL PHYSICAL LABORATORY

Function: Development and maintenance of national measurement standards of physical quantities, calibration services and research on standards for engineering material and information technology.

Launched: July 1990.

Chief Executive: Dr Peter Clapham. Educated: Ashville College, Harrogate; University College, London. Previous posts include scientific officer, NPL, Deputy Chief Scientific Officer, DTI, and Head of Optical Metrology, before becoming Chief Executive as an internal candidate in 1989.

Accountable to: Trade and Industry Department.

115

Address: Teddington, Middlesex TW11 0LW.
Telephone: 081-977 3222 Fax: 081-943 2155

NATIONAL WEIGHTS & MEASURES LABORATORY

Function: Facilitate fair trade by setting standards for accurate measurement, and advice and guidance to equipment manufacturers and trading standards officers.
Launched: April 1989.
Chief Executive: Dr Seton Bennett. Born: 1945. Educated: Queen Elizabeth's School; Oriel College, Oxford; Imperial College, London. Previous posts include Branch Head, National Physical Laboratory, and Deputy Director NWML, before becoming Chief Executive as an internal candidate in 1990.
Accountable to: Trade and Industry Department.
Address: Stanton Avenue, Teddington, Middlesex TW11 0JZ.
Telephone: 081-943 7272 Fax: 081-943 7270

NATURAL RESOURCES INSTITUTE

Function: Provision of assistance to developing countries to improve productivity and sustainable management of renewable resources, including farming, forestry and fisheries.
Launched: April 1990.
Chief Executive: Anthony Beattie. Born: 1944. Educated: Stationers' Company School, London; Trinity College, Cambridge. He held posts in the Economic Planning Division, Malawi, Economic Planning Staff, ODA, Director of the Tropical Development and Resources Institute, and Director of the Overseas Resources Institute before becoming Chief Executive in 1990 as an internal appointment.
Accountable to: Overseas Development Administration.
Address: Central Avenue, Chatham Maritime, Chatham, Kent ME4 4TB.
Telephone: 0634-880088 Fax: 0634-880066-77

NAVAL AIRCRAFT REPAIR ORGANISATION DEFENCE AGENCY

Function: Repair, modify, overhaul and provide storage facilities for all UK Armed Forces' helicopter fleets, engines and components.
Launched: April 1992.
Chief Executive: Captain NJ Pearson. Born: 1947. Educated: Sherborne School; the RN Engineering College; Southampton University. He held various naval posts before being appointed Chief Executive as an internal candidate in 1994.
Accountable to: Defence Ministry.
Address: Royal Naval Aircraft Yard, Fleetlands, Gosport PO13 0AW.
Telephone: 0329-826225

NATIONAL ENGINEERING LABORATORY (NEL)

Function: Provision of engineering technology services for government and private-sector customers.
Launched: October 1990.
Chief Executive: William Edgar. Born: 1938. Educated: Strathclyde University, and

Birmingham University. He held posts at the British Aircraft Corporation, Weir Pumps, Glasgow, Seaforth Maritime, Vickers Marine Engineering, and Chief Executive of Cochrane Shipbuilders, before becoming Chief Executive as an external candidate in 1990.
Accountable to: Trade and Industry Department.
Address: East Kilbride, Glasgow G75 0QU.
Telephone: 03552-72221 Fax: 03552-721132

NHS ESTATES

Function: Healthcare property and estate management, design and construction.
Launched: April 1991.
Chief Executive: John Locke. Born: 1947. Educated: Pangbourne College; Regent Street Polytechnic; Brixton School of Building; Northern Polytechnic. Previous posts include director of estate management, Prudential Assurance, director of Prudential Portfolio Managers, and chairman of City Aviation Insurance Tenancies, before becoming Chief Executive as an external candidate in 1991.
Accountable to: Health Department.
Address: 1 Trevelyan Square, Boar Lane, Leeds LS1 6AE.
Telephone: 0532-547000 Fax: 0532-547299

NHS PENSIONS AGENCY

Function: Administration of the NHS Occupational Pensions Scheme, collection and distribution of payments, and provision of advice on pension matters.
Launched: November 1992.
Chief Executive: Alec Cowan. Born: 1946. Educated: Gateshead Grammar School. His previous posts include Senior Pensions Administrator (Teachers), and Director of Information Systems (DFE), before becoming Chief Executive as an internal candidate in 1992.
Accountable to: Health Department.
Address: Hesketh House, 200-220 Broadway, Fleetwood, Lancashire FY7 8LG.
Telephone: 0253-774401 Fax: 0253-774860

NORTHERN IRELAND CHILD SUPPORT AGENCY

Function: Assessment, collection and payment of child maintenance to ensure parents maintain their children wherever possible.
Launched: April 1993.
Chief Executive: Pat Devlin. Born: 1938. Educated: Abbey Grammar School, Newry. Previous appointments include Regional Manager Social Security Offices, and Head of IT Services, before being appointed Chief Executive in 1991.
Accountable to: Northern Ireland Office.
Address: Great Northern Tower, 17 Great Victoria Street, Belfast BT2 7AD.
Telephone: 0232-896896 Fax: 0232-896693

OCCUPATIONAL HEALTH SERVICE

Function: Promotion of health and safety at work, including the provision of a range of health and safety services to government departments, executive agencies and other public bodies.

Launched: April 1990.

Chief Executive: Dr Elizabeth McCloy. Born: 1945. Educated: Guilford County Grammar School; University College, London; University College Hospital, London University. Previous posts include Consultant in Occupational Medicine, Manchester Royal Infirmary, and Director of Health and Safety, Central Manchester Health Care Trust, before becoming Chief Executive as an external candidate in 1993.

Accountable to: Cabinet Office.

Address: 19-20 Hill Street, Edinburgh EH2 3NB.

Telephone: 031-220 4177 Fax: 031-220 4183

ORDNANCE SURVEY

Function: Production of topographic data and maps of Britain, including the revision of existing maps, for public- and private-sector customers.

Launched: May 1990.

Chief Executive: Professor David Rhind. Born: 1943. Educated: Berwick Grammar School; the Universities of Bristol, Edinburgh and London. His previous posts include Head of Resource Centre, Birkbeck College, Professor of Geography, London University, Head of Geography, Birkbeck College, before becoming Chief Executive in 1992 as an external entrant.

Accountable to: Environment Department.

Address: Romsey Road, Maybush, Southampton SO9 4DH.

Telephone: 0703-792559 Fax: 0703-792660

ORDNANCE SURVEY OF NORTHERN IRELAND

Function: Production of topographic data and maps, and street plans and atlases for Northern Ireland.

Launched: April 1992.

Chief Executive: Michael Brand. Born: 1939. Previous posts include Director of Ordnance Survey NI, and Chairman of the National Association for Geographic Information, before being appointed Chief Executive in 1992.

Accountable to: Northern Ireland Office.

Address: Colby house, Stranmillis Court, Belfast BT9 5BJ.

Telephone: 0232-661244 Fax: 0232-683211

PATENT OFFICE

Function: Granting patents, registering designs and trademarks for goods and services, and protecting intellectual property rights.

Launched: October 1991.

Chief Executive: Paul Hartnack. Born: 1943. Educated: Hastings Grammar School. He held posts in the DTI, the British Embassy in Paris, and the National Enterprise Board,

before becoming Chief Executive in 1990.
Accountable to: Trade and Industry Department.
Address: Concept House, Cardiff Road, Newport, Gwent NP9 1RH.
Telephone: 0633-814000 Fax: 0633-814504

PAYMASTER

Function: Provision of banking, pensions and financial information service for government departments, executive agencies and other public bodies, and the provision of statistics on public expenditure to the Treasury and the Central Statistical Office.
Launched: April 1993.
Chief Executive: Keith Sullens. Born: 1944. Educated: Hove Grammar School. He held a series of posts, including Head of Banking and Computer Services, Establishment Officer, and Assistant Paymaster General, before being appointed Chief Executive as an internal candidate in 1993.
Accountable to: Chancellor of the Exchequer.
Address: Sutherland House, Russell Way, Crawley, West Sussex RH10 1UH.
Telephone: 0293-560999 Fax: 0293-538979

PESTICIDES SAFETY DIRECTORATE

Function: Protection of health of humans, animals and plants, safeguard the environment, and establish safe, efficient, and humane methods of pest control.
Launched: April 1993.
Chief Executive: Geoff Bruce. Born: 1944. Educated: George Stephenson Grammar School. He joined the Ministry of Agriculture in 1962, and worked as Head of Agricultural Resources Policy Division, Head of Research and Development, and Regional Director, before being appointed Chief Executive in 1992.
Accountable to: Ministry of Agriculture, Fisheries and Food.
Address: MAFF, Whitehall Place, London SW1A 2HH
Telephone: 071-270 3000

PLANNING INSPECTORATE

Function: Appeals against the decisions of local authorities on planning applications, and the provision of inspectors to hold inquiries into objections to local authority plans.
Launched: April 1992.
Chief Executive: Christopher Shepley. Born: 1944. Educated: Stockport Grammar School; London School of Economics. Planner with Manchester City and Greater Manchester Councils, becoming city planning officer, Plymouth, in 1985. He is a past president of the Royal Town Planning Institute and was appointed chief executive as an external candidate in 1994.
Accountable to: Environment Department.
Address: Tollgate House, Houlton Street, Bristol BS2 9DJ.
Telephone: 0272-218927 Fax: 0272-218408

119

PUBLIC RECORD OFFICE

Function: Preservation of central government and central law court records from the Domesday Book to the present day, and providing access to records to members of the public.
Launched: April 1992.
Chief Executive: Sarah Tyacke. Born: 1945. Educated: Chelmsford County High School; London University. Her previous appointments include Assistant Keeper, Map Room, British Museum, Deputy Map Librarian, British Library, and Director of Special Collections, British Library, before being appointed Chief Executive in 1992.
Accountable to: Lord Chancellor.
Address: Ruskin Avenue, Kew, Richmond, Surrey TW9 4DU.
Telephone: 081-876 3444 Fax: 081-878 8905

PUBLIC TRUST OFFICE

Function: To protect and manage the property and affairs of people with mental disability, and to provide a trustee and executorship service for the general public.
Launched: July 1994
Chief Executive: Julia Lomas. Born: 1955. Educated: Pontefract and District High School, Coventry University and the College of Law, Guildford. A former Deputy Borough Solicitor for Waltham Forest, she became the Borough Solicitor of Haringey in April 1989, before being appointed to her current position in May 1994.
Accountable to: Lord Chancellor's Department.
Address: Stewart House, 24 Kingsway, London WC2B 6JX
Telephone: 071-269 7300 Fax: 071-831 0060

QUEEN ELIZABETH II CONFERENCE CENTRE

Function: Provision and management of secure conference facilities for national and international government meetings and private-sector customers.
Launched: July 1989.
Chief Executive: Marcus Buck. Born: 1938. Educated: Cheltenham Grammar School; University of Western Ontario; British Transport Staff College. Previous posts with BOAC and British Airways include manager Japan and Korea, Singapore and Indonesia, marketing manager Japan, manager Victoria, South Australia, Tasmania and Northern Territory, manager Malaysia and Brunei, Trinidad and Tobago, and district manager Guyana and Ethiopia. He was appointed Chief Executive in 1992 as an external candidate.
Accountable to: Environment Department.
Address: Broad Sanctuary, London SW1P 3EE.
Telephone: 071-798 4012 Fax: 071-798 4033

QUEEN VICTORIA SCHOOL

Function: Educational facility for the sons of Scottish soldiers, sailors and airmen.
Launched: April 1992.
Chief Executive: Brian Raine. Born: 1946. Educated: Durham Grammar School; Durham University. Previous posts include Head of History and Housemaster at Strathallen School, before being appointed Chief Executive in 1994.

Accountable to: Defence Ministry.
Address: Dunblane, Perthshire FK15 OYJ.
Telephone: 0786-822288 Fax: 031-310 2519

RADIO COMMUNICATIONS AGENCY

Function: Management of the civil radio spectrum, including monitoring and enforcement with particular priority given to tackling interference which could endanger lives of disrupt commercial operations.
Launched: April 1990.
Chief Executive: Dr Jim Norton. Born: 1952. Educated: Sheffield University. He worked for more than two decades in the Telecommunications and Information Technology Industries, including British Telecom and Cable and Wireless, before becoming Chief Executive as an external candidate in 1993.
Accountable to: Trade and Industry Department.
Address: Waterloo Bridge House, Waterloo Road, London SE1 8UA.
Telephone: 071-215 5000 Fax: 071-928 4309

RAF TRAINING GROUP DEFENCE AGENCY

Function: To provide trained servicemen and civilians to meet RAF requirements.
Launched: April 1994.
Chief Executive: Air Vice-Marshal CCC Colville. Born: 1945. Educated: the RAF College, Cranwell; the Open University; RAF Staff College, Bracknell. He served as a Lightning and Phantom pilot, member of the UK delegation to NATO, OC Operations Wing RAF Stanley, the Falkland Islands, Commander No 111 (Fighter) Squadron, Group Captain Headquarters 11 Group, Strike Command, and Air Commodore Flying Training before being appointed Chief Executive in 1994.
Accountable to: Defence Ministry.
Address: RAF Innsworth, Gloucestershire GL3 1EZ.
Telephone: 0452-512612 Fax: 0452-510825

RAF SUPPORT COMMAND'S MAINTENANCE GROUP
DEFENCE AGENCY

Function: Provision of aerosystems engineering, storage and distribution, and communications electronic services to the RAF and other UK and foreign armed services.
Launched: April 1991.
Chief Executive: Air Vice-Marshal Richard Kyle. Born: 1943. Educated: Southampton University. He held a series of RAF appointments before becoming Chief Executive as an internal candidate in 1991.
Accountable to: Ministry of Defence.
Address: RAF Support Command, RAF Brampton, Huntingdon, Cambs, PE18 8QL.
Telephone: 0480-52151 6306 Fax: 0480-52151 ext. 6498

RATE COLLECTION AGENCY

Function: Collection of rates for Northern Ireland's 26 district councils, and administration of the housing benefit scheme for domestic ratepayers.

Launched: April 1991.

Chief Executive: David Gallagher. Born: 1944. Previous posts include Divisional Finance and Administrative Officer in the Water Service, and Principal of Finance Division of the Environment Department NI, before becoming Chief Executive as an internal candidate in 1991.

Accountable to: Northern Ireland Office.

Address: Oxford House, 49-55 Chichester Street, Belfast BT1 4HH.

Telephone: 0232-235211 Fax: 0232-231936

RECRUITMENT AND ASSESSMENT SERVICES AGENCY

Function: Recruitment of qualified personnel for government departments, executive agencies and other public bodies.

Launched: April 1991.

Chief Executive: Michael Geddes. Born: 1944. Educated: Sherborne School, Dorset, and British Columbia University. He held posts in the Cranfield Institute of Technology, the Royal Military College of Science and Ashridge Management College, before being appointed Chief Executive in 1990.

Accountable to: Cabinet Office.

Address: Alençon Link, Basingstoke RG21 1JB.

Telephone: 0256-29222 Fax: 0256-846315

REGISTERS OF SCOTLAND

Function: Responsible for the public registers of Scotland, including the Register of Sasines and the Land Register, the two national registers of land interests in Scotland.

Launched: April 1990.

Chief Executive: James Barron. Born: 1944. Educated: Broughton Secondary School. He joined the Civil Service in 1951, and held posts in the Admiralty, the Department of Registers, the Lands Tribunal for Scotland, and the Scottish Office before being appointed Chief Executive as an internal candidate in 1990.

Accountable to: Scottish Office.

Address: Meadowbank House, 153 London Road, Edinburgh EH8 7AU.

Telephone: 031-659 6111 Fax: 031-459 1221

RESETTLEMENT AGENCY

Function: Provision of hostels for single homeless people, and grant aiding voluntary organisations and local authorities to provide similar services.

Launched: May 1989.

Chief Executive: Tony Ward. Born: 1940. Educated: Devonport High School. He joined the National Assistance Board in 1959, and held posts in the Social Security Department, and the Cabinet Office, before being appointed Chief Executive in 1989.

Accountable to: Social Security Department.

Address: Euston Tower, 286 Euston Road, London NW1 3DN.
Telephone: 071-388 1188 Fax: 071-383 7199

ROYAL MINT

Function: Production of circulating coinage for the UK, other national governments, and collectors of coins and medals.
Launched: April 1990.
Chief Executive: Roger Holmes. Born: 1938. Educated: Huddersfield New College; Balliol College, Oxford. He joined the Civil Service in 1969, and transferred to the private sector where he held a variety of posts, including British Leyland, Mercury Communications, ICL, Dunlop, Euroroute, Chloride Group, Power Electronics and Cygnet Health Care, before becoming Chief Executive as an external candidate in 1993.
Accountable to: Chancellor of the Exchequer.
Address: Llantrisant, Pontyclun, Mid-Glamorgan CF7 8YT.
Telephone: 0443-222111 ext. 445 Fax: 0443-228799

ROYAL PARKS AGENCY

Function: Management and protection of London's nine Royal Parks, including St James's Park, The Green Park, Hyde Park, Regent's Park, Kensington Gardens, Greenwich Park, Primrose Hill, Richmond Park and Bushy Park.
Launched: April 1993.
Chief Executive: David Welch. Educated: the Royal Horticultural Society, Wisley. Previous posts include Director of Leisure and Recreation, City of Aberdeen, before being appointed Chief Executive as an external candidate in 1992.
Accountable to: National Heritage Department.
Address: The Old Police House, Hyde Park, London W2 2UH.
Telephone: 071-298 2000 Fax: 071-298 2005

SCOTTISH AGRICULTURAL SCIENCE AGENCY

Function: Provision of information and advice on agricultural crops, horticultural crops, and the environment.
Launched: April 1992.
Chief Executive: Dr Robert Hay. Born: 1946. Educated: Forres Academy, Moray; Aberdeen and East Anglia Universities. He held University posts in Malawi, Edinburgh, Lancaster, Norway, and Western Australia, before being appointed Chief Executive as an external candidate in 1990.
Accountable to: Scottish Office.
Address: East Craigs, Edinburgh EH12 8NJ.
Telephone: 031-556 8400 Fax: 031-244 8940

SCOTTISH FISHERIES PROTECTION AGENCY

Function: Responsible for enforcement of fisheries regulations to conserve stocks in 200,000 square miles of sea around Scotland.
Launched: April 1991.

Chief Executive: Andrew MacLeod. Born: 1950. Educated: Fettes College, Edinburgh; St John's College and Nuffield College, Oxford. He held posts in the National Economic Development Office, the Manpower Services Commission, and the Scottish Office, before becoming Chief Executive in 1991.
Accountable to: Scottish Office.
Address: Pentland House, 47 Robbs Loan, Edinburgh EH14 1TW.
Telephone: 031-244 6059 Fax: 031-244 6001

SCOTTISH OFFICE PENSION AGENCY

Function: Administration of pension schemes for the NHS and teaching service in Scotland.
Launched: April 1993.
Chief Executive: Norman MacLeod. Born: 1938. Educated: Oban High School. He has held various posts in the Department of Health and Social Security and the Scottish Office before becoming Chief Executive in 1992 as an internal candidate.
Accountable to: Scottish Office.
Address: St Margaret's House, 151 London Road, Edinburgh EH8 7TG.
Telephone: 031-244 3579 Fax: 031-244 3334

SCOTTISH PRISON SERVICE

Function: Custody of those committed by the courts, maintenance of prisoner order and discipline, and care and rehabilitation of inmates.
Launched: April 1993.
Chief Executive: Edward Frizzell. Born: 1946. Educated: Paisley Grammar School; Glasgow University. He held a series of posts at the Scottish Office, the UK Representation in Brussels, returning to the Scottish Office, before becoming Chief Executive in 1991 as an internal candidate.
Accountable to: Scottish Office.
Address: Calton House, 5 Redheughs Rigg, Edinburgh EH12 9HW.
Telephone: 031-556 8400 Fax: 031-244 8774

SCOTTISH RECORD OFFICE

Function: Selection, preservation and presentation to public of the national archives of Scotland.
Launched: April 1993.
Chief Executive: Patrick Cadell. Born:1941. Educated: Merchiston Castle School; Trinity College, Cambridge; Toulouse University. He held a variety of posts at the National Library of Scotland, before being appointed Chief Executive in 1991.
Accountable to: Scottish Office.
Address: HM General Register House, Edinburgh EH1 3YY.
Telephone: 031-556 6585 Fax: 031-556 6044

SECURITY FACILITIES EXECUTIVE

Function: Provision of security services to government departments and public-sector customers, including the government car service, dispatch collection and delivery service, and custody service.

Launched: October 1993.

Chief Executive: John King. Born: 1940. Educated: Newquay Grammar School; Regent Street Polytechnic. Previous posts include Business Administration and Personnel Director for PSAS Special Services, and Head of Transport and Security Services, Environment Department, before becoming Chief Executive as an internal appointment in 1993.

Accountable to: Environment Department.

Address: St Christopher House, Southwark Street, London SE1 0TE.

Telephone: 071-921 4813 Fax: 071-921 4012

SERVICE CHILDREN'S SCHOOL (NORTH WEST EUROPE)

Function: Provision of schooling for dependent children of Defence Ministry personnel living in North West Europe.

Launched: April 1991.

Chief Executive: Ian Mitchelson. Born: 1936. Educated: Morecambe Grammar School; Downing College, Cambridge. He held teaching posts in Devon and the West Midlands, education management posts in Worcestershire, North Riding and North Yorkshire, before becoming Chief Executive as an external candidate in 1991.

Accountable: Ministry of Defence.

Address: HQ BAOR BFPO 140.

Telephone: 010-492161-4723296 Fax: 010-492161-4723487

SOCIAL SECURITY AGENCY (NI)

Function: Administration of social security benefits, fraud prevention and collection of National Insurance contributions in Northern Ireland.

Launched: July 1991.

Chief Executive: Alec Wylie.

Accountable to: Northern Ireland Office.

Address: Castle Buildings, Stormont, Belfast BT4 3SJ.

Telephone: 0232-520520 Fax: 0232-523337

STUDENT AWARDS AGENCY FOR SCOTLAND

Function: To administer awards and grants and other related services for Scottish domiciled students in full-time higher education.

Launched: April 1994.

Chief Executive: Ken MacRae. Born: 1939. Previous posts include Head of the Scottish Office Education Department since 1987 before being appointed Chief Executive as an internal candidate in 1994.

Accountable to: Scottish Office.

Address: Gyleview House, 3 Redheughs Rigg, Edinburgh EH12 9HH.

Telephone: 031-244 5823 Fax: 031-244 5887

125

TEACHERS' PENSIONS AGENCY

Function: Administration of the Teachers' Superannuation Scheme for teachers in England and Wales.

Launched: April 1992.

Chief Executive: Denyse Metcalfe. Born: 1953. Educated: Convent of the Assumption, Manchester; Manchester University. Previous posts include Principal Finance and Administration Officer, Newcastle City Council, Assistant Director of Finance, Middlesbrough, and Deputy Finance Director, Gateshead, before becoming Chief Executive as an external candidate in 1991.

Accountable to: Education Department.

Address: Mowden Hall, Staindrop Road, Darlington, County Durham DL3 9EE.

Telephone: 0325-392929 Fax: 0325-92216

THE BUYING AGENCY

Function: Procurement of products and services, including catering equipment, engineering and building equipment, and residential, office and restaurant furniture for government departments, local government, NHS, universities, and other public bodies.

Launched: October 1991.

Chief Executive: Stephen Sage. Born: 1953. Educated: Bristol Grammar School; Peterhouse, Cambridge. He held posts in the Crown Agents, the Environment Department, and Controller of the Merseyside Task Force, before becoming Chief Executive as an internal candidate in 1993.

Accountable to: Environment Department.

Address: Royal Liver Building, Pier Head, Liverpool L3 1PE.

Telephone: 051-227 4262 Fax: 051-227 3315

TRAINING AND EMPLOYMENT AGENCY (NI)

Function: Provision of training and employment services to Northern Ireland labour force and private-sector companies.

Launched: April 1990.

Chief Executive: Julian Crozier. Born: 1935. Educated in Australia and Hong Kong; Campbell College, Belfast; Queen's College, Cambridge. He joined the Northern Ireland Office in 1965, and held posts in Agriculture, Health and Social Services, Manpower Services, Finance and Personnel, and Economic Development before becoming Chief Executive in 1990.

Accountable to: Northern Ireland Office.

Address: Clarendon House, 19-21 Adelaide Street, Belfast BT2 8NR.

Telephone: 0232-239944 Fax: 0232-234417

TRANSPORT RESEARCH LABORATORY

Function: Research and development in support of government policies on highway and road design, road safety, vehicle design and environmental protection.

Launched: April 1992 (to be privatised).

Chief Executive: John Wootton. Born: 1936. Educated: Queen Mary College; London

University; University of California, Berkeley. Previous posts include Chairman, Wootton Jeffreys Consultants, and Visiting Professor in Transport Studies, University College, London, before becoming Chief Executive as an external candidate in 1991.
Accountable to: Transport Department.
Address: Old Wokingham Road, Crowthorne, Berkshire RG11 6AU.
Telephone: 0344-770001 Fax: 0344-770761

UNITED KINGDOM PASSPORT AGENCY

Function: Issue passports to British nationals in the UK through regional passport offices in Belfast, Glasgow, Liverpool, London, Newport and Peterborough.
Launched: April 1991.
Chief Executive: John Hayzelden. Born: 1936. Educated: Merchant Taylors School, Northwood; St John's College, Oxford. He held posts in Shell and BP, the Home Office, Urwick Orr and Partners, the Central Computer Agency, and the Home Office, before becoming Chief Executive in 1988.
Accountable to: Home Office.
Address: Clive House, 70-78 Petty France, London SW1H 9HD.
Telephone: 071-271 3000 Fax: 071-271 8581

VALUATION AND LANDS AGENCY

Function: Provision of Valuation List for rating purposes, along with estate management and property information in Northern Ireland.
Launched: April 1993.
Chief Executive: David Bell. Born: 1938. Educated: Regent House School, Newtownards; Belfast College of Technology. He joined the Civil Service in 1963 where he held a variety of posts, including Divisional Estates Surveyor, Superintending Estates Surveyor, Chief Lands Officer, and Assistant and Deputy Commissioner, Lands Service, before becoming Chief Executive in 1993 as an internal candidate.
Accountable to: Northern Ireland Office.
Address: Queen's Court, 56-66 Upper Queen Street, Belfast BT4 6FD.
Telephone: 0232-439303 Fax: 0232-235897

VALUATION OFFICE

Function: Provision of land and buildings valuation, and specialist advice on minerals to government departments, local authorities and other public bodies.
Launched: September 1991.
Chief Executive: John Langford. Born: 1936. Educated: Soham Grammar School. Previous posts include District Valuer and Valuation Officer, Camden, Regional Superintending Valuer, North East, Assistant Chief Valuer Operations, and Deputy Chief Valuer, before becoming Chief Executive as an internal candidate in 1994.
Accountable to: Inland Revenue.
Address: New Court, Carey Street, London WC2A 2JE.
Telephone: 071-324 1012 Fax: 071-324 1073

VEHICLE CERTIFICATION AGENCY

Function: Test and certification of vehicle types to UK and international standards.
Launched: April 1990.
Chief Executive: Derek Harvey. Born: 1948. Educated: Royal Grammar School, Worcester; Swansea University. Previous posts include Superintending Engineer, Vehicle Inspectorate, Transport Department, before becoming Chief Executive in 1990.
Accountable to: Transport Department.
Address: 1 The Eastgate Office Centre, Eastgate Road Bristol BS5 6XX.
Telephone: 0272-515151 Fax: 0272-524103

VEHICLE INSPECTORATE

Function: To conduct annual tests on heavy goods vehicles, public service vehicles, supervision of MOT testing of motorcycles, cars and light goods vehicles, and enforcement of law on roadworthiness, vehicle weights, and drivers' hours.
Launched: August 1988.
Chief Executive: Ron Oliver. Born: 1945. Educated: Windsor Grammar School; Brunel University. He worked for Wilkinson Sword and British Leyland before joining the Transport Department in 1974, where he held posts in vehicle engineering and safety before becoming Chief Executive in 1988.
Accountable to: Transport Department.
Address: Berkeley House, Croydon Street, Bristol BS5 ODA.
Telephone: 0272-554300 Fax: 0272-543212

VETERINARY MEDICINES DIRECTORATE

Function: Enforcement of safety, quality and efficacy of animal medicines in the UK, including licensing and control of the manufacture and marketing of animal medicines, post-licensing surveillance, and monitoring suspected adverse reactions.
Launched: April 1990.
Chief Executive: Dr Mike Rutter. Born: 1941. Educated: Edinburgh University. Previous posts include Head of Microbiology and then Head of Laboratory, Institute for Research on Animal Diseases, Berkshire, and Director of Veterinary Medicines, MAFF, before being appointed Chief Executive in 1990 as an internal candidate.
Accountable to: Ministry of Agriculture.
Address: Woodham Lane, New Haw, Addlestone, Surrey KT15 3NB.
Telephone: 0932-336911 Fax: 0932-336618

WAR PENSIONS AGENCY

Function: To administer the payment of war disablement pensions, and provide welfare services to war disablement pensioners, war widows and dependants.
Launched: April 1994.
Chief Executive: Peter Mathison. Born: 1946. Educated: Quarry Bank High School, Liverpool. He worked in a wide variety of industries, including food, soft drinks, automotive, aerospace and defence weapons, and held senior management positions in Rover and Lucas Aerospace and Royal Ordnance before being appointed Chief Executive as an

external candidate in 1994.
Accountable to: Social Security Department.
Address: War Pensions Agency, Norcross, Blackpool FY5 3TA.
Telephone: 0253-858858 Fax: 0253-62391

WILTON PARK

Function: Organisation of conferences on international affairs for politicians, officials, diplomats, business executives and academics.
Launched: September 1991.
Chief Executive: Richard Langhorne. Born: 1940. Educated: St Edward's School, Oxford; St John's College, Cambridge. He held posts as History Tutor, Exeter University, Research Student, St John's College, Cambridge, Master of Rutherford College, Kent University, and Director of the Centre for International Studies, Cambridge university, before being appointed Chief Executive as an external candidate in 1993.
Accountable to: Foreign and Commonwealth Office.
Address: Wiston House, Steyning, Sussex BN44 3DZ.
Telephone: 0903-815020 Fax: 0903-815931

THE MEDICAL DEVICES AGENCY

Function: The Medical Devices Agency is responsible for ensuring the safety and ethicality of a range of products used in the health service, from heart valves and hospital beds to radio therapy machines, surgical instruments and syringes.
Launched: September 1994.
Chief Executive: Alan Kent. He was recruited by open competition from the medical devices manufacturing industry where he has worked in research and general management.
Accountable to: Health Department.
Address: 14 Russell Square, London, WC1 5EP.
Telephone: 071-972 2000

4
THE PERIPHERAL STATE: NON-DEPARTMENTAL PUBLIC BODIES

Non-departmental public bodies (NDPBs) are part of that vast archipelago of the government's non-elected executive, administrative and advisory machinery, popularly known as quangos. The acronym stands for quasi-autonomous non-governmental organisation, despite strenuous attempts by the *Daily Telegraph* to rename them 'quite unacceptable and nasty government off-shoots'. The term quango appears to have been imported from America in the 1960s, achieved great notoriety during the Callaghan years in the late 1970s, was then used to describe a bewildering range of new organisations created during the 1980s, and has been so overused by the 1990s as to be almost meaningless. The term now embraces everything from the Apple and Pear Research Council to NHS hospital trusts, and from the Natural History Museum to the Training and Enterprise Councils. Each of these bodies have widely different powers, responsibilities and relationships with central government. Some have government functions, others do not. But all attempts to refine the nomenclature of public bodies have been resisted by MPs, the media and the general public alike. For better or worse, the term quango, used generically to describe anything and everything that occupies the terrain between the public and the private sector, is here to stay.

By popular demand, therefore, non-departmental public bodies are a species of the genus quango. They are defined by the Cabinet Office as bodies which have a role in the processes of national government, but are not government departments or part of one, and which operate at arm's length from ministers. Both ministerial government departments, such as the Trade and Industry Department, and non-ministerial government departments, such as the Office of Electricity Regulation (Offer), have the power to create non-departmental public bodies. This definition excludes, however, other public-sector bodies, such as nationalised industries, public corporations, the Next Steps executive agencies, health authorities and hospital trusts, self-governing schools, police authorities, training and enterprise councils, local authorities, and universities and colleges – all of which have separate accountability, audit and review regimes, and, in the words of the Cabinet Office, are not properly regarded as 'adjuncts to government'.

According to the Whitehall manual, *Non-Departmental Public Bodies: A Guide for Departments*, there are three distinct categories of NDPB: executive bodies, advisory bodies, and tribunals and other bodies.

(a) Executive bodies, such as the Medical Research Council, the Commission for Racial Equality, the Housing Corporation, the Occupational Pensions Board, and the United Kingdom Atomic Energy Authority, exercise executive, administrative, regulatory or commercial functions on behalf of the government. Executive bodies are usually set up by statute, with powers conferred by legislation, are headed by boards appointed by government, and normally employ their own staff, occupy their own premises, and are responsible for their own budgets. There are some 358 executive bodies served by 4,066 appointees, which account for most of the £12 billion spent by the government on NDPBs every year.

(b) Advisory bodies, such as the Advisory Committee on Conscientious Objectors, the Spongiform Encephalopathy Advisory Committee, the Citizen's Charter Panel of Advisers, the Industrial Injuries Advisory Council, and the Royal Commissions, are set up to advise ministers and their departments on specific areas of expertise. There are 829 advisory bodies served by 10,022 appointees, most of which are made up of outside experts working part-time. Advisory bodies may meet weekly, monthly or at longer intervals, and normally do not have their own premises, staff or budgets.

(c) Tribunals and other bodies, such as the Central Arbitration Committee, the Social Security Appeal Tribunals, the Disability Appeal Tribunals and the Value Added Tax Tribunal, are all quasi-judicial bodies with jurisdiction in a specialised field of law. There are 68 such tribunals which are responsible for deciding the rights and obligations of individuals to each other and to the state, and are served by 22,265 appointees. In addition, there are 134 other bodies, including boards of visitors to penal establishments, which are responsible for monitoring the conditions of prisons and prisoners, and which are served by 1,804 appointees.

Although it is unrealistic to try and stamp out popular usage of the terms quango, quangoland and quangocrat, it is necessary to make a distinction between traditional and new quangos. The former are non-departmental public bodies set up to help provide the government with expertise and advice in a particular field, while the latter includes all those bodies designed to take away responsibilities hitherto exercised by local authorities, devolve power to the grass roots, and improve the efficiency of the public sector, such as Housing Action Trusts, Grant Maintained schools, and NHS hospital trusts. Much of the debate about quangos has been vitiated by a failure to make this distinction clear.

Under guidelines set out by the Cabinet Office in 1992, non-departmental public bodies are created for one or more of the following reasons:

(a) The need to distance particular administrative or regulatory activities from central government in order to highlight their independence, such as the Audit

Commission for England and Wales, the Monopolies and Mergers Commission, and the Data Protection Registrar.

(b) The need to co-opt external interests and expertise in executive or advisory functions, such as the Arts Council, the Research Councils, the Sports Council and the Trustee Museums.

(c) The need to discharge a clearly defined task through powers it would be inappropriate for central government to exercise directly, such as the Urban Development Corporations.

(d) The need to distance quasi-commercial activities from the direct control of central government, such as Scottish Enterprise, the Welsh Development Agency and the Urban Development Corporations.

New non-departmental public bodies are created only where they can be demonstrated to be 'the most appropriate and cost-effective solution' to meet government requirements. They are all accountable to Parliament through the minister of their sponsor department, and are subject to review every five years. In addition, since 1985, the Parliamentary Commissioner for Administration or Ombudsman has the power to investigate allegations of maladministration by the top 50 or so non-departmental public bodies. Finally, like the Next Steps executive agencies, NDPBs are covered by the principles outlined in the Citizen's Charter, and are subject to the market testing initiative of the government's public-sector reform programme.

QUANGO HUNTS AND QUANGO CULLS

Sir Philip Holland, the Conservative MP for Carlton, Nottinghamshire, is usually credited as the man who first drew attention to the dramatic growth in the number of public bodies or quangos. After conducting a three-month investigation in 1976 into the extent of government patronage, he discovered that a baffling variety of bodies had sprung up virtually unnoticed all over Whitehall, providing full or part-time work for an army of the great and the good, often at the taxpayers' expense. His timing could not have been more apposite. By demanding that Whitehall yield its secrets on how many union bosses had benefited from the growth of state patronage, Sir Philip's exposé of the expansion of this secondary bureaucracy was exploited by Margaret Thatcher to highlight what she branded as the bankrupt corporatism of the post-war era, and a ruthless cull was promised.

Following the Conservatives' 1979 general election victory, Sir Leo Pliatzky, a former Permanent Secretary at the Trade and Industry department, was appointed to carry out a review. His report on non-departmental public bodies (the first time the new phrase appeared), was published in 1980, and heralded the demise of a swathe of quangos, including the Hadrian's Wall Advisory Committee, the Advisory Committee on Bird Sanctuaries in Royal Parks, the Furniture Development Council, the Location of Offices Bureau, the Metrication Board, the Price Commission and a host of other exotic Whitehall creatures. Of the 2,117 public bodies examined by the Pliatzky review, a total of 246 were terminated, further culls were promised, stringent rules were established for the creation of new public bodies, and most of the remaining 1,871 organisations were made subject to scrutiny by the National Audit Office, the national public expenditure watchdog.

But Sir Philip would not let the issue rest there. In February 1981 he sponsored an unsuccessful private member's bill designed to open up quangos to parliamentary scrutiny, and compel Whitehall to publish an annual register of non-departmental public bodies. Launching another campaign for tougher government action against quangos the same year, he began to question the utility of individual public bodies, and cast a spotlight on their expenditure – such as the Equal Opportunities Commission's decision to spend £5,681 on the restoration of Emily Pankhurst's house in Chorlton-on-Meadlock, Manchester. By the time he published his pamphlet, *The Governance of Quangos*, which accused Mrs Thatcher of backtracking on her election promise to cut them back, the issue of quango hunts and quango culls had become part of the cut and thrust of day-to-day politics.

For a government committed to trim back the non-elected state, the establishment of new quangos was particularly embarrassing. The creation of the Audit Commission in November 1983, for example, was justified by ministers as an attempt to control the extravagant spending of local authorities. But the revelation that the new local government spending watchdog was to pay its staff twice the salaries paid to town hall officials caused an outcry, especially as the commission's money was to come from fees levied on local councils, so that the ratepayers would ultimately have to pick up the bill. Similarly, the Government took the credit for winding down the English New Town Development Corporations and the Manpower Services Commission, only to find itself accused of creating a new tier of quangos in the form of the Urban Development Corporations and the Training and Enterprise Councils (Cabinet Office insists that the latter are not quangos but private-sector companies, limited by guarantee, working on contract to the Employment Department).

In addition, the new organisations created to regulate the newly privatised industries, including Oftel, Ofwat, Offer and Ofgas, whose role was to represent consumer interests in the telecommunications, water, electricity and gas industries, were also dubbed as quangos. These bodies are officially classified as non-ministerial government departments (NMGDs), a term rarely heard outside the cloistered corridors of Whitehall, and never likely to catch on. Housing Action Trusts, on the other hand, which were created to help renovate the nation's run-down public housing estates, are non-departmental public bodies, managed by boards appointed by the Environment Secretary. Similarly, the abolition of the Greater London Council in 1986, led to the creation of new non-elected bodies such as the London Residuary Body and the London Docklands Development Corporation, and prompted further accusations that far from reducing the number of non-elected public bodies, the Conservative party had actually presided over a massive expansion of quangos.

Many of these bodies, such as the Health Department's Committee on the Ethics of Gene Therapy, the Environment Department's Radioactive Waste Management Advisory Committee, and Agriculture Ministry's Advisory Committee on

Pesticides, carry out valuable work. Others are singled out by the media for a spot of harmless public ribbing simply because of their names, such as the Agriculture Ministry's Banana Trade Advisory Committee (now abolished), and the Foreign Office's Government Hospitality Fund Advisory Committee for the Purchase of Wine. Some, like the Health Department's Advisory Panel on the Importation of Sexually Explicit Films for Health Purposes, are pilloried because they do not appear to do anything. The role of this august body was to examine the pornography which doctors, psychotherapists and psychiatrists wanted to import to help treat psychosexual conditions. It was finally abolished in February 1994 after it was discovered that it had not received a single request to vet such material in almost a decade.

Most of this criticism was, however, directed at the proliferation of new quangos rather than the persistence of traditional quangos. Every year, the Cabinet Office proclaims that the number of non-departmental public bodies (Whitehall officials cannot bring themselves to refer to NDPBs as quangos) has been cut back further, only to be met with a crop of newspaper articles proclaiming that quangos are on the march again. According to official figures, the number of non-departmental public bodies has fallen from 2,167 in 1979 to 1,389 in 1993. Such figures are never a precise guide because by the time they are published new public bodies have been created and others abolished. Critics insist, however, that these statistics are misleading because they fail to take into account the huge changes that have taken place since 1979 in the way the public sector is organised.

Such criticisms were inspired largely by John Stewart, professor of public policy at Birmingham University, in his paper, *Accountability to the Public*, published in December 1992 by the European Policy Forum, the market studies think-tank. Professor Stewart warned that the growth of quangos had resulted in the gradual replacement of elected officials with a new elite of appointed officials who were now responsible for overseeing the provision of a wide range of public services, including health, education and other social services. Moreover, this 'new magistracy' had created a 'crisis of accountability' because it could not be called to account for its actions by local electors, and because the ministers to whom the new bodies were theoretically accountable could not be realistically expected to shoulder the additional burden of responsibility.

Indeed, the *Guardian* warned in November 1993 that if the transformation of the British state continues on its present path, there would be 7,700 quangos responsible for £54 billion worth of public money by 1996. The article noted that 'the bulk of the quango creation results from the onslaught upon local government and the de facto colonisation by quango of Scotland, Wales and Northern Ireland'. But that figure included traditional quangos, new quangos, Next Step executive agencies and a good deal else. Nevertheless, it was clear that by the early 1990s, the criticisms first set in motion by Sir Philip Holland against non-departmental public bodies in the 1970s had rebounded on the wider organisational changes implemented in the public sector by the Conservatives during the 1980s.

PATRONAGE AND CORRUPTION

There is nothing novel about accusations that the large number of non-elected public bodies provides the government of the day with substantial powers of patronage which it abuses to promote its friends and supporters. The situation in which a Labour Prime Minister and Cabinet were able to appoint thousands of people to hundreds of bodies whose salaries and allowances cost the taxpayer millions of pounds a year was described by Sir Philip in 1976 as 'the growth industry of political appointments'. Similar reservations about this so-called 'Old Boy Network' were also expressed by Labour MPs. Gwilyn Roberts, for example, said in 1977 that the government's power of patronage was 'not exactly a nepotistic system but one which is outside the system of democratic government and extremely disturbing'. But such accusations have grown in ferocity as a result of the protracted period of one-party rule, and the vast increase in patronage that has occurred since 1979, which was branded by John Smith, the former Labour leader, as the emergence of the 'quango state'.

When Harold Wilson set up the Cabinet Office's Public Appointments Unit in 1975, his objective was to systematise the list of prospective candidates for non-elected public office, cast the net wider to draw in new and young talent, and take the sting out of criticisms that the bulk of appointees were middle-class worthies from the Home Counties who were 'nice safe people who kept their noses clean'. But the initiative did little to mitigate accusations that the government was ruthlessly exploiting its powers of patronage to fill quango posts with union bosses and other Labour party supporters, thanks largely to the work of Sir Philip. Almost a decade later, however, the Conservative party found itself facing similar accusations. In 1989, for instance, the *Guardian* said: 'Ten years ago they were called quangos. Now Mrs Thatcher calls them non-departmental public bodies, appoints her political friends to them, and thinks creating them can be cost effective.'

The issue hit the headlines once again in February 1994, following a series of damning revelations about financial mismanagement and misappropriation of public funds in a number of non-departmental public bodies under the jurisdiction of the Welsh Office. Win Griffiths, the Labour MP for Brighead, insisted that Tory appointees to quangos 'outnumber by at least five to one those appointed from other parties'. Rhodri Morgan, the Labour MP for Cardiff West, added that: 'there were now more quangos in Cardiff than there were gondolas in Venice'. John Redwood, the Welsh Secretary, replied angrily that: 'There are fair shares for the other parties but above all we appoint people who are right for the job, regardless of political affiliation.' In recognition of the growing sensitivity over appointments to non-elected public bodies, Mr Redwood did, however, undertake to talk 'privately' to Ron Davies, Labour's Welsh spokesman, about the scope for increasing co-operation with the Labour party over future appointments to non-elected public office, although this has done little to appease the growing number of critics of the growth of the quango state.

Indeed, by May 1994, it was being claimed that quangos now exercise more power and influence than the entire structure of local government in Britain. A report by six constitutional experts, published by the Charter 88 Trust, lumped together every conceivable public body and claimed that the number of quangos had grown to in excess of 5,000 – three times the official figure – giving them control of one-third of all public spending, and putting an estimated 73,000 jobs into the hands of ministers. The report said that there was now one quango for every 10,000 people in Britain; they were responsible for spending in excess of £46 billion of taxpayers' money, and the people who staff them outnumbered locally elected officials by nearly three to one. Moreover, it warned that the growth of quangos since the Conservatives came to power in 1979 had been so 'phenomenal' that 'the essential democratic underpinnings of scrutiny, accountability, and openness' were all under threat. In addition, it attacked William Waldegrave's attempt to replace traditional notions of accountability to the electorate with accountability to the market. The citizen as consumer is a poor substitute for the citizen as elector 'who is entitled to choose who runs his or her services, to participate and be consulted in the way they are run, and to know what decisions are being taken in his or her name', the report added.

Alongside claims that quangos are stuffed with Tory party placemen run allegations that Tories who contribute to Conservative party funds are even more likely to be appointed to non-elected public office. George Howarth, the Labour MP for Knowsley North, reported in September 1993 that one in three appointments is an employee or a director of companies that make donations to Tory party coffers. His report described 'a sleazy picture of a government which whenever possible, to borrow Mrs Thatcher's phrase, appoints "one of us" – which in John Major's era seems to be tested against financial donations to the Tory Party'. This allegation was robustly denied by John Major during the Commons all-day debate on quangos in February 1994. The Prime Minister cited a number of Labour politicians who have benefited from such appointments, including Bob Cryer, the Labour MP for Bradford South, who sits on the board of the British Film Institute.

Criticisms have also been levelled at the salaries and expenses paid to such office holders. The £92,000 received by Lord Wyatt as Chairman of the Tote, and the £98,000 paid to Sir David Rees, the Chairman of the Medical Research Council, are among the highest salaries paid to the heads of executive non-departmental public bodies in the land. But many such salaries, including the £45,000 paid to Lord Belstead, the Chairman of the Parole Board, and the £35,150 paid to Lord Cranbrook, the Chairman of English Nature, are considerably more modest by private-sector standards. Appointees to advisory non-departmental public bodies, such as James Blyth, the Chairman of Boots, who receives £13,125 as Chairman of the Citizen's Charter Advisory Panel, tend to be much lower, although membership of a handful of such bodies can bring in handsome rewards. None the less, there are thousands of so-called quangocrats who receive very modest remuneration, and many more who receive no salary at all and are entitled to claim only their expenses.

Anyone with expertise in a particular field can be appointed to a quango, either by being nominated by someone else or by nominating themselves. Each government department has its own procedures for making these appointments, although the Cabinet Office Public Appointments Unit maintains its own data-base of some 20,000 potential candidates which is made available to ministers when required. Candidates are asked to complete a public appointments nomination form, providing details of their previous experience, areas of interest, ability to work full-time or part-time, and their ethnic origin. No details of political affiliation are requested. Ostensibly, the appointments system appears to be based on merit, and free of political interference. Critics have long insisted, however, that appearances are deceptive.

Such criticism appeared to be vindicated in March 1993 when Baroness Denton of Wakefield, the junior Trade and Industry Minister with a say in an estimated 800 public appointments, brazenly said: 'I can't remember knowingly appointing a Labour supporter' to non-elected public office. Baroness Denton's outburst lent credence to allegations that the formal system in which prospective candidates were put forward by the Public Appointments Unit was little more than a facade behind which political back-channels were in operation. At the time, the *Independent* quoted an anonymous politician who claimed: 'The Cabinet Office suggests names and a fig-leaf of impartiality is maintained. But when they get to a government department the minister will veto some names and accept others. He either knows the candidates or gets his political researcher to run the names past Central Office.'

The objective of this informal system for staffing quangos, Sir Philip said in an interview in the *Daily Telegraph* in 1992, was naked political influence. 'What is crucial is the power of patronage they give a minister. Quangos pretend to be independent, but the minister selects people who are going to say what he wants them to say', he added. But while claims that all non-elected appointments are made in this way would be quite ludicrous, it is clear that there is enough evidence of corruption at the margins to tarnish the way the public appointments system works as a whole.

Few critics argue that Labour has not done the same kind of thing in the past or would not do so again in the future. But there is growing concern that the growth in the number of public appointments, due largely to the creation of the new quangos, has conferred immense powers of patronage on the Government without any democratic checks and balances. Indeed, in July 1993, *The Times* suggested that the time had now come for Britain to adopt a system similar to the American 'advise and consent procedure' in which key public appointments are vetted by Congressional committee. Such a system would always entail the risk that politicians on the select committees, who would be best suited for carrying out this role, would be also tempted to turn every public appointment into a partisan issue. Nevertheless, the feeling that Parliament should have some say in the appointment of people to key public bodies and other non-elected big-spending quangos is becoming more and more widespread.

The same point was picked up by the Public Accounts Committee report, 'The Proper Conduct of Public Business', published in January 1994. Robert Sheldon, the committee chairman, called for the prevailing 'culture of patronage' surrounding non-elected public office to be replaced with one based on greater consultation. The report highlighted 26 cases of declining levels of public stewardship by both non-departmental public bodies, such as the Welsh Development Agency's waste of public money on dubious redundancy and employee car schemes, along with shortcomings of some of the new quangos, such as the West Midlands Regional Health Authority's waste of £10 million which should have been spent on patient care. But when pressed on this question, a Cabinet Office official told *The Times* that: 'There has never been cross-party consultation for these appointments'. Giving evidence to the Treasury and Civil Service select committee in February 1994, Sir John Bourn, the head of the National Audit Office, the government spending watchdog, said that private-sector managers brought in to run public-sector services were often surprised to discover that they were subject to scrutiny when handling public money. Consequently, what better way could there be for rectifying this lack of awareness than by making appointments to non-elected public office, at least those which exercise executive powers or command large budgets, subject to a new 'advise and consent procedure' by the appropriate select committee?

The government does not keep a national register of non-departmental public bodies enabling the public to identify who they are, what they do, who they are run by, and how they can be contacted, although the Cabinet Office is presently considering compiling such a list. At the time of writing, few Whitehall departments have all of these details readily to hand. Some of this information is available in the Cabinet Office's annual publications, *Public Bodies* and the *Civil Service Year Book*. But neither is exhaustive.

NON-DEPARTMENTAL PUBLIC BODIES

AGRICULTURE FISHERIES AND FOOD EXECUTIVE BODIES

AGRICULTURAL TRAINING BOARD

Function: To provide training for those engaged in commercial agriculture and horticulture, and help farmers diversify their activities.
Chairman: Andy Stewart
Address: National Agricultural Centre
Kenilworth
Warwickshire CV8 2UG
Telephone: 0203-696996

AGRICULTURE WAGES BOARD FOR ENGLAND AND WALES
Function: To fix minimum wage rates and holiday entitlement for workers employed in agriculture.
Chairman: Professor J S Marsh
Address: Room 320D
Nobel House
17 Smith Square
London SW1 3RJ
Telephone: 071-238 6540

AGRICULTURE WAGES COMMITTEES FOR ENGLAND
Function: The 16 AWCs authorise premium pay arrangements between employers and workers, issue craft certificates and revalue farm workers' houses.
Address: East Malling Research Station
Maidstone
Kent ME19 6DZ
Telephone: 0732-844828

CUMBRIA AWC
Chairman: M G Barnes
Address: Eskdale House
Shap Road, Kendal
Cumbria LA9 6NQ
Telephone: 0539-721741

LANCASHIRE, GREATER
MANCHESTER AND
MERSEYSIDE AWC
Chairman: H M Booth JP
Address: As above

CLEVELAND DURHAM,
NORTHUMBERLAND AND TYNE
AND WEAR AWC
Chairman: Sir J L Pumphery
Address: Hadrian House
21 Market Place, Hexham
Northumberland NE46 3NT
Telephone: 0434-604213

SOUTH AND WEST YORKSHIRE
AWC
Chairman: Dr W Belfield
Address: Government Buildings
Crosby Road, Northallerton
North Yorkshire
Telephone: 0609-773751

NORTH YORKSHIRE AWC
Chairman: T Mills
Address: As above

HUMBERSIDE AWC
Chairman: I Patter
Address: As above

CHESHIRE AND
STAFFORDSHIRE AWC
Chairman: C W Blagg
Address: Berkeley Towers, Crewe
Cheshire CW2 6PT
Telephone: 0270-69211

SHROPSHIRE AWC
Chairman: R A H Lloyd
Address: As above

HEREFORD AND WORCESTER,
GLOUCESTERSHIRE,
WARWICKSHIRE AND WEST
MIDLANDS AWC
Chairman: A Brown
Address: Block C
Government Buildings
Whittington Road
Worcester WR5 2LQ
Telephone: 0905-763355

DERBYSHIRE,
LEICESTERSHIRE,
LINCOLNSHIRE,
NORTHAMPTONSHIRE AND
NOTTINGHAMSHIRE AWC
Chairman: A L Morgan
Address: Block 7
Government Buildings
Chalfont Drive
Nottingham NG8 3SN
Telephone: 0602-291191

NORFOLK AND SUFFOLK AWC
Chairman: K Buckley
Address: Block B
Government Buildings
Brooklands Avenue
Cambridge CB2 2DR
Telephone: 0223-462727

BEDFORDSHIRE,
CAMBRIDGESHIRE, ESSEX AND
HERTFORDSHIRE AWC
Chairman: Cannon F Scuffham
Address: As above

KENT, SURREY, EAST SUSSEX
AND WEST SUSSEX AWC
Chairman: B J Youngman
Address: Block A
Government Buildings

Coley Park
Reading RG1 6DT
Telephone: 0734-581222

BERKSHIRE,
BUCKINGHAMSHIRE,
HAMPSHIRE, ISLE OF WIGHT
AND OXFORDSHIRE AWC
Chairman: JG Gillies
Address: As above

AVON, DORSET, SOMERSET AND
WILTSHIRE AWC
Chairman: A Pendlebury
Address: Burghill Road
Westbury-on-Trym
Bristol BS10 6NJ
Telephone: 0272-591000

DEVON, CORNWALL AND ISLES
OF SCILLY AWC
Chairman: D M Ansari
Address: Government Buildings
Alphington Road
Exeter EX2 8NQ
Telephone: 0392-77951

APPLE AND PEAR RESEARCH COUNCIL
Function: To commission research and development in the apple and pear sector.
Chairman: Professor Sir Colin Spedding
Address: The Stable Block, Bradbourne House
East Malling Research Station
Maidstone, Kent ME19 6DZ
Telephone: 0732-844828

FOOD FROM BRITAIN
Function: To provide a consultancy service to British food exporters seeking to break into and expand foreign markets.
Chairman: Geoffrey John
Address: Market Towers, New Covent Garden Market
1 Nine Elms Lane, London SW8 5NQ
Telephone: 071-720 2144

HOME GROWN CEREALS AUTHORITY

Function: To improve the production and marketing of home grown cereals, support exports, and act as an agent of the Intervention Board.
Chairman: GB Nelson
Address: Hamlyn House
Highgate Hill
London N19 5PR
Telephone: 071-263 3391

HORTICULTURAL DEVELOPMENT COUNCIL

Function: To commission research and development in horticulture on behalf of the industry.
Chairman: Margaret Charrington
Address: 18 Lavant Street
Petersfield
Hampshire GU32 3EW
Telephone: 0730-263736

HORTICULTURAL RESEARCH INTERNATIONAL

Function: To conduct research and development to advance plant and microbial science of relevance to horticulture.
Chairman: GT Pryce
Address: RTI
Wellesbourne
Warwick CV35 9EF
Telephone: 0789-470552

MEAT AND LIVESTOCK COMMISSION

Function: To improve the efficiency of the livestock, meat, and meat product industries.
Chairman: Donald Curry (Acting)
Address: PO Box 44
Winterhill House
Snowdon Drive
Milton Keynes MK6 1AX
Telephone: 0908-677577

ROYAL BOTANIC GARDENS KEW

Function: Maintain Kew Gardens as a centre for the study and conservation of living plants, for research into taxonomy and the properties of plants, and for public instruction and recreation.
Chairman: Robin Herbert
Address: Royal Botanic Gardens, Kew
Richmond, Surrey TW9 3AE
Telephone: 081-332 5414

REGIONAL FLOOD DEFENCE COMMITTEES

Function: The regional flood defence committees (RFDCs) were created under the provisions of the 1989 Water Act to arrange, under the auspices of the National Rivers Authority, for all flood defence precautions, including land drainage, defences against sea water, irrigation and flood warnings.

ANGLIAN REGION RFDC
Address: Regional Headquarters
Kingfisher House
Goldhay Way
Orton Goldhay
Peterborough PE2 0ZR
Telephone: 0733-371811

BRISTOL HEAD OFFICE RFDC
Address: Rivers House
Waterside Drive
Aztec West
Almondsbury
Bristol BS12 4UD
Telephone: 0454-624400

LONDON HEAD OFFICE RFDC
Address: Eastbury House
30-34 Albert Embankment
London SE1 7TL
Telephone: 071-820 0101

NORTH WEST REGION RFDC
Address: Richard Fairclough House
Knutsford Road
Warrington WA4 1HG
Telephone: 0925-53999

**NORTHUMBRIA AND
YORKSHIRE REGION RFDC**
Address: Regional Headquarters
Rivers House
21 Park Square South
Leeds LS1 2QG
Telephone: 0532-440191

SEVERN TRENT REGION RFDC
Address: Regional Headquarters
Sapphire East
550 Streetsbrook Road
Solihull
West Midlands
Telephone: 021-711 2324

SOUTHERN REGION RFDC
Address: Regional Headquarters
Guildbourne House
Chatsworth Road
Sussex BN11 1LD
Telephone: 0903-820692

SOUTH WESTERN REGION RFDC
Address: Regional Headquarters
Manley House, Kestral Way
Exeter EX2 7LQ
Telephone: 0392-444000

THAMES REGION RFDC
Address: Regional Headquarters
Kings Meadow House
Kings Meadow Road
Reading RG1 8DQ
Telephone: 0734-535000

WELSH REGION RFDC
Address: Regional Headquarters
Rivers House-Plas-yr-Afon
St Mellons Business Park
St Mellons
Cardiff CF3 0LT
Telephone: 0222-770088

SEA FISH INDUSTRY AUTHORITY

Function: To undertake research and development, advise, provide training, and promote the marketing and consumption of fish.

Chairman: vacant

Address: SFIA

18 Logie Mill

Logie Green Road

Edinburgh EH2 4HG

Telephone: 031-558 3331

WINE STANDARDS BOARD OF THE VINTNERS' COMPANY

Function: Responsible for enforcing European Community regulations governing the production, transport and labelling of wine.

Chairman: Peter Purton

Address: The Wine Standards Board

Five King's House

1 Queen Street Place

London EC4R 1QS

Telephone: 071-236 9512

AGRICULTURE FISHERIES AND FOOD ADVISORY BODIES

Advisory Committee on Novel Foods and Processes

Advisory Committee on Pesticides

Agricultural Dwelling House Advisory Committees

Committee on Agricultural Evaluation

Consultative Panel on Badgers and Tuberculosis

Consumers' Committee for England and Wales

Consumers' Committee for Great Britain

Consumer Panel

Farm Animal Welfare Council

Food Advisory Committee

Hill Farming Advisory Committee

National Food Survey Committee

Priorities Board for Research and Development in Agriculture and Food

Regional Panels

Salmon Advisory Committee

Spongiform Encephalopathy Advisory Committee

Sugar Beet Research and Education Committee

Veterinary Products Committee

Telephone: 071-917 3704

AGRICULTURE FISHERIES AND FOOD TRIBUNALS

Agricultural Land Tribunal (England)
Dairy Produce Quota Tribunal
Milk and Dairies Tribunal
Plant Varieties and Seeds Tribunal
Telephone: 071-917 3704

CABINET OFFICE AND OFFICE OF PUBLIC SERVICE AND SCIENCE
EXECUTIVE BODIES

BIOTECHNOLOGY AND BIOLOGICAL SCIENCES RESEARCH COUNCIL
Function: To promote and support basic, strategic and applied research and related post-graduate training in biological systems.
Chairman: Sir Alistair Grant
Address: Polaris House, North Star Avenue
Swindon SN2 1ET
Telephone: 0793-413200

ENGINEERING AND PHYSICAL SCIENCES RESEARCH COUNCIL
Function: To promote and support basic, strategic and applied research and related post-graduate training in engineering and the physical sciences.
Chairman: Dr Alan Rudge
Address: Polaris House, North Star Avenue
Swindon SN2 1ET
Telephone: 0793-444000

ECONOMIC AND SOCIAL RESEARCH COUNCIL
Function: To promote and support basic, strategic and applied social science research and related postgraduate training.
Chairman: Dr Bruce Smith
Address: Polaris House, North Star Avenue
Swindon SN2 1ET
Telephone: 0793-413062

MEDICAL RESEARCH COUNCIL
Function: To promote and support basic, strategic and applied research and related post-graduate training in all brances of biomedical science.
Chairman: Sir David Plastow
Address: MRC
20 Park Crescent, London W1N 4AL
Telephone: 071-637 6037

NATURAL ENVIRONMENTAL RESEARCH COUNCIL
Function: To support basic, strategic and applied research, long-term environmental monitoring and related postgraduate training in terrestrial and freshwater biology and earth, atmospheric, ocean and polar sciences, and earth observation.
Chairman: Robert Malpas
Address: Polaris House
North Star Avenue
Swindon SN2 1ET
Telephone: 0793-411500

PARTICLE PHYSICS AND ASTRONOMY RESEARCH COUNCIL
Function: To promote and support basic research and related postgraduate training in astronomy, planetary science and particle physics.
Chairman: Dr Peter Williams
Address: Polaris House
North Star Avenue
Swindon SN2 1ET
Telephone: 0793-444200

CABINET OFFICE AND OFFICE OF PUBLIC SERVICE AND SCIENCE ADVISORY BODIES

Advisory Committee on Business Appointments
Advisory Panel on Equal Opportunities
Civil Service Appeal Board
Security Commission
Advisory Committee on Human Genome Research
Council for Science and Technology
Citizen's Charter Panel of Advisers
LINK (industry and engineering) Steering Group
Political Honours Scrutiny Committee
Telephone: 071-270 5986

CENTRAL OFFICE OF INFORMATION ADVISORY BODIES

ADVISORY COMMITTEE ON ADVERTISING
Function: To provide advice on suitable advertising agencies to undertake government information and publicity campaigns.
Chairman: Sir Brian Nicholson
Telephone: 071-261 8247

DEFENCE MINISTRY
EXECUTIVE BODIES

FLEET AIR ARM MUSEUM
Function: To preserve aircraft documents and general exhibits of Royal Navy Air Service and the Fleet Air Arm.
Director: Captain WJ Fundell RN
Address: Fleet Air Arm Museum
RNAS Yeovilton, Yeovil
Somerset BA22 8HT
Telephone: 0935-840565

NATIONAL ARMY MUSEUM
Function: To explain the social history of the British Army from 1485
Director: Ian Robertson
Address: The National Army Museum
Royal Hospital Road, Chelsea
London SW3 4HT
Telephone: 071-730 0717

OIL AND PIPELINES AGENCY
Function: Management of the network of petroleum pipelines and storage facilities held by the Crown on behalf of the Defence Secretary.
Director: Geoff Richards
Address: Oil and Pipelines Agency
35-38 Portman Square
London W1H OEU
Telephone: 071-935 2585

ROYAL AIR FORCE MUSEUM
Function: To collect, preserve and exhibit Royal Air Force equipment and records.
Director: Dr Michael Fopp
Address: Royal Air Force Museum, Hendon
London NWG 5LL
Telephone: 081-205 2266

ROYAL MARINES MUSEUM
Function: To preserve and exhibit equipment and records of the Royal Marines.
Director: Colonel Keith Wilkins
Address: Royal Marines Museum
Royal Marines Eastney, Southsea
Hampshire PO4 9PX
Telephone: 0705-819385

ROYAL NAVAL MUSEUM
Function: To preserve and exhibit equipment and records of the Royal Navy.
Director: H Murray
Address: Royal Naval Museum
Portsmouth PO1 3LR
Telephone: 0705-733060

ROYAL NAVY SUBMARINE MUSEUM
Function: Repository of the heritage of the submarine service.
Director: Commander Richard Compton Hall
Address: Royal Navy Submarine Museum
Haslar Jetty Road
Gosport
Hampshire PO12 2AS
Telephone: 0705-510354

SERVICES SOUND AND VISION CORPORATION
Function: Provision of audio-visual equipment and corporate training videos for the Armed Services.
Director: Air Vice Marshall David Crwys Williams
Address: Services Sound and Vision Corporation
Chalfont Grove
Gerrards Cross
Buckinghamshire SL9 8TH
Telephone: 049-4871769

DEFENCE MINISTRY
ADVISORY BODIES

Advisory Committee on Conscientious Objectors
Advisory Council for the Royal Navy Engineering College
Anglo-Scottish-Welsh-American Community Relations Committees
Dartmoor Steering Group and Working Party
Defence Scientific Advisory Council and Committees
Independent Board of Visitors for Military Corrective Training Centre
Meteorological Committees
Meteorological Research Sub-Committee
National Employers' Liaison Committee
Nuclear Weapons Safety Committee
Review Board for Government Contracts
Royal College of Defence Studies Advisory Board
Royal Military College of Science Advisory Council
United Kingdom Polar Medal Assessment Committee
Telephone: 071-218 4014

EDUCATION DEPARTMENT
EXECUTIVE BODIES

CENTRAL BUREAU FOR EDUCATIONAL VISITS AND EXCHANGES

Function: Promotion of international educational visits and exchanges at all educational levels.
Director: Tony Male
Address: Seymour Mews House
Seymour Mews
London W1H 9PE
Telephone: 071-486 5101

CENTRE FOR INFORMATION AND LANGUAGE TEACHING AND RESEARCH

Function: Promotion of greater national capability in foreign languages through conferences, training programmes and publications.
Director: Dr L King
Address: 20 Bedfordbury
London WC2N 4LB
Telephone: 071-379 5101

EDUCATION ASSETS BOARD

Function: Responsible for the transfer of property, rights and liabilities from local authorities to higher education institutions and grant maintained schools.
Director: Roger Suddards
Address: Dudley House
Albion Street
Leeds LS2 8PN
Telephone: 0532-461221

FURTHER EDUCATION FUNDING COUNCIL

Function: Responsible for ensuring there is sufficient provision of full-time education for 16 to 18-year-olds, and distributing funds between further education colleges in England.
Chief Executive: Sir William Stubbs
Address: Cheylesmore House
Quinton Road
Coventry CV1 3WT
Telephone: 0203-863000

FURTHER EDUCATION UNIT

Function: A limited company with charitable status responsible for the promotion and development of further education.
Director: Allan Ainsworth
Address: Citadel Place
Tinworth Street
London SE11 5EH
Telephone: 071-962 1266

HIGHER EDUCATION FUNDING COUNCIL FOR ENGLAND

Function: Responsible for distributing state funds for the provision of education and of research by the higher educational institutions of England.
Chief Executive (until September 1995): Professor Graeme Davies
Address: Northavon House
Coldharbour Lane
Bristol BS16 1QD
Telephone: 0272-317317

NATIONAL COUNCIL FOR EDUCATIONAL TECHNOLOGY

Function: Promotion of effective application of technologies to improve the process of learning and its management.
Chief Executive: Margaret Bell
Address: Milburn Hill Road
Science Park
Coventry CV4 7JJ
Telephone: 0203-416994

SCHOOL CURRICULUM AND ASSESSMENT AUTHORITY

Function: Provision of advice to the Secretary of State on the curriculum and examinations for maintained schools in England.
Chief Executive: Chris Woodhead
Address: Newcombe House
Notting Hill Gate
London W11 3JB
Telephone: 071-229 1234

NATIONAL YOUTH AGENCY

Function: Responsible for the training, development and accreditation of youth and community worker staff development.
Director: Janet Paraskeva
Address 17-23 Albion Street
Leicester LE1 6GD
Telephone: 0533-471043

149

TEACHING AS A CAREER UNIT

Function: Promotion of teaching and teacher training to potential recruits.
Director: Jack Dodds
Address: 35 Great Smith Street
London SW1P 3BJ
Telephone: 071-227 2867

COUNCIL FOR THE ACCREDITATION OF TEACHER EDUCATION

Function: Provision of advise on the nature, organisation and length of courses and examinations for Specialist Teacher Assistants.
Director: Professor Malcolm Frazer
Address: Elizabeth House
York Road
London SE1 7PH
Telephone: 071-934 0946

FUNDING AGENCY FOR SCHOOLS

Function: Calculation and payment of grants to grant maintained schools.
Chief Executive: Michael Collier
Address: Albion Wharf
25 Skeldergate
York YO1
Telephone: 0904-661661

OFFICE OF ELECTRICITY REGULATION (OFFER)

Function: Offer was established under the 1989 Electricity Act to regulate the electricity industry, and promote competition in electricity generation and supply. Offer's Director General is assisted by the 14 regional electricity consumers' committees who represent consumers' interests, and whose chairmen make up the National Consumers' Consultative Committee (NCCC).
Director: General of Electricity Supply: Geoffrey Horton
Address: Hagley House
Hagley Road, Edgbaston
Birmingham B16 8QG
Telephone: 021-456 2100

OFFICE OF ELECTRICITY REGULATION (OFFER)
REGIONAL COMMITTEES

**EASTERN ELECTRICITY
CONSUMERS' COMMITTEE**
Chairman: R Grierson
Address: 4th Floor
Waveney House
Handford Road
Ipswich, Suffolk IP1 2BJ
Telephone: 0473-216101

**EAST MIDLANDS ELECTRICITY
CONSUMERS' COMMITTEE**
Chairman: Professor N C L Weedon
Address: Suite 3c
Langford House
40 Friar Lane
Nottingham NG1 6DQ
Telephone: 0602-508738

**LONDON ELECTRICITY
CONSUMERS' COMMITTEE**
Chairman: Y Constance
Address: 2nd Floor
11 Belgrave Road
London SW1V 1RB
Telephone: 071-233 6366

**MERSEYSIDE AND NORTH
WALES ELECTRICITY
CONSUMERS' COMMITTEE**
Chairman: C S Myers
Address: 4th Floor
Hamilton House, Hamilton Place
Chester CH1 2BH
Telephone: 0244-320849

**MIDLANDS ELECTRICITY
CONSUMERS' COMMITTEE**
Chairman: L Olphin
Address: 11th Floor
Hagley House
83-85 Hagley Road
Birmingham B16 8QG
Telephone: 021-456 4424

**NORTH EASTERN ELECTRICITY
CONSUMERS' COMMITTEE**
Chairman: J S Craigs
Address: 1st Floor
St Cuthbert's Chambers
35 Nelson Street
Newcastle upon Tyne NE1 5AN
Telephone: 091-221 2071

**NORTH WEST ELECTRICITY
CONSUMERS' COMMITTEE**
Chairman: Professor L F Baric
Address: 1st Floor
Boulton House
17-21 Chorlton Street
Manchester M1 3HY
Telephone: 061-236 3484

**SOUTHERN ELECTRICITY
CONSUMERS' COMMITTEE**
Chairman: K H Prior
Address: 30-31 Friar Street
Reading
Berkshire RG1 1DX
Telephone: 0734-560211

**SOUTH EASTERN ELECTRICITY
CONSUMERS' COMMITTEE**
Chairman: S E Goulden
Address: 1-4 Lambert's Yard
Tonbridge
Kent TN9 1WR
Telephone: 0732-351356

**SOUTH WALES ELECTRICITY
CONSUMERS' COMMITTEE**
Chairman: T H Keen
Address: 5th Floor (West Wing)
St David's House
Wood Street
Cardiff CF1 1ES
Telephone: 0222-228388

SOUTH WESTERN
ELECTRICITY CONSUMERS'
COMMITTEE
Address: Unit 1
Hide Market, West Street
Old Market
Bristol BS2 OBH
Telephone: 0272-540934

YORKSHIRE ELECTRICITY
CONSUMERS' COMMITTEE
Chairman: C S Woods
Address: 4th Floor
Fairfax House, Merrion Street
Leeds LS2 8JU
Telephone: 0532-341866

SCOTLAND
SOUTH OF SCOTLAND
ELECTRICITY CONSUMERS'
COMMITTEE
Chairman: Professor T F Carbery
Address: 48 St Vincent Street
Glasgow G2 5TS
Telephone: 041-248 5588

NORTH OF SCOTLAND
ELECTRICITY CONSUMERS'
COMMITTEE
Chairman: J M Mathisson
Address: 24 Marshall Place
Perth PH2 8AG
Telephone: 0738-36669

EMPLOYMENT DEPARTMENT
EXECUTIVE BODIES

ADVISORY CONCILIATION AND ARBITRATION SERVICE

Function: Responsible for providing facilities for conciliation, mediation and arbitration in an attempt to avoid and resolve industrial disputes.
Chairman: J W Hougham
Address: 27 Wilton Street
London SW7X 7AZ
Telephone: 071-210 3000

COMMISSIONER FOR THE RIGHTS OF TRADE UNION MEMBERS

Commissioner: Gill Rowlands
Function: To assist individuals taking proceedings against their union, its officials or trustees.
Address: 2nd Floor
Bank Chambers,
2a Rylands Street
Warrington WA1 1EN
Telephone: 0925-414128

COMMISSIONER FOR THE PROTECTION AGAINST UNLAWFUL INDUSTRIAL ACTION

Commissioner: Gill Rowlands
Function: To grant assistance to individuals taking proceedings against a trade union under the new 'citizen's right' created by the Trade Union Reform and Employment Rights Act.
Address: as above

EQUAL OPPORTUNITIES COMMISSION
Function: To promote equality of opportunity, work towards the elimination of discrimination, and review the sex discrimination and equal pay legislation.
Chairman: Kamlesh Bahl
Address: Swan House
52 Poland Street
London W1V 3DF
Telephone: 071-287 3953

HEALTH AND SAFETY COMMISSION
Function: Responsible for overseeing the work of the Health and Safety Executive. It has the power to delegate any of the HSE's functions but it cannot direct the HSE to interpret the Health and Safety at Work Act.
Chairman: Sir John Cullen
Address: Baynards House
1 Chepstow Place
Westbourne Grove
London W2 4TF
Telephone: 071-243 1000

HEALTH AND SAFETY EXECUTIVE
Function: Responsible for the protection of health, safety and the welfare of employees, and to safeguard others who may be exposed to risks from industrial activity.
Director General: J D Rimington
Address: As above

NATIONAL COUNCIL FOR VOCATIONAL QUALIFICATIONS
Function: To promote national vocational qualifications, with the objective of covering 90 per cent of the work-force by 1995.
Chairman: Mike Heron
Address: NCVQ
222 Euston Road
London NW1 2BZ
Telephone: 071-728 1893

INVESTORS IN PEOPLE UK
Function: To provide national ownership, leadership and direction to ensure the establishment of national standards with employers as investors in people.
Chairman: Sir Brian Wolfson
Address: Investors in People UK
Employment Department, W819
Moorfoot, Sheffield S1 4PQ
Telephone: 0742-739190

REMPLOY LTD

Function: To employ people with severe disabilities who can work but because of their disability are likely to have limited productivity.
Contact: John Carr
Address: Remploy
415 Edgware Road
London NW2
Telephone: 081-452 8020

WOMEN'S NATIONAL COMMISSION

Function: To ensure that the views of women are properly considered by Government.
Co-chairman: Maureen Rooney
Address: WNC Secretariat
Employment Department
Level 4 Tothill Street
London SW1H 9NF
Telephone: 071-273 5466

CONSTRUCTION INDUSTRY TRAINING BOARD

Function: An employer-led organisation responsible for providing training in the construction sector.
Chairman: Sir Clifford Chetwood
Address: CITB
Bircham Newton
Near Kings Lynn
Norfolk PE31 6RH
Telephone: 0553-775677

ENGINEERING CONSTRUCTION INDUSTRY TRAINING BOARD

Function: An employer-led organisation responsible for providing training in the engineering construction sector.
Chairman: Norman Dunlop
Address: Engineering Construction ITB
Blue Court, Kings Langley
Herts WD4 8JP
Enquiries: 0923-260000

EMPLOYMENT DEPARTMENT ADVISORY BODIES

National Advisory Council on Employment of People with Disabilities
Race Relations Advisory Group
Employment Service Bodies
Telephone: 071-273 5466

EMPLOYME NT DEPARTMENT TRIBUNALS

CENTRAL ARBITRATION COMMITTEE
Function: To provide boards of arbitration for the settlement of trade union disputes.
Chairman: Professor Sir John Wood
Address: 39 Grosvenor Place
London SW1 7BD
Telephone: 071-210 3000

EMPLOYMENT APPEAL TRIBUNAL
Function: The Superior Court of Record dealing with employment appeals.
Chairman: Sir John Mummery
Address: Audit House
58 Victoria Embankment
London EC4Y 0DS
Telephone: 071-273 1041

CERTIFICATION OFFICE FOR TRADE UNION ANDEMPLOYER'S ASSOCIATIONS
Function: An independent body appointed by the Secretary of State to carry out the provisions specified under the 1975 Employment Protection Act.
Certification Officer: EG Whybrew
Address: 27 Wilton Street
London SW7X 7AZ
Telephone: 071-210 3000

INDUSTRIAL TRIBUNALS
Telephone: 071-273 5466

ENVIRONMENT DEPARTMENT EXECUTIVE BODIES

AUDIT COMMISSION
Function: Overall responsibility for auditing the accounts of local authorities and the National Health Service.
Chairman: Sir David Cooksey
Address: 1 Vincent Square
London SW1P 2PN
Telephone: 071-828 1212

BRITISH BOARD OF AGREMENT
Function: Responsible for assessing building and construction products.
Chairman: William Courtney
Address: PO Box 195, Bucknalls Lane
Garston, Watford
Hertfordshire: WD2 7NG
Telephone: 0923-670844

COMMISSION FOR THE NEW TOWNS
Function: Disposal of assets of the 21 former English new town development corporations.
Chairman: Sir Neil Shields
Address: Glen House, Stag Place
London SW1E 5AJ
Telephone: 071-828 7722

COUNTRYSIDE COMMISSION
Function: To conserve and enhance the beauty of the English countryside.
Chairman: Sir John Johnson
Address: John Dower House
Crescent Place, Cheltenham
Gloucestershire GL50 3RA
Telephone: 0242-521381

HOUSING ACTION TRUSTS (HATS)
HATs were established to help tenants renovate rundown housing estates (*see* Chapter 5, The New State, for further details).

HOUSING CORPORATION
Function: Registration, supervision and funding of housing associations in England.
Chairman: Sir Brian Pearse
Address: Maple House
149 Tottenham Court Road
London W1P OBN
Telephone: 071-387 9466

JOINT NATURE CONSERVATION COMMITTEE
Function: A joint committee of the Countryside Council for Wales, English Nature, and Scottish Natural Heritage, responsible for nature conservation.
Chairman: The Earl of Selbourne
Address: Monkstone House, City Road
Peterborough PE1 1JY
Telephone: 0733-62626

LETCHWORTH GARDEN CITY CORPORATION
Function: Responsible for the management and development of the world's first garden city in Letchworth.
Chairman: Eric Lyall
Address: Broadway, Letchworth Garden City
Hertfordshire SG6 3AB
Telephone: 0462-482424

LOCAL GOVERNMENT COMMISSION
Function: Advisory body set up to review the structure, boundaries and electoral arrangements of English local authorities.
Chairman: Sir John Banham
Address: Dolphyn Court, 10-11 Great Turnstile
Lincoln's Inn Fields
London WC1V 7JU
Telephone: 071-430 8400

LONDON PENSIONS FUND AUTHORITY
Function: Responsible for paying the pensions of former GLC employees.
Chairman: Cholmeley Messer
Address: Dexter House
2 Royal Mint Court
London EC3N 4LP
Telephone: 071-488 6000

LONDON RESIDUARY BODY
Function: Responsible for winding up the affairs of the GLC and the Inner London Education Authority.
Chairman: Sir Godfrey Taylor
Address: c/o The Town Hall
Hornton Street, Kensington
London W8 7NX
Telephone: 071-938 4028

NATIONAL RIVERS AUTHORITY
Function: Responsible for water resources, pollution control, flood defence, conservation and navigation in England and Wales.
Chairman: Lord Crickhowell
Address: Rivers House, Waterside Drive
Aztec West, Almondsbury
Bristol BS12 4UD
Telephone: 0454-624400

NATURE CONSERVANCY COUNCIL FOR ENGLAND (ENGLISH NATURE)

Function: Conservation of English wildlife and natural features.
Chairman: The Earl of Cranbrook
Address: Northminster House
Peterborough PE1 1UA
Telephone: 0733-340345

RURAL DEVELOPMENT COMMISSION

Function: Promotion of job creation and essential services in the countryside.
Chairman: Lord Shuttleworth
Address: 11 Cowley Street
London SW1P 3NA
Telephone: 071-276 6969

UK ECOLABELLING BOARD

Function: To promote use of products which have reduced impact on the environment.
Chairman: Dr Elizabeth Nelson
Address: 7th Floor, Eastbury House
30-34 Albert Embankment
London SE1 7TL
Telephone: 071-820 1199

URBAN DEVELOPMENT CORPORATIONS

These bodies were set up to help promote inner-city regeneration.

BIRMINGHAM HEARTLANDS DEVELOPMENT CORPORATION

Chairman: Sir Reginald Eyre
Address: Waterlinks House
41 Richard Street, Heartlands
Birmingham B7 4AA
Telephone: 021-333 3060

BLACK COUNTRY DEVELOPMENT CORPORATION

Chairman: Sir William Francis
Address: Black Country House
Rounds Green Road, Oldbury
West Midlands B69 2RD
Telephone: 021-511 2000

BRISTOL DEVELOPMENT CORPORATION

Chairman: Christopher Thomas
Address: Techno House, Redcliffe Way
Bristol BS1 6NX
Telephone: 0272-255222

CENTRAL MANCHESTER DEVELOPMENT CORPORATION

Chairman: Dr James Grigor
Address: PO Box 42, Churchgate House
56 Oxford Road
Manchester M1 6EU
Telephone: 061-236 1166

158

LEEDS DEVELOPMENT CORPORATION
Chairman: Peter Hartley
Address: South Point
South Accommodation Road
Hunslett
Leeds LS10 1PP
Telephone: 0532-446273

LONDON DOCKLANDS DEVELOPMENT CORPORATION
Chairman: Michael Pickard
Address: Thames Quay
191 Marsh Wall, London E14 9TJ
Telephone: 071-512 3000

DOCKLANDS LIGHT RAILWAY
Chairman: Sir Peter Levene
Address: PO Box 154
Castor Land, Poplar
London E14 ODX
Telephone: 071-538 0311

MERSEYSIDE DEVELOPMENT CORPORATION
Chairman: Desmond Pitcher
Address: Royal Liver Buildings
Pier Head
Liverpool L3 1JH
Telephone: 051-236 6090

PLYMOUTH DEVELOPMENT CORPORATION
Chairman: Sir Robert Gerken
Address: Royal William Yard
Plymouth PL1 3RP
Telephone: 0752-256132

SHEFFIELD DEVELOPMENT CORPORATION
Chairman: Hugh Sykes
Address: Don Valley House
Savile Street East
Sheffield S4 7UQ
Telephone: 0742-720100

TEESIDE DEVELOPMENT CORPORATION
Chairman: Ron Norman
Address: Dunedin House
Riverside Quay, Stockton-on-Tees
Cleveland TS17 6BJ
Telephone: 0642-677123

TRAFFORD PARK DEVELOPMENT CORPORATION
Chairman: JWH Morgan
Address: Trafford Wharf Road,
Wharfside, Trafford Park
Manchester M17 1EX
Telephone: 061-848 8000

URBAN REGENERATION AGENCY
Function: Responsible for making the 150,000 acres of vacant and derelict land in English towns and cities available for housing, regeneration and employment.
Chairman: Lord Walker
Address: Room N19/12
2 Marsham Street
London SW1P 3EB
Telephone: 071-276 0600

ENVIRONMENT DEPARTMENT ADVISORY BODIES

Advisory Committee on Business and the Environment
Advisory Committee on Hazardous Substances
Advisory Committee on Releases of Genetically Modified Organisms

Black Country Limestone Advisory Panel
Building Regulations Advisory Committee
Inland Waterways Amenity Advisory Council
HM Inspectorate of Pollution Advisory Committee
Property Advisory Group
Radioactive Waste Management Advisory Committee
Royal Commission on Environmental Pollution
Telephone: 071-276 3840

ENVIRONMENT DEPARTMENT TRIBUNALS

Commons Commissioners
Rent Assessment Panels
Valuation Tribunals
Telephone: 071-276 3840

EXPORT CREDITS GUARANTEE DEPARTMENT ADVISORY BODIES

EXPORT GUARANTEES ADVISORY COUNCIL
Function: To provide advice to ECGD on sovereign risk underwriting, including portfolio and debt management.
Chairman: Robin Fox
Telephone: 071-512 7421

FOREIGN AND COMMONWEALTH OFFICE AND OVERSEAS DEVELOPMENT ADMINISTRATION EXECUTIVE BODIES

COMMONWEALTH INSTITUTE
Function: To promote the Commonwealth within United Kingdom educational establishments.
Director General: Stephen Cox
Address: Kensington High Street
London W8 6NQ
Telephone: 071-603 4535

GREAT BRITAIN-CHINA CENTRE
Function: Forum for advancing mutual co-operation and understanding between Britain and China.
Director: Nicola MacBean
Address: 15 Belgrave Square, London SW1
Telephone: 071-235 6696

BRITISH ASSOCIATION FOR CENTRAL AND EASTERN EUROPE

Function: To promote parliamentary, cultural and trade contacts between Britain and Central Europe, including the former Soviet Union and the republics of former Yugoslavia.

Director: Alan Brooke-Turner

Address: 4th Floor

50 Hans Crescent

London SW1 0NB

Telephone: 071-584 0766

WESTMINSTER FOUNDATION FOR DEMOCRACY

Function: To provide assistance to build and strengthen pluralistic and democratic institutions overseas.

Chairman: Sir James Spicer MP

Address: 3rd Floor

Queen Anne's Chambers

3 Dean Farrar Street

London SW1H 9LG

Telephone: 071-210 3318

BRITAIN-RUSSIA CENTRE

Function: To promote links between Britain and Russia.

Director: Dr Ian Elliott

Address: 14 Grosvenor Place

London SW1X 7HW

Telephone: 071-235 2116

MARSHALL AID COMMEMORATION COMMISSION

Function: To administer the Marshall Scholarships Scheme to bring postgraduate students from the United States to the UK.

Chairman: Sir Donald Tebbitt

Address: John Foster House

36 Gordon Square

London WC1H 0PF

Telephone: 071-387 8572

BBC WORLD SERVICE

Function: To provide a reliable and independent news service, and a balanced British view of national and international events.

Managing Director: Robert Phillis

Address: Bush House

PO Box 79, The Strand

London WC2B 4PH

Telephone: 071-240 3456

161

BRITISH COUNCIL

Function: To promote cultural, educational and technical co-operation between Britain and other countries.
Chairman: Sir Martin Jacomb
Address: 10 Spring Gardens
London SW1A 2BN
Telephone: 071-389 4878

COMMONWEALTH SCHOLARSHIP COMMISSION

Function: Selection of Commonwealth students for postgraduate study in the United Kingdom.
Chairman: Sir Michael Caine
Address: 36 Gordon Square, London WC1H 0PF
Telephone: 071-387 8572

CROWN AGENTS FOR OVERSEAS GOVERNMENT AND ADMINISTRATION

Function: Provision of financial, commercial and technical assistance for more than 120 countries in the developing world.
Chairman: David Probert
Address: St Nicholas House, St Nicholas Road
Sutton, Surrey SM1 1EL
Telephone: 081-643 3311

FOREIGN AND COMMONWEALTH OFFICE AND OVERSEAS DEVELOPMENT ADMINISTRATION ADVISORY BODIES

Diplomatic Service Appeals Board
Government Hospitality Fund Advisory Committee for the Purchase of Wine
Wilton Park Academic Council
Wilton Park International Advisory Council
Advisory Committee on Overseas Economic and Social Research
Indian Family Pension Funds Body of Commissioners
Overseas Service Pensions Scheme Advisory Body
Telephone: 071-210 0425

FOREIGN AND COMMONWEALTH OFFICE AND OVERSEAS DEVELOPMENT ADMINISTRATION TRIBUNAL

Foreign Compensation Commission
Telephone: 071-210 0425

OFFICE OF GAS SUPPLY (OFGAS)
Function: A non-ministerial government department established to monitor and regulate the gas supply industry and to protect the interests of customers.
Director General: Clare Spottiswoode
Address: Office of Gas Supply
Southside
105 Victoria Street
London SW1E 6QT
Telephone: 071-828 0898

GAS CONSUMERS COUNCIL (GCC)
Function: Investigation of problems arising out of gas appliances inside customer's homes.
Address: Gas Consumers Council
Abford House
15 Wilton Road
London SW1V 1LT
Telephone: 071-931 0977

HEALTH DEPARTMENT EXECUTIVE BODIES

CENTRAL COUNCIL FOR EDUCATION AND TRAINING IN SOCIAL WORK
Function: Statutory authority responsible for approving and promoting education and training for social work.
Chairman: Jeffrey Greenwood
Address: Derbyshire House
St Chad's Street
London WC1H 8AD
Telephone: 071-278 2455

ENGLISH NATIONAL BOARD FOR NURSING MIDWIFERY AND HEALTH VISITING
Function: Approval of educational institutions conducting courses leading to admission to the professional register.
Chairman: Maureen Theobald
Address: Victory House
170 Tottenham Court Road
London W1
Telephone: 071-388 3131

HUMAN FERTILISATION AND EMBRYOLOGY AUTHORITY
Function: Regulation of certain types of infertility treatment and research.
Address: Paxton House
30 Artillery Lane
London E1 7LS
Telephone: 071-377 5077

MEDICAL PRACTICES COMMITTEE
Function: Control of the distribution of general medical practitioners in England and Wales.
Chairman: Dr JG Ball
Address: 9th Floor
Euston Tower
286 Euston Road
London NW1 3DN
Telephone: 071-388 6471

NATIONAL BIOLOGICAL STANDARDS BOARD
Function: To safeguard and enhance public health through the standardisation and control of biological substances used in medicine.
Chairman: Dr John Evans
Address: Blanche Lane
South Mimms
Potters Bar
Hertfordshire EN6 3QD
Telephone: 0707-654753

NATIONAL RADIOLOGICAL PROTECTION BOARD
Function: Research, development and advice to professionals responsible for radiological protection.
Chairman: Sir Richard Southwood
Address: Chilton Didcot
Oxon OX11 0RQ
Telephone: 0235-831600

PUBLIC HEALTH LABORATORY SERVICES BOARD
Function: Laboratory services for the diagnosis, prevention and control of infectious and communicable diseases in England and Wales.
Chairman: Dr M P W Godfrey
Address: 61 Colindale Ave
London NW9 5DF
Telephone: 081-200 1295

STANDING COMMITTEE ON POSTGRADUATE MEDICAL AND DENTAL EDUCATION

Function: Responsible for advising the Health Secretary on standards for medical and dental education.
Chairman: Professor Dame Barbara Clayton
Address: 26 Park Crescent
London WN 3PB
Telephone: 071-323 1289

UK CENTRAL COUNCIL FOR NURSING MIDWIFERY AND HEALTH VISITING

Function: To maintain the professional register and improve standards of education and conduct.
President: Mary Uprichard
Address: 23 Portland Place
London W1N 3AF
Telephone: 071-637 7181

HEALTH DEPARTMENT ADVISORY BODIES

Administration of Radioactive Substances Advisory Committee
Advisory Board on the Registration of Homeopathic Products
Advisory Committee on Borderline Substances
Advisory Committee on Breast Cancer Screening
Advisory Committee on Distinction Awards
Advisory Committee on Micro-biological Safety of Food
Advisory Committee on NHS Drugs
Advisory Group on Hepatitis
Advisory Group on Rehabilitation
British Pharmacopoeia Commission
Clinical Standards Advisory Group
Committee on Carcinogenicity of Chemicals in Food
Committee on Dental and Surgical Materials
Committee on the Ethics of Gene Therapy
Committee on Medical Aspects of Food Policy
Committee for Monitoring Agreements on Tobacco Advertising
Committee on Medical Aspects of Radiation in the Environment
Committee on Mutagenicity of Chemicals in Food
Committee on the Safety of Medicines
Committee on Toxicity of Chemicals in Food
Dental Rates Study Group
Expert Advisory Group on Aids
Health Advisory Service
Joint Action for Implementation Group

165

Joint Committee on Vaccination and Immunisation
Joint Planning Advisory Committee
Medicines Commission
National Disability Information Project Steering Group
Standing Dental Advisory Committee
Standing Medical Advisory Committee
Standing Nursing and Midwifery Advisory Committee
Standing Pharmaceutical Advisory Committee
Steering Committee on Pharmacy Postgraduate Education
Supraregional Services Advisory Group
Secretary of State's Advisory Group on the Youth Treatment Service
Unrelated Live Transplant Regulatory Authority
Telephone: 071-210 5695

HEALTH DEPARTMENT
TRIBUNALS

Mental Health Review Tribunal
National Health Service Tribunal
Registered Homes Tribunal
Telephone: 071-210 5695

HOME OFFICE
EXECUTIVE BODIES

ALCOHOL EDUCATION AND RESEARCH COUNCIL

Function: To finance educational and research projects on alcohol misuse, and to provide financial assistance to charities active in the same field.
Chairman: Rt Hon Christopher Chataway
Address: Room G6, Abell House
John Islip Street
London SW1P 4LN
Telephone: 071-217 5276

COMMISSION FOR RACIAL EQUALITY

Function: To work for the elimination of racial discrimination and promote good relations between different racial groups.
Chairman: Herman Ouseley
Address: Elliot House
10-11 Allington Street
London SW1E 5EH
Telephone: 071-828 7022

COMMUNITY DEVELOPMENT FOUNDATION
Function: A registered charity offering consultancy work in community relations.
Chairman: Alan Haselhurst
Address: 60 Highbury Grove
London N5 2AG
Telephone: 071-226 5375

FIRE SERVICE EXAMINATIONS BOARD
Function: Responsible for setting and monitoring the examinations required for promotion to leading fire-fighter, sub-officer and station officer.
Chairman: Bryan Collins
Address: Arndale House
Arndale Centre
Luton LU1 2TS
Telephone: 0582-451166

FIRE SERVICES RESEARCH AND TRAINING TRUST
Function: A registered charity administering funds to assist research and training for the British Fire Service.
Chairman: RFD Shuffrey
Address: 5 Sheraton Drive
Tilehurst
Reading RG3 5UZ
Telephone: 0734-420945

GAMING BOARD FOR GREAT BRITAIN
Function: To ensure that gaming is run fairly, and to ensure that those involved in gaming and lotteries are fit and proper to do so, and to keep criminals out of the industry.
Chairman: Lady Littler
Address: Berkshire House
168-173 High Holborn
London WC1V 7AA
Telephone: 071-306 6200

HORSERACE BETTING LEVY BOARD
Function: Assessment and collection of monetary contributions from bookmakers and the Horserace Totalisator Board for the improvement of horse racing.
Chairman: Sir John Sparrow
Address: 52 Grosvenor Gardens
London SW1 0AU
Telephone: 071-333 0043

HORSERACE TOTALISATOR BOARD (TOTE)

Function: A statutory body with exclusive powers to carry out pool betting on approved racecourses under the 1963 Betting, Gaming and Lotteries Act.
Chairman: Lord Wyatt of Weeford
Address: Tote House
74 Upper Richmond Road
London SW1S 2SU
Telephone: 081-874 6411

OFFICE OF THE DATA PROTECTION REGISTRAR

Function: Administration and enforcement of the 1984 Data Protection Act.
Registrar: Elizabeth France
Address: Wycliffe House
Water Lane
Wilmslow
Cheshire SK9 5AF
Telephone: 0625-535777

POLICE COMPLAINTS AUTHORITY

Function: Supervision of investigations and disciplinary procedures resulting from complaints against the police.
Chairman: Sir Leonard Peach
Address: 10 Great George Street
London SW1P 3AB
Telephone: 071-273 6479

POLICE PROMOTION EXAMINATIONS BOARD

Function: Supervision of formal qualifications required by constables seeking promotion to sergeant and sergeants seeking promotion to inspector.
Chairman: Professor John Andrews
Address: F5 Division
Home Office
50 Queen Anne's Gate
London SW1 1AT
Telephone: 071-273 2676

HOME OFFICE
ADVISORY BODIES

Advisory Board on Restricted Patients
Advisory Committee on Service Candidates
Advisory Council on Race Relations
Advisory Council on the Misuse of Drugs
Animal Procedures Committee

Central Fire Brigades Advisory Council
Local Review Committees
Parliamentary Boundary Commission for England
Parliamentary Boundary Commission for Wales
Parole Board
Pensions Board
Police Advisory Board
Police Negotiating Board
Police Staff College Board of Governors
Telephone: 071-273 2639

HOME OFFICE
TRIBUNALS

Criminal Injuries Compensation Board
Data Protection Tribunal
Horserace Betting Levy Appeals Tribunal
Interception of Communications Tribunal
Misuse of Drugs Advisory Board
Misuse of Drugs Professional Panel
Misuse of Drugs Tribunal
Police Arbitration Tribunal
Police Discipline Appeals Tribunal
Security Services Tribunal
Telephone: 071-273 2639

HOME OFFICE:
OTHER BODIES

129 Boards of Visitors to Penal Establishments
Telephone: 071-273 2639

INLAND REVENUE
TRIBUNALS

GENERAL AND SPECIAL COMMISSIONERS OF INCOME TAX
Function: Responsible for resolving each year more than one million tax disputes between the Inland Revenue and taxpayers.
Telephone: *See* local tax office.

169

LORD CHANCELLOR'S DEPARTMENT EXECUTIVE BODIES

AUTHORISED CONVEYANCING PRACTITIONERS BOARD
Function: Responsible for regulation and promoting competition in the provision of conveyancing services.
Chairman: John Sadler CBE
Address: Suspended

LEGAL AID BOARD
Function: Responsible for the administration of the Legal Aid fund.
Chief Executive: Steve Orchard
Address: 29 Red Lion Street
London WC1R 4PP
Telephone: 071-831 4209

LORD CHANCELLOR'S DEPARTMENT ADVISORY BODIES

Advisory Committees on General Commissioners of Income Tax
Advisory Committees on General Commissioners of Income Tax (NI)
Advisory Committees on Justices of the Peace in England and Wales
Advisory Committees on Justices of the Peace (NI)
Advisory Committee on Juvenile Court Lay Panel (NI)
Advisory Committee on Legal Education and Conduct
Advisory Council on Public Records
Council on Tribunals
Country Court Rule Committee
Crown Court Rule Committee
Family Proceedings Rules Committee
Insolvency Rules Advisory Committee
Judicial Studies Board
Land Registration Rule Committee
Law Commission
Legal Aid Advisory Committee
Supreme Court Rule Committee
Telephone: 071-210 8603

LORD CHANCELLOR'S DEPARTMENT
TRIBUNALS

IMMIGRATION APPELLATE AUTHORITIES
Function: Independent judicial bodies responsible for hearings and appeals against immigration decisions in the United Kingdom.
President: G W Farmer
Address: Thanet House
231 Strand, London WC2R 1DA
Telephone: 071-353 8060

LANDS TRIBUNAL
Function: Responsible for non-domestic rating appeals, compensation for compulsory purchase, and other issues of land valuation and law.
President: Judge Bernard Marder QC
Address: 48-49 Chancery Lane
London WC2A 1JR
Telephone: 071-936 7200

PENSIONS APPEAL TRIBUNALS
Function: Responsible for hearing appeals on War Pensions
President: R T Holt
Address: 48-49 Chancery Lane
London WC2A 1JR
Telephone: 071-936 7034

VALUE ADDED TAX TRIBUNAL
Function: Responsible for hearing appeals against Customs and Excise.
President: Stephen Oliver QC
Address: 15 Bedford Avenue
London WC1B 3AS
Telephone: 071-631 4242

NATIONAL HERITAGE DEPARTMENT
EXECUTIVE BODIES

ARTS COUNCIL OF GREAT BRITAIN
Function: Promotion of knowledge, understanding and accessibility of the arts.
Chairman: Lord Palumbo
Address: 14 Great Peter Street, London SW1P 3NQ
Telephone: 071-333 0100

BRITISH LIBRARY

Function: National centre for reference study and bibliography for science, technology and the humanities.
Chairman: Sir Anthony Kenny
Address: 96 Euston Road
London NW1 2BD
Telephone: 071-323 7111

BRITISH MUSEUM

Function: Houses the national collections of art and archaeology from prehistoric times to the twentieth century.
Chairman: Lord Windlesham
Address: Great Russell Street
London WC1B 3DG
Telephone: 071-636 1555

BRITISH FILM INSTITUTE

Function: Promotion of moving image culture in all its forms.
Chairman: Jeremy Thomas
Address: 21 Stephen Street
London W1P 1PL
Telephone: 071-255 1444

BRITISH TOURIST AUTHORITY

Function: Promotion of overseas visitors to Britain.
Chairman: Adele Biss
Address: Thames Tower
Black's Road, Hammersmith
London W6 9EL
Telephone: 081-846 9000

BROADCASTING COMPLAINTS COMMISSION

Function: Examination of complaints over unjust or unfair treatment and invasions of privacy in broadcast programmes.
Chairman: Rev Canon Peter Pilkington
Address: Grosvenor Gardens House
35-37 Grosvenor Gardens
London SW1W 0BS
Telephone: 071-630 1966

BROADCASTING STANDARDS COUNCIL
Function: Monitoring and research into standards of taste and decency in broadcast programmes.
Chairman: Lady Howe
Address: 5-8 The Sanctuary
London SW1P 3JS
Telephone: 071-233 0544

CRAFTS COUNCIL
Function: To encourage the creation of fine works of craft, and promote public interest in works of craftspeople.
Chairman: Sir Nigel Broackes
Address: 44a Pentonville Road
London N1 9BY
Telephone: 071-278 7700

ENGLISH HERITAGE (HISTORIC BUILDINGS AND MONUMENTS COMMISSION)
Function: Protection and promotion of England's architectural and archaeological heritage.
Chairman: Jocelyn Stevens
Address: Fortress House
23 Savile Row
London W1X 1AB
Telephone: 071-973 3000

ENGLISH TOURIST BOARD
Function: Promotion of foreign tourism in England.
Chairman: Adele Biss
Address: Thames Tower
Black's Road, Hammersmith
London W6 9EL
Telephone: 081-846 9000

FOOTBALL LICENSING AUTHORITY
Function: Enforcement of government policy on safety at grounds where football matches are played.
Chairman: Norman Jacobs
Address: 27 Harcourt House
19 Cavendish Square
London W1M 9AD
Telephone: 071-491 7191

173

GEFFRYE MUSEUM
Function: Displays of English domestic furniture and interiors.
Chairman: The Baroness Brigstocke
Address: Kingsland Road
London E2 8EA
Telephone: 071-739 9893

HORNIMAN MUSEUM AND PUBLIC TRUST
Function: Holds collections of musical instruments and ethnographic material.
Chairman: Dame Margaret Weston
Address: 100 London Road
Forest Hill
London SE23 3PQ
Telephone: 081-699 1872

IMPERIAL WAR MUSEUM
Function: Holds collections of armed conflicts involving Britain and the Commonwealth since 1914.
Chairman: Lord Bramall
Address: Lambeth Road
London SE1 6HZ
Telephone: 071-416 5000

MANCHESTER MUSEUM OF SCIENCE AND INDUSTRY
Function: Displays collections dealing with the industrial revolution and the history of science.
Chairman: John Lee
Address: Liverpool Road
Castlefield, Manchester M3 4JP
Telephone: 061-832 2244

MUSEUM OF LONDON
Function: Displays collections of the history of London.
Chairman: Peter Revell-Smith
Address: London Wall
London EC2Y 5HN
Telephone: 071-600 3699

MUSEUM AND GALLERIES COMMISSION
Function: Responsible for distribution of grants for the 1,000 minor museums in England.
Chairman: Graham Greene
Address: 16 Queen Anne's Gate
London SW1H 9AA
Telephone: 071-233 4200

NATIONAL FILM AND TELEVISION SCHOOL
Function: Provides training for the freelance film and television production sector.
Chairman: David Puttnam
Address: Station Road
Beaconsfield
Buckinghamshire HP9 1LJ
Telephone: 0494-671234

NATIONAL GALLERY
Function: Holds the national collection of Western European painting to 1900.
Chairman: Nicholas Hugo Baring
Address: Trafalgar Square
London WC2N 5DN
Telephone: 071-839 3321

NATIONAL HERITAGE MEMORIAL FUND
Function: Assists with the acquisition and preservation of land, buildings and objects of importance to the national heritage.
Chairman: Lord Rothschild
Address: 10 St James's Street
London SW1A 1EF
Telephone: 071-930 0963

NATIONAL MARITIME MUSEUM
Function: Illustration of Britain's maritime history through its collection of nautical artefacts.
Chairman: Admiral of the Fleet The Lord Lewin
Address: Greenwich
London SE10 9NF
Telephone: 081-858 4422

NATIONAL MUSEUMS AND GALLERIES ON MERSEYSIDE
Function: Includes the Walker Art Gallery, the Merseyside Maritime Museum, the Liverpool Museum and the Lady Lever Art Gallery.
Chairman: Sir Leslie Young
Address: Liverpool Museum
William Brown Street, Liverpool L3 8EN
Telephone: 051-207 0001

NATIONAL PORTRAIT GALLERY
Function: Holds the national collection of portraits of famous British men and women.
Chairman: Rev Prof Owen Chadwick
Address: 2 St Martin's Place, London WC2H 0HE
Telephone: 071-306 0055

NATURAL HISTORY MUSEUM
Function: Displaying and researching the natural sciences.
Chairman: Sir Walter Bodmer
Address: Cromwell Road
London SW7 5BD
Telephone: 071-938 9123

PUBLIC LENDING RIGHT
Function: Provides for registered authors to receive payment for the loan of their books from a sample of 30 library authorities.
Chairman: David Whitaker
Address: Bayheath House
Prince Regent Street
Stockton-on-Tees
Cleveland TS18 1DF
Telephone: 0642-604699

REDUNDANT CHURCHES FUND
Function: Preservation of selected churches which had fallen into disuse.
Chairman: Gordon Burrett
Address: 89 Fleet Street
London EC4Y 1DH
Telephone: 071-936 2285

ROYAL ARMOURIES
Function: Preservation of the national collection of arms and armour.
Chairman: Rt Hon The Lord Eden of Winton PC
Address: HM Tower of London
London EC3N 4AB
Telephone: 071-480 6358

ROYAL COMMISSION ON HISTORICAL MANUSCRIPTS
Function: Provides investigation and advice on the preservation and study of historical manuscripts in the United Kingdom.
Chairman: Dr Gerald Aylmer
Address: Quality House
Quality Court
Chancery Lane
London WC2A 1HP
Telephone: 071-242 1198

ROYAL COMMISSION ON THE HISTORICAL MONUMENTS OF ENGLAND

Function: Compiles the register of England's ancient monuments and historic buildings.
Chairman: Baroness Park of Monmouth
Address: Fortress House
23 Savile Row
London W1X 2JQ
Telephone: 071-973 3500

ROYAL FINE ART COMMISSION

Function: Provides advice on developments that could affect amenities of a national character.
Chairman: Lord St John of Fawsley
Address: 7 St James's Square
London SW1Y 4JU
Telephone: 071-839 6537

SCIENCE MUSEUM

Function: Holds the national collections on science, technology, transport and medicine.
Chairman: Sir Austin Pearce
Address: Exhibition Road
South Kensington, London SW7 2DD
Telephone: 071-938 8000

SIR JOHN SOANE'S MUSEUM

Function: Holds the collection of antiques, furniture and paintings collected by the architect Sir John Soane.
Chairman: His Grace the Duke of Grafton
Address: 13 Lincoln's Inn Fields, London WC2A 3BP
Telephone: 071-405 2107

SPORTS COUNCIL

Function: Promotion of participation in sport and physical recreation.
Chairman: Rodney Walker
Address: 16 Upper Woburn Place
London WC1H 0QP
Telephone: 071-388 1277

TATE GALLERY

Function: Holds the national collection of British painting and 20th-century painting and sculpture.
Chairman: Dennis Stevenson
Address: Millbank, London SW1P 4RG
Telephone: 071-887 8000

THE MILLENNIUM COMMISSION
Function: Responsible for the distribution of 20 per cent of the net proceeds of the National Lottery to projects to mark the millennium.
Chief Executive: Nicholas Hinton
Address: Vincent House
Vincent Square
London SW1P 2NB
Telephone: 071 416 8070

VICTORIA AND ALBERT MUSEUM
Function: The national museum of art and design.
Chairman: Lord Armstrong of Ilminster
Address: Cromwell Road
South Kensington
London SW7 2RL
Telephone: 071-938 8500

THE WALLACE COLLECTION
Function: Collection of paintings, furniture, ceramics and armour bequeathed to the nation by Lady Wallace.
Chairman: The Hon Simon Sainsbury
Address: Manchester Square
London W1M 6BN
Telephone: 071-935 0687

NATIONAL HERITAGE DEPARTMENT ADVISORY BODIES

Advisory Committee on Historic Wreck Sites
Advisory Committee on the Government Art Collection
Advisory Committee for the Public Lending Right
Library and Information Services Council
Regional Councils for Sport and Recreation
Reviewing Committee on the Export of Works of Art
Royal Fine Art Commission
Theatres Trust
Telephone: 071-211 2006

OFFICE OF THE NATIONAL LOTTERY (OFLOT)

Function: OFLOT is a non-ministerial government department established to choose the licensee to operate the national lottery for seven years, and to regulate the licensee for the duration of the licence. Money from the operation of the lottery will be transferred to the National Lottery Distribution Fund, run by the National Heritage Department, and distributed

to the Arts Councils, the Sports Councils, the National Heritage Memorial Fund, the National Lotteries Charities Board and the Millennium Commission.
Director General: Peter Davis
Address: 2-4 Cockspur Street, London SW1Y 5DH
Telephone: 071-211 2132

OFFICE OF PASSENGER RAIL FRANCHISING (OPRAF)

Function: OPRAF is a non-ministerial government department responsible for improving railway passenger services by issuing franchise agreements to private-sector companies, distributing public subsidy to uneconomic lines, and monitoring standards of performance of franchise operators.
Director of Franchising: Roger Salmon
Address: 26 Old Queen Street, London SW1H 9HP
Telephone: 071-799 8800

OFFICE OF THE RAIL REGULATOR

Function: The Rail Regulator is a non-ministerial government department responsible for the interests of the users of railway services, the promotion of the railway network, and the promotion of competition in railway services. It is served by the regional Rail Users Consultative Committees, formerly known as the Transport Users Consultative Committees.
Director: John Swift QC
Address: 1 Waterhouse Square
Holborn Bars, 138-140 Holborn, London EC1N 2SU
Telephone: 071-427 6000

CENTRAL RAIL CONSULTATIVE COMMITTEE
Function: Responsible for monitoring the national performance and policies of British Rail, and co-ordinating the work of regional committees.
Chairman: Major General Lennox Napier
Address: Golden Cross House, Duncannon Street, London WC2N 4JF
Telephone: 071-839 7338

OFFICE OF THE RAIL REGULATOR REGIONAL COMMITTEES

LONDON REGIONAL RAIL USERS' CONSULTATIVE COMMITTEE
Chairman: Dr Eric Midwinter
Address: Golden Cross House
Duncannon Street, London WC2N 4JF
Telephone: 071-839 1898

EASTERN ENGLAND RAIL USERS' CONSULTATIVE COMMITTEE
Chairman: David Bertram
Address: Midgate House
Midgate, Peterborough PE1 1TN
Telephone: 0733-312188

179

**MIDLANDS RAIL USERS'
CONSULTATIVE COMMITTEE**
Chairman: Dr P Pritchard Jones
Address: 77 Paradise Circus
Queensway
Birmingham B1 2DT
Telephone: 021-212 2133

**NORTH EASTERN ENGLAND
RAIL USERS'
CONSULTATIVE COMMITTEE**
Chairman: Professor P B Fairest
Address: 16 St Saviour's Place
York YO1 2PL
Telephone: 0904-625615

**NORTH WESTERN ENGLAND
RAIL USERS' CONSULTATIVE
COMMITTEE**
Chairman: Frank Dolphin
Address: Room 112
17-21 Chorlton Street
Manchester M1 3HY
Telephone: 061-228 6247

**SCOTLAND RAIL USERS'
CONSULTATIVE COMMITTEE**
Chairman: J A Corrie
Address: 249 West George Street
Glasgow G2 4QE
Telephone: 041-221 7760

**SOUTHERN ENGLAND RAIL
USERS' CONSULTATIVE
COMMITTEE**
Chairman: Ann Hooper
Address: Golden Cross House
Duncannon Street
London WC2N 4JF
Telephone: 071-839 1851

**WALES RAIL USERS'
CONSULTATIVE COMMITTEE**
Chairman: C A Hogg
Address: St David's House
East Wing
Wood Street
Cardiff CF1 1ES
Telephone: 0222-227247

**WESTERN ENGLAND RAIL
USERS' CONSULTATIVE
COMMITTEE**
Chairman: Sir Robert Wall
Address: 13th Floor
Tower House
Fairfax Street
Bristol BS1 3BN
Telephone: 0272-265703

ROYAL MINT
ADVISORY BODIES

ROYAL MINT ADVISORY COMMITTEE
Function: To advise on the design of coins, medals and decorations.
Chairman: HRH The Duke of Edinburgh
Telephone: 0443-222111

SOCIAL SECURITY DEPARTMENT
EXECUTIVE BODIES

OCCUPATIONAL PENSIONS BOARD
Function: Administration of contracting out of occupational pensions from the State
Earnings Related Pensions Scheme (SERPS).

Chairman: C H Dawes
Address: Secretariat and Executive Office
PO Box 2EE
Newcastle upon Tyne NE99 2EE
Telephone: 091-225 6414

SOCIAL SECURITY DEPARTMENT ADVISORY BODIES

Central Advisory Committee on War Pensions
Disability Living Allowance Advisory Board
Industrial Injuries Advisory Council
Social Security Advisory Committee
War Pensions Committees
Telephone: 071-962 8147

SOCIAL SECURITY DEPARTMENT TRIBUNALS

Child Support Tribunals
Disability Appeals Tribunals
Medical Appeals Tribunals
Social Security Appeals Tribunals
Vaccine Damage Tribunals
Central Adjudications Services (Social Security Benefits)
Telephone: 071-962 8147

OFFICE OF TELECOMMUNICATIONS (OFTEL)

Function: Independent Regulatory body for monitoring and enforcement of licences to operate public telecommunications systems.
Chairman: Don Cruickshank
Address: Export House, 50 Ludgate Hill
London EC4M 7JJ
Telephone: 071-634 8700

OFFICE OF TELECOMMUNICATIONS (OFTEL) ADVISORY COMMITTEES

ENGLISH ADVISORY COMMITTEE ON TELECOMMUNICATIONS
Address: 50 Ludgate Hill
London EC4M 7JJ
Telephone: 071-634 8770

SCOTTISH ADVISORY
COMMITTEE ON
TELECOMMUNICATIONS
Address: 43 Jeffrey Street
Edinburgh EH1 1DN
Telephone: 031-244 5576

WELSH ADVISORY COMMITTEE
ON TELECOMMUNICATIONS
Address: Caradog House
St Andrew's Place
Cardiff CF1 3BE
Telephone: 0222-374028

NORTHERN IRELAND
ADVISORY COMMITTEE ON
TELECOMMUNICATIONS
Address: Chamber of Commerce and Industry
22 Great Victoria Street
Belfast BT2 7QA
Telephone: 0232-244113

TRADE AND INDUSTRY DEPARTMENT EXECUTIVE BODIES

BRITISH HALLMARKING COUNCIL
Function: Responsible for ensuring that adequate facilities exist for the assaying and hallmarking of articles of precious metals.
Chairman: R S Burman
Address: St Philips House, St Philips Place
Birmingham B3 2PP
Telephone: 021-200 3330

COAL AUTHORITY
Function: As part of the privatization of Britain's coal, this body will take over its ownership of coal reserves and be responsible for licensing coal mining operations.
Chief Executive designate: Neville Washington
Address: Mansfield, Nottinghamshire.
Telephone: c/o DTI 071-215 5000

DESIGN COUNCIL
Function: To improve the performance of British industry by improving the design of its products.
Director General: Evelyn Ryle
Address: 28 Haymarket, London SW1Y 4SU
Telephone: 071-839 8000

DOMESTIC COAL USERS' COUNCIL
Function: Monitors coal supply, prices and quality, and consumer protection.
Chairman: Ann Scully
Address: 52 Horseferry Road, London SW1P 2AG
Telephone: 071-233 0582

ENGLISH INDUSTRIAL ESTATES CORPORATION
Function: Development and management of industrial and commercial premises throughout Britain.
Chairman: Sir Idris Pearce
Address: Sir George's House, Kingsway
Team Valley, Gateshead
Tyne and Wear NE11 0NA
Telephone: 091-487 8941

HEARING AID COUNCIL
Function: Responsible for maintaining the register of qualified hearing aid dispensers.
Chairman: W M Fernie
Address: 201 Silbury Boulevard
Central Milton Keynes MK9 1LZ

MONOPOLIES AND MERGERS COMMISSION
Function: Responsible for the investigation of monopolies, mergers and takeovers.
Chairman: Graeme Odgers
Address: New Court, 48 Carey Street, London WC2A 2JT
Telephone: 071-324 1467

NATIONAL CONSUMER COUNCIL
Function: Responsible for safeguarding the interests of consumers.
Chairman: Lady Wilcox
Address: 20 Grosvenor Gardens, London SW1W 0DH
Telephone: 071-730 3469

POLICYHOLDERS PROTECTION BOARD
Function: To protect policyholders affected by the inability of insurance companies to meet their liabilities.
Chairman: R A G Neville
Address: 51 Gresham Street, London EC2V 7HQ
Telephone: 071-600 3333

POST OFFICE UNIONS COUNCIL
Function: To conduct negotiations with the unions on pay and conditions.
Chairman: Bobby Devine

Address: 80-86 Old Street
London EC1V 9PP
Telephone: 071-490 5290

POST OFFICE USERS' NATIONAL COUNCIL
Function: The Council must be consulted by the Post Office on all policy proposals affecting services.
Chairman: Thomas Corrigon
Address: Waterloo Bridge House
London SE1 8UA
Telephone: 071-928 9458

SIMPLER TRADE PROCEDURES BOARD
Function: To rationalise documentation needed for the trade and the cross-frontier movement of goods.
Chairman: J G Davies
Address: 29 Glasshouse Street
London W1R 5RG
Telephone: 071-287 3525

UNITED KINGDOM ATOMIC ENERGY AUTHORITY
Function: Responsible for the production, use and disposal of atomic energy, atomic energy research and development, and the disposal of radioactive material.
Chairman: Sir Anthony Cleaver
Address: Harwell
Oxfordshire OX11 0RA
Telephone: 0235-821111

TRADE AND INDUSTRY DEPARTMENT ADVISORY BODIES

Advanced Manufacturing Technology Committee
Advisory Committee on Arbitration Law
Advisory Committee on Telecommunications for England
Advisory Council on Research and Development
Advisory Panel on Deregulation
Aviation Committee
British Overseas Trade Board
Coal Task Force
Engineering Technology Advisory Committee
Fuel Cell Advisory Panel
Industrial Development Advisory Board
Information Technology Advisory Board
Innovation Advisory Board

Monitoring Committee on Misleading Price Indications
Offshore Industry Advisory Board
Overseas Projects Board
Regional Industrial Developments Boards
Renewable Energy Advisory Committee
Standards Quality and Measurement Advisory Committee
Standing Advisory Committee on Industrial Property
Telephone: 071-215 5000

TRADE AND INDUSTRY DEPARTMENT TRIBUNALS

Copyright Tribunal
Insolvency Practitioners' Tribunal
Consumer Credit Licensing Appeals
Estate Agents Appeals
Telephone: 071-215 5000

TRANSPORT DEPARTMENT EXECUTIVE BODIES

NORTHERN LIGHTHOUSE BOARD
Function: Responsible for navigational aids outside immediate area of ports around Scotland and the Isle of Man.
Chief Executive: Captain James Taylor
Address: 84 George Street
Edinburgh EH2 3DA
Telephone: 031-226 7051

TRINITY HOUSE
Function: Responsible for navigational aids outside immediate area of ports in England, Wales and the Channel Islands.
Managing Director: Captain David Orr
Address: Trinity House
Tower Hill
London EC3 N4DH
Telephone: 071-480 6601

TRANSPORT DEPARTMENT ADVISORY BODIES

Disabled Persons Transport Advisory Committee
Landscape Advisory Committee

Standing Advisory Committee on Trunk Road Assessment
Street Works Advisory Committee
Telephone: 071-276 3578

TREASURY EXECUTIVE BODIES

BUILDING SOCIETIES COMMISSION
Function: Monitoring and regulating Building Societies.
Chairman: Geoffrey Fitchew
Address: 15 Great Marlborough Street, London W1V 2AY
Telephone: 071-437 9992

TRANSPORT DEPARTMENT TRIBUNALS

Traffic Commissioners-Licensing Authorities
Telephone: 071-276 3578

TREASURY ADVISORY BODIES

Armed Forces Pay Review Body
Doctors' and Dentists' Review Body
Nurses' Midwives' and other NHS Professions' Review Body
Pharmacists' Review Body
School Teachers' Review Body
Top Salaries Review Body
The Private Finance Panel
The Panel of Independent (Economic) Forecasters
Telephone: 071-270 5082

TREASURY TRIBUNALS

Financial Services Tribunal
Telephone: 071-270 5082

OFFICE OF WATER SERVICES (OFWAT)

Function: Ofwat was set up in 1989 as the regulator of the water and sewerage companies in England and Wales. It is supported by 10 regional Customer Service Committees (CSCs) who represent the interests of domestic and non-domestic customers.
Director General: Ian Byatt
Address: Office of Water Services, Centre City Tower, 7 Hill Street, Birmingham B5 4UA
Telephone: 021-625 1300

OFWAT EASTERN CSC
Chairman: David Edwards
Address: Ground Floor
Carlyle House
Carlyle Road
Cambridgeshire CB4 3DN
Telephone: 0223-323889

OFWAT NORTHUMBRIA CSC
Chairman: Jim Gardner
Address: 2nd Floor
35 Nelson Street
Newcastle NE1 5AN
Telephone: 091-221 0646

OFWAT NORTH WEST CSC
Chairman: Anthony Goldstone
Address: 1st Floor
Boulton House
17-21 Chorlton Street
Manchester M1 3HY
Telephone: 061-236 6112

OFWAT CENTRAL CSC
Chairman: Clive Wilkinson
Address: 1st Floor
77 Paradise Circus
Queensway
Birmingham B1 2DZ
Telephone: 021-212 5202

OFWAT SOUTHERN CSC
Chairman: Professor Judith Rees
Address: 15-17 Ridgmount Street
London WC1E 7AH
Telephone: 071-636 3656

OFWAT SOUTH WEST CSC
Chairman: Jessica Thomas
Address: 1st Floor
Broadwalk House
Southernhay West
Exeter EX1 1TS
Telephone: 0392-428028

OFWAT THAMES CSC
Chairman: Elizabeth Monck
Address: 15-17 Ridgmount Street
London WC1E 7AH
Telephone: 071-636 3656

OFWAT WALES CSC
Chairman: Archdeacon Raymond
Roberts
Address: Room 140, Caradog House
1-6 St Andrews Place
Cardiff CF1 3BE
Telephone: 0222-239852

OFWAT WESSEX CSC
Chairman: Anthony Clothier
Address: Unit 2
The Hide Market
West Street, St Philips
Bristol BS2 0BH
Telephone: 0272-557001

OFWAT YORKSHIRE CSC
Chairman: Diana Scott
Address: 10th Floor
Dudley House, Upper Albion Street
Leeds LS2 8PN
Telephone: 0532-340874

5
THE NEW STATE

No blueprint exists for the reorganisation of government into what we are calling the 'new state'. This is the creation of councils, committees, trusts, governing boards and associations occupying the intermediate ground between – on one side – ministers, civil servants and the bodies which answer to them, and – on the other – elected local authorities. No minister or policy adviser or think-tank guru sat down and drew up a chart. If they had, it would have been fearsomely complicated, an exercise in social engineering as ambitious as anything ever attempted in the totalitarian East. For the creation of Training and Enterprise Councils, City Technology Colleges, health service trusts and grant-maintained schools, together with the parallel expansion of housing associations has involved the mobilisation (not yet complete) of large numbers of people who answer the traditional descriptions neither of civil servants nor council employees. Some of them belong to the state, in that they depend for their livelihood not just on public money but the exercise of coercive public powers. Others have volunteered: as new-look school governors, for example, unpaid but required to take on onerous responsibilities for managing their school. Yet others are paid a little – members of health authorities can expect up to £5,000 a year. This is considerably more than elected councillors claim in expenses and attendance allowances but it is not quite a job.

The new state is accidental. In political terms these organisations happened to be created at the same time, but for different reasons. In employment, the Government was impatient with its own in-house organisation, the Manpower Services Commission, and sought an alternative means of delivering training schemes. In education Mrs Thatcher and several Secretaries of State for Education were antagonistic to local education authorities and cast around for a means, as they saw it, of freeing schools from council control. The reorganisation of the National Health Service in successive waves from the later 1980s answered, some might say, the frustration of the Thatcher government at being unable to proceed with privatisation. The split into 'purchasing' and 'providing' elements followed from the Government's wish to introduce some elements of a market into health care without seeming to jeopardise the existence of a National Health Service free at the point of delivery.

The very absence of a guiding philosophy has meant that the relationship between these new state bodies – and between them and the central government, let alone local authorities – is overlapping and ambiguous. Since their creation, no 'machinery of government' official in the Cabinet Office has, at least in documents to be put before the eyes of the public, examined how this plethora of new bodies is working. How they spend public money has only, so far, been the subject of disjointed and ad hoc inquiries by the statutory spending watchdogs, the National Audit Office and the Audit Commission, who initially at least were barking at each other over which one of them should have the bone.

The origins of the 'new state' are, in important part, negative. The Government led by Lady Thatcher and (to a diminished extent) that led by Mr Major have been antagonistic to aspects of local government. The size, spending and often the political colour of local authorities have vexed ministers. After coming to office in 1979 the Thatcher Government made successive efforts to curb local spending by altering council grants and eventually councils' own tax base.

Councils were meanwhile held responsible for apparent failures of performance, especially in education, even though many local education authorities had for years existed semi-independently of town and county halls and enjoyed close links with the Ministry, later the Department of Education; the post-war catch-phrase said that education was a 'national service, locally administered'. Indeed when education reform came, the role of the centre was enhanced in matters of curriculum at the same time as, in ministers' rhetoric, local control was wrested from bureaucrats and councillors and given back to local communities, through plans for self-governing schools completely independent of councils, or at least given wide powers of delegated spending by local authorities.

A similar train of thought was apparent in housing. Generous discounts and a 'right to buy' had been available to council tenants since 1980. Later this was extended to tenants of publicly assisted not-for-profit housing associations. By the end of the decade most of those tenants who wished to buy had done so. The Government, still oppressed by the size of the municipal stock, was thinking of ways in which tenants could be mobilised, like parents, to wrest control from local councils. Policy proceeded down two tracks: the creation of new Housing Action Trusts which would, temporarily, at least take over estates and ensure their physical refurbishment, possibly to hand them back to local authorities, possibly to pass them on to new tenants co-operatives or even the private sector. Another was to encourage the wholesale transfer of council housing to alternative landlords. Again, the private sector was favoured but in the event stock transfer has been in favour of housing associations, which are regulated in England by a non-departmental body, the Housing Corporation, on behalf of the Environment Department.

Robert Jackson, the former Education Minister, has claimed there is philosophy behind these changes. In education it was, he said, given a classical form in the Education Reform Act of 1988, a new marriage of central state power and the delegated authority of local, but non-elected groups. This Act established a new national curriculum, the standards and content of which would be specified by the central government. It would put in place arrangements for testing pupils, but schools would get their own budgets, and some capacity to run their own show, provided they can attract sufficient numbers of children and their parents.

The same philosophy – stronger centre, stronger local unit, but outside elected local government – has been developed in the National Health Service with the shift of power from the health authorities (and the exclusion from them of elected councillors) to GP fundholders and health trusts running hospitals, ambulance and specialist services.

One aspect of these changes, half considered by the government, was the great extension they implied in the range of lay people involved in running public bodies – as activist school governors, as employer members of TECs, as appointees to the health trusts. How big is the pool of civic spirits waiting to be fished in? Would candidates come forward without the inducement of salaries and expense allowances?

The Government has been anxious to deny these new bodies can be called 'quangos'. William Waldegrave has sought to make a clear distinction between non-departmental public bodies set up to help provide the government with expertise and advice in a particular field, and bodies designed to take away responsibilities hitherto exercised by local authorities, to devolve power to the grass roots (as he put it), and improve the efficiency of the public sector.

To sum up, the 'new state' encompasses the health service, divided into semi-autonomous local trusts, health districts where the old regime is still relatively intact, new central regulatory and management bodies; housing associations and trusts; the new governance of training, urban development and industrial assistance; and education. To critics, recent years have seen 'a transformation in the structure of local governance – that network of institutions by which local communities are governed. Responsibilities have been taken from elected councillors and given to appointees so that the structure of local governance becomes an increasingly complex array of appointed bodies'.

Part of this process has been the removal of councillors from bodies on which they previously sat (such as District Health Authorities); the removal of entire local functions from the public sector (for example, water); the transfer of organisations previously run by local authorities to alternative public status (further education and sixth-form colleges); the creation of new organisations with local responsibilities but little or no local authority participation (such as Urban Development Corporations and Housing Action Trusts).

THE NEW LOCAL GOVERNANCE

There is widespread public confusion about the exact distribution of powers and functions within the state, and especially about boundaries between respective public bodies. There is nothing new in this public ignorance about public administration. When they enjoyed a plenitude of powers, local authorities were not exactly well understood. For example, people do and did confuse the functions of district councils with those of county councils. About 60 per cent of those asked in a survey for the Widdicombe Committee enquiry in the mid-1980s into the conduct of local author - ity business thought that their local authority was responsible for the hospitals. Will people in future be equally confused about where responsibility for the schools lies, shared as it increasingly will be between Department for Education at the core, the Funding Agency for Schools, residual local education authorities and grant-maintained schools with trust status?

In recent months, academics and commentators have mounted a criticism of the 'new state' by emphasising the lack of ballot box accountability for the new organisations. Howard Davis of the University of Birmingham says elected representatives are excluded from most of these bodies. Even where as in grant-maintained schools there are parental representatives the wider community has no role – for example the views of parents of children below the relevant school age or people without children go unheard. How, critics ask, can a minister at the end of a long and convoluted chain of payments and reports be responsible or accountable to local people? In local authorities, by contrast, however imperfect their administrative record, local people have a regular opportunity to inspect the record of their councillors and eject them if it is found wanting.

'The local authority stands in the middle of it all', according to Graham Mather of the European Policy Forum and Professor Michael Clarke in their introduction to the pamphlet 'The New Local Governance'. 'It is the only elected body and the one which has the legitimacy to take a broad view. It should be well placed to lead, enthuse and enable.' With an eye on the future of the new state, they argue 'increasingly those involved in the plethora of appointed bodies have come to value its unique contribution'.

Can councillors be in some sense brought back in? In the spring of 1994, the district council at Newport in Gwent established a scrutiny committee to monitor the quangos which affect the town, having estimated that central government dispenses a total of £2.2 billion to quangos in Wales compared with the £2.7 billion it pays in grants to local authorities. Meanwhile Lancashire County Council told its officers to monitor the establishment of any executive agencies in the Civil Service which might affect the county. Other councils, including the Conservative party's flagship of Wandsworth in south-west London have been arguing that they could perform a valuable role in purchasing health care, by replacing unelected District Health Authorities or District Health Commissions.

There are some glaring anomalies. Elected councillors can be surcharged and disqualified from office if the district auditor finds they have misused their powers. No such sanction hangs over people appointed to 'new state' organisations such as health authorities and trusts even though their financial decision-making powers are not dissimilar. Councils meet in public; many 'new state' bodies are secretive by comparison.

191

EDUCATION AND TRAINING

The new economy of education is based on the 1988 Education Reform Act and the Education Act 1992. It embodies a division between those state schools that are no longer maintained by local authorities and receive grants directly from the centre, and those that remain with the local authority, albeit with much more discretion than they used to have over how they spend and budget. Education Secretary John Patten was hinting in early summer 1994 that he might legislate to force all schools to move out of local authority control. Mr Patten was turfed out but the Department for Education announced, in August, that the 1,000th school had been given the go-ahead to opt out. 'A milestone' it said, 'which clearly demonstrates the popularity of self-governing schools'. At that point, some 580,000 pupils were being educated in self-governing schools in England. That is about 18 per cent of pupils of secondary school age and 2 per cent of primary school children. The Government's plan is that, over time, more and more parents and schools will perceive the advantages of grant-maintained status and force the issue. The Government has put in place a mechanism by which after a set proportion of local schools have 'opted out', the Funding Agency rather than the local authority becomes responsible for them all.

GRANT MAINTAINED SCHOOLS FOUNDATION
36 Great Smith Street
London SW1P 3BU
Telephone: 071-233 4666
Director: Andrew Turner

The Government had earlier created the City Technology Colleges, a special class of grant-maintained schools, intended to be showcases for both technology and the involvement of private-sector finance in education. There are currently 15 of them; they are funded directly by the Government. Ministers quickly realised the unit costs of these schools were too high to permit their numbers to grow much, given that the large sums of capital expected from the private sector were slow in materialising.

CITY TECHNOLOGY COLLEGES TRUST
15 Young Street
London W8 5EH
Telephone: 071-376 2511
Chairman: Sir Cyril Taylor
Chief Executive: Kathleen Lund

ADT COLLEGE
100 West Hill
London SW15 2UT
Telephone: 081-877 0357

BACON'S COLLEGE
Timber Pond Road
London SE16 2XB
Telephone: 071-231 4647

BRIT PERFORMING ARTS AND TECHNOLOGY SCHOOL
60 The Crescent,
Croydon CR0 2HN
Telephone: 081-665 5242

BROOKE CITY TECHNOLOGY COLLEGE
Coomb Road
Great Oakley
Corby NN18 8LA
Telephone: 0536-460110

DIXONS BRADFORD CITY TECHNOLOGY COLLEGE
Ripley Street
Bradford BD5 7RR
Telephone: 0274-395140

DJANOGLY CITY TECHNOLOGY COLLEGE
Sherwood Rise
Nottingham NG7 7AR
Telephone: 0602-424422

EMMANUEL COLLEGE
Consett Road
Lobley Hill
Gateshead NE11 0AN
Telephone: 091-460 2099

HABERDASHERS' ASKE'S HATCHAM COLLEGE TRUST
PO Box167
London SE14 5AA
Telephone: 071-277 9333

HARRIS CITY TECHNOLOGY COLLEGE
Maberley Road
Upper Norwood
London SE19 2JH
Telephone: 081-771 2261

JOHN CABOT CITY TECHNOLOGY COLLEGE
Potterwood
Britannia Road
Kingswood
Bristol BS1 2DB
Telephone: 0272-763000

KINGSHURST CITY TECHNOLOGY COLLEGE
PO Box 1017
Cooks Lane
Kingshurst
Birmingham B37 6NZ
Telephone: 021-770 8923

LANDAU FORTE COLLEGE
Fox Street
Derby DE1 2LF
Telephone: 0332-204040

LEIGH CITY TECHNOLOGY COLLEGE
Green Street
Dartford
Kent DA1 1QE
Telephone: 0322-228635

MACMILLAN COLLEGE
PO Box 8
Stockton Road
Middlesborough TS5 4YU
Telephone: 0642-244144

THOMAS TELFORD SCHOOL
Old Park
Telford
Shropshire
Telephone: 0925-200000

Grant-maintained schools are governed on oligarchic lines with the governors inherited from the school before it opted out (minus those governors appointed by the local council) staying on and ensuring others, for example representatives of local business, are subsequently added.

The Government's principal tool in funding the schools is the Funding Agency established in April 1994.

FUNDING AGENCY
Albion Wharf
25 Skeldergate
York YO1 2XL
Telephone: 0904-661608
Chairman: Sir Christopher Benson
Chief Executive: Michael Collier

The agency calculates grants and loans to grant-maintained schools; monitors their spending and conducts value for money studies; it also has to ensure sufficient school places are provided. When, eventually, 75 per cent of pupils in state primary or secondary schools are attending GM schools in any given area, the Secretary of State for Education can order that responsibility for ensuring sufficient schools places passes from the local education authority to the Funding Agency.

At summer 1994, the agency had responsibility, either sole or shared with a local authority for ensuring secondary school places in 44 local education authority areas.

FURTHER EDUCATION FUNDING COUNCIL
Cheylesmore House
Quinton Road
Coventry CV1 3WT
Telephone: 0203-863000
Director: Bob Gunn

Through the 1992 Further and Higher Education Act, the Government wrested control of post-16 education from local authorities entirely, creating a new generation of sixth form and further education colleges answerable to governors and paid for by grants from the Further Education Funding Council. Governors appoint members of governing bodies, though the Secretary of State for Education has the power to appoint additional members.

Until the late 1980s, the Government was the principal provider of training schemes for the young unemployed and older workers without jobs, through the Manpower Services Commission, an early example of an arm's length agency, created in 1973. But the MSC was originally a 'tripartite' body, giving trade unions a voice alongside employers. Its ambitions for young people were often limited to keeping them off the streets but it did succeed in establishing a nation wide programme of youth training which officials and ministers had hoped to dovetail with new vocational qualifications offered under the auspices of the National Council for Vocational Qualifications (an example of a new, 1980s quango).

194

Under the Employment and Training White Paper 1988, training was revolutionised. The MSC was abolished and a new vehicle for training and job schemes set up in the shape of the Training and Enterprise Council, on which local employers would have a leading role under the general supervision of the Department of Employment. Introduced in phases in different parts of the country from April 1990, the 82 English and Welsh TECs represented the Conservatives' faith that business leaders do know best. Two-thirds of TEC members are drawn from private companies, one-third from local authorities, unions and voluntary bodies. In practice TEC chairmen and chairwomen have to be approved by the Secretary of State for Employment or Secretary of State for Wales.

Through them private-sector employers were handed managerial control of key skills and jobs programmes; the TECs also allocate funds on behalf of government initiatives for small firms. They now handle some £2.3 billion of public money a year. The National Audit Office found surpluses of over £200 from providing programmes for the unemployed. 'Surpluses are intended to act as an incentive for TECs to maximise efficiency, increase employer investment and provide TECs as private companies with the reserves they need to protect them from the risk of insolvency ...'

TECs became responsible for organising Youth Training (YT). In England and Wales some 65 per cent of 16-year-olds generally stay on in full-time education at school or college; just under 8 per cent get jobs and the rest become eligible for YT. Costing some £844 million in 1993-4, YT seeks to provide broad vocational education and training mainly for 16 and 17 year olds and to produce 'better qualified young entrants into the labour market'. TECs are responsible for the planning and delivery of YT to meet the needs of their local labour markets.

Payments to TECs, some of which have the status of companies limited by guarantee rather than more conventional public bodies, are calculated on trainee weeks and positive outcomes – that is to say vocational qualifications attained. The Department of Employment contracts with TECs through its regional offices.

TECs inherited staff who had been Department of Employment civil servants who transferred to the TECs on secondment. The Department of Employment assured them they would keep their Whitehall terms and conditions and pension rights. Grievances and career planning were handled as much by the DE as the TECs themselves.

Secondment of civil servants to the TECs is supposed to end by April 1996 but a study by Professor Bob Bennett of the London School of Economics published in 1994 found that many still had no staff of their own. Over 85 per cent of all TEC staff were still on secondment from the Department. Administration costs in TECs appear to be high. Start-up costs for a TEC are of the order of £1.3 million, before any training is done. Meanwhile the annual rate of resignation of TEC directors is about 20 per cent. This has created problems of continuity. Many of these private-sector recruits have been apparently disillusioned about their relative lack of freedom to manage TECs.

TECs' financial systems have been dictated to them by the National Audit

195

Office. The Treasury has restricted TECs' budgets, tying them tightly to targets for training outputs – reducing the scope for TECs to take a wider role in the economic development of their communities.

THE TEC NATIONAL COUNCIL
Chairman: Michael Bett, deputy chairman of British Telecommunications plc.
Secretary: Nigel Chilcott
Address: 10/F Westminster Tower
3 Albert Embankment
London SE1 7SP
Telephone: 071-735 0010

TEC ASSESSORS COMMITTEE
Chair: Sir Anthony Cleaver, Chairman
of AEA Technology
Rex House
4-12 Regent St
London SW1Y 4PE
Telephone: 071-389 6565

AVON TEC
St Lawrence House
29-31 Broad Street
Bristol BS99 7HR
Telephone: 0272-277116
Chairman: Colin Green
Chief Executive: Pat Hall

AZTEC
Manorgate House
2 Manorgate Road
Kingston upon Thames KT2 7AL
Telephone: 081-547 3934
Chairman: David Hill
Chief Executive: Judith Rutherford

BARNSLEY AND DONCASTER TEC
Conference Centre
Eldon Street
Barnsley S70 2JL
Telephone: 0226-248088
Chairman: Peter Wetzel
Chief Executive: Tony Goulbourn

BEDFORDSHIRE TEC
Woburn Court
2 Railton Road
Kempston
Bedfordshire MK42 7PN
Telephone: 0234-843100
Chairman: John Barber
Chief Executive: Diana McMahon

BIRMINGHAM TEC
Chaplin Court
80 Hurst Street
Birmingham B5 4TG
Telephone: 021-622 4419
Chairman: Charles Darby
Chief Executive: David Cragg

BOLTON AND BURY TEC
Clive House
Clive Street
Bolton BL1 1ET
Telephone: 0204-397350
Chairman: Michael Smyth
Chief Executive: Geoff Critchley

BRADFORD AND DISTRICT TEC
Fountain Hall
Fountain Street
Bradford BD1 3RA
Telephone: 0274-723711
Chairman: Judith Donovan
Chief Executive (acting): Mike Lowe

CALDERDALE AND KIRKLEES TEC
Park View House
Woodvale Office Park
Woodvale Road
Brighouse HD6 4AB
Telephone: 0484-400770
Chairman: Jill Wilson
Chief Executive: Alastair Graham

CAMBSTEC
Units 2-3 Trust Court
Chivers Way, The Vision Park
Histon
Cambridge CB4 4PW
Telephone: 0223-235633
Chairman: Robert Mallindine
Managing Director: Alan Maltpress

CENTEC
12 Grosvenor Crescent
London SW1X 7EE
Telephone: 071-411 3500
Chairman: Lord Stockton
Chief Executive: Gwynneth Flower

CENTRAL ENGLAND TEC
The Oaks
Clewes Road
Redditch
Worcestershire B98 7ST
Telephone: 0527-545415
Chairman: Terry Morgan
Chief Executive: Rodney Skidmore

CEWTEC
Block 4
Woodside Business Park
Birkenhead
Wirral L41 1EH
Telephone: 051-650 0555
Chairman: John Conland
Chief Executive: Alan Moody

CILNTEC
80 Great Eastern Street
London EC2A 3DP
Telephone: 071-324 2424

Chairman: David Peake
Chief Executive: Peter Box

COUNTY DURHAM TEC
Valley Street North
Darlington DL1 1TJ
Telephone: 0325-351166
Chairman: Bernard Robinson
Chief Executive: David Hall

**COVENTRY AND
WARWICKSHIRE TEC**
Brandon Court
Progress Way
Coventry CV3 2TE
Telephone: 0203-635666
Chairman: Aaron Jones
Chief Executive: Scott Glover

CUMBRIA TEC
Venture House
Regents Court
Guard Street
Workington
Cumbria CA14 4EW
Telephone: 0900-66991
Chairman: Arthur Sanderson
Chief Executive: Steve Palmer

DEVON AND CORNWALL TEC
Foliot House
Brooklands
Budshead Road
Crownhill
Plymouth PL6 5XR
Telephone: 0752-767929
Chairman: Tim Legood
Chief Executive: John Mannell

DORSET TEC
25 Oxford Road
Bournemouth BH8 8EY
Telephone: 0202-299284
Chairman: Rex Symons
Chief Executive: John Morrison

DUDLEY TEC
Dudley Court South
Waterfront East
Lever Street
Brierly Hill
West Midlands DY5 1XN
Telephone: 0384-485000
Chairman: Philip White
Chief Executive: John Woodall

ELTEC
Red Rose Court
Clayton Business Park
Clayton Le Moors
Accrington
Lancashire BB5 5JR
Telephone: 0254-301333
Chairman: Tony Cann
Chief Executive: Mark Price

ESSEX TEC
Redwing House
Hedgerows Business Park
Colchester Road
Chelmsford
Essex CM2 5PB
Telephone: 0245-450123
Chairman: Roy Lawrence
Chief Executive: Michael Clegg

GLOUCESTERSHIRE TEC
Conway House
33-35 Worcester Street
Gloucester GL1 3AJ
Telephone: 0452-524488
Chairman: John Hazlewood
Chief Executive: Graham Hoyle

GREATER NOTTINGHAM TEC
Marina Road
Castle Marina Park
Nottingham NG7 1TN
Telephone: 0602-413313
Chairman: John Williams
Chief Executive: Jim Potts

GREATER PETERBOROUGH TEC
Unit 4 Blenheim Court
Peppercorn Close
off The Lincoln Road
Peterborough PE1 2DU
Telephone: 0733-890808
Chairman: Philip Salisbury
Chief Executive: Mike Styles

HAMPSHIRE TEC
25 Thackeray Mall
Fareham
Hants PO16 0PQ
Telephone: 0329-230099
Chairman: Alan Philpott
Chief Executive: Max Wilson

HAWTEC
Hazwell House
St Nicholas Street
Worcester WR1 1UW
Telephone: 0905-723200
Chairman: Barrie Carter
Chief Executive: Alan Curless

HEART OF ENGLAND TEC
26-27 The Quadrant
Abingdon Science Park
Abingdon OX14 3YS
Telephone: 0235-553249
Chairman: Julian Blackwell
Chief Executive: Brian McCarthy

HERTFORDSHIRE TEC
45 Grosvenor Road
St Albans
Herts AL1 3AW
Telephone: 0727-813600
Chairman: Philip Groves
Chief Executive: Chris Humphries

HUMBERSIDE TEC
The Maltings
Silvester Square
Silvester Street
Hull HU1 3HL
Telephone: 0482-226491
Chairman: Tony Hailey
Chief Executive: Peter Fryer

KENT TEC
5th Floor
Mountbatten House
28 Military Road
Chatham
Kent ME4 4JE
Telephone: 0634-844411
Chairman: Sir Alastair Morton
Chief Executive: John Forsdyke

LAWTEC
4th Floor
Duchy House
96 Lancaster Road
Preston PR1 1HE
Telephone: 0772-200035
Chairman: Jonathan Taylor
Chief Executive: Tony Bickerstaffe

LEEDS TEC
Belgrave Hall
Belgrave Street
Leeds LS2 8DO
Telephone: 0532-347666
Chairman: Clive Leach
Chief Executive: Derek Pearce

LEICESTERSHIRE TEC
Meridian East
Meridian Business Park
Leicester LE3 2WZ
Telephone: 0533-651515
Chairman: Martin Henry
Chief Executive: David Nelson

LINCOLNSHIRE TEC
Beech House
Witham Park

Waterside South
Lincoln LN5 7JH
Telephone: 0522-567765
Chairman: Paul Hodgkinson
Chief Executive: David Rossington

LONDON EAST TEC
Cityside House
40 Adler Street
London E1 1EE
Telephone: 071-377 1866
Chairman: Dick Goddard
Chief Executive: Susan Fey

MANCHESTER TEC
Boulton House
17-21 Chorlton Street
Manchester H1 3HY
Telephone: 061-236 7222
Chairman: David Compston
Chief Executive: Paul Read

MERSEYSIDE TEC
3rd Floor
Tithebarn House
Tithebarn Street
Liverpool L2 2NZ
Telephone: 051-236 0026
Chairman: Barry Moult
Chief Executive: Linda Bloomfield

METROTEC (WIGAN) LTD
Buckingham Row
Northway
Wigan WN1 1XX
Telephone: 0942-36312
Chairman: Richard Vincent
Chief Executive: Bill Badrock

**MILTON KEYNES AND
NORTH BUCKS TEC**
Old Market Halls
Creed Street
Wolverton
Milton Keynes MK12 5LY
Telephone: 0908-222555
Chairman: Peter Muir
Chief Executive: Michael Hind

199

NORFOLK AND WAVENEY TEC
Partnership House
Unit 10, Norwich Business Park
Whiting Road
Norwich NR4 6DJ
Telephone: 0603-763812
Chairman: Martin Rickard
Chief Executive: John Wooddissee

NORMIDTEC
Spencer House
Dewhurst Road
Birchwood
Warrington WA3 7PP
Telephone: 0925-826515
Chairman: Peter Clarke
Chief Executive: Andrew Gurr

NORTH DERBYSHIRE TEC
Block C
St Marys Court
St Marys Gate
Chesterfield S41 7TD
Telephone: 0246-551158
Chairman: Derrick Penrose
Chief Executive: Stuart Almond

NORTH LONDON TEC
Dumayne House
1 Fox Lane
Palmers Greeen
London N13 4AB
Telephone: 081-447 9422
Chairman: John Wilkinson
Chief Executive: Mike Nixon

NORTH NOTTINGHAMSHIRE TEC
1st Floor Block C
Edwinstone House
High Street
Edwinstone
Notts NG21 9PR
Telephone: 0623-824624
Chairman: Tony Wilkinson
Chief Executive: Pat Richards

NORTH WEST LONDON TEC
Kirkfield House
118-120 Station Road
Harrow
Middx HA1 2RL
Telephone: 081-424 8866
Chairman: Declan O'Farrell
Chief Executive: Roy Bain

NORTH YORKSHIRE TEC
TEC House
7 Pioneer Business Park
Amy Johnson Way
Clifton Moorgate
York YO3 8TN
Telephone: 0904-691939
Chairman: Colin Shepherd
Chief Executive: Roger Grasby

NORTHAMPTONSHIRE TEC
Royal Pavilion
Summerhouse Pavilion
Summerhouse Road
Moulton Park
Northampton NN3 1WD
Telephone: 0604-671200
Chairman: Tony Stoughton-Harris
Chief Executive: Martyn Wylie

NORTHUMBERLAND TEC
Suite 2
Craster Court
Manor Walk Shopping Centre
Cramlington NE23 6XX
Telephone: 0670-713303
Chairman: Bill Clark
Chief Executive: Stephen Cowell

OLDHAM TEC
Meridian Centre
King Street
Oldham OL8 1EZ
Telephone: 061-620 0006
Chairman: Norman Stoller
Chief Executive (acting): Lynne Clough

QUALITEC (ST HELENS) LTD
7 Waterwise Court
Technology Campus
St Helens WA9 1UE
Telephone: 0744-24433
Chairman: Gordon Spencer
Chief Executive: John Gracie

ROCHDALE TEC
St James Place
160-162 Yorkshire Street
Rochdale OL16 2DL
Telephone: 0706-44909
Chairman: Harry Moore
Chief Executive: Anne Martin

ROTHERHAM TEC
Moorgate House
Moorgate Road
Rotherham S60 2EN
Telephone: 0709-830511
Chairman: Giles Bloomer
Chief Executive: Christopher Duff

SANDWELL TEC
1st Floor
Kingston House
438/450 High Street
West Bromwich B70 9LD
Telephone: 021-525 4242
Chairman: Michael Worley
Chief Executive: John Bedingfield

SHEFFIELD TEC
St Mary's Court
55 St Mary's Road
Sheffield S2 4AQ
Telephone: 0742-701911
Chairman: Doug Liversidge
Chief Executive: Keith Davie

SHROPSHIRE TEC
2nd Floor
Hazledine House
Central Square
Telford TF3 4JJ

Telephone: 0952-291471
Chairman: Michael Lowe
Chief Executive: Stephen Jury

SOLOTEC
Lancaster House
7 Elmfield Road
Bromley BR1 1LT
Telephone: 081-313 9232
Chairman: Ralph Ellis
Chief Executive: Chris Hubbard

SOMERSET TEC
Crescent House
3-7 The Mount
Taunton TA1 3TT
Telephone: 0823-321188
Chairman: David Gwyther
Chief Executive: Roger Phillips

SOUTH AND EAST CHESHIRE TEC
PO Box 37
Middlewich Industrial and Business Park
Dalton Way
Middlewich
Cheshire CW10 0HU
Telephone: 0606-734244
Chairman: Tom Booth
Chief Executive: Richard Guy

SOUTH THAMES TEC
200 Great Dover Street
London SE1 4YB
Telephone: 071-403 1990
Chairman: Tim Hoult
Chief Executive: Mike Hanson

SOUTHERN DERBYSHIRE TEC
St Helen's Court
St Helen's Street
Derby DE1 3GY
Telephone: 0332-290550
Chairman: Eric Betsworth
Chief Executive: Joy Street

STAFFORDSHIRE TEC
Festival Way
Festival Park
Stoke on Trent ST1 5TQ
Telephone: 0782-202733
Chairman: Charles Mitchell
Chief Executive: Richard Ward

STOCKPORT-HIGH PEAK TEC
1 St Peters Square
Stockport SK1 1NN
Telephone: 061-477 8830
Chairman: Iain Parker
Chief Executive: Trevor Jones

SUFFOLK TEC
2nd Floor
Crown House
Crown Street
Ipswich IP1 3HS
Telephone: 0473-218951
Chairman: Robin Chesterman
Chief Executive: Mike Bax

SURREY TEC
Technology House
48-54 Goldsworth Road
Woking
Surrey GU21 1LE
Telephone: 0483-728190
Chairman: Colin Harris
Chief Executive: Richard Wormell

SUSSEX TEC
2nd Floor
Electrowatt House
North Street
Horsham
West Sussex RH12 1RF
Telephone: 0403-271471
Chairman: James Stewart
Chief Executive: Malcolm Allen

TEESSIDE TEC
Training and Enterprise House
2 Queen's Square
Middlesborough TS2 1AA
Telephone: 0642-231023

Chairman: Les Bell
Chief Executive: John Howell

THAMES VALLEY ENTERPRISE
6th Floor Kings Point
120 Kings Road
Reading RG1 3BZ
Telephone: 0734-568156
Chairman: Russell Nathan
Chief Executive: Roy Knott

TYNESIDE TEC
Moongate House
5th Avenue Business Park
Team Valley,
Gateshead NE11 0HF
Telephone: 091-491 6000
Chairman: Chris Sharp
Chief Executive: Olivia Grant

WAKEFIELD TEC
Grove Hall
60 College Grove Road
Wakefield WF1 3RN
Telephone: 0924-299907
Chairman: John Wesson
Chief Executive: Geoffrey Badcock

WALSALL TEC
5th Floor
Townend House
Townend Square
Walsall WS1 1NS
Telephone: 0922-32332
Chairman: Peter Burton
Chief Executive: John Hyde

WEARSIDE TEC
Derwent House
New Town Centre
Washington NE38 7ST
Telephone: 091-416 6161
Chairman: John Anderson
Chief Executive: Jules Preston

WEST LONDON TEC
Sovereign Court
15-21 Staines Road
Hounslow TW3 3HA
Telephone: 081-577 1010
Chairman: Anne Hacker
Chief Executive: Phil Blackburn

WIGHT TEC
Mill Court
Furrlongs
Newport
Isle of Wight PO30 2AA
Telephone: 0983-822818
Chairman: Francis Dabell
Chief Executive: Derek Kozel

WILTSHIRE TEC
The Bora Building
Westlea Campus
Westlea Down
Swindon SN5 7EZ
Telephone: 0793-513644
Chairman: John Briffitt
Chief Executive: John Selway

WOLVERHAMPTON TEC
Pendeford Business Park
Wobaston Road
Wolverhampton WV9 5HA
Telephone: 0902-397787
Chairman: David Thompson
Chief Executive: Peter Latchford

HOUSING

Ever since the Conservative government took office in 1979, it has sought to shrink the size of the municipal estate and reduce the role of local authorities as the providers of subsidised housing for rent. The introduction of a statutory right to buy at a discount for local authority tenants (Housing Act 1980; Housing and Building Control Act 1984) was succeeded by measures to stimulate the not-for-profit housing associations not only into building homes, but to take over and manage local authority stock. These measures did change the nature of the housing stock – by the end of 1992, for example, more than two million public-sector tenants in Great Britain had applied to buy their homes and seven out of ten of these had actually made a purchase. But the local authority housing stock remains substantial. Although around two-thirds of the housing stock is now owner-occupied, one in five dwellings in Great Britain is still owned by a local authority; one in ten belong to housing associations. Housing associations in England are supervised by one of the larger quangos, the Housing Corporation.

THE HOUSING CORPORATION
149 Tottenham Court Road
London W1P 0BN
Telephone: 071-393 2000
Chairman: Sir Brian Pearse
Chief Executive: Anthony Mayer

THE NATIONAL FEDERATION OF HOUSING ASSOCIATIONS
175 Gray's Inn Road
London WC1X 8UP
Telephone: 071-278 6571
Chief Executive: Jim Coulter

The Housing Act 1988 gave the Government powers to establish Housing Action Trusts, designed to take over and manage concentrations of rundown local authority housing where a range of physical, social and other problems were proving 'beyond the capacity of the local authority to tackle'. HATs have several statutory objects, including not just improving the condition and management of estates but also wider regeneration initiatives. They are meant to diversify tenure, selling properties into owner occupation or to other landlords. The Department of the Environment pays a annual grant but HATs are meant to attract private-sector finance as far as possible.

The creation of a HAT depends on a local vote. For example on the Stonebridge estate in the London Borough of Brent 65 per cent of residents lodged valid votes in a contest conducted by Electoral Reform Ballot Services. Of this number, 68 per cent of residents voted in favour of the HAT.

After a set period – probably seven years – the HAT should ballot tenants about the future ownership and management of the properties. Housing Action Trusts are established by orders made under the Housing Act 1988. Six have been formed.

HATs are run by boards appointed by the Secretary of State for the Environment though local authorities are expected to nominate about half the members – provided they include residents as well as councillors. Chairs and board members are paid.

CASTLE VALE HOUSING ACTION TRUST
Chairman: Richard Temple Cox
Concorde House, Hawker Drive
Castle Vale, Birmingham B35 7ED
Telephone: 021-776 6784

LIVERPOOL HOUSING ACTION TRUST
Chairman: Paula Ridley
7th Floor, Silkhouse Court
Tithebarn Street
Liverpool L2 2LZ
Telephone: 051-236 5263

NORTH HULL HOUSING ACTION TRUST
Chairman: David Liggins
PO Box 601
Hull HU6 9YZ
Telephone: 0482-472843

STONEBRIDGE HOUSING ACTION TRUST
Chairman: Lucy Robinson
Telephone: 081-961 2096

TOWER HAMLETS HOUSING ACTION TRUST
Chairman: Dr Michael Barraclough
279 Lefevre Walk, Bow
London E3 2RH
Telephone: 081-983 4698

WALTHAM FOREST HOUSING ACTION TRUST
Chairman: John Chumrow
4th Floor, Kirkdale House
Kirkdale Road, Leytonstone
London E11 1HP
Telephone: 081-539 5533

NEW GOVERNMENT OF HEALTH

It is debatable whether Mrs Thatcher ever intended to 'privatise' health care. What she did become determined to do was knock the administration of health into a more business like shape. The inquiry in the early 1980s into the management of the National Health Service led by Sir Roy Griffiths on Mrs Thatcher's behalf laid the basis for what became the 1989 White Paper *'Working for Patients'* and its ambitious plan, still incompletely enacted, to divide the health service up into a new tripartite structure – of doctors, nurses and other health providers; of local health purchasers; and a skeleton framework of health governors in the regions and at the Department of Health. Local authorities had appointed members of the health authorities which existed up to 1982; they now have no formal role in the National Health Service though in recent months some have been arguing that they could make a better job of health purchasing than the health authorities set up for that purpose.

From April 1991 on the pace of change quickened as the NHS bifurcated into purchasing and providing trusts and agencies. At the same time the Government sought to put pressure on both purchasers and providers to improve services to patients, by means of the Patient's Charter (from April 1992), establishing new norms for waiting periods and the way patients are treated by hospital staff.

Formally, the Secretary of State for Health is accountable to Parliament for health, and her agents are the purchasing authorities and the providing agents; the Department oversees the appointment of chairmen and women of district authorities, and of NHS Trusts, and the chairs and non executive members of the regional authorities.

Nomenclature has been changing rapidly. The structure emerging in most areas of England and Wales consists on the purchasing side of new health 'commissions' – often formed from the merger of District Health Authorities and family health services authorities (which formerly supervised general practitioners and similar local services); on the providing side trusts (hospital, ambulance, specialist services) and GPs, a proportion of whom are 'fund-holders', contracting with hospitals to supply patients with services. Meanwhile there still exist Community Health Councils to represent the public interest in the NHS.

NHS Trusts have the freedom to acquire, own and dispose of assets to ensure the most effective use is made of them; make their own cases for capital development direct to the National Health Service Management Executive (NHS top management based in the Department of Health); borrow money within limits for new buildings and equipment; create own management structures; employ own staff, set out terms and conditions of employment; advertise their services within guidelines.

Central bodies remain important in health provision. For example the new National Blood Authority, with 4,500 staff, has taken over from the 13 regional transfusion centres. The NHS transfusion tradition had been one of regional autonomy, leading – it is argued – to a lack of common standards on the coding or testing of blood products.

After politically embarrassing computer and management failure, the Government stepped firmly in to manoeuvre the London Ambulance Service back from control by a free-standing, arm's-length board to its former status as a service run by a regional health authority.

The centre remains extensive. The total manpower costs for the NHS Management Executive in 1992-3 were £29 m. The NHS Service Supplies Authority employs 4,500 people, transferred from NHS regional and district authorities. Other central bodies include the Prescription Pricing Authority, the Medical Advisers' Support Group and the Medicines Research Centre.

The Department of Health retains large reserve powers. The Secretary of State can make directions to trusts as laid down in the NHS and Community Care Act 1990, for example on appointments of consultants and speech therapists, and order the production of accounts.

NATIONAL HEALTH SERVICE MANAGEMENT EXECUTIVE

Quarry House
Quarry Hill
Leeds LS2 7UE

Chief Executive: Alan Langlands (Grade 1). Born: 1952. Educated: Allan Glen's School; University of Glasgow. Joined the NHS in Scotland 1974. Administrator at Middlesex Hospital 1981 before moving to Harrow HA in 1985 and becoming General Manger of North West Thames, 1991.

Director of Planning and Performance Management: Alasdair Liddell. Born: 1949. Educated: University of Oxford. Joined NHS in 1972, serving in administration in Hammersmith and Fulham, and Bloomsbury. Later he became Regional General Manager of East Anglia Region.

Director of Corporate Affairs: John Shaw (Grade 2). Born: 1936. Educated: Loretto School; Worcester College, Oxford. Joined the Church Commissioners in 1960 and moved to the Department of Health and Social Security in 1973.

Medical Director: Dr Graham Winyard

Director of Nursing/Chief Nursing Officer: Yvonne Moores. Born: 1941. Educated: Itchen Grammar; Royal South Hampshire Hospital. Hospital appointments: District Nursing Office N Manchester 1974; chief Nursing Officer Welsh Office 1982.

Director of Finance and Corporate Information: C Reeves

Director of Human Resources: Ken Jarrold (Grade 2). Born 1948. Educated: University of Cambridge. Joined NHS in 1970, serving as an administrator in Gloucester, Cleveland and Nottingham before becoming Chief Executive of Wessex Region.

Director of Research and Development: Professor Michael Peckham (for details *see* Department of Health)

Special authorities, closely monitored by the centre, are responsible for certain hospitals and functions.

SPECIAL HEALTH AUTHORITIES
(with budgets for 1993-4)

NATIONAL BLOOD AUTHORITY
Oak House
Reeds Crescent
Watford
Herts WD1 1QH
Telephone: 0923-212121
£8.649m

NHS SUPPLIES AUTHORITY
Apex Plaza
Forbury Road
Reading RG1 1AX
Telephone: 0734-595085
£16.630m

UK TRANSPLANT SPECIAL SERVICES AUTHORITY
Southmead Road
Southmead
Bristol BS10 5NO
Telephone: 0272-314777
£5.37m (does not include money allocated to the SHA for reimbursing donor hospitals)

BETHLEM ROYAL AND MAUDSLEY
The Maudsley Hospital
Denmark Hill SE5 8AZ
Telephone: 071-703 6333
£36.64m

EASTMAN DENTAL HOSPITAL
256 Gray's Inn Road
London WC12X 8LD
Telephone: 071-837 3646
£9.926m

HAMMERSMITH AND QUEEN CHARLOTTE'S (& ACTON)
Hammersmith Hospital
150 Du Cane Road
London W12 0HS
Telephone: 081-743 2030
£83.64m

MOORFIELDS EYE HOSPITAL
City Road
London EC1V 2PD
Telephone: 071-253 3411
£22.87m

HOSPITALS FOR SICK CHILDREN (GT ORMOND ST AND QUEEN ELIZABETH'S)
Great Ormond Street
London WC1N 3JH
Telephone: 071-405 9200
£67.65m

NATIONAL HEART AND LUNG HOSPITALS (BROMPTON AND LONDON CHEST)
Brompton Hospital
Fulham Road
London SW3 6HP
Telephone: 071-352 8121
£50.56m

NATIONAL HOSPITALS FOR NEUROLOGY AND NEUROSURGERY (QUEEN SQUARE, MAIDA VALE, FINCHLEY AND CHALFONT)
Queen Square
London WC1N 3BG
Telephone: 071-837 3611
£37.30m

ROYAL MARSDEN HOSPITAL (FULHAM AND SUTTON)
Fulham Road,
London SW3 6JJ
Telephone: 071-352 8171
£39.98m

The governance of health also includes an array of organisations, some classified as non-departmental public bodies, with specialist remits. These include

HEALTH EDUCATION AUTHORITY
Hamilton House
Mabledon Place
London WC1H 9TX
Telephone: 071-383 3833
Function: To advise the government on health education.
Chief Executive: Dr Spencer Hagard

THE NATIONAL HEALTH SERVICE ESTATE MANAGEMENT AND HEALTH BUILDING AGENCY
1 Trevelyan Square
Boar Lane, Leeds LS1 6AE
Function: Property advisers and consultants to providers of health care.
Chief Executive: J C Locke

PUBLIC HEALTH LABORATORY SERVICE
PHLS Communicable Disease Surveillance Centre
61 Colindale Avenue
London NW9 5EQ
Telephone: 081-200 6868
Function: To co-ordinate a network of district and hospital based consultants in communicable disease control and public health.

Ninety-six per cent of hospitals and community units had trust status by 1 April 1994, which gave them managerial independence and the ability to set pay and conditions. These 400 or so trusts had turnovers ranging from £15 to £230 million a year; they were responsible for delivering £17 billion of health service care, equivalent to 7 per cent of total government spending. Trusts have been required to earn a return on their capital of 6 per cent, to break even and to operate within external financing limits.

But their financial health has been a subject of continuing controversy. A report in April 1994 suggested one trust in ten faced a parlous financial situation, and increasing numbers were likely to merge. Mergers or takeover by stronger hospitals could be the pattern of the future, resulting from financial imperative. Half were said to be failing to meet one or more of the targets mentioned above. The National Association of Health Authorities and Trusts suggested that one in five trusts might not be financially viable. Mergers thus become inevitable.

But some commentators points out that the health service changes of the past three years could be seen as one of the most wide-ranging organisational restructurings in British industry. In that light, the lack of disasters has been notable. However, there is no hard evidence yet that as a result of these changes hospitals are delivering higher-quality or lower-cost health care.

NHS REGIONAL AUTHORITIES
ANGLIA AND OXFORD

Union Lane
Chesterton
Cambridge CB4 1RF
Telephone: 0223-375375

Old Road
Headington
Oxford OX3 7LF
Telephone: 0865-742277
Chairman: Dr Stuart Burgess
Chief Executive: Barbara Stocking. Age 42. Educated: Universities of Cambridge and Wisconsin. Joined Health Service in 1977, later becoming director of King's Fund Centre. She has written widely on health issues.

BEDFORDSHIRE HA (BEDFORDSHIRE HEALTH COMMISSION)
3 Kimbolton Road
Bedford MK40 2NU
Telephone: 0234-355122
Chief Executive: Miss M E Goose

BEDFORDSHIRE FAMILY HEALTH SERVICES AUTHORITY
65 De Parys Avenue
Bedford
MK40 2TR
Telephone: 0234-354694

BERKSHIRE HA
Prospect Park Hospital
Honey End Lane
Tilehurst
Reading RG3 4EJ
Telephone: 0734-586161

BERKSHIRE FAMILY HEALTH SERVICES AUTHORITY
Pendragon House
59 Bath Road
Reading
RG3 2BA
Telephone: 0734-503094

BUCKINGHAMSHIRE HA
Ardenham Lane
Aylesbury HP19 3DX
Telephone: 0296-394022

BUCKS FAMILY HEALTH SERVICES AUTHORITY
1/7 The Courtyard
Merlyn Centre
Gatehouse Close
Aylesbury HP19 3DP
Telephone: 0296-24626

CAMBRIDGE/HUNTINGDON HEALTH COMMISSION
Fulbourn Hospital,
Fulbourn,
Cambridge CB1 5EF
Telephone: 0223-248074
District General Manager: Dr P A Troop

CAMBRIDGESHIRE FAMILY HEALTH SERVICES AUTHORITY
Vinery Road
Cambridge CB1 3DX
Telephone: 0223-242731

NORFOLK FAMILY HEALTH
SERVICES AUTHORITY
St Mary's House
Duke Street
Norwich NR3 1PH
Telephone: 0603-615726

NORTHAMPTONSHIRE HA
Highfield
Cliftonville Road
Northampton NN1 5DN
Telephone: 0604-34700

NORTHANTS FAMILY HEALTH
SERVICES AUTHORITY
Pyramid Close
Weston Favell
NN3 4PA
Telephone: 0604-406531

NORTH WEST ANGLIA HA
41 Priestgate
Peterborough PE1 1LN
Telephone: 0733-882288
District General Manager: A R Burns

OXFORD HA
Manor House
Headley Way
Oxford OX3 9DZ
Telephone: 0865-741741

OXFORDSHIRE FAMILY HEALTH
SERVICES AUTHORITY
Old Road
Headington
Oxford OX3 7LG
Telephone: 0865-741174

SUFFOLK HA
PO Box 55 Foxhall Road
Ipswich IP3 8NN
Telephone: 0473-712272

SUFFOLK FAMILY HEALTH
SERVICES AUTHORITY
PO Box 7
Ipswich IP3 8NJ
Telephone: 0473-720211

NORTHERN AND YORKSHIRE
Benfield Road
Newcastle upon Tyne NE6 4PY
Telephone: 091-224 6222

The Queen Building
Park Parade
Harrogate HG1 5AH
Telephone: 0423-500066
Chairman: John Greetham
Chief Executive: Professor Liam Donaldson. Age: 44. Educated: University of Bristol.
A qualified medical practitioner who has written widely on health and health policy.

BRADFORD HA
New Mill
Victoria Road
Saltaire
Shipley BD18 3LD
Telephone: 0274-366007
Acting Chief Executive: Melvyn Ellis

BRADFORD FAMILY HEALTH
SERVICES AUTHORITY
Joseph Brennan House
Sunbridge Road
Bradford BD1 2SY
Telephone: 0274-724575

210

CALDERDALE FAMILY HEALTH SERVICES AUTHORITY
Royal Halifax Infirmary
Free School Lane
Halifax HX1 2YP
Telephone: 0422-362946

CLEVELAND FAMILY HEALTH SERVICES AUTHORITY
PO Box 93
West Lane Hospital
Acklam Road
Middlesborough TS5 4EP
Telephone: 0642-812321

CUMBRIA FAMILY HEALTH SERVICES AUTHORITY
Wavell Drive
Rosehill Business Park
Carlisle CA1 2ST
Telephone: 0228-511009

DURHAM FAMILY HEALTH SERVICES AUTHORITY
Green Lane
Old Elvet
Durham DH1 3JX
Telephone: 091-386 2326

EAST RIDING HA
Grange Park Lane
Willoughby
Hull H10 6DT
Telephone: 0482-658822
Chief Executive: George Barnes

GATESHEAD FAMILY HEALTH SERVICES AUTHORITY
Aidan House
Tynegate Precinct
Sunderland Road
Gateshead NE8 3EP
Telephone: 091-478 1111

GRIMSBY AND SCUNTHORPE HA (UNITED HEALTH)
Rawby Road
Brigg

South Humberside DN20 8GS
Telephone: 0652-659659
Chief Executive: Clive Dench

HUMBERSIDE FAMILY HEALTH SERVICES AUTHORITY
Grange Park Lane
Willerby
North Humberside HU10 6DT
Telephone: 0482-650700

KIRKLEES FAMILY HEALTH SERVICES AUTHORITY
Mill Hill
Dalton Green Lane
Huddersfield HD5 9TT
Telephone: 0484-540141

LEEDS HA
St Mary's House
St Mary's Road
Leeds LS7 3JX
Telephone: 0532-781341
Chief Executive: Bill Swan

LEEDS FAMILY HEALTH SERVICES AUTHORITY
Brunswick Court
Bridge Street
Leeds LS2 7RJ
Telephone: 0532-450271

NEWCASTLE HA
Scottish Life House
2-10 Archbold Terrace
Newcastle upon Tyne NE2 1EF
Telephone: 091-281 5011
District General Manager: C Marshall

NEWCASTLE FAMILY HEALTH SERVICES AUTHORITY
2nd Floor
Pearl Assurance House
7 New Bridge Street
Newcastle upon Tyne NE1 8BY
Telephone: 091-261 2884

211

NORTH CUMBRIA HA
Unit 2
The Lakeland Business Park
Lamplugh Road
Cockermouth CA13 0QT
Telephone: 0900-822155

NORTH DURHAM HA
Appleton House
Lanchester Road
Durham DH1 5XZ
Telephone: 091-386 4911
District General Manager:
W A H Holroyd

**NORTH TYNESIDE HA
(NORTH TYNE HEALTH)**
Tynemouth Victoria Jubilee Infirmary
Hawkeys Lane
North Shields NE29 0SF
Telephone: 091-259 6660
District General Manager:
Tony Jamieson

**NORTH TYNESIDE FAMILY
HEALTH SERVICES AUTHORITY**
9 Albion House
Sidney Street
North Shields NE29 0DW
Telephone: 091-258 5865

NORTH YORKSHIRE HA
Sovereign House
Kettlestring Lane
Clifton Moor
York YO3 4XF
Telephone: 0904-693322
Chief Executive: Barry Fisher

**NORTH YORKSHIRE FAMILY
HEALTH SERVICES AUTHORITY**
Third Floor
Ryedale Building
Piccadilly
York YO1 1PE
Telephone: 0904-631345

NORTHUMBERLAND HA
East Cottingwood
Morpeth NE61 2PD
Telephone: 0670-514331
Chairman: R Harbottle
District General Manager: J P O'Brien

**NORTHUMBERLAND FAMILY
HEALTH SERVICES AUTHORITY**
East Cottingwood
Morpeth NE61 2PD
Telephone: 0670-519039

SOUTH DURHAM HA
Appleton House
Lanchester Road
Durham DH1 5XZ
Telephone: 091-386 4911

SOUTH OF TYNE HA
Aidan House
Tynegate Precinct
Sunderland Road
Gateshead NE8 3EP
Telephone: 091-478 3811
District General Manager: W F Worth

**SOUTH TYNESIDE FAMILY
HEALTH SERVICES AUTHORITY**
Horsley Hill Road
South Shields NE33 3BN
Telephone: 091-427 6926

**SUNDERLAND HA
(SUNDERLAND HEALTH
COMMISSION)**
The Children's Centre
Durham Road
Sunderland SR3 4AF
Telephone: 091-522 8671

**SUNDERLAND FAMILY HEALTH
SERVICES AUTHORITY**
11 Humbledon View
Tunstall Road
Sunderland SR2 7RY
Telephone: 091-528 2540

TEES HA (TEES HEALTH)
Poole Hospital
Nunthorpe
Middlesborough TS7 0NH
Telephone: 0642-320000
District General Manager:
I A Donaldson

WAKEFIELD HA
White Rose House
West Parade
Wakefield WF1 1LT
Telephone: 0924-814400
Chief Executive: Keith Salsbury

**WAKEFIELD FAMILY HEALTH
SERVICES AUTHORITY**
White Rose House
West Parade
Wakefield WF1 1LT
Telephone: 0924-814400

WEST YORKSHIRE HA
St Luke's House
Blackmoorfoot Road
Huddersfield HD4 5RH
Telephone: 0484-654777
Chief Executive: Tony P E Wood

NORTH THAMES
40 Eastbourne Terrace
London W2 3QR
Telephone: 071-725 5300
Chairman: Sir William Staveley
Chief Executive: Ron Kerr. Age: 44. Educated: University of London. Joined NHS in 1974 working for South-East London Commissioning Agency and was district general manager in Hounslow and in North Herts.

BARKING AND HAVERING HA
The Grange
Harold Wood Hospital
Gubbins Lane
Harold Wood RM3 0DD
Telephone: 0708-349511
Chief Executive: Stephen Eames

**BARKING AND HAVERING
FAMILY HEALTH SERVICES
AUTHORITY**
St George's Hospital
117 Suttons Lane
Hornchurch RM12 6SD
Telephone: 0708-472011
General Manager: Mike Fox

**BARNET HA (BARNET HEALTH
AGENCY)**
Colindale Hospital
Colindale Avenue
London NW9 5HG
Telephone: 081-200 1555
Chief Executive: Simon Robbins

**BARNET FAMILY HEALTH
SERVICES AUTHORITY**
313 Ballards Lane
London N12 8NQ
Telephone: 081-446 5351
Director of Primary Care:
Peter Gregory

**BRENT AND HARROW HA
(BRENT AND HARROW
COMMISSIONING AGENCY)**
Grace House
Bessborough Road
Harrow HA1 3EX
Telephone: 081-422 6644
Chief Executive: M Whitty

**BRENT AND HARROW FAMILY
HEALTH SERVICES AUTHORITY**
The 21 Building
21 Pinner Road
Harrow HA1 4BB
Telephone: 081-427 7888
General Manager: John Tate

213

CAMDEN AND ISLINGTON HA
110 Hampstead Road
London NW1 2LJ
Telephone: 071-383 4888
Chief Executive: Victoria Hardman

**CAMDEN AND ISLINGTON
FAMILY HEALTH SERVICES
AUTHORITY**
Hobson House
155 Gower Street
London WC1E 6BJ
Telephone: 081-383 4155
General Manager: Caroline Taylor

**EALING, HAMMERSMITH AND
HOUNSLOW HA (EALING,
HAMMERSMITH AND
HOUNSLOW COMMISSIONING
AGENCY)**
1 Armstrong Way
Southall UB2 4SA
Telephone: 081-893 0303
Chief Executive: M Bellamy

EAST LONDON AND THE CITY HA
Tredegar House
97-99 Bow Road
London E3 2AN
Telephone: 071-377 7944
Chief Executive: Peter Coe

**CITY AND EAST LONDON
FAMILY HEALTH SERVICES
AUTHORITY – BOW ROAD**
Tredegar House
97-99 Bow Road
London E3 2AN
Telephone: 081-983 2900

**CITY AND EAST LONDON
FAMILY HEALTH SERVICES
AUTHORITY – NUTTALL STREET**
St Leonard's Hospital
Nuttal Street
London N1 5LZ
Telephone: 071-730 6566

**EAST AND NORTH
HERTFORDSHIRE HA
(HERTFORDSHIRE HEALTH
AGENCY)**
Charter House
Parkway
Welwyn Garden City
Hertfordshire AL8 6JL
Telephone: 0707-390855

**ENFIELD AND HARINGEY
FAMILY HEALTH SERVICES
AUTHORITY**
Holbrook House
Cockfosters Road
Barnet EN4 0DR
Telephone: 081-440 9384
General Manager: Christine Outram

**ESSEX FAMILY HEALTH
SERVICES AUTHORITY**
Carnarvon House
Carnarvon Road
Clacton on Sea CO15 6QD
Telephone: 0255-221222
General Manager: Graham Butland

**HILLINGDON HA (HILLINGDON
COMMISSIONING AGENCY)**
St John's
Kingston Lane
Uxbridge UB8 3PL
Telephone: 0895-258191
Chief Executive: Maureen Dalziel

**HILLINGDON FAMILY HEALTH
SERVICES AUTHORITY**
Cromwell House
43/45 High Street
Ruislip
Middlesex
Telephone: 0895-678383
**Director of Primary and
Community Care:** Bryan Allen

KENSINGTON, CHELSEA AND
WESTMINSTER HA
(KENSINGTON, CHELSEA AND
WESTMINSTER
COMMISSIONING AGENCY)
Bay 10
16 South Wharf Road
London W2 1PF
Telephone: 071-725 1151
Chief Executive: John James

KENSINGTON AND CHELSEA
AND WESTMINSTER FAMILY
HEALTH
Services Authority
88/94 Westbourne Grove
London W2
Telephone: 071-221 9061
Chief Executive: (as above)

NEW RIVER HA
85 Tanners End Lane,
London N18 1SB
Telephone: 081-803 1444
Chief Executive: David Kleeman

NORTH ESSEX HA
8 Collingwood Road
Witham CM8 2TT
Telephone: 0376-516515
Chief Executive: David Johnson

REDBRIDGE AND WALTHAM
FOREST HA
West Wing
(King George Hospital)
713 Eastern Avenue
Newbury Park
Ilford IG2 7SJ
Telephone: 081-518 2299
Chief Executive: Geoffrey Shepherd

REDBRIDGE AND WALTHAM
FOREST FAMILY HEALTH
SERVICES AUTHORITY
Ilford Chambers
11 Chapel Road
Ilford IG1 2QU
Telephone: 081-478 5151
General Manager: Laura Noel

SOUTH ESSEX HA
Charles House
Norsey Road
Billericay CM11 1AG
Telephone: 0277-633006
Chief Executive: K Sharp

NORTH WEST
Gateway House
Piccadilly South
Manchester M60 7LP
Telephone: 061-236 9456
Chairman: Sir Donald Wilson
Regional General Manager: Robert Tinston. Age: 42. Educated University of Edinburgh. Joined NHS as administrative trainee in 1975; was general manager of Leeds General Infirmary and subsequently Chief Executive of Mersey Regional Health Authority and Chief Executive of the Royal Liverpool University Hospital Trust.

BOLTON HA
43 Churchgate
Bolton NL1 1JF
Telephone: 0204-22444
Chief Executive: M Ruane

CHESTER HA
PO Box 41 1829 Building
Countess of Chester Health Park
Liverpool Road
Chester CH2 1UL
Telephone: 0244-365000
Chief Executive: N Large

215

EAST LANCASHIRE HA
31/33 Kenyon Road
Lonshay Estate
Nelson BB9 5S2
Telephone: 0282-619909
Chief Executive: R Crail

LIVERPOOL HA
1st Floor
8 Mathew Street
Liverpool L2 6RE
Telephone: 051-236 4747
Chief Executive: A Doran

MANCHESTER HA
Darbishire House
293a Upper Brook Street
Manchester M13 0FW
Telephone: 061-276 1234
Chief Executive: R Popplewell

MORECAMBE BAY HA
Tenterfield
Brigsteer Road
Kendal LA9 5EA
Telephone: 0539-735565
Chief Executive: B Abram

NORTH CHESHIRE HA
Victoria House
Holloway
Runcorn
Cheshire WA7 4TH
Telephone: 0928-714567
Chief Executive: G Greenfield

NORTH WEST LANCASHIRE HA
Victoria Hospital
Whinney Heys Road
Blackpool FY3 8NR
Telephone: 0253-300000
Chief Executive: P Carter

ROCHDALE HEALTHCARE
Starring Offices
Birch Hill Hospital
Rochdale OL12 9QB
Telephone: 0706-377777
Chief Executive: D Kenny

SALFORD AND TRAFFORD HA
Peel House
Albert Street
Eccles M30 0NJ
Telephone: 061-7897373
Chief Executive: Dr I Greatorex

SEFTON HA
Burlington House
Crosby Road N
Waterloo, Liverpool L22 0QP
Telephone: 051-9205056
Chief Executive: R Wall

SOUTH AND EAST CHESHIRE HA
324 Chester Road
Hartford
Cheshire CW8 2AH
Telephone: 0606-301025
Chief Executive: Mrs Chris Hannah

ST HELENS AND KNOWSLEY HA
Cowley Hill Lane
St Helens WA 10 2AP
Telephone: 0744-33722
Chief Executive: D Fillingham

STOCKPORT HA
Springwood House
Poplar Grove
Hazel Grove
Stockport SK7 5BY
Telephone: 061-419 4600
Chief Executive: P Milnes

WEST PENNINE HA
Westhulme Avenue
Oldham OL1 2PL
Telephone: 061-624 0420
Chief Executive: D Common

WIGAN HA
Bryan House
61 Standishgate
Wigan WN1 1AH
Telephone: 0942-44000
Chief Executive: R Pilkington

WIRRAL HA
Clock Tower
St Catherine's Hospital
Church Road
Birkenhead L42 0LQ
Telephone: 051-6785111
Chief Executive: P Butler

SOUTH AND WEST

King Square House,
26/27 King Square
Bristol BS2 8EF
Telephone: 0272-423271

Highcroft
Romsey Road
Winchester
Hants SO22 5DH
Telephone: 0962-863511
Chairman: Rennie Fritchie
Chief Executive: Ian Carruthers (on secondment from Dorset HA)

BRISTOL AND DISTRICT HA
10 Dighton Street
Bristol BS2 8EE
Telephone: 0272-766600
Chief Executive: Dr G Johnson

AVON FAMILY HEALTH SERVICES AUTHORITY
27 Tyndalls Park Road
Clifton
Bristol BS8 1PT
Telephone: 0272-744242

CORNWALL AND ISLES OF SCILLY HA
John Keay House
St Austell
Cornwall PL25 4DJ
Chief Executive: R Spencer
Telephone: 0726-71777

CORNWALL AND ISLES OF SCILLY FAMILY HEALTH SERVICES AUTHORITY
John Keay House
St Austell
Cornwall PL25 4DJ
Telephone: 0726-77777

DORSET HA (DORSET HEALTH COMMISSION)
Herrison House
Herrison Hospital
Dorchester DT2 9RL
Telephone: 0305-251851
District General Manager (acting):
Ian Titey

DORSET FAMILY HEALTH SERVICES AUTHORITY
Victoria House
Princes Road
Ferndown
Dorset BH22 9JR
Telephone: 0202-893000

217

EXETER AND NORTH DEVON HA
Dean Clarke House
Southernhay East
Exeter EX1 1PQ
Telephone: 0392-411222
Chief Executive: P Jackson

DEVON FAMILY HEALTH
SERVICES AUTHORITY
Cecil Boyall House
Southernhay Rast
Exeter EX1 1RB
Telephone: 0392-75242

GLOUCESTERSHIRE HA
(GLOUCESTERSHIRE HEALTH)
Victoria Warehouse
The Docks
Gloucester GL1 2EL
Telephone: 0452-300222
Chief Executive: Peter Colclough

ISLE OF WIGHT HA (ISLE OF
WIGHT HEALTH COMMISSION)
Whitecroft Hospital
Sandy Lane
Newport IOW PO30 3ED
Telephone: 0983-526011
Chief Executive: Peter Mankin

NORTH AND MID HAMPSHIRE
HA (NORTH AND MID
HAMPSHIRE HEALTH
COMMISSION)
Harness House
Basingstoke District Hospital
Basingstoke RG24 9NB
Telephone: 0256-473202
Chief Executive: Dr Kate Barnard

HAMPSHIRE FAMILY HEALTH
SERVICES AUTHORITY
Friarsgate
Winchester SO23 8EE
Telephone: 0962-853361
General Manager: Alice Harding

PLYMOUTH AND TORBAY HA
Powisland Drive
Plymouth PL6 6AB
Telephone: 0752-793793
Chief Executive: J C Minty

PORTSMOUTH AND SOUTH
EAST HAMPSHIRE HA
St Mary's Hospital
Milton Road
Portsmouth PO3 6AD
Telephone: 0706-822331
Chairman: Dr A J Taylor
Chief Executive: Chris West

SOMERSET HA
Wellsprings Road
Taunton TA2 7PQ
Telephone: 0823-333491
Chief Executive: I N Smith

SOMERSET FAMILY HEALTH
SERVICES AUTHORITY
Osborne House
Trull Road
Taunton TA1 4PX
Telephone: 0823-321381
Chief Executive: Tony Langham

SOUTHAMPTON AND SOUTH-
WEST HAMPSHIRE HA
(SOUTHAMPTON AND SOUTH-
WEST HAMPSHIRE HEALTH
COMMISSION)
Western Hospital
Oakley Road
Southampton SO9 4WQ
Telephone: 0703-780911
Chief Executive: Tony Shaw

WILTSHIRE AND BATH HA
(WILTSHIRE AND BATH HEALTH
COMMISSION)
Newbridge Hill
Bath BA1 3QE
Telephone: 0225-313640
Chief Executive: Trevor Goodman

**WILTSHIRE FAMILY HEALTH
SERVICES AUTHORITY**
Red Gables
Hilperton Road
Trowbridge BA14 7JF
Telephone: 0225-752561
General Manager: Mike Warner

SOUTH THAMES
Thrift House
Collington Avenue
Bexhill-on-Sea TN39 3NQ
Telephone: 0424-730073

40 Eastbourne Terrace
London W2
Telephone: 071-725 2500
Chairman: William Wells
Regional General Manager: Chris Spry. Age 47. Educated: University of Essex. Joined NHS in 1969, serving as administrator in South Nottingham and Newcastle.

**BEXLEY AND GREENWICH HA
(BEXLEY AND GREENWICH
HEALTH)**
221 Erith Road
Bexleyheath DA7 6HZ
Telephone: 081-302 2678
Chief Executive: Michael Kerin

**GREENWICH AND BEXLEY
FAMILY HEALTH SERVICES
AUTHORITY**
Marlow House
109 Station Road
Sidcup DA15 7EU
Telephone: 081-300 3303
Chief Executive: John Potter

CHICHESTER HA
Royal West Sussex Hospital
Broyle Road
Chichester PO19 4AS
Telephone: 0243-781411
Chief Executive: Peter Catchpole

CROYDON HA
Croydon General Hospital
London Road
Croydon CR9 2RH
Telephone: 081-410 3914
Chairman: Adrienne Fresko
Chief Executive: Terry Hanafin

**CROYDON FAMILY HEALTH
SERVICES AUTHORITY**
Windsor House
1270 London Road
Croydon SW16 4DL
Telephone: 081-764 9949
General Manager: Rebecca Sparks

EAST KENT HA
7-9 Cambridge Terrace
Dover CT16 1JT
Telephone: 0304-227227
Chief Executive: Mark Outhwaite

EAST SURREY HA
Maple House
East Surrey Hospital
Three Arch Road
Redhill RH1 5RH
Telephone: 0737-768511
Chief Executive: Ken Gilbert

EAST SUSSEX HA
Westlords
250 Willingdon Road
Eastbourne BN20 9BG
Telephone: 0323-520000
Chief Executive: John Sully

EAST SUSSEX FAMILY HEALTH SERVICES AUTHORITY
Springman House
8 North Street
Lewes BN7 2PB
Telephone: 0273-476262
Chief Executive: Leon Screene

KINGSTON AND RICHMOND HA
17 Upper Brighton Road
Surbiton
Surrey KT6 6LH
Telephone: 081-390 1111
Chief Executive: Dr Richard Gibbs

KINGSTON AND RICHMOND FAMILY HEALTH SERVICES AUTHORITY
Cooper House
40/46 Surbiton Road
Kingston K1 2HX
Telephone: 081-547 0011
Chief Executive: Peter Hornby

MERTON, SUTTON AND WANDSWORTH HA
Harewood House
61 Glenburnie Road
London SW17 7DJ
Telephone: 081-672 5970
Chief Executive: George Gibson

MERTON, SUTTON AND WANDSWORTH FAMILY HEALTH SERVICES AUTHORITY
Wellington House
154-160 Upper Richmond Road
London SW15 2SW
Telephone: 081-788 7255
Chief Executives: Sue Osborn/
Susan Williams

MID DOWNS HA
Linwood
Butlers Green Road
Haywards Heath
West Sussex
RH16 4BE
Telephone: 0444-441666
Chief Executive: Peter Catchpole

MID SURREY HA
West Park Hospital
Horton Lane
Epsom
Surrey KT19 8PB
Telephone: 03727-27811
Chief Executive: Richard Congdon

SURREY FAMILY HEALTH SERVICES AUTHORITY
187 Ewell Road
Surbiton
KT6 6AU
Telephone: 081-399 5133
Chief Executive: Anne Sutcliffe

NORTH WEST SURREY HA
The Ridgewood Centre
Old Bisley Road
Frimley
Surrey GU16 5QF
Telephone: 0276-671718
Chief Executive: Simon Strachan

SOUTH-EAST LONDON HA
No 1 Lower Marsh
London SE1 7RJ
Telephone: 071-716 7000
Chief Executive: Martin Roberts

LAMBETH, SOUTHWARK AND LEWISHAM FAMILY HEALTH SERVICES AUTHORITY
No 1 Lower Marsh
London SE1 7RJ
Telephone: 071-716 7000

SOUTH-WEST SURREY HA
Farnham Road Hospital
Farnham Road
Guildford GU2 5LX
Telephone: 0483-61612
Chief Executive: Crispin Kirkman

WEST KENT HA
Preston Hall
Maidstone ME20 7NJ
Telephone: 0622-710161
Chief Executive: Ruth Carnall

**KENT FAMILY HEALTH
SERVICES AUTHORITY**
11 Station Road
Maidstone ME20 1QH
Telephone: 0622-655000
Chief Executive: Fedelma Winkler

WORTHING DHA
Courtlands
Parklands Avenue
Worthing BN12 4NQ
Telephone: 0903-502566
Chief Executive: Peter Catchpole

**WEST SUSSEX FAMILY HEALTH
SERVICES AUTHORITY**
175 Broyle Road
Chichester PO19 4AD
Telephone: 0243-781441
Chief Executive: Roger Townsend

TRENT

Fulwood House
Old Fulwood Road
Sheffield S10 3TH
Telephone: 0742-630300
Chairman: Keith Ackroyd.
Regional director: Keith MacLean. Age: 47. Joined NHS in 1964, specialising in finance. Was Director of Finance for North Derbyshire Health Authority and director of finance for Yorkshire Region.

BARNSLEY HA
Hillder House
49-51 Gawber Road
Barnsley S75 2PY
Telephone: 0226-730000
District General Manager: R Akroyd

**BARNSLEY FAMILY HEALTH
SERVICES AUTHORITY**
Hillder House
49-51 Gawber Road
Barnsley S75 2PY
Telephone: 0226-730000
General Manager: D Quinney

**DONCASTER HA (DONCASTER
HEALTH)**
White Rose House
Ten Pound Walk
Doncaster DN4 5DL
Telephone: 0302-320111
Chief Executive: C J M Newton

LEICESTERSHIRE HA
Gwendolen Road
Leicester LE5 4QS
Telephone: 0533-588613
Chief Executive: M Froggatt (joint
Chief Executive: Leicestershire Family
Health Services Authority)

LINCOLNSHIRE HA
Cross O'Cliff Court
Bracebridge Heath
Lincoln LN4 2HL
Telephone: 0522-513355
Chief Executive: R G Smith

**LINCOLNSHIRE FAMILY
HEALTH SERVICES AUTHORITY**
Cross O'Cliff Court
Bracebridge Heath
Lincoln LN4 2HL
Telephone: 0522-513355

NORTH DERBYSHIRE HA
Scarsdale Hospital
Newbold Road
Chesterfield S41 7PF
Telephone: 0246-231255
District General Manager:
C Fewtrell

**DERBYSHIRE FAMILY HEALTH
SERVICES AUTHORITY**
Derwent Court
Stuart Street
Derby DE1 2FZ
General Manager: K A Houghton

NORTH NOTTINGHAMSHIRE HA
Ransom Hospital
Rainworth
Mansfield NG21 0ER
Telephone: 0623-22515
Chief Executive: N Clifton

NOTTINGHAM HA
Forest House
Berkeley Avenue
Nottingham NG3 5AF
Telephone: 0602-691691
District General Manager:
Dr I P Reynolds

**NOTTINGHAMSHIRE FAMILY
HEALTH SERVICES AUTHORITY**
111 The Ropewalk
Nottingham NG1 5EP
Telephone: 0602-473473

ROTHERHAM HA
220 Badsley Moor Lane
Rotherham S65 2QU
Telephone: 0709-382647
Chief Executive: J G Hinchcliffe
(joint with Rotherham Family Health
Services Authority)

SHEFFIELD HA
Westbrooke House
Sharrow Vale Road
Sheffield S11 8EU
Telephone: 0742-670333
Chief Executive: Ms C Hamlyn (joint
with Sheffield Family Health Services
Authority)

**SHEFFIELD FAMILY HEALTH
SERVICES AUTHORITY**
Brincliffe House
90 Osborne Road
Sheffield S11 9BD
Telephone: 0742 588211

SOUTHERN DERBYSHIRE HA
Boden House
Main Centre
Derby DE1 2PH
Telephone: 0332-363971
District General Manager: B S Blissett

WEST MIDLANDS

Arthur Thomson House
146 Hagley Road
Birmingham B16 9PA
Telephone: 021-456 1444
Chairman: Bryan Baker
Chief Executive: Brian Edwards. Age: 52. He worked in the NHS for 30 years, visiting professor at the University of Keele.

COVENTRY HA
Christchurch House
Greyfriars Lane
Coventry
CV1 2GQ
Telephone: 0203-224055
Chief Executive:
Chris Howgrave-Graham

COVENTRY FAMILY HEALTH SERVICES AUTHORITY
Parkshire House
Quinton Road
Coventry CV1 2NJ
Telephone: 0203-553344

DUDLEY HA
12 Bull Street
Dudley DY1 2DD
Telephone: 0384-256911
Chief Executive: H T Foster

DUDLEY FAMILY HEALTH SERVICES AUTHORITY
2nd Floor
East Wing
Falcon House
6 The Minories
Dudley DY2 8PG
Telephone: 0384-239376

HEREFORDSHIRE HA
Victoria House
Eign Street
Hereford HR4 0AN
Telephone: 0432-272012
District General Manager: D Caldwell

HEREFORD AND WORCESTER FAMILY HEALTH SERVICES AUTHORITY
99 High Street
Worcester WR1 2HP
Telephone: 0905-25881

NORTH BIRMINGHAM HA (NORTH BIRMINGHAM PURCHASING HEALTHCARE CONSORTIUM)
1 Vernon Road
Edgbaston
Birmingham B16 9SA
Telephone: 021-456 5566
Chief Executive: Graham Coomber

NORTH STAFFORDSHIRE HA
Princes Road
Hartshill
Stoke on Trent
Telephone: 0782-715444
Chief Executive: R T Priestley

STAFFORDSHIRE FAMILY HEALTH SERVICES AUTHORITY
Britannia House
6/7 Eastgate Street
Stafford ST16 2NJ
Telephone: 0785-56341

NORTH WORCESTERSHIRE HA
The Croft
Sutton Park Road
Kidderminster DY11 6JJ
Telephone: 0562-824711
Chief Executive: Malcolm Cooper

SANDWELL HA
PO Box 1953
Lewisham Street
West Bromwich B71 4NA
Telephone: 021-553 6151
Chief Executive: Neil Lockwood

SANDWELL FAMILY HEALTH
SERVICES AUTHORITY
Kingston House
438 High Street
West Bromwich B70 9LD
Telephone: 021-553 1774

SHROPSHIRE HA
Cross Houses Hospital
Cross Houses
Shrewsbury SY5 6JN
Telephone: 0743-52277
Chief Executive: Colin Hayton

SHROPSHIRE FAMILY HEALTH
SERVICES AUTHORITY
Abbeydale
39 Abbey Foregate
Shrewsbury SY2 6BN
Telephone: 0743-23515

SOLIHULL HA
21 Poplar Road
Solihull B91 3AH
Telephone: 021-704 5191
Chief Executive: Colin Jackson

SOLIHULL FAMILY HEALTH
SERVICES AUTHORITY
Clarendon House
High Street
Solihull B91 3QP
Telephone: 021-704 2555

SOUTH BIRMINGHAM HA
27 Highfield Road
Edgbaston
Birmingham B15 3DP
Telephone: 021-456 5600
Chief Executive: Stuart Dickens

BIRMINGHAM FAMILY HEALTH
SERVICES AUTHORITY
Aston Cross
Rocky Lane
Birmingham B6 5RQ
Telephone: 021-333 4444

SOUTH STAFFORDSHIRE HA
Mellor House
Corporation Street
Stafford ST16 3SR
Telephone: 0785-52233
Chief Executive: Dr J A Sorrell

WALSALL HA
Lichfield House
27-31 Lichfield Street
Walsall WS1 1TE
Telephone: 0922-720255
Chief Executive: J Chandra

WALSALL FAMILY HEALTH
SERVICES AUTHORITY
Greybury House
Bridge Street
Walsall WS1 1ET
Telephone: 0922-29861

WARWICKSHIRE HA
Lewes House
Heath End Road
Nuneaton CV10 7QX
Telephone: 0203-351122
Chief Executive: Mrs P S Stansbie

WARWICKSHIRE FAMILY
HEALTH SERVICES AUTHORITY
Westgate House
Market Street
Warwick CV34 4DH
Telephone: 0926-493491

WOLVERHAMPTON HA
New Cross Hospital
Wolverhampton WV10 0QP
Telephone: 0902-307721
Chief Executive: Michael Jackson

WOLVERHAMPTON FAMILY
HEALTH SERVICES AUTHORITY
Upper Ground Floor
St John's House
St John's Square
Wolverhampton WV2 4BP
Telephone: 0902-20281

WORCESTER AND DISTRICT HA
Isaac Maddox House
Shrub Hill Road
Worcester WR1 9RW
Telephone: 0905-763333
Managing Director Jim Watts

NATIONAL HEALTH SERVICE TRUSTS

NATIONAL ASSOCIATION OF HEALTH AUTHORITIES AND TRUSTS
Birmingham Research Park,
Vincent Drive,
Birmingham B15 2SQ
Telephone: 021-471 4444
Director: Philip Hunt

**ASSOCIATION OF COMMUNITY HEALTH COUNCILS FOR ENGLAND
AND WALES**
30 Drayton Park
London N5 1PB
Telephone: 071-609 8405
Function: Established under statutory instrument to provide a forum for the exchange of views between the CHCs, which exist to provide a forum for the expression of public views on health administration.
Director: Toby Harris

NHS TRUST FEDERATION
3 Robert Street
London WC2N 6BH
Telephone: 071-895 8823
Director: Ross Tristem

6
THE EUROPEAN STATE

The Treaty of Maastricht, which was signed by the 12 member states of the European Community in February 1992, and which came into effect in Britain in November 1993, marked a profound turning point in the evolution of European co-operation. Maastricht simultaneously augments the Community's power by extending its competence into areas not hitherto embraced by existing treaties. These include defence, economic and monetary union, and environmental protection. The treaty also imposes limits on the scope of Community initiatives by enshrining the principle of subsidiarity, while at the same time transforming 58 million British Crown subjects into citizens of the new European Union.

Much of the national debate about this development has focused on whether Britain's much vaunted 'national sovereignty' is being surreptitiously eroded by federalists plotting in Brussels to breathe new life into some sort of Napoleonic vision of European integration. Surprisingly, comparatively little attention has been paid to how the Community's institutional structure functions, and how it has been altered by the Maastricht treaties. More alarmingly, however, even less attention has been paid to how Britain fits into that institutional structure, and how it might better organise its own institutions to ensure that British interests are more effectively catered for. Yet Britain's class of administrative civil servants have been working on a routine basis alongside Brussels officials and civil servants from other member states, on a wide range of policy issues, for many years.

Newspaper editors and broadcasters have long kept their readers and viewers amused with hoary tales about attempts by 'barmy Brussels bureaucrats' on the rampage, trying to ban dogs in public houses, abolish sawdust on butchers' floors, and prohibit the sale of round cheeses. Even among the more serious commentators, the debate about the destiny of Europe has been curiously one-dimensional. Arguments about the implications of such vital issues as economic and monetary union are, of course, essential. Too often, however, Britain seems to arrive at these debates late, concentrates excessive amounts of effort discussing them once the horse has bolted, and then compounds this error by failing to devote sufficient – if any – attention to anticipating new developments approaching on the distant horizon. Ironically, it is usually those who complain most about creeping Euro-federalism who display the greatest ignorance about how the European Community or Union works. But Europe's institutions are transparent, if a little complex, and there is no substitute for mastering them in pursuit of Britain's long-term national interest.

THE ORIGINS OF EUROPEAN UNION

The idea of a Europe-wide system of government can be traced back to the medieval concept of a united Christendom. Scholars such as Aquinas and Erasmus, for example, thought of themselves as European, and moved freely between Europe's flourishing universities. The Quaker William Penn, just a little prematurely, even proposed the establishment of a European Parliament. For the most part, however, European unification has generally meant unification by coercion, whether by Charlemagne, Napoleon or Hitler. But it was the last of these upheavals which precipitated an unprecedented desire among continental political leaders to rise above Europe's destructive national rivalry by pooling their sovereignty and binding Germany in a democratic Europe. This post-war supranational enterprise has its roots in the 1948 Benelux Union between Belgium, The Netherlands and Luxembourg. Over a period of six years it grew into a Community of Six: Benelux, France, West Germany and Italy. It was given added impetus by the emerging Superpowers: positive support from the United States in the form of the Marshall Aid programme to foster European reconstruction; negative support from the former Soviet Union in the form of an armed menace (real or imagined) pushing Western Europe closer together for common protection.

Britain, despite Winston Churchill's rhetoric about the need for a united Europe, remained aloof. The reasons for this detachment are bound up with Britain's peculiar wartime experience. But they also go a long way to explain current British attitudes towards European integration. As Vernon Bogdanor, a reader in government at Oxford University, highlighted in a lecture in December 1993, the founders of the European experiment were motivated by a reaction against nationalism. Britain, on the other hand, saw its 'island home' as the fortress which kept it safe from invasion. Consequently, there was little incentive or reason to restrain British nationalism or confine it in supranational European institutions.

As a result, he observed: 'Although we joined the European Community over twenty years ago, our basic attitudes have changed very little. We remain as far as ever from sharing the psychology of the other member states. In particular, we find it difficult to grasp the importance of the principle of power-sharing, the fundamental leitmotif of Community institutions. For the Community is based not only upon a division of powers between itself and member states, but also upon a separation of powers within its own institutions – the Commission, the Council of Ministers and the European Parliament.' This observation is misleading in that it fails to acknowledge the extent to which continental Europeans have exhibited great anxieties about the loss of national sovereignty inherent in increased European co-operation. But it is none the less true that most British politicians, by contrast, seem to have been pre-occupied with the concept of the 'sovereignty of

Parliament'. As a result, they are almost incapable of recognising, let alone accommodating, the principle of power-sharing.

But power-sharing was the foundation stone on which Jean Monnet and Robert Schuman, the French architects of the new Europe, laboured to build the European Community. Like many Frenchmen, Monnet and Schuman feared that Germany would once again dominate Europe, through its possession of key coal and iron industries in the Saarland, the source of much bitter rivalry in the past. Their plan for a European Coal and Steel Community, to oversee these industries, came to fruition in 1952, and was joined by Italy and Benelux. In 1955, the Six began work on a new treaty, laying the foundations for the European Atomic Energy Commission, and the European Economic Community, which was signed in Rome in 1957. All three Communities, the European Coal and Steel Community (ECSC), the European Atomic Energy Commission (Euratom), and the European Economic Community (EEC) were merged in 1967, giving rise to the European Communities. But in practice, it was the EEC, later shortened to European Community or EC, which really mattered.

Because of the stability of the post-war Franco-German rapprochement, sustained largely by the personal relationship between Charles de Gaulle, the French President, and Konrad Adenauer, the German Chancellor, the EC made rapid progress towards the realisation of its first goal: the removal of all internal tariffs and the creation in 1968 of a common external tariff to protect the nascent common market. It also fulfilled the Treaty of Rome's provision for a Common Agricultural Policy, designed to protect and foster European agriculture. But a series of early attempts to honour the treaty's goal of laying 'the foundations of an ever closer union among the peoples of Europe ... to ensure economic and social progress by common action to eliminate the barriers which divide Europe', proved more difficult to realise. Nothing eventually came of the 1961 Fouchet Plan for a joint foreign policy, the 1970 Werner Plan for economic and monetary union, and the 1976 Tindemans Plan for European Union. Unlike old soldiers, however, plans for increased European integration refuse to fade away, and the subsequent history of the Community has been a history of lurches towards the original goal of the Treaty of Rome.

The centripetal allure that the Community exercised on member states, including Britain, became apparent at the beginning of the 1960s. Under Harold Macmillan's premiership, Britain first decided to apply for full membership in 1961, barely a year after taking the lead in setting up the rival European Free Trade Association (EFTA). This application was rejected by de Gaulle in 1963 on the grounds that Britain was an Atlantic not a European power – much to the irritation of the other member states. Britain renewed its application under Harold Wilson in 1966. This was again vetoed by de Gaulle. The third and final application was made under the premiership of Edward Heath. This time he succeeded in bringing Britain into the Community in 1973 (a decision ratified by popular referendum under Harold Wilson's premiership in 1975), along with Denmark and Ireland. Greece joined in 1981, and Spain and Portugal followed in 1986. Following the anticipated accession of Finland, Norway, Sweden and Austria in January 1995, membership will be increased to 16, and further accessions from central and possibly eastern Europe are expected around the turn of the century.

By the early 1980s, however, it was clear that the Community had lost its way. The early enlargements had proved difficult to digest, both financially and institutionally. The Common Agricultural Policy had become bloated and unmanageable as the system of subsidies for both production and storage gave rise to huge agricultural surpluses, ridiculed as food mountains. The twin oil crises of the 1970s appeared to have brought an end to the boom years of the 1950s and 1960s. Increased national rivalries left the Community's decision-making apparatus in a state of acute paralysis. In short, the EC was suffering from an absence of overall direction, guidance and leadership.

THE SINGLE EUROPEAN ACT

In January 1985, Jacques Delors, the new European Commission President, who was destined to become the first French politician to become a household name in Britain since de Gaulle, embarked upon a tour of European capitals to sound out opinion on four ways of lifting the Community out of this impasse. These were: the revival of the idea of a defence union; the revival of the idea of monetary union; reform of the Community's institutional structure; and the completion of the common, or as it later became known, the internal market. Consensus was achieved on the last goal, although that quickly came to embrace all the other suggestions as well. Problems began, however, when Delors insisted that the completion of the internal market would require a mass of new legislation which could only be enacted by the deadline if the Treaty of Rome was reformed. Herein lie the origins of the Single European Act.

The logic behind Delors' idea was simple and far-reaching. Previous attempts to create a common market by harmonising Community business standards and practices had repeatedly come up against the deep-rooted national instincts to protect home markets from external competition. A ruling by the European Court of Justice in 1979, in the Cassis de Dijon case, offered a solution. The case arose after a complaint by a German trader that he had been prohibited from importing Cassis de Dijon, the basis of a popular aperitif called kir, because the cassis allegedly did not conform to national standards for liqueurs. But the court ruled that Bonn could only prevent the import of the French product if it could prove that it was harmful to health or contravened tax or consumer protection laws. It could not.

In formulating their new plan for the internal market, Delors and his co-Commissioners seized on the 'Cassis de Dijon Principle' which laid down that goods (and services) should be allowed to circulate freely around the Community providing they conformed to commonly agreed standards. With this principle in mind, Lord Cockfield, Britain's senior Commissioner, drafted the Internal Market White Paper after the Milan Summit in June 1985. This listed some 300 separate pieces of legislation designed to eliminate the technical, physical and fiscal barriers to intra-Community trade, through the extension of majority voting (a more detailed account of this process can be obtained from *The Times Guide to the Single European*

229

Market). The Single European Act, which was endorsed at the Luxembourg Summit in December 1985, laid down that: 'The Community shall adopt measures with the aim of progressively establishing the internal market over a period expiring on December 31 1992 ... The internal market shall comprise an area without internal frontiers in which the free movement of goods, persons, services and capital is ensured ...' In the course of 1987, the Single European Act, which involved a partial loss of national sovereignty (more accurately described as a pooling of sovereignty) to the Community, was ratified in all member states, including Britain.

But the impetus towards the realisation of the original aspirations of the Community in the form of the 1992 programme also breathed new life into the related goals of economic and monetary union, political union, and institutional reform. The decision to proceed with plans for economic and monetary union was taken at the Strasbourg Summit in December 1989. At the Dublin Summit in June 1990, it was also decided to press ahead with political union and institutional reform. As with the Single European Act, the preparatory work was undertaken by an inter-governmental conference (IGC). In fact two IGCs were proposed, to run in parallel and deal with two reforms – one on political union and the other on economic and monetary union. The results were presented to the Maastricht Summit in December 1991, and finally signed by all Community heads of state or government in February 1992. The result of the Maastricht negotiations was a disappointment for the advocates of European federalism, partly because Britain succeeded in having the word 'federal' dropped from the final text of the treaty on political union, but also because of the UK's ability to negotiate an 'opt out' clause from the creation of a single European currency by 1999. In addition, Britain prevented the so-called Social Chapter, extending the Community's competence into social legislation, from being incorporated into the Treaty on Political Union (it exists as a separate protocol signed by the Eleven). None the less, Britain retains the option to 'opt in' to the single currency, subject to Parliament's approval.

THE MAASTRICHT TREATIES
Maastricht heralds a new stage in the process of European integration set in motion by the original Treaty of Rome. The new European Union (EU) is based on the existing structure of the European Community. This is known as the Treaty of Rome 'pillar'. But it has been augmented by the creation of new institutional structures dealing with the creation of a common foreign and security policy on the one hand, and a common interior and justice policy on the other. These are known as the non-Treaty of Rome pillars – hence the so-called three pillars. Strictly speaking, foreign and interior policy is not part of the EC but part of the EU as these issues are an inter-governmental responsibility and do not fall within the competence of the Commission. The distinction is important for member states such as Britain which are reluctant to see the Commission's powers of initiative extended into new policy-making areas. For the sake of simplicity, however, all three pillars tend to be referred to as the EU.

230

The Treaty on Economic and Monetary Union, which comes under the Treaty of Rome pillar of the Community's new tripartite structure, is seen as the core of the Maastricht agreements. Under its provisions, progress towards full economic and monetary union (EMU) is envisaged in three distinct but cumulative stages. Stage One began in July 1990, with the beginnings of increased co-operation and co-ordination between the member states in the fields of economic and monetary policy. Stage One was also intended to strengthen the role of the European Monetary System, boost the use of European Currency Unit (Ecu), and extend the work of the Committee of Central Bankers. But the virtual collapse of the EMS in the autumn of 1992 raised severe doubts among observers that the EMU timetable can be adhered to.

Stage Two begins with the establishment of the European Monetary Institute (EMI) in January 1994, designed to further strengthen co-operation between European Central Banks, boost co-ordination of monetary policies of member states, and oversee the development of the Ecu. In addition, the EMI is responsible for preparing the way for Stage Three of EMU by establishing the 'regulatory, organisational and logistical framework' for the proposed European System of Central Banks (ESCB) by December 1996. The date for Stage Three, including the introduction of the ECU as a common currency, should be fixed during 1997. But if no date has been agreed, the treaty lays down that 'the third stage will start "irrevocably" in January 1999'. The irrevocability clause may, however, be regarded as a working assumption rather than any iron-clad guarantee that EMU will take place in accordance with the timetable set at Maastricht.

The Treaty on Political Union defines the creation of a common foreign and security policy as being 'central' to the future development of the EU. The treaty makes it incumbent on member states to assert the identity of the EU on the international stage 'through the implementation of a common foreign and security policy which shall include the eventual framing of a common defence policy'. The new common foreign and security policy is to be developed through the inter-governmental procedures of the Council of Ministers, although both the European Commission and the European Parliament are to be consulted. The new policy will cover all questions related to the security of the Union. This includes the framing of a common defence policy 'which might in time lead to a common defence'. The Western European Union (WEU), founded in 1955 to provide a defence dimension to the nascent process of European integration but which became moribund because of the success of the 1949 North Atlantic Treaty Organisation (NATO), now becomes 'the defence component of the Union'. It has moved from London to Brussels.

Under the Treaty on Political Union, the new common interior and justice policy embraces a wide range of issues, including asylum policy, the policing of external borders, immigration, combating drugs trafficking and fraud, judicial co-operation in civil and criminal affairs, and customs and police co-operation. Initiatives can be taken in any of these areas by the Council of Ministers, acting on the basis of majority voting where agreed, effective from January 1996. The European Commission is to be associated with decisions taken in each area, while the European Parliament must be kept fully informed. However, Council must decide unanimously, on the basis of a proposal from the Commission, which Third World countries require a visa to enter the EU. Finally, the common interior and justice policy also provides for the creation of Europol, a Union-wide system for exchanging information between European police forces.

The Treaty on European Union also introduces the concept of Union Citizenship, defines the limits of Community action through the principle of subsidiarity, and augments the powers of the European Parliament. From the day the Maastricht treaties were ratified, 'every person holding the nationality of a member shall be a citizen of the Union', entitling him or her to move and reside freely within the territory of the member states; granting the right to stand as a candidate in local elections outside the country of origin; granting a similar right to vote and stand as a candidate for the European Parliament; entitling everyone to diplomatic or consular protection from any member state, and conferring on him or her a right to petition the European Parliament or Ombudsman to seek redress of grievance.

Following the growing clamour over what Douglas Hurd, the Foreign Secretary, described as the Community's increasing intervention in the 'nooks and crannies' of national life, Article 3b of the Treaty on Political Union lays down that for policy areas outside the Community's exclusive jurisdiction, it will act 'only if and in so far as the objectives of the proposed action cannot be sufficiently achieved by the member states'. This is the famous so-called principle of 'subsidiarity'. This principle is, however, a double-edged sword. For while Maastricht has put a brake on the centralising tendency of the EU in certain respects by drawing a line between the competences of the EU and national governments, it has done nothing to decide on how competences are distributed within member states between national, regional and local government. Nor could it. However, the Maastricht decision to create a new Committee of the Regions could lead to growing pressures within Britain for greater devolution of power from Westminster to the regional and local level.

The Treaty on Political Union also enhances the powers of the European Parliament (EP). The EP is granted new powers of joint decision-making with the Council of Ministers in 13 areas of legislative activity, including the internal market, the right of establishment, labour mobility, research and development, trans-European networks (transport and communications), training, culture, consumer affairs and environmental protection.

THE EUROPEAN COUNCIL

The European Council, which came into being in 1974, partly in an attempt to overcome the decision-making impasse of the Council of Ministers, is a body made up of national presidents, prime ministers, and foreign ministers (hence the formal reference to the heads of state and government in summit communiques) which is responsible for mapping out the overall direction of the Community on contentious issues such as the Common Agricultural Policy, the annual budget and the Community's relations with the rest of the world. Because European Councils, or summits, were not formally provided for by the Treaty of Rome, the European Council is not, strictly speaking, a Community institution. But its bi-annual and extraordinary meetings or summits were, however, formally recognised by the Single European Act.

European Councils, which meet behind closed doors, have frequently been criticised for being non-democratic and unaccountable. But its members invariably announce their progress to the international media after each session, and report back to their national parliaments or assemblies on their decisions. European Councils are normally held every six months in whichever country holds the rotating presidency of the Council of Ministers. Extraordinary summits are usually convened when the Community is confronted by an internal or external crisis, as occurred with the Brussels Summit in February 1988 (called to solve the Community's budgetary crisis), or the Rome Summit in October 1990 (called to discuss aid to the former Soviet Union – but which ended up setting a timetable for economic and monetary union).

THE COUNCIL OF MINISTERS

Council Secretariat
Secretary General: Doctor Jürgen Trumpf
Function: Co-ordination of Council business
Address in Brussels: Rue de la Loi 170, B-1048 Brussels, Belgium
Telephone: 010 322-234 6111
Address in Luxembourg: Plateau du Kirchberg, L-2929 Luxembourg
Telephone: 010 352-430 011

Under the provisions of the Treaty of Rome, the Council of Ministers is the effective decision-maker of the European Community. It does not sit in permanent session, although it does have its own permanent secretariat with some 2,000 staff, and a Committee of Permanent Representatives (referred to by its French acronym COREPER) made up of member states' ambassadors to the Community, who collectively are responsible for taking the day-to-day decisions when Council is not in session, and preparing the workload for when it is. Sir John Kerr, the British Ambassador to Brussels, is the current head of the United Kingdom's Permanent Representation, known as UKRep.

The Council of Ministers meets regularly at the Charlemagne building in Brussels or at the Kirchberg in Luxembourg (only during April, June and October) in some two dozen formats, ranging from foreign ministers to agriculture ministers, and from environment ministers to trade ministers. Over time, ministers working together in a particular Council will get to know each other quite intimately, and sometimes seem to take on the appearance of a European government. Ultimately, however, all ministers, whatever their nationality, tend to feel that they owe their first duty of loyalty to their respective national electorates. Once back home from a Council meeting in Brussels or Luxembourg, they invariably disguise the extent to which they co-operate in the European cause, and emphasise instead the role they have played, whether imagined or real, in defending the national interest.

The Council of Ministers is chaired by each member state in turn for a period of six months, and it is responsible for organising the work of the individual Councils, setting priorities and building compromises. This rotating chairmanship is referred to as the presidency of the Council of Ministers, and the President of the Council is the head (President or Prime

Minister) of whichever country holds the rotating presidency at any given time. Traditionally, the presidency has been held by the member states in alphabetical order (in the language of each member state). Following a Council decision in December 1993, however, it was agreed that when the Accession Treaty bringing Austria, Norway, Finland and Sweden into the Community comes into force, and after the French and Spanish presidencies in 1995, the office of President will be held by the member states in the following order: Italy, Ireland, Netherlands, Luxembourg, United Kingdom, Austria, Norway, Germany, Finland, Portugal, France, Sweden, Belgium, Spain, Denmark, Greece. Therefore, Britain, which last held the presidency in the second half of 1992, will not hold it again until the first six months of 1998.

The primary task of the Council of Ministers, in its various forms, is to examine the legislative proposals put forward by the European Commission, and to amend, accept or reject them, in conjunction with the European Parliament. Commission proposals are usually examined first by COREPER. These meetings are attended by a representative of the Commission. When COREPER agrees unanimously on a particular measure, it is endorsed by Council on the nod, appearing on the agenda as what is known in the jargon as an 'A Point'. If COREPER cannot reach a compromise, a report is generally drawn up outlining which elements of the Commission's proposal have been agreed and which are still in dispute, and the issue is then passed up to Council for resolution. Ministers then arrive in Brussels or Luxembourg, flanked by civil servants from their respective departments, who try to thrash out a compromise.

As the number of the Community's competences have been extended, more and more home civil servants have found themselves drawn into the activities of Brussels. Indeed, in a speech describing the challenges facing Britain's Civil Service given to Leicester University in April 1993, Sir Robin Butler, the Cabinet Secretary and Head of the Home Civil Service, pointed out that: 'The days are long gone when only a handful of departments such as the Ministry of Agriculture and the Department of Trade and Industry had to worry about the EC and its doings: almost every department of the Civil Service now quite regularly has to deal with the issues arising from Commission directives, rulings of the European Court of Justice, and so on.' Anticipating the consequences of increased co-operation between the national and the supra-national bureaucracy, he added: 'This relationship will clearly continue to grow, and I believe the gradual effect of inter-acting closely with other European bureaucracies will be profound.'

The Single European Act saw the introduction of qualified majority voting (QMV) on a wide range of issues which come before Council (with key exceptions such as fiscal policy). Decisions are much easier to reach than had been the case hitherto. Issues can now be decided by a system of voting under which each member state is given a number of votes more or less consonant with its size and importance. Britain, therefore, wields ten votes, along with Germany, France and Italy; Spain has eight votes; Belgium, Greece, The Netherlands and Portugal have five votes each; Denmark and Ireland wield three votes each, and Luxembourg can cast only two votes.

Consequently, of the 76 votes available, 54 are needed to obtain what is referred to as a qualified majority. At the same time, however, only 23 votes have to be mustered to obtain the so-called 'blocking minority' needed to prevent Commission proposals from passing into law. Prior to the accession of Austria, Norway, Finland and Sweden, a blocking minority could be obtained by the combination of three large states, two large and one medium or small state, or five medium states. After accession (assuming all accession treaties are ratified), the threshold for a blocking minority will increase from 23 to 27, as Austria, Sweden, Finland and Norway were allocated four, four, three and three votes respectively, bringing the total number of possible votes to 90. The increased threshold caused alarm in Britain for fear that the national veto had been further diluted. Despite attempts in March 1994 by Douglas Hurd, the Foreign Secretary, to suggest that the Commission would not press ahead with a proposal which had 23 votes against it, 27 votes is now the threshold for a blocking minority. This arrangement will only last until the inter-governmental conference in 1996, which is scheduled to review the Community's institutional arrangements – including QMV. But it is unlikely to be reduced.

COMMISSION OF THE EUROPEAN COMMUNITIES

Address in Brussels: Rue de la Loi 200, B-1049 Brussels, Belgium
Telephone: 010 322-235 1111
Address in Luxembourg: Bâtiment Jean Monnet, Rue Alcide de Gasperi
L-2920 Luxembourg
Telephone: 010 352-430 011

The European Commission is the engine room of the Community. It is often described as its executive branch or central bureaucracy, and is the best known of all the Community's institutions. It is, none the less, an appointed body, and therefore frequently criticised for being 'unaccountable' by those jealous or resentful of its powers and prerogatives. A Commission is made up of 17 Commissioners, nominated by the governments of the member states. Britain, Germany, France, Italy and Spain each have two Commissioners, and the remaining member states have one. After the accession of Austria, Norway, Finland and Sweden in 1995, the number of Commissioners will be increased to an unwieldy 21. The Delors Commission left office at the end of 1994, and was replaced by a new Commission in January 1995. But the inter-governmental conference in 1996 is expected to examine the number of Commissioners and their portfolios as part of the wider review of Community institutions.

From 1995, each Commission will last for five years, with each Commissioner serving a five-year term, thereby bringing it into line with the five-year term of the European Parliament. Commissioners are supposed to be independent of the government which has appointed them. On arriving in Brussels, Commissioners are required to take a solemn oath, committing them to perform their duties 'in complete independence, in the general interests of the Communities'. They also vow in carrying out their duties 'neither to take instructions from any Government or body'. The oath pointedly adds that member states have undertaken to respect the independence of their Commissioners, and 'not to seek to influence Members of the Commission in the performance of their task'. From Britain's island perspective, however, its Commissioners almost always seem to 'go native' – a charge frequently levelled at Stanley Clinton Davis and Lord Cockfield, neither of whom were renominated because they were seen to have strayed too far from the government line.

The President of the Commission is chosen by the European Council. He must then be approved by the Council of Ministers and the European Parliament. In theory, the Commission can be dismissed en masse in a vote of censure by the European Parliament under Article 144 of the Treaty of Rome. This has never happened, and is most unlikely to ever do so. The powers of the Commission President are considerable, but he is not the President of Europe, as some British tabloid newspapers pretend. The Commission President has little or no influence over the appointment of his fellow Commissioners, but he does wield substantial influence over the distribution of their portfolios. These cover one or more areas of Community responsibility such as economic and financial affairs, agriculture, transport, environment or social

affairs. These have traditionally been allocated by the Commission President (after heavy lob-
bying by member states) over dinner at a chateau in the Belgian countryside in what has been
dubbed by the media as a 'night of the long knives'. The more powerful member states are
generally given the key portfolios, and the less powerful have to make do with what is left.
Even before the 1995 accession there was simply not enough work to go around, leaving some
Commissioners somewhat underemployed. This problem is likely to get worse as the number
of Community members increases.

The Commission has four broad areas of jurisdiction: policy initiation; guardianship of the
Community treaties; management and administration of core policies; and external relations.

The Treaty of Rome confers on the Commission a virtual monopoly right to initiate legislative proposals (draft directives), which are then submitted to the Council of Ministers for
approval: hence the maxim – the Commission proposes and Council disposes. In addition, the
Commission has the power to issue regulations or decisions in limited areas, which are not subject to Council's approval. It is also responsible for ensuring that all member states comply with
Community law (the so-called acquis communautaire), and for bringing them to book if they
refuse to do so. The Commission carries out this function by delivering a 'reasoned opinion' in
cases where it believes a Treaty infringement has occurred. If member states fail to rectify the
situation the Commission can initiate legal action against the offending member state in the
European Court of Justice. This is an inescapable legal duty, although some member states,
notably Britain, frequently act as if the Commission is singling them out for 'special attention'.

The Commission's administrative and managerial functions are considerable. It is directly responsible for the administration of the Common Agricultural Policy through the European
Agricultural Guidance and Guarantee Fund; the administration of regional policy through the
European Regional Development Fund; and the distribution of overseas aid through the
European Development Fund. Finally, the Commission is also responsible for conducting
external trade negotiations on behalf of all member states, and is the primary contact point for
other international organisations dealing with the Community. It has also become the first
point of call for non-member states, and currently has more than 130 diplomatic missions
accredited to its Brussels headquarters.

Contrary to popular misconception, the Commission bureaucracy is not large. Altogether
there are some 17,000 staff (most of which are translators and interpreters), less than the number
employed to run an average city council in Britain. Allegations of high tax-free salaries and
perks for Commission officials have helped to create an image of a bloated Euro-bureaucracy.
In fact, while the salaries are high, and the perks good, all Community employees are subject
to a Community tax, ranging from around 10 per cent at the bottom of the salary scale to 45 per
cent at the top. A small number of high-flying administrative officials are employed by each
Commissioner to make up their staff or cabinet, a political and administrative body responsible
for managing the Commissioner's portfolio. Like the Council of Ministers, the European
Commission also has its own Secretariat, which is responsible for providing the Commission's
spokesman's service, legal service, joint interpreting and conference service, statistical
service, and the translation service – without which the Community would rapidly grind to a
halt. The remainder are employed by the bureaucracy proper – the 22 so-called Directorates-
General, or DGs, into which the Commission's work is divided. These are directly answerable
to their respective Commissioner.

Britain has finally embarked upon what will prove to be a long march on European
Community institutions in an attempt to reverse its under-representation among Brussels

bureaucrats. Following the launch of the Cabinet Office's European fast-stream initiative in October 1991, two dozen British graduates passed the Commission's 1993 recruitment examination (which has a 35-year age limit) for 248 top administrative posts, significantly exceeding the tally in previous years when the intake of British officials fell as low as one. The improved performance reflects the belated attempt by Whitehall policy-makers to boost the number of British administrators in Brussels where French and Germans have long dominated. Britons now account for 11.5 per cent of the Commission's 3,500 administrators, still below the 15 per cent target but well above the 3 per cent at the end of the 1980s. As one Whitehall official told *The Times*: 'Whatever your views on Europe, we need more Brits over there.'

The Commission, including its Commissioners and most of its officials, have traditionally resided in the Berlaymont, the bureaucracy's star-shaped plate-glass headquarters at the Rond Point Schuman on the Rue de la Loi. This home has been temporarily abandoned following the Commission's decision at the end of 1991 to refurbish its headquarters and remove the asbestos used in its construction. The resulting diaspora has meant that the Commission has been scattered throughout a large number of buildings in Brussels and Luxembourg, although the Commissioners, their cabinets and spokesmen, are situated near the Berlaymont in the Breydel Building in the Avenue d'Auderghem. Largely thanks to the efforts of the Belgian postal service in redirecting mail, the chaos is much less than might otherwise have been the case.

GENERAL SECRETARIAT

Secretary General: David Williamson
Function: Organisation of Commission business, including the provision of legal, translation and interpreting services.
Address: Breydel Building
Avenue d'Auderghem 45
Rue Belliard 68
Rue Archimède 17
Brussels
Telephone: 010 322-235 3914

DIRECTORATES-GENERAL

DG I: EXTERNAL RELATIONS

Function: Responsible for general external trade relations; negotiations with the General Agreement on Tariffs and Trade (GATT); relations with the Organisation for Economic Co-operation and Development (OECD); commercial issues affecting agriculture and fisheries; export credit policy; export promotion; relations with North America, Australia, South Africa, New Zealand, China, Japan, the Far East, Mediterranean, Near and Middle East, and Latin America; assistance programmes for the Commonwealth of Independent States (CIS), and Central and Eastern Europe; relations with state trading companies; North South issues; Enlargement; political co-operation and human rights.
Director General: Horst Günther Krenzler
Address: Rue de la Loi 200, B-1049 Brussels, Belgium
Telephone: 010 322-299 0097

DG II: ECONOMIC AND FINANCIAL AFFAIRS
Function: Responsible for monitoring national economic policies; evaluation of Community economic policies; macroeconomic analysis; monetary issues, including domestic and international aspects of economic and monetary union; promotion of the European Currency Unit (Ecu); financial interventions and capital movements; international economic and financial issues.
Director General: Giovanni Ravasio
Address: Rue de la Loi 200, B-1049 Brussels, Belgium
Telephone: 010 322-299 4366

DG III: SINGLE MARKET AND INDUSTRIAL AFFAIRS
Function: Responsible for industrial policy (state aids); technical standards and certification; steel, shipbuilding, chemicals, pharmaceuticals, textiles and construction etc; foodstuff legislation; biotechnology, information technology, and research and development.
Director-General: Riccardo Perissich
Address: Rue de la Loi 200, B-1049 Brussels, Belgium
Telephone: 010 322-235 4022

DG IV: COMPETITION POLICY
Function: Responsible for overall competition policy, including legal questions, infringement procedures, anti-dumping, application of Treaty competition rules to state enterprises and monopolies, policing restrictive practices, dominant positions, and other market distortions.
Director-General: Claus Dieter Ehlermann
Address: Rue de la Loi 200, B-1049 Brussels, Belgium
Telephone: 010 322-236 2178

DG V: EMPLOYMENT AND SOCIAL AFFAIRS
Function: Responsible for industrial relations; working conditions and labour law; initiative to counter structural unemployment; freedom of movement and migration policies; health and safety; co-ordination, evaluation and verification of European Social Fund initiatives.
Director-General: Hywell Ceri Jones
Address: Rue de la Loi 200, B-1049 Brussels, Belgium
Telephone: 010 322-235 5245

DG VI: AGRICULTURE
Function: Responsible for administering the Common Agricultural Policy; crop products and animal nutrition legislation; veterinary and zoo technical legislation; rural development; and international agricultural issues.
Director-General: Guy Legras
Address: Rue de la Loi 200, B-1049 Brussels, Belgium
Telephone: 010 322-235 3315

DG VII: TRANSPORT
Function: Promotion of European-wide transport networks and infrastructures; roads, rail, combined transport and internal waterways; air transport policy; international maritime transport policy.

Director-General: Robert Coleman
Address: Rue de la Loi 200, B-1049 Brussels, Belgium
Telephone: 010 322-236 8245

DG VIII: DEVELOPMENT
Function: Responsible for promoting economic development in the 69 African, Caribbean and Pacific group of nations (Lomé countries); management of the Stabex (Stability in export revenue) and Sysmin (System for safeguarding and developing mineral production) programmes; emergency food aid, technical co-operation, and private investment schemes.
Director-General: Peter Pooley
Address: Rue de la Loi 200, B-1049 Brussels, Belgium
Telephone: 010 322-299 3270

DG IX: PERSONNEL AND ADMINISTRATION
Function: Responsible for all aspects of Community staff recruitment, training and employment requirements; building management and maintenance, and the supply of office equipment.
Director-General: Frans de Koster
Address: Rue de la Loi 200, B-1049 Brussels, Belgium
Telephone: 010 322-235 2355

DG X: INFORMATION COMMUNICATION AND CULTURE
Function: Responsible for the development and co-ordination of the Community's audiovisual policy; promotion of the People's Europe information and public awareness programmes, and the promotion of Europe's cultural heritage.
Director-General: Colette Flesch
Address: Rue de la Loi 200, B-1049 Brussels, Belgium
Telephone: 010 322-299 9222

DG XI: ENVIRONMENT NUCLEAR SAFETY AND CIVIL PROTECTION
Function: Responsible for all aspects of environmental protection; nuclear safety, including radiation protection, emissions from industry, waste management, and civil protection.
Director-General: Laurens Jan Brinkhorst
Address: Rue de la Loi 200, B-1049 Brussels, Belgium
Telephone: 010 322-299 9253

DG XII: SCIENCE RESEARCH AND DEVELOPMENT
Function: Responsible for overseeing all Community research and development programmes, and co-ordinating international co-operation schemes.
Director-General: Paolo Fasella
Address: Rue de la Loi 200, B-1049 Brussels, Belgium
Telephone: 010 322-235 3570

DG XIII: TELECOMMUNICATIONS INFORMATION INDUSTRY AND INNOVATION
Function: Responsible for telecommunications policy; the audiovisual sector, including satellite broadcasting; high definition television; technology transfer and innovation;

information technology, and postal systems.
Director-General: Michel Carpentier
Address: Rue de la Loi 200, B-1049 Brussels, Belgium
Telephone: 010 322-236 8045

DG XIV: FISHERIES
Function: Responsible for all aspects of the Common Fisheries Policy, including fishing fleet sizes and conservation.
Director-General: José Almedia Serra
Address: Rue de la Loi 200, B-1049 Brussels, Belgium
Telephone: 010 322-235 9564

DG XV: INTERNAL MARKET AND FINANCIAL SERVICES
Function: Responsible for all aspects of the Single Market programme, including the free movement of goods, services, capital and labour; the elimination of the technical, physical and fiscal barriers to intra-Community trade; and the regulation of financial institutions and services.
Director-General: John Mogg
Address: Rue de la Loi 200, B-1049 Brussels, Belgium
Telephone: 010 322-235 3719

DG XVI: REGIONAL POLICY
Function: Responsible for the formulation and implementation of regional development policies, including assistance to declining industrial regions.
Director-General: Eneko Landaburo Illarramendi
Address: Rue de la Loi 200, B-1049 Brussels, Belgium
Telephone: 010 322-235 1968

DG XVII: ENERGY
Function: Responsible for energy planning; fossil fuels, including renewable energy; non-fossil energy; energy conservation, and energy industry and markets.
Director-General: Constantine Maniatopoulos
Address: Rue de la Loi 200, B-1049 Brussels, Belgium
Telephone: 010 322-235 1959

DG XVIII: CREDIT AND INVESTMENTS
Function: Responsible for finance and accounting; investments and loans; Treasury management, receipts and payments.
Director-General: Enrico Cioffi
Address: Rue de la Loi 200, B-1049 Brussels, Belgium
Telephone: 010 322-236 0341

DG XIX: BUDGETS
Function: Responsible for the Community budget; budget forecasts; structural funds; borrowing policy; forecasting and management of revenues.
Director-General: Jean-Paul Mingasson
Address: Rue de la Loi 200, B-1049 Brussels, Belgium
Telephone: 010 322-235 1684

DG XX: FINANCIAL CONTROL
Function: Responsible for the control of administrative, research, energy and industrial expenditure; borrowing and lending operations, and agricultural expenditure.
Director-General: Lucien de Moor
Address: Rue de la Loi 200, B-1049 Brussels, Belgium
Telephone: 010 322-235 3613

DG XXI: CUSTOMS UNION AND INDIRECT TAXATION
Function: Responsible for the external tariff; combating fraud; circulation and origin of goods; indirect taxation, and the elimination of fiscal frontiers.
Director-General: Peter Graham Wilmott
Address: Rue de la Loi 200, B-1049 Brussels, Belgium
Telephone: 010 322-236 1170

DG XXII:
Following reorganisation, DG XXII has been abolished and its responsibilities for co-ordinating structural policies has been distributed amongst the other DGs.

DG XXIII: ENTERPRISE POLICY, DISTRIBUTIVE TRADES, TOURISM AND CO-OPERATIVES
Function: Promotion of enterprise, commerce and distribution; assistance to small and medium enterprises, and promotion of tourism.
Director-General: Heinrich von Moltke
Address: Rue de la Loi 200, B-1049 Brussels, Belgium
Telephone: 010 322-235 2394

EC COMMISSION OFFICES IN THE UK
Commission of the European Communities
Jean Monnet House
8 Storey's Gate
London SW1P 3AT
Telephone: 071-973 1992

Commission of the European Communities
Windsor House
9-15 Bedford Street
Belfast BT2 7EG
Telephone: 0232-240708

Commission of the European Communities
4 Cathedral Road
Cardiff CF1 9SG
Telephone: 0222-371631

Commission of the European Communities
9 Alva Street
Edinburgh EH2 4PH
Telephone: 031-225 2058

THE EUROPEAN PARLIAMENT
Palais de l'Europe
BP 1024, F-67070
Strasbourg, France
Telephone: 010 3388 174001

Rue Belliard 97-113
B-1047 Brussels, Belgium
Telephone: 010 322-284 2111

The European Parliament (EP) is the only representative institution of the European Union, and is therefore much despised by British MPs in Westminster – largely for the perceived threat it poses to their position. The EP grew out of the European Assembly, which was created as part of the European Coal and Steel Community in 1952 before the EEC was established, and to which national MPs were seconded. A major change in the EP's fortunes occurred in 1979 when the first direct elections took place to a body of 410 seats, enabling Euro-MPs or MEPs to claim that they were the only authentic democratic voice of the peoples of Europe – a claim which has since become a mantra which MEPs recite at every available opportunity, much to the irritation of their counterparts in national parliaments. Following the accession of Spain and Portugal in 1986, the number of seats was increased to 518. That figure was again increased for the 1994 Euro-elections to 567, largely to give Germany more seats following reunification (although the number of British seats was increased from 81 to 87), and the number of seats will increase further after the accession of the four new members in 1995.

The EP is administered by an elected President and 14 vice-presidents, who sit collectively in what is known as the Bureau. Their work is supported by the EP's own Secretariat and Directorates-General. Members of the European Parliament sit in political groupings, rather than national blocs, and generally meet once a month in Strasbourg at the Palais de l'Europe for their plenary sessions. Following the Edinburgh Summit in 1992, Council provisionally agreed that Parliament would continue to meet in Strasbourg, although it was granted leave to hold extraordinary sessions in Brussels. However, the Parliament's Secretariat is based in Luxembourg, while MEPs work in the EP's buildings in Brussels, where most meetings of its committees and political groups are held. This confusing arrangement is largely due to the failure of member states to take a definitive decision on the permanent seat of the EP or, for that matter, any of the other central EU institutions.

Prior to the passage of the Single European Act, the EP was little more than an advisory body. Under Article 137 of the Treaty of Rome, the EP is granted 'advisory and supervisory powers', enabling it to offer only 'opinions' in nearly all policy areas, which the Council could (and did) ignore. The sole exception was the annual Community budget where MEPs exercise joint control with Council over non-obligatory expenditure. Even here, however, its powers are circumscribed, as non-obligatory expenditure excludes the cost of financing the Common Agricultural Policy (for which there is a legal obligation). Even after the recent reforms this still accounts for more than half the Community budget.

None the less, the final budget cannot be adopted without the EP's approval, in effect conferring on it the power of veto.

The significance of the EP has, however, been considerably enhanced by the ratification of the Single European Act and the Maastricht treaties. The Single European Act gave the EP two further important roles in addition to its budgetary powers. Under the so-called 'co-operation' or second reading procedure, Council takes a common position on a legislative proposal, after taking into account Parliament's opinion. Parliament now has three months to decide whether to accept Council's views. If it does, or takes no action, the proposal passes into law. But if the EP proposes amendments or rejects the proposal, Council can only pass its original version by unanimous agreement. Otherwise it must accept Parliament's version or drop the proposal altogether. Consequently, the EP can now influence the Community's legislative process by proposing amendments which Council and the Commission must take seriously. Second, under the new 'assent procedure', the EP has the final say in accession and economic co-operation agreements with non-member states.

The Single European Act undoubtedly emboldened MEPs in their bid to eliminate what they call the 'democratic deficit', by demanding the right of 'co-decision' with Council and the Commission. Indeed, as work was under way on the draft Maastricht treaties, David Martin, a British MEP, and the rapporteur on the EP's institutional reform committee, produced a report which alleged: 'If the EC was a state and applied to join the Community it would be turned down on the grounds that it was not a democracy.' In the event, the Maastricht Treaty on Political Union gave the EP powers of co-decision through the so-called 'negative assent procedure'. This effectively enables the EP to reject a Commission proposal by an overall majority of its members if agreement cannot be reached between the two institutions in a joint conciliation committee. The negative assent procedure covers a wide range of policy areas, mainly where the Council decides by qualified majority voting, including the free movement of workers, the right of establishment, mutual recognition of professional qualifications, single market proposals, aspects of education, research and development framework programmes, environmental protection, trans-European networks, culture and consumer protection.

Although suspicion and hostility have been the dominant features of relations between Westminster MPs and their British counterparts in Strasbourg, some attempts have been made to improve this situation. In 1991, new arrangements were agreed between the two representative institutions enabling MPs to travel to visit Community institutions, and British MEPs were given greater access to the Commons, including reserved seats in the front two rows of the public gallery (MEPs previously had to queue along with members of the public). Yet this falls far short of what some critics feel is needed to enable Westminster to assume a more effective role in the Community's decision-making process. In his 1993 lecture, Vernon Bogdanor warned: 'If Westminster is to defend British interests successfully, it will have to alter its mental attitude to the Community. MPs must cease to regard MEPs with condescension, as winners of some kind of consolation prize. They must come to appreciate that Westminster and Strasbourg are complementary rather than competitive institutions', he said.

Bogdanor pointed out that the so-called 'scrutiny reserve', under which the government has undertaken not to agree to legislative proposals in Council until they have been debated in Parliament, has been seriously undermined by the extension of qualified majority voting. Moreover, this loss of power has yet to be compensated for by greater efforts by the select committee system to influence the Commission and the EP over new legislative proposals at a sufficiently early stage. At present, scrutiny is exercised largely by the Select Committee on

European Legislation, as if Europe was 'a separate box distinct from other policy issues'. In order to rectify this flaw, Bogdanor recommended that Parliament should develop better ways of exerting influence on Community institutions by transferring the task of examining legislative proposals to the select committee responsible for the policy area in question, and by greater co-operation between MPs and MEPs since MEPs have greater and earlier access to information than MPs. Belgium and Germany, for example, include MEPs on their parliamentary committees. As yet, however, there is little sign that Westminster is prepared to embark upon the kind of reforms of its own institutional structure which would give it the influence in the Community's legislative process that it so desperately desires.

SECRETARIAT-GENERAL
European Parliament
Centre Européen
Plateau de Kirchberg BP 1601
L-2929 Luxembourg
Telephone: 010 352-430 011

EUROPEAN PARLIAMENT UK OFFICE
No 2 Queen Anne's Gate
London SW1H 9AA
Telephone: 071-222 0411

THE EUROPEAN COURT OF JUSTICE
Palais de la Cour de Justice
L-2925 Luxembourg
Telephone: 010 352-4303 3441
President: Ole Due

The European Court of Justice (ECJ), which is based in Luxembourg, is the guardian of all the European Treaties, and the Community's supreme legal authority. It is not to be confused with the European Court of Human Rights in Strasbourg, which is a Council of Europe body, or the International Court of Justice in The Hague. The ECJ was established by the Treaty of Rome to ensure that Community law is correctly interpreted and implemented by Council, the Commission, and the individual member states. It is a collegiate body made up of 13 judges (one from each member state with the 13th member nominated by one of the large member states in rotation), and six advocates-general. Its members serve for a six-year term, and are required to be persons of the highest legal qualification 'whose independence is beyond doubt'. Since 1989 it has been assisted by a Court of First Instance, designed to relieve the increasing workload on the main court, and which is made up of one judge from each member state, all of whom serve for a six-year term.

The ECJ is empowered to settle disputes within the Community, including disputes between member states; disputes between member states and Community institutions, and disputes between Community institutions. As a result, member states can initiate legal proceedings against other member states; member states can initiate legal proceedings against Community institutions; Community institutions can initiate legal proceedings against member states, and Community institutions can initiate legal proceedings against other Community institutions on grounds of error, infringement of the Treaties, failure to implement Community legislation, or abuse of power. The ECJ thus has the power to annul decisions made by Council, the Commission, and individual member states, as indeed occurred with Britain's 1988 Merchant Shipping Act, which was struck down for illegally discriminating against other Community nationals. In practice, however, most legal actions are initiated by the Commission, which is legally obliged to act as guardian of the Treaties.

Because Community law takes precedence over national law, one of the main functions of the ECJ is to give rulings on cases referred to it by the national courts on points of Community law, decisions on which are binding. As a result, decisions and rulings by the ECJ are gradually contributing to the emergence of a common European legal system, which is increasingly being used by way of precedent by the national courts, companies, and even private individuals. Finally, although the Treaties are primarily a matter of relations between member states, under the doctrine of 'direct effect' Community law can be invoked by individuals in the national courts against the decisions of their own government.

TRIBUNAL OF FIRST INSTANCE
Palais de la Cour de Justice
L-2925 Luxembourg
Telephone: 010 352-4303 3441
President: Jose Luis da Cruz Vilaca

THE COURT OF AUDITORS
Address: 12 Rue Alcide de Gasperi
L-1615 Luxembourg
Telephone: 010 352-43981
President: Andre Middlehoek

The Court of Auditors was established in Luxembourg in 1977, and was made a full institution of the Community under the Maastricht Treaties. Its role is to examine the accounts of all Community institutions, ensure that all revenue has been received, that all expenditure is lawful, and that financial management is effective and efficient. It therefore carries out the same role in the Community that the National Audit Office, the government spending watchdog, carries out in Britain. The court is made up of one representative from each of the member states, appointed by Council, who are independent of their country of origin. It has the power to request any document or information from any Community institution or government department – on the spot if necessary – in order to execute its legal audit responsibilities. As well as publishing annual reports on the accounts of Community institutions, it has the power to examine any issue at any time in order to ensure that Community finances are kept free of fraud and corruption. Such a situation occurred in 1988 when a report on fraud in the Common Agricultural Policy forced Council and the Commission to tighten controls. It also assists Council and the European Parliament in exercising controls over the Community budget.

THE ECONOMIC AND SOCIAL COMMITTEE (ECOSOC)

Address: Rue Ravenstein 2
B-100 Brussels, Belgium
Telephone: 010 322-519 9011
Secretary-General: Simon-Pierre Northomb

The Economic and Social Committee is a consultative body established under the Treaty of Rome with the intention of involving a wide range of economic and social groups in the development of the Community. It is made up of 189 members (which will increase after the 1995 accession) representing employers (Group I), workers (Group II), and a variety of other interest groups including agriculture, transport, trade, small and medium enterprises, the professions and consumers (Group III). Its members are proposed by national governments, and appointed by Council for a term of four years which is renewable. Council and the Commission are legally required to consult ECOSOC on a wide range of issues such as agriculture, labour movement, the right of establishment, transport, approximation of laws, social policy and vocational training. Under the Euratom Treaty, ECOSOC also plays a consultative role in the fields of health and safety, investment, the nuclear common market, and research and training. Under the Single European Act, it must also be consulted on issues relating to the internal market, social policy, economic and social cohesion, research, technological development and the environment. The committee can also issue opinions on its own initiative on any matter of interest to the Community.

BRITISH MEMBERS

John Andrews
General Secretary
Professional Associaton of Teachers
2 St James Court
Friar Gate
Derby DE1 1BT
Telephone: 0322-372337

Wilfred Aspinall
Managerial Professional and Staff
Liason Group
Tavistock House
Tavistock Square
London WC1H 9JP
Telephone: 071-387 4499

Jocelyn Barrow
Deputy Chairman
Broadcasting Standards Council
5-8 The Sanctuary
London SW1P 3JS
Telephone: 071-233 0544

Neville Beale
Independent Consultant
Flat 20
Chelsea Towers
Chelsea Manor Street
London SW3 5PN
Telephone: ex-directory

Beata Brookes
Chairman
Welsh Consumer Council
Castle Buildings
Womanby Street
Cardiff CF1 2BN
Telephone: 0222-396056

Campbell Christie
General Secretary
Scottish Trades Union Congress
Middleton House, 16 Woodlands Terrace
Glasgow G3 6DF
Telephone: 041-332 4946

Ann Davidson
Executive Director
Fairtrade Foundation
105-111 Euston Street
London NW1 2ED
Telephone: 071-383 4025

Kenneth Gardner
Consultant in Food Law
Bishops Orchard
Oakley Green
Near Windsor
Berkshire SL4 5UN
Telephone: 0753-860904

Angela Guillaume
Chairwoman European Union of Women
Camelot
Ramley Road
Lymington SO41 8LH
Telephone: 0590-678466

Tom Jenkins
Assistant Secretary
Trades Union Congress
Congress House
23-28 Great Russell Street
London WC1B 3LS
Telephone: 071-636 4030

Malcolm Levitt
EU advisor to Barclays Bank
Murray House
1 Royal Mint Court
London EC3N 4HH
Telephone: 071-488 1144

John Little
Former Chairman Scottish Confederation
of British Industries
8 Wateryett Loan
Strathaven
Lanarkshire ML10 6EJ
Scotland
Telephone: 0357-20762

John Lyons
General Secretary
Engineers and Managers Association
305 Salmon Street
London NW9

Ada Maddocks
National Organising Officer
National Association of Local
Government Officers (Unison)
68 Barley Lane
Ilford
Essex IG3 8XF
Telephone: 081-388 2366

Michael Mobbs
Chairman and Managing Director
ML Aviation
Hamilton House
1 Temple Avenue
Victoria Embankment
London SW1

Robert Moreland
Westminster City Council
7 Vauxhall Walk
London SE11 5JT
Telephone: 071-828 8070

Peter Morgan
Director General
Institute of Directors
116 Pall Mall
London SW1Y 5ED
Telephone: 071-839 1233

Richard Pickering
National President
General and Municipal Boilermakers
Union
22-24 Worple Road
Wimbledon
London SW19 4DD
Telephone: 081-947 3131

Roy Sanderson
National Secretary
Electrical Engineering and
Staff Association
West Common Road
Bromley
Kent BR2 7AU
Telephone: 071-226 0112

John Simpson
Economist
Former Chairman
NI Probation Board

Michael Strauss
Former Policy Co-ordinator
National Farmers Union
Birch Cottage
Common Road, Ightham
Sevenoaks
Kent TN15 9AY
Telephone: 0732-882036

Kenneth Walker
Independent Management Consultant

John Whitworth
Chairman
Merchant Navy Officers Pension Fund
The Old School House
Farley Chamberlayne
Romsey
Hampshire SO51 0QR
Telephone: 0794-368538

George Wright
Regional Secretary
Transport and General Workers Union
(Wales)
1 Cathedral Road
Cardiff CF1 9SD
Telephone: 0222 394521

THE COMMITTEE OF THE REGIONS

President: Jacques Blanc
Address: Rue Ravenstein 2
1000-Brussels, Belgium
Telephone: 010 322-519 9243

The Committee of the Regions (COR) was established under the Maastricht Treaty on Political Union as a consultative organisation made up of representatives of local or regional bodies. Its objective is to give a greater voice to local authorities in the development of the Community, and is seen by Brussels as a practical expression of the principle of subsidiarity. Critics have insisted that with a budget of £9 million a year, it is at best a Tower of Babel with no discernible purpose other than to provide all expenses-paid trips to Brussels for local councillors, and at worst an attempt to subvert national government by encouraging a direct dialogue between Brussels and the regions. Such criticisms are generally heard only in Britain, where local or regional government is either weak or non-existent, and are usually made by national politicians suspicious of Brussels' involvement at the local level. Although, to be fair, some Scottish and Welsh representatives see the COR as the thin edge of devolution. Like ECOSOC, the Committee of the Regions is made up of 189 representatives, 24 from Britain, plus 24 alternates, who are appointed for a four-year renewable term. The Committee must be consulted by Council and the Commission on a wide range of subjects, including education, public health, trans-European networks, economic and social cohesion and culture.

BRITISH MEMBERS

Simon Day
Devon County Council
Telephone: 0752-382000

Lady Elizabeth Anson
Waverley Borough Council
Telephone: 0252-792724

Sir Peter Bowness
London Borough of Croydon
Telephone: 081-686 4433

Colin Warbrick
Trafford City Borough Council
Telephone: 061-872 2101

Christopher Penn
Suffolk County Council
Telephone: 0502-562262

Toby Harris
London Borough of Haringey
Telephone: 081-975 9700

Albert Bore
Birmingham City Borough Council
Telephone: 021-235 9944

Josie Farrington
Lancashire County Council
Telephone: 0772-254868

George Gill
Gateshead City Borough Council
Telephone: 091-477 1011

Dennis Pettit
Nottinghamshire County Council
Telephone: 0602-823823

Janet Sillett
Norwich City District Council
Telephone: 0606-622233

Graham Tope
London Borough of Sutton
Telephone: 081-770 5000

David Belotti
East Sussex County Council
Telephone: 0273-481000

Roy Cross
Richmondshire District Council
Telephone: 0748-850222

Charles Gray
Strathclyde Regional Council
Telephone: 041-204 2900

Rosemary McKenna
Cumbernauld and Kilsyth District Council
Telephone: 0236-722131

Brian Meek
Edinburgh District Council
Telephone: 031-225 2424

Duncan McPherson
Highland Regional Council
Telephone: 0463-702000

Daniel Coffey
Kilmarnock and Loudon District Council
Telephone: 0563-21140

John Evans
Rhymney Valley District Council
Telephone: 0443-815588

Lord Lloyd Kenyon
Wrexham Borough Council
Telephone: 0978-292000

Eurig Wyn
Gwynedd County Council
Telephone: 0286-672225

Reg Empey
Belfast City Council
Telephone: 0232-320202

Dennis Haughey
Cookstown Borough Council
Telephone: 0648-62205

ALTERNATES
John Morgan
Test Valley District Council
Telephone: 0794-515117

Doreen Fleming
Fenland District Council
Telephone: 0354-54321

Fraser Mitchell
Solihull City Council
Telephone: 021-704 6000

Elgar Jenkins
Bath City Council
Telephone: 0225-461111

Paul White
Essex County Council
Telephone: 0245-492211

John Battye
Oldham City Borough Council
Telephone: 061-624 0505

Hedley Salt
Barnsley City Borough Council
Telephone: 0226-770770

Kenneth Bodfish
East Sussex County Council
Telephone: 0273-481000

Ian Swithinbank
Northumberland County Council
Telephone: 0670-533000

Sally Powell
London Borough of Hammersmith
and Fulham
Telephone: 081-748 3020

Peter Soulsby
Leicester City Council
Telephone: 0533-549922

Peter Cocks
Cornwall County Council
Telephone: 0892-74282

Tony Prior
South Somerset District Council
Telephone: 0935-75272

Milner Whiteman
Bridgnorth District Council
Telephone: 0746-765131

Keith Geddes
Lothian Regional Council
Telephone: 031-229 9292

Jean McFadden
Glasgow City Council
Telephone: 041-221 9600

Marcus Humphrey
Glasgow City Council
Telephone: 0224-312718

Peter Peacock
Highland Regional Council
Telephone: 0463-702000

Clive Sneddon
North East Fife District Council
Telephone: 0592-754411

Keith Griffiths
Gwent County Council
Telephone: 0633-838838

Bill Hughes
Swansea City Council
Telephone: 0792-301301

Simpson Gibson
Ards Borough Council
Telephone: 0247-812215

Jill Evans
Rhondda Borough Council
Telephone: 0443-434551

Sean Neeson
Carrickfergus Borough Council
Telephone: 0960-351604

THE EUROPEAN INVESTMENT BANK
Boulevard Konrad Adenauer 100
L-2950 Luxembourg
Telephone: 010 352-43791
President: Sir Brian Unwin

The European Investment Bank (EIB) was established in 1958 to provide long-term loans for public- and private-sector capital investment projects within the Community on a non-profit making basis. It is made up of a Board of Governors (usually the Finance Ministers of the member states), a Board of Directors and a permanent management committee. Member states provide the EIB with guarantee capital, enabling it to borrow on the international capital markets (where it has a AAA rating) at the lowest rate of interest. The bank then re-loans the money for projects which could not be financed by the capital markets direct. Within the Community, the EIB is responsible for promoting economic development by improving transport and communications links, such as the Channel Tunnel, ensuring the security of energy supplies, and enhancing the internal and external competitiveness of European industry. Outside the Community, the EIB finances projects in the 69 African, Caribbean and Pacific members of the Lomé Convention, the Mediterranean countries, Latin America and the Far East, and more recently, Central and Eastern Europe.

EIB LONDON OFFICE
68 Pall Mall
London SW1Y 5ES
Telephone: 071-839 3351

EUROPEAN COAL & STEEL COMMUNITY
The European Coal & Steel Community (ECSC) was established in August 1952 by Belgium, France, West Germany, Italy, Luxembourg and the Netherlands, as the first of the three organisations making up the European Communities. Its role is to control the production and marketing of coal and steel, provide a common market for coal and steel, and eliminate duties, subsidies, and other anti-competitive practices. In 1967 the ECSC's High Authority was merged into the European Commission, enabling a greater co-ordination of energy policy. The original ECSC treaty expires in 2002, and its functions are expected to be incorporated into the Treaty of Rome.

DIRECTORATE-GENERAL III
Commission of the European Communities
Rue de la Loi 200
B-1049 Brussels, Belgium
Telephone: 010 322-299 1111

EUROPEAN ATOMIC ENERGY COMMUNITY (EURATOM)
Rue du Luxembourg 46
B-1040 Brussels, Belgium
Telephone: 010 322-295 7894

The European Atomic Energy Community (Euratom) was founded in 1958 by Belgium, France, Germany, Italy, Luxembourg and the Netherlands, thus becoming the third of the three treaties making up the European Communities (the European Economic Community came into existence on the same day). It was responsible for creating the technical and industrial conditions required to exploit nuclear discoveries and produce nuclear energy for peaceful purposes on a large scale. This is now carried out by the Joint Research Centre (JRC), which conducts nuclear research throughout Europe. Euratom's supply agency is responsible for the supply of nuclear fuels, exercises a monopoly on nuclear contracts with third world countries, and is also responsible for setting standards for health and safety throughout the Community. Like the ECSC, it was in effect merged with the Commission in 1967.

JOINT RESEARCH CENTRE
Commission of the European Communities
Directorate-General XII
Rue de la Loi 200
B-1049 Brussels, Belgium
Telephone: 010 322-295 8527

THE UNITED KINGDOM PERMANENT REPRESENTATION (UKREP)
Rond-Point Schuman 6
B-1040 Brussels, Belgium
Telephone: 010 322-287 8211

The UK Permanent Representation or UKRep is the long arm of Whitehall in Brussels. It is made up of British civil servants, drawn from across Whitehall departments, who are responsible for fighting Britain's corner in the day-to-day negotiations over the Commission's legislative programme on behalf of the Council of Ministers. UKRep staff are in constant touch with the Commission, the Permanent Representatives of the other member states on COREPER, the Council Secretariat, and the European Parliament, and are therefore best placed to give advice on any Community issue.

Permanent Representative: Sir John Kerr
Ambassador Extraordinary and Plenipotentiary
Function: Overall responsibility for UKRep
Deputy Permanent Representative: David Durie

Function: Responsible for all Councils excluding Foreign Affairs, Agriculture, Industry, Development and Economic and Financial Affairs.

KEY SUPERVISORY STAFF
Agriculture: Kate Timms
Industry, Energy, Internal Market and Transport: Anne Lambert
Economic Affairs, Finance and Taxation: Bob Bonney
External Affairs: John Grant
Social, Environmental and Regional Policy: Chris Capella
Political and Institutional Affairs: Nigel Sheinwald
Home and Justice Affairs: Ian Hendry
Media Spokesman: Robert Court

THE NEW EUROPEAN INSTITUTIONS

During a meeting of Community leaders in Brussels in October 1993, agreement was reached on the siting of a dozen or so new institutions, organisations and other bodies throughout Europe. At the time of writing, most of these organisations were still in the process of being set up, and details about staff, location and contact numbers were not available.

THE EUROPEAN ENVIRONMENT AGENCY

The new European Environment Agency will be situated in Copenhagen, and will be responsible for providing the technical and scientific support needed for European-wide environmental protection initiatives. The new body is expected to pay particular attention to air quality, atmospheric emissions, water quality, pollutants, water resources, soil conditions, flora and fauna, biotopes, land use, natural resources, waste management, noise emissions, hazardous substances and coastal protection. It will publish a report on the state of the environment every three years in an attempt to inform and influence the public debate on environmental issues.

THE EUROPEAN TRAINING FOUNDATION

The European Training Foundation will be based in Turin, and will be responsible for developing the vocational training systems, including initial and continuing vocational training, youth and adult retraining, and management retraining, in Central and East European countries.

THE OFFICE FOR VETERINARY AND PLANT HEALTH INSPECTION AND CONTROL

This new body, which is responsible for monitoring and enforcing Community policies on plant and animal health, will be located in Ireland as part of the European Commission rather than a decentralised organisation.

THE EUROPEAN MONITORING CENTRE FOR DRUGS AND DRUG ADDICTION

The Centre will be situated in Lisbon, and will be responsible for providing objective and comparative data on drugs, drug addiction and its consequences. The statistical, documentary and technical information gathered by the centre will be used in the formulation of policies to combat the problem.

THE EUROPEAN AGENCY FOR THE EVALUATION OF MEDICINAL PRODUCTS

The Agency will be based in London, and will be responsible for providing scientific advice to Community institutions and member states needed for the authorisation and supervision of new medicinal products, including monitoring adverse reactions to newly authorised products.

THE AGENCY FOR HEALTH AND SAFETY AT WORK

The Agency will be situated in Bilbao, and will be responsible for promoting health and safety at work throughout the Community.

THE EUROPEAN MONETARY INSTITUTE

The institute was established in Frankfurt in January 1994, under the provisions of the Maastricht Treaty on Economic and Monetary Union. The EMI is responsible for preparing the groundwork for stage three of economic and monetary union, including the co-ordination of monetary policy, the development of the Ecu, and the preparation for the European System of Central Banks. It is intended that the EMI will be replaced by the proposed European Central Bank, which will also be located in Frankfurt.

OFFICE FOR HARMONISATION IN THE INTERNAL MARKET

The office will be located in Alicante, and will concentrate on methods of harmonising trade within the EU.

EUROPOL

The new European Police Office (Europol), which will be situated in the Hague, was created under the provisions of the Maastricht Treaty on Political Union, and will be responsible for co-ordinating cross-border police co-operation to prevent or combat terrorism, drug-trafficking and crime.

EUROPEAN CENTRE FOR THE DEVELOPMENT OF VOCATIONAL TRAINING (CEDEFOP)

The centre, which was originally established in 1975 to assist the Commission in encouraging the promotion and development of vocational training throughout the Community, will be moved from Berlin to Thessaloniki.

254

FOUNDATION FOR THE IMPROVEMENT OF LIVING AND WORKING CONDITIONS

The foundation was set up in Dublin in 1975 to research into the medium- and long-term improvement of living and working conditions.

TRANSLATION CENTRE

The centre will be situated in Luxembourg to meet the translation needs of the new institutions and will be financed by contributions from them.

7
THE REGIONAL STATE

The tendrils of government reach far and wide. One level of government, directly or on contract, sweeps the streets and empties dustbins. To many people local authorities are as much part of 'the state' as central government. Surveys show many make no distinction between the local authority responsible for, say, social services and the National Health Service. Yet local government is special. The existence of local democratic elections gives its decisions a character different from those of appointed and non-departmental public bodies. Its spending is accounted differently. Although important local authority functions have recently been switched away, at £30 billion a year in net spending the municipal empire demands to be treated separately.

Central government has its own local dimension. Branches of the state reach close to the ground in the regions. The state has its outposts, in hundreds of local offices dispensing welfare benefits or assessing tax. Non-departmental public bodies have out-stations. In addition there is an English provincial apparatus of state. In the 'regional capitals' such as Manchester and Birmingham there are heavy concentrations of administrative power, spread between the offices of those departments such as Employment or Trade and Industry with local programmes. It is worth noting how absent from the regions are certain major departments of state, notably the Home Office and the Treasury. The fact that the Home Office needs no local presence to ensure co-ordination and control of the police forces it largely pays for is a testimony to the informal nature, still, of much public administration in Britain.

In the three other nations which make up the United Kingdom there are statelets. Government in Cardiff, Edinburgh and Belfast has some of the characteristics of vice-royalty with a very powerful Secretary of State commanding administrative empires like Whitehall in miniature. Administration often seems 'thicker' in Scotland and Northern Ireland, reflecting a tradition of more intensive government involvement in social and economic life.

ENGLAND

For official purposes, such as the collection of statistics, the map of England has long been divided up into eight standard regions. The special urban problems of the Liverpool area have more recently led to the creation of another and London, a perennial problem for the central government, is the tenth. It has suited those departments delivering grants and benefits locally to follow roughly the same regional structure but the financial departments – Customs and Excise and Inland Revenue – have organised the country quite differently for their own purposes. Over the years some regions have been the focus of specific measures, as when the Macmillan government in the early 1960s designated Lord Hailsham as the Minister for the North East or 1981 when Michael Heseltine created a new Merseyside task force. London is too close to the centres of power and influence to escape detailed and continuous political and administrative inspection. Since the abolition of the directly elected Greater London Council in 1986, ministers have sought various ways of dealing with problems and opportunities – transport, tourism – which span the entire conurbation.

In its 1992 manifesto the Conservative party promised to tidy up regional governance and in doing so to make central government more responsive to the regional voice – without in any way suggesting that voice might need some kind of election to express it. After much internal argument within Whitehall, a new network was created, but involving only some of the Whitehall departments. New Government Offices for the Regions were established in April 1994 to work in partnership with local authorities and private firms to 'maximise the competitiveness, prosperity and quality of life of their region'. The reform is meant to give DTI, Employment, Environment and Transport the same regional boundaries. The new offices are together administering programmes with a total value of £4.5 billion. The different departments are meant to relocate their officials to the same buildings 'as and when circumstances permit'.

The Offices are intended to look two ways: upwards to Whitehall, contributing local views and experience to the formation and communication of policy; and downwards, providing a single point of contact for local people and delivering high-quality services. The new Regional Directors will be accountable to the relevant Secretary of State for the programmes their offices carry out and also to a Cabinet committee. A new Single Regeneration Budget is, in parallel, bringing together 20 existing 'inner city' and development programmes.

When the plan was announced newspaper headlines spoke of 'Whitehall commissars'; they probably exaggerate the likely power of the new regional directors even within Whitehall. The Labour party said that while the new network was an admission that a regional dimension was needed, these officials were unelected and lacked legitimacy in making decisions for their regions.

Ministers have high hopes for the new offices. The Government Office for London 'will ensure that Londoners are better served by Government in the capital', according to the Environment Secretary. Some regional programmes remain outside the new framework, for example the unemployment programmes of the Employment Service, now an executive agency. There has been some discussion in Whitehall about whether the Department for Education needs to grow a regional 'arm' to allocate money to the grant-maintained schools.

The regional picture ought also to include a number of organisations which offer to other public bodies a local presence. The Regional Arts Boards, for example, are intended to be strategic bodies with charitable status working in partnership with local authorities and other bodies; they receive grants from the Arts Council, the British Film Institute and the Crafts Council. The regional directors of the Sports Council double as secretaries of the regional council for sport and recreation. Regional machinery exists to bring local authorities and government together for planning and the administration of national parks.

SOUTH-WEST
Bristol BS1 2NQ
Telephone: 0272-273710
Senior Regional Director: Brian Leonard. Born: 1948. Educated: Dr Challoner's Grammar, Amersham; London School of Economics. Joined the Department of the Environment in 1974 specialising in public spending and the private rented sector housing, he became a Hubert Humphrey Fellow in Minnesota in 1987. He later became Northern regional controller for the Departments of Environment and Transport.

EMPLOYMENT DEPARTMENT: TRAINING, ENTERPRISE AND EDUCATION DIRECTORATE
The Pithay
Bristol BS1 2NQ
Telephone: 0272-273710
Assistant Regional Director: Wendy Mauger

EMPLOYMENT SERVICES
Ken Pascoe
The Pithay
Bristol BS1 2NQ
Telephone: 0272-273710

DTI BRISTOL OFFICE
The Pithay
Bristol BS1 2NQ
Telephone: 0272-272666
Devon: 0752-221891
Cornwall: 0736-60440

SOUTH-WESTERN REGIONAL COUNCIL FOR SPORT AND RECREATION
P G Barson
Ashlands House
Ashlands, Crewkerne
Somerset TA18 7LQ
Telephone: 0460-73491

SOUTH-WEST ARTS
Bradninch Place
Gandy Street
Exeter
Devon EX4 3LS
Telephone: 0392-218188
Chief Executive: C Bates

SOUTH-WEST REGIONAL PLANNING CONFERENCE
County Hall
Taunton TA1 4DY
Telephone: 0823-333451
Secretary: B M Tanner

SOUTH-WEST ASSOCIATION FOR FURTHER EDUCATION AND TRAINING
Bishops Hull House, Bishops Hull
Taunton TA1 5RA
Telephone: 0823-335491
Chief Officer: F S Fisher

NATIONAL PARKS
DARTMOOR
Established: 1951 (984 sq km, 380 sq miles)
Dartmoor National Park Authority
Parke, Haytor Road
Bovey Tracey, Newton Abbot TQ13 9JQ
Telephone: 0626-832093

EXMOOR
Established: 1954 (686 sq km, 265 sq miles)
Severns House
20 Middle Pavement
Nottingham NG1 7DW

Exmoor National Park
Exmoor House
Dulverton, Somerset TA22 9HL
Telephone: 0398-23665
Keith Bungay

259

MERSEYSIDE

Graeme House
Derby Square
Liverpool L2 7SU
Telephone: 051-227 4111

Senior Regional Director: John Stoker. Born: 1950. Educated: King Edward's School, Birmingham; Brasenose College, Oxford. Served in Department of Environment Yorks and Humberside Regional Office and subsequent portfolios included housing, finance and environmental protection. Served as Civil Service Selection Board assessor and recently became Director of Government Office for Merseyside and, in 1992, the Merseyside Task Force.

EMPLOYMENT DEPARTMENT: TRAINING, ENTERPRISE AND EDUCATION DIRECTORATE

Washington House
New Bailey Street
Manchester M3 5ER
Telephone: 061-833 0251
Assistant Regional Director: Felicity Everiss

DTI

Graeme House
Derby Square
Liverpool L2 7UP
Telephone: 051-224 6300

MERSEYSIDE ARTS TRUST

Bluecoat Chambers
School Lane
Liverpool L1 3BX
Telephone: 051-709 0671
Director: P Booth

WEST MIDLANDS

Paradise Circus
Queensway
Birmingham B1 2DT
Telephone: 021-212-5000

Senior Regional Director: David Ritchie. Born: 1948. Education: Manchester Grammar School; St John's College, Cambridge. Joined Ministry of Transport in 1970 and served in the North West Regional Office later becoming Regional Director, West Midlands (DoE/DpT).

EMPLOYMENT DEPARTMENT
TRAINING, ENTERPRISE AND EDUCATION DIRECTORATE

Alpha Tower
Suffolk Street

Queensway
Birmingham B1 1UR
Telephone: 021-631 3555
Assistant Regional Director: Paul Thomas

EMPLOYMENT SERVICE
2 Duchess Place
Hagley Road
Birmingham B16 8NF
Telephone: 021-456 4411
Regional Director: Martin Raff

DEPARTMENT OF TRADE AND INDUSTRY
Paradise Circus
Queensway
Birmingham B1 2DT
Telephone: 021-212 5000
Warwickshire and Coventry: Martin Morris: 0203-632328
Hereford and Worcester: Richard Chalk: 0905-765339
Staffordshire: 0782-285171
Shropshire: 0952-290422

REGIONAL COUNCIL FOR SPORT AND RECREATION WEST MIDLANDS
D Pryor
1 Hagley Road
Five Ways
Birmingham B16 8TT
Telephone: 021-456 3444

WEST MIDLANDS REGIONAL FORUM LOCAL AUTHORITIES
12 Martin Street
Stafford ST16 2LH
Telephone: 0785-223121
Principal Officer: G Moran

WEST MIDLANDS ARTS
82 Granville Street
Birmingham B1 2LH
Telephone: 021-631 3121
Chief Executive: M Elliott

WEST MIDLANDS EXAMINATION BOARD (FE ADVISORY COUNCIL)
Mill Wharf
Mill Street
Birmingham B6 4BU
Telephone: 021-628 2000
Secretary: B Swift

EAST MIDLANDS
Severns House
20 Middle Pavement
Nottingham NG1 7DW

Senior Regional Director: Mark Lanyon. Born: 1939. Educated: University of St Andrews. By training an engineer, he joined the Civil Service in 1963 entering the Department of Trade and Industry South West Regional Office and becoming in 1982 Regional Director for the West Midlands. After serving in the Office of Fair Trading he became Department of Trade and Industry director in Yorkshire and Humberside in 1993.

EMPLOYMENT DEPARTMENT
TRAINING, ENTERPRISE AND EDUCATION DIRECTORATE
(also covers Eastern Region)
21-23 Castlegate
Nottingham NG1 7AQ
Telephone: 0602-410360
Assistant Regional Director: Peter Lauener

EMPLOYMENT SERVICE
New Town House
Maid Marian Way
Nottingham NG1 6GT
Telephone: 0602-483308
Regional Director: Ann Le-Sage

DEPARTMENT OF TRADE AND INDUSTRY
Severns House, 20 Middle Pavement
Nottingham NG1 7DW
Regional office: 0602-506181
Derbyshire: Craig Jones: 0332-47031/0246-239905
Leicestershire: Diane Robertson: 0533-559944
Lincolnshire: Bob Hudson: 0522-512002
Northamptonshire: Paul Rigby: 0604-791105

REGIONAL COUNCIL FOR SPORT AND RECREATION EAST MIDLANDS
Grove House
Bridgford Road, West Bridgford
Nottingham NG2 6AP
Telephone: 0602-821887
T Garfield

EAST MIDLANDS FURTHER EDUCATION COUNCIL
Robins Wood House
Robins Wood Road , Aspley
Nottingham NG8 3NH
Telephone: 0602-293291
Secretary: R Ainscough

NATIONAL PARK
PEAK DISTRICT
Established: 1951 (1,438 sq km, 555 sq miles)
Peak Park Jt Planning Board
Peak NP Office
Baslow Road
Bakewell DE4 1AE
Telephone: 0629-814321

EAST MIDLANDS ARTS BOARD
Mountfields House
Forest Road
Loughborough LE11 3HU
Telephone: 0509-218292
Chief Executive: J Buston

NORTH-EAST
Wellbar House
Gallowgate
Newcastle upon Tyne NE1 4TD
Telephone: 091-201 3300
Senior Regional Director: Pamela Denham. Educated: Central Newcastle High School; took a doctorate in physics at Kings College, London. Joined the Department of Trade and Industry in 1967 taking positions in quality design and education. After a secondment in management and development at the Cabinet Office she became Regional Director for the DTI in the North East in 1990.

EMPLOYMENT DEPARTMENT
TRAINING, ENTERPRISE AND EDUCATION DIRECTORATE
Wellbar House, Gallowgate
Newcastle upon Tyne NE1 4TP
Telephone: 091-232 7575
Assistant Regional Director: Keith Heslop

EMPLOYMENT SERVICE
Broadacre House, Market Street
Newcastle upon Tyne NE1 6HH
Telephone: 091-232 6181
Regional Director: Alan Brown

DEPARTMENT OF TRADE AND INDUSTRY
Stanegate House, 2 Groat Market
Newcastle upon Tyne NE1 1YN
Telephone: 091-232 4722
(Consultancy for firms)
Northumberland, Tyne and Wear and Co Durham: Peter Blackburn: 091-232 4722
Cleveland: Bernard Wilson: 0642-232220

NORTHERN REGIONAL COUNCIL FOR SPORT AND RECREATION
Aykley Heads
Durham DH1 5UU
Telephone: 091-384 9595
D Dunlop

NORTHERN ARTS
9-10 Osborne Terrace
Newcastle upon Tyne NE2 1NZ
Telephone: 091-281 6334

NORTHERN COUNCIL FOR FURTHER EDUCATION
5 Grosvenor Villas , Grosvenor Road
Newcastle upon Tyne NE2 2RU
Telephone: 091-281 3242
Secretary: J F Pearce

NORTHERN REGIONAL COUNCILS ASSOCIATION
Guildhall Quayside
Newcastle upon Tyne NE1 3AF
Telephone: 091-261 7388
Secretary: Adrian Smith

NATIONAL PARK
NORTHUMBERLAND NATIONAL PARK
Established: 1956 (1,030 sq km, 398 sq miles)
Northumberland National Park and Countryside Dept
South Park, Hexham NE46 1BS
Telephone: 0434-605555

NORTH-WEST

Sunley Tower
Piccadilly Plaza
Manchester M1 4BE
Telephone: 061-832 9111

Senior Regional Director: Marianne Neville-Rolfe. Born: 1944. Educated: St Mary's Convent, Shaftesbury; Oxford University. Joined the Confederation of British Industry, moving to the DTI in 1973 becoming head of the European Policy Unit there. She became Chief Executive of the Civil Service College, newly an executive agency in 1990, and Director of the Cabinet Office's Top Management Programme.

EMPLOYMENT DEPARTMENT
Washington House
New Bailey Street
Manchester M3 5ER
Telephone: 061-833 0251
Assistant Regional Director: Paul Keen

EMPLOYMENT SERVICE
Julian Roberts
Ontario House
2 Furness Quay
Salford M5 2XZ
Telephone: 061-873 7077

DEPARTMENT OF TRADE AND INDUSTRY
Sunley Tower
Piccadilly Plaza
Manchester M1 4BE
Telephone: 061-838 5000
(Consultancy for firms)
Cheshire: Alan Pierce: 0606-737247
Cumbria: Ken Wright: 0900-828328
Lancashire: Frank Duffy: 0772-653000

NORTH-WEST REGIONAL COUNCIL FOR SPORT AND RECREATION
5th Floor
Astley House, Quay Street
Manchester M3 4AE
C C Clark

CENTRAL: NORTH WESTERN RAC FOR FURTHER EDUCATION
Town Hall
Walkden Road, Worsley
Manchester M28 4QE
Telephone: 061-702 8700
Manager: R S Welsh

NORTH-WEST ARTS BOARD
12 Charter Street
Manchester M1 6HY
Telephone: 061-228 3062

NATIONAL PARK
LAKE DISTRICT NATIONAL PARK
Established: 1951 (2,279 sq km, 880 sq miles)
Lake District National Park Authority
National Park Office
Busher Walk
Kendal LA9 4RH
Telephone: 0539-724555

SOUTH-EAST

Charles House
375 Kensington High Street
London W14 8QH
Telephone: 071-605 9000

Senior Regional Director: Gillian Ashmore. Born: 1949. Educated: Cambridge University. Joined Civil Service in 1971 serving subsequently in the Departments of the Environment, Transport, Employment and Trade & Industry becoming deputy director Enterprise and Deregulation Unit (DTI). At Transport she was seconded to assist with British Rail privatisation.

EMPLOYMENT DEPARTMENT
TRAINING, ENTERPRISE AND EDUCATION DIRECTORATE

Telford House
Hamilton Close
Basingstoke RG21 2UZ
Telephone: 0256-29266
Assistant Regional Director: David Main

EMPLOYMENT SERVICE

236 Grays Inn Road
London WC1X 8HL
Telephone: 071-278 0363
Regional Director, London and South-East Region: Richard Foster

DEPARTMENT OF TRADE AND INDUSTRY

Bridge Place
88-89 Eccleston Square
London SW1V 1PT
Telephone: 071-215 5000
(Consultancy for firms)
Greater London: 071-627 7800
Kent, Sussex and Surrey: Martin Payne: 0737-226913
Berkshire, Bucks, Oxford, Hants, IOW: Glenis Barnes: 0734-395616
East Kent: Judith Coates: 0843-290511
North Kent: Tony Mills: 0634-829299
South Hants: Lyn Stevens: 0705-294111

SOUTH-EAST EGIONAL COUNCIL FOR SPORT AND RECREATION

PO Box 480
Crystal Palace National Sports Centre
Ledrington Road
London SE19 2BQ
Telephone: 081-778 8600
M Lockhart

SOUTHERN EGIONAL COUNCIL FOR SPORT AND RECREATION
51a Church Street
Caversham
Reading RG4 8AX
Telephone: 0734-483311
L J Bridgeman

SOUTH-EAST: THE LONDON AND SOUTH-EAST REGIONAL PLANNING
CONFERENCE, SERPLAN
50-64 Broadway
London SW1H 0DB
Telephone: 071-799 2191

SOUTH-EAST ARTS BOARD
10 Mount Ephraim
Tunbridge Wells
Kent TN4 8AS
Telephone: 0892-515210
Director: C Cooper

SOUTHERN ARTS
13 St Clement Street
Winchester SO23 9DQ
Telephone: 0962-55099
Executive Director: W Dufton

SOUTHERN REGIONAL COUNCIL FOR FURTHER EDUCATION AND TRAINING
26 Bath Road
Reading RG1 6NT
Telephone: 0734-572120
Secretary: B Knowles

LEE VALLEY REGIONAL PARK AUTHORITY
Myddleton House
Bulls Cross
Enfield EN2 9HG
Telephone: 0992-717711
(Under the Lee Valley Regional Park Act 1966 levies on local authority council tax payers.)

YORKSHIRE AND HUMBERSIDE
City House
New Station Street
Leeds LS1 4JD
Telephone: 0532-836300
Senior Regional Director: Jeremy Walker. Born: 1949. Educated: Birmingham University;
Joined Department of Employment 1971 and with subsequent positions in the Cabinet
Office's economic secretariat and, in 1978, the Manpower Services Commission. After

267

service with the Australian Government in Canberra became (Employment) Regional Manager for Yorks and Humberside and leader of Leeds and Bradford City Action team.

DEPARTMENT OF EMPLOYMENT
TRAINING, ENTERPRISE AND EDUCATION DIRECTORATE
City House
New Station Street
Leeds LS1 4JD
Telephone: 0532-341044
Assistant Regional Director: Greg Dyche

EMPLOYMENT SERVICE
Jubilee House
33-41 Park Places
Leeds LS1 2RE
Telephone: 0532-446299
Regional Director: Geoff Humphreys

DEPARTMENT OF TRADE AND INDUSTRY
25 Queen Street
Leeds LS1 2TW
Telephone: 0532-443171
(Consultancy for firms)
Yorks N and W, Humberside: Keith Thompson: 0532-338300
Humberside: Keith Marson: 0482-465741
South Yorks: John Whitehouse: 0742-729849

REGIONAL COUNCIL FOR SPORT AND RECREATION YORKSHIRE AND HUMBERSIDE
Coronet House, Queen Street
Leeds LS1 4PW
Telephone: 0532-422189
C Villiers

YORKSHIRE AND HUMBERSIDE ARTS
21 Bond Street
Dewsbury WF13 1AX
Telephone: 0924-455555
Executive Director: R Lancaster

YORKSHIRE AND HUMBERSIDE REGIONAL ASSOCIATION (PLANNING)
Barnsley MBC
Town Hall
Barnsley S70 2TA
Telephone: 0226-770770
Hon Secretary: J A Edwards

NATIONAL PARKS
NORTH YORK MOORS NATIONAL PARK
Established: 1952 (1,438 sq km, 555 sq miles)
North York Moors National Park
NYCC
The Old Vicarage
Bondgate
Helmsley YO6 5BP

YORKSHIRE DALES NATIONAL PARK
Established: 1954 (1,761 sq km, 680 sq miles)
Yorkshire Dales National Park
Bainbridge
Leyburn DL8 3BP

YORKSHIRE AND HUMBERSIDE ASSOCIATION FOR FURTHER AND HIGHER EDUCATION
Business Centre
13 Wellington Street
Dewsbury WF13 1XG
Telephone: 0924-450900
Chief Officer: Pam Cole

EASTERN
Room 306
Heron House
49-53 Goldington Road
Bedford MK40 3LL
Telephone: 0234-363131

Senior Regional Director: John Turner. Born: 1946. Educated: Ramsey Abbey, Northwood Hills Grammar Schools. Joined Civil Service 1967 and served in the Department of Trade and Industry and the Department of Employment before moving to the Manpower Services Commission where, after serving in Private Office with Lord Young and Sir Norman Fowler, he became deputy Chief Executive of the Employment Service in 1989.

EMPLOYMENT DEPARTMENT
Victory House, Histon
Cambridge CB4 4ZR
Telephone: 0223-202000
Celia Johnson

DEPARTMENT OF TRADE AND INDUSTRY
Building A, Westbrook Centre
Milton Road, Cambridge CB4 1YG
Telephone: 0223-461939
(Consultancy for firms): Stuart Ellis
Essex: Jenny Middleton: 0245-492385

EASTERN REGIONAL COUNCIL FOR SPORT AND RECREATION EASTERN
26 Bromham Road
Bedford MK40 2QP
Telephone: 0234-45222

EAST ANGLIAN RAC FOR FURTHER EDUCATION
2 Looms Lane
Bury St Edmunds
Suffolk IP33 1HE
Telephone: 0284-764977
Secretary: Helen Herrington

BROADS AUTHORITY
Thomas Harvey House
18 Colegate
Norwich NR3 1BQ
Telephone: 0603-610734
(Established in 1978 as a joint local authority committee; under Norfolk and Suffolk
Broad Act 1988 a statutory board with 75 per cent of funding from central government.)
Chief Executive: M A Clark

EASTERN ARTS BOARD
Cherry Hinton Hall
Cherry Hinton , Cambridge CB1 4DW
Telephone: 0223-213355
Director: J Newton

STANDING CONFERENCE OF EAST ANGLIAN LOCAL AUTHORITIES
County Hall
Ipswich IP4 2JS
Telephone: 0473-230000

LONDON
236 Grays Inn Road
London WC1X 8HL
Telephone: 071-211 4193

Senior Regional Director: Robin Young (Grade 2). Born: 1948. Educated: Fettes College,
Edinburgh; University College, Oxford. Joined Department of the Environment 1973
later serving in the Minister for Housing's Private Office in 1980. His work included
housing and environmental policy and he became head of the Local Government
Directorate in 1992 dealing with local government reorganisation.

Director, Government Office for London (Transport): Irving Yass. Born: 1935.
Educated: Harrow County Grammar; Balliol College, Oxford. Joined HM Treasury mov-
ing to the DoE in 1971 serving as Secretary of the Committee on Local Government
Finance 1974. His jobs in the Department of Transport have included director of finance.

EMPLOYMENT DEPARTMENT: TRAINING, ENTERPRISE AND
EDUCATION DIRECTORATE
236 Grays Inn Road
London WC1X 8HL
Telephone: 071-211 3000
Win Harris

LONDON REGIONAL COUNCIL FOR SPORT AND RECREATION
PO Box 480
Crystal Palace National Sports Centre
Ledrington Road
London SE19 2BQ
Telephone: 081-778 8600
A D Sutch

LONDON AND SOUTH-EAST RAC FOR EDUCATION AND TRAINING
232 Vauxhall Bridge Road
London SW1V 1AU
Telephone: 071-233 6199
Director: Laurie South

LONDON ARTS BOARD
3rd Floor, Elm House
133 Long Acre
London WC2
Telephone: 071-240 1313
Chief Executive: T Mason

The abolition of the Greater London Council in 1986 left the map of London's government complicated. A series of special and ad hoc bodies provide services which in other areas still fall within the purview of elected councils.

LONDON BOROUGHS GRANTS UNIT
5th Floor
Regal House
London Road
Twickenham TW1 3QS
Telephone: 081-891 5021
Director: Gerald Oppenheim

LONDON PLANNING ADVISORY COMMITTEE
Eastern House
8-10 Eastern Road
Romford RM1 3PN
Telephone: 0708-724515
Chief Planning Officer: M Simmons

LONDON RESEARCH CENTRE
81 Black Prince Road
London SE1 7SZ
Telephone: 071-735 4250
Chief Executive: Ann Page

LONDON RESIDUARY BODY
Globe House
Temple Place
London WC2R 3HP
Telephone: 071-633-5000
Secretary: John Howes

LONDON WASTE REGULATION AUTHORITY
Established by government order to control the movement of hazardous waste.
Hampton House
20 Albert Embankment
London SE1 7TJ
Telephone: 071-587 3601
Director: J Ferguson

EAST LONDON WASTE AUTHORITY
c/o Town Clerk
Barking and Dagenham LBC
Dagenham RM10 7BN
Telephone: 081-592 4500

NORTH LONDON WASTE AUTHORITY
c/o Edmonton Solid Waste Incineration Plant
Angel Road
London N18 3AG

WEST LONDON WASTE AUTHORITY
West London Waste Office
Mogden Works, Mogden Lane
Isleworth, London TW7
Telephone: 081-847 5555

WESTERN RIVERSIDE WASTE AUTHORITY
Smugglers Way
London SW18 3JU
Telephone: 081-871 2788

LOCAL GOVERNMENT BODIES IN ENGLAND

Local government is part of 'the state', in its broadest definition. Nowadays central government has considerable leverage over local authorities especially in terms of their spending, some 85 per cent of which comes from central grants. Yet local authorities retain by dint of the electoral process a special legitimacy and some autonomy. For certain services, such as the police and probation, identifying where local authority influence ends and central government's starts is very difficult – a fact exploited by the more astute chief constables. Those joint police forces such as Thames Valley covering areas larger than a single local authority seem occasionally to exist in an administrative space of their own.

Here are some of the principal national bodies associated with local government.

THE ASSOCIATION OF COUNTY COUNCILS
Eaton House
66a Eaton Square
London SW1W 9BH
Telephone: 071-235 1200
Secretary: Robin Wendt

LONDON BOROUGHS ASSOCIATION
College House
Great Peter Street
London SW1P 3LN
Telephone: 071-799 2477
Secretary: John Hall

ASSOCIATION OF LONDON AUTHORITIES
36 Old Queen Street
London SW1H 9JF
Telephone: 071-222 7799
Secretary: John McDonnell

ASSOCIATION OF METROPOLITAN AUTHORITIES
35 Great Smith Street
London SW1P 3BJ
Telephone: 071-222 8100
Secretary: Rodney Brooke

ASSOCIATION OF DISTRICT COUNCILS
26 Chapter Street
London SW1P 4ND
Telephone: 071-233 6868
Secretary: Geoffrey Filkin

THE LOCAL AUTHORITIES' MUTUAL INVESTMENT TRUST
St Alphage House
2 Fore Street
London EC2Y 5AQ
Telephone: 071-588 1815
Chairman: H Purcell
Secretary: D Fitton

THE NATIONAL ASSOCIATION OF LOCAL COUNCILS
108 Great Russell Street
London WC1B 3LD
Telephone: 071-637 1865
Secretary: John Clark
(Federation of parish councils and 'town councils'.)

LOCAL GOVERNMENT MANAGEMENT BOARD
41 Belgrave Square
London SW1X 8NZ
Telephone: 071-235 6081
and
Arndale House, Arndale Centre
Luton LU1 2TS
Telephone: 0582-451166
Chief Executive: Judith Hunt

POLICE AND PROBATION
COMBINED FORCES IN ENGLAND

AVON AND SOMERSET
37 Valley Road
Portishead
Bristol BS20 8QY
Telephone: 0272-277777

DEVON AND CORNWALL
Force HQ
Middlemoor
Exeter EX2 7HQ
Telephone: 0392-52101

HAMPSHIRE CONSTABULARY (HANTS AND IOW)
Police HQ
West Hill, Winchester SO22 5DB
Telephone: 0962-868133

NORTHUMBRIA POLICE FORCE
HQ Ponteland
Newcastle upon Tyne NE20 0BL
Telephone: 0661-72555

SUSSEX POLICE
Police HQ
Malling House
Lewes BN7 2DZ
Telephone: 0273-475432

THAMES VALLEY POLICE
Oxford Road
Kidlington
Oxford OX5 2NX
Telephone: 0865-846000

WEST MERCIA CONSTABULARY
PO Box 55
Hindlip Hall
Worcester WR3 8SP
Telephone: 0905-723000

PROBATION

Probation Committees made up of magistrates and councillors and co-opted members oversee the work of probation officers; while these committees are corporate bodies independent of central and local government the Home Secretary is responsible to Parliament for their work. Four-fifths of the spending of the committees is provided by the Home Office by way of specific grants to councils which provide the remainder.

ASSOCIATION OF CHIEF OFFICERS OF PROBATION
Head Office:
20-30 Lawefield Lane
Wakefield WF2 8SP
Telephone: 0924-361156

LONDON OFFICE:
212 Whitechapel Road,
London E1 1BJ
Telephone: 071-377 9141
General Secretary: W R Weston

SCOTLAND

The Scottish Office
St Andrew's House
Edinburgh EH1 3DG
Telephone: 031-556 8400

London:
Dover House, Whitehall
London SW1A 2AU
Telephone: 071-270 3000

Since the Act of Union, the government of Scotland has had a certain distinctiveness within the United Kingdom but within bounds. In the twentieth century the 'welfare state' functions of government have largely been administrated on a UK- or Great-Britain-wide basis and social security payments are made no differently in Aberdeen than in Abingdon. But the Scottish Office in Edinburgh has come to have a particular administrative culture. Most of its officials spend most of their Civil Service careers in Scotland. The Office is directly responsible for a variety of functions which in England are handled by separate departments and so the complex of buildings around New St Andrews House has the air of a Whitehall in miniature.

Traditionally the Secretary of State 'spoke for' Scotland to his Cabinet colleagues to whom he often appears as a kind of viceroy, and until recently managed to secure relatively generous treatment in successive public expenditure rounds. There was talk in the 1980s of 'Keynesianism north of the Border' while economic disciplines to the South were drier. The impact in Scotland of certain measures, with the exception of the poll tax which was 'piloted' north of the border, has often blunted in response to the relatively weak position of the Conservative party in Scottish politics. For example, while water was privatised in England, the Government has stopped short of selling 'Scotland's water' after loud outcry.

The Scottish Office is divided into a number of substantive sub-departments and has responsibility for the activities in Scotland of several statutory bodies whose functions extended throughout Great Britain, such as the Forestry Commission.

Permanent Under-Secretary of State: Sir Russell Hillhouse (Grade 1). Born: 1938. Educated: Hutchesons' Grammar, Glasgow; Glasgow University. Joined the Scottish Education Department in 1962 and after a secondment to HM Treasury in the early 1970s joined the Scottish Home and Health Department in 1977.

Principal Establishment Officer: Colin MacDonald. Born: 1943. Educated: Allan Glen's School, Glasgow; University of Strathclyde. Joined the Scottish Development Department 1967, taking charge of the housing division in 1988.

Director of Administrative Services: Robert Gordon.

Principal Finance Officer: Eileen Mackay. Born: 1943. Educated: Dingwall Academy; Edinburgh University. Joined Department of Employment, Scotland in 1965 and, after secondments to HM Treasury and the Central Policy Review Staff (the 'Think-tank') she became Under-Secretary for housing in 1988.

Solicitor: Robert Brodie (Grade 2). Born: 1938. Educated: Morgan Academy, Dundee; St Andrews University. Qualified as a solicitor and joined the Scottish Office in 1965 becoming deputy director of Scottish Courts Administration in 1975.

Deputy Solicitor: Norman Boe. Born: 1943. Educated: George Heriot's School, Edinburgh; Edinburgh University. Qualified as a solicitor and worked in private practice before joining the Scottish Office in 1970.

AGRICULTURE AND FISHERIES

Pentland House
47 Robb's Loan
Edinburgh EH14 1TW
Telephone: 031-556 8400

Secretary: Kenneth MacKenzie (Grade 2). Born: 1943. Educated: Birkenhead School; Pembroke College, Oxford. Joined the Scottish Home and Health Department in 1965, serving in Private Office four years later. After joining the Scottish Education Department, he became Principal Finance Officer in 1985.

Commodities and Land: Tony Cameron. Born: 1947. Educated: Stranraer High School.

Joined the Department of Agriculture for Scotland in 1966, becoming an Assistant Secretary in 1982.

Fisheries Secretary: Alastair Findlay. Born: 1944. Educated: Kelso High School; University of Edinburgh. Joined the Department of Agriculture for Scotland in 1966. After Private Office experience, he was seconded to the Foreign Office, later moving to higher education within the SO's Education Deptment.

EDUCATION

New St Andrew's House
Edinburgh EH1 3TG
Telephone: 031-556 8400

Secretary: Gerald Wilson (Grade 2). Born: 1939. Educated: Holy Cross Academy, Edinburgh; University of Edinburgh. Joined the Scottish Home and Health Department in 1961. After Private Office experience beginning in 1965, he became Counsellor, UK Permanent Representative to the European Communities. He was later Under-Secretary at the Industry Department for Scotland.

Schools: John Martin. Born: 1946; Educated: Bell-Baxter High School, Cupar; University of St Andrews. Joined the Scottish Education Department in 1968 and was seconded to the Rayner Scrutiny team in 1979.

Higher and Further Education: Alastair Weatherston. Born: 1935. Educated: Peebles High School; Edinburgh University. Joined the Department of Health for Scotland in 1959; seconded to the Cabinet Office in 1972. In 1982 he became Director, Scottish Courts Administration.

HM Senior Chief Inspector of Schools: Nisbet Gallacher. Born: 1936. Educated: Kilmarnock Academy; Glasgow University; Jordanhill College of Education. Maths teacher and lecturer, appointed to HM Inspectorate in 1969, becoming HM Senior Chief Inspector in 1987.

ENVIRONMENT

New St Andrew's House
Edinburgh EH1 3TG
Telephone: 031-556 8400

Secretary: Harold Mills (Grade 2). Born: 1938. Educated: Greenock High School; University of Glasgow. After doing scientific research joined the Scottish Home and Health Dept in 1970. After secondment to the Privy Council Office in 1981, became Principal Finance Officer in the Scottish Office in 1988.

Local Government: John Graham. Born: 1950. Educated: Edinburgh Academy; Corpus Christi College, Oxford. Joined the Scottish Office in 1972, serving in ministers' Private Offices in 1975 and 1983.

Rural Affairs and Environment: Stephen Hampson. Born: 1946. Educated: Leys School, Cambridge; University College, Oxford. Joined Civil Service in 1975, working in the Department of Industry, with a spell overseas in HM Diplomatic Service.

Housing: Muir Russell. Born: 1949. Educated: High School of Glasgow; University of Glasgow. Joined the Scottish Office in 1970 and served in Private Office in 1981. He was seconded to the Cabinet Office in 1990.

Director, Building and Chief Architect: Dr John Gibbons. Born: 1940. Educated: Oldbury Grammar; Birmingham University; Edinburgh University PhD. After private practice and academic work he joined the Scottish Development Department in 1972.

Director, Engineering and Chief Engineer: Alasdair Paton. Born: 1944. Educated: John Neilson Institution, Paisley; University of Glasgow. After working for the Clyde Port Authority he joined the Department of Agriculture for Scotland in 1971; seconded to the Hong Kong government in 1977.

Chief Reporter (planning inquiries): Gillian Pain. Born: 1936. Educated: Felixstowe College, Suffolk; University of St Andrews; University College, London. After teaching and service with Essex County joined the Department of the Environment in London and became Principal Planning Inspector in 1977.

HOME AND HEALTH
St Andrew's House
Edinburgh EH1 3DG
Telephone: 031-556 8400
Secretary: Hamish Hamill (Grade 2).

Police, Fire: David Essery. Born: 1938. Educated: Royal High School, Edinburgh. Joined the Department of Health for Scotland in 1956, serving in Private Office in 1968. He joined the Scottish Development Department in 1981.

Criminal Justice: Gillian Stewart. Born: 1945. Educated: Blyth Grammar; University of Durham. Joined the Scottish Office in 1970, taking posts in education, social work and local government.

Health, Police: David Belfall.

INDUSTRY
New St Andrew's House
Edinburgh EH1 3TG
Telephone: 031-556 8400

Secretary: Peter Mackay (Grade 2). Born: 1940. Educated: Glasgow High School; St Andrews University. After teaching, joined the Scottish Office in 1963, serving with the Manpower Services Commission in Scotland and later with the Department of Employment.

Urban Regeneration, New Towns: Edward Weeple. Born: 1945. Educated: St Aloysius' College, Glasgow; University of Glasgow. Joined the Ministry of Health in 1968 serving three years later in Private Office. He joined the Scottish Economic Planning Department in 1978 and the Department of Agriculture for Scotland in 1985.

European Funds, Transport: John Elvidge. Born: 1951. Educated: Sir George Monoux School, London; St Catherine's College, Oxford. Joined Civil Service in 1973, working in Scottish OFfice, on urban regeneration, industry and, later, European co-ordination.

Director, Road and Chief Road Engineer: John Dawson. Born: 1950. Educated: Mill Hill School; Southampton University. Served with Departments of Environment and Transport and joined their joint London Regional Office in 1985.

Industrial Expansion: Godfrey Robson. Born: 1946. Educated: St Joseph's College, Dumfries; Edinburgh University. Joined the Scottish Office in 1970 serving nine years later in Private Office and later taking a position overseeing local government finance.

Secretary of Commissions for Scotland (appointments of Justices of the Peace, etc.):
Edward Fraser. Born: 1931. Educated: Aberdeen Grammar; University of Aberdeen; Christ's College, Cambridge. Joined the Scottish Home Department in 1957, seconded to the Cabinet Office in 1964 and later headed the local government finance group in the Scottish Office.

EMPLOYMENT SERVICE SCOTLAND
Alan Brown
Argyll House, 3 Lawson Street
Edinburgh EH3 9SD
Telephone: 031-229 9191

SCOTTISH LAW

LORD ADVOCATE'S DEPARTMENT
2 Carlton Gardens
London SW1Y 5AA
Telephone: 071-210 1010

THE CROWN OFFICE
25 Chamber Street
Edinburgh EH1 1LA
Telephone: 031-226 2626
(The Lord Advocate and the Solicitor General for Scotland are the Law Officers for the Crown for Scotland and chief advisers on legal questions. They handle legislation exclusively for Scotland and the adaptation of other legislation to Scotland. The Crown Office is responsible for public prosecutions in Scotland.)

Lord Advocate: The Rt Hon the Lord Rodger of Earlsferry QC (Alan Rodger). Born: 1944. Educated: Kelvinside Academy; Glasgow University; New College Oxford (DPhil). After an academic career, became QC in 1985 and Solicitor General for Scotland in 1989.

Solicitor General for Scotland: Thomas Dawson QC. Born: 1948. Educated: Royal High School of Edinburgh; Edinburgh University. Became an advocate in 1973 and Advocate Deputy ten years later.

Legal Secretary and First Scottish Parliamentary Counsel: John McCluskie QC. Born: 1946. Educated: Hyndland School, Glasgow; Glasgow University. Qualified as a solicitor in 1970; worked for the South of Scotland Electricity Board and joined the Lord Advocate's Department in 1972.

Assistant Legal Secretaries and Scottish Parliamentary Counsel: Gregor Clark. Born: 1946. Educated: Queen Park Secondary, Glasgow; St Andrews University. Joined the Faculty of Advocates in 1972 and the Lord Advocate's Department in 1974.

Gregor Kowalski. Born: 1949. Educated: Airdrie Academy; Strathclyde University. Became Procurator Fiscal depute, in Glasgow in 1974 and joined the Lord Advocate's Department in 1978.

Patrick Layden. Born: 1949. Educated: Holy Cross Academy, Edinburgh; Edinburgh University. Called to Scottish bar in 1973 and joined the Lord Advocate's Department in 1977.

C A M Wilson.

Crown Agent: J D Lowe (Grade 2).
Regional Procurator Fiscal Glasgow and Strathkelvin: A C Normand.
Regional Procurator Fiscal Lothian and Borders: R F Lees.
Regional Procurator Fiscal Grampian Highlands and Islands: A D Vannet (Grade 4).
Regional Procurator Fiscal Tayside, Central and Fife: B K Heywood (Grade 4).
Regional Procurator Fiscal North Strathclyde: J D Friel (Grade 4).
Regional Procurator Fiscal South Strathclyde: W G Carmichael (Grade 4).

SUPREME COURTS, SCOTLAND
Parliament House
11 Parliament Square
Edinburgh EH1 1RQ
Telephone: 031-225 2595

Lord Justice General of Scotland and Lord President of the Court of Session: The Rt Hon Lord Hope (David Hope). Born: 1938. Educated: Edinburgh Academy; Rugby School; St John's College, Cambridge; Edinburgh University. Joined the Faculty of Advocates in 1965 and became QC in 1978.
The Principal Clerk of Session and Justiciary: H S Foley (Grade 5).

SCOTTISH COURTS ADMINISTRATION
26/27 Royal Terrace
Edinburgh EH7 5AH
Telephone: 031-556 0755

Director: Gordon Murray. Born: 1935. Educated: Kirkcaldy High School; Edinburgh University (PhD). After doing research, joined the Scottish Home and Health Department in 1970 and took responsibility for Central Services in the Scottish Office in 1979.

SCOTTISH LAND COURT
1 Grosvenor Crescent
Edinburgh EH12 5ER
Telephone: 031-225 3595

Function: dealing with agricultural and crofting cases.
Chairman: The Hon Lord Philip QC. Born: 1942. Educated: High School of Glasgow; St Andrews University. Qualified as a solicitor and became an advocate in 1973 and QC in 1984.
Principal Clerk: K H R Graham (Grade 6).

SCOTTISH LAW COMMISSION
140 Causewayside
Edinburgh EH9 1PR
Telephone: 031-668 2131
Chairman: The Lord Davidson
Commissioners: Dr E M Clive, Professor P N Love, Sheriff I D Macphail QC, W A Nimmo Smith QC.
Secretary: K F Barclay.

SCOTTISH LEGAL AID BOARD
44 Drumsheugh Gardens
Edinburgh EH3 7SW
Telephone: 031-226 7061
Chairman: Mrs C A Davis
Chief Executive: A E M Douglas

LANDS TRIBUNAL FOR SCOTLAND
Function: Responsible for resolving land and title disputes, and awarding compensation
for compulsory purchases.
President: The Hon Lord Philip QC
1 Grosvenor Crescent
Edinburgh EH12 5ER
Telephone: 031-225 3595

PENSIONS APPEAL TRIBUNAL FOR SCOTLAND
Function: Responsible for hearing appeals on war pensions.
President: Arthur Hamilton QC
20 Walker Street
Edinburgh EH7 7HS
Telephone: 031-220 1404

EXECUTIVE AGENCIES IN SCOTLAND
(For details *see* Chapter Three.)
HISTORIC SCOTLAND
QUEEN VICTORIA SCHOOL
REGISTERS OF SCOTLAND
SCOTTISH AGRICULTURAL SCIENCE AGENCY
SCOTTISH FISHERIES PROTECTION AGENCY
SCOTTISH OFFICE PENSION AGENCY
SCOTTISH PRISON SERVICE
SCOTTISH RECORD OFFICE
STUDENT AWARDS AGENCY FOR SCOTLAND

TRIBUNALS
CHILDREN'S PANEL
HORSERACE BETTING LEVY APPEAL TRIBUNAL
RENT ASSESSMENT PANEL
Telephone: 031-244 4999

SCOTTISH HEALTH SERVICE
Chief Executive: G R Scaife.
Chief Medical Officer: Dr R E Kendell (Grade 2).
Deputy Chief Medical Officer: Dr A B Young.
Chief Nursing Officer: Miss A Jarvie.

COMMON SERVICES AGENCY FOR THE SCOTTISH HEALTH SERVICE
Trinity Park House
South Trinity Road
Edinburgh EH5 3SE
Telephone: 031-552 6255
General Manager: J T Donald

SCOTTISH AMBULANCE SERVICE
National HQ
Tipperlinn Road
Edinburgh EH10 5RF

HEALTH SERVICE COMMISSIONER FOR SCOTLAND
Second Floor
11 Melville Crescent
Edinburgh EH3 7LU
Telephone: 031-225 7465
Unit Leader (Grade 7): G Keil

HEALTH EDUCATION BOARD FOR SCOTLAND
Woodburn House
Canaan Lane
Edinburgh EH10 4SG
Telephone: 031-447 8044

SCOTTISH HEALTH BOARDS

ARGYLL AND CLYDE
Gilmour House
Paisley PA1 1DU
Telephone: 041-887 0131
Chairman: R R Reid
General Manager: I C Smith

AYRSHIRE AND ARRAN
PO Box 13
1 Seafield House, Doonfoot Road
Ayr KA7 4DW
Telephone: 0292-611040
Chairman: W S Fyfe
General Manager: J M Eckford

BORDERS
Huntlyburn, Melrose
Roxburgh TD6 9BP
Telephone: 0896-822662
Chairman: D H Pringle
General Manager: D A Peters

DUMFRIES AND GALLOWAY
Nithbank
Dumfries DG1 2SD
Telephone: 0387-46246
Chairman: J A McIntyre
General Manager: M D Cook

FIFE
Glenrothes House
North Street, Glenrothes
Telephone: 0592-754355
Chairman: Mrs A H Ferguson
General Manager: M Murray

FORTH VALLEY
33 Spittal St
Stirling FK8 1DX
Chairman: Mrs J I D Isbister
General Manager: Miss L Barrie

GRAMPIAN
1-7 Albyn Place
Aberdeen AB9 8QP
Telephone: 0224-589901
Chairman: J Kyle
General Manager: F E L Hartnett

GREATER GLASGOW
112 Ingram Street
Glasgow G1 1ET
Telephone: 041-552 6222
Chairman: Sir Thomas Thomson
General Manager: L E Peterken

HIGHLAND
Reay House
17 Old Edinburgh Road
Inverness IV2 3HG
Telephone: 0463-239851
Chairman: J Robertson
General Manager: R R W Stewart

LANARKSHIRE
Board Offices
14 Beckford Street
Hamilton ML3 OTA
Telephone: 0698-281313
Chairman: Mrs B M Gunn
General Manager: F Clark

LOTHIAN
148 Pleasance
Edinburgh EH8 9RS
Telephone: 031-668 3940
Chairman: J W Baynham
General Manager: J Lusby

ORKNEY
New Scapa Road
Kirkwall
Orkney
Telephone: 0586-872763
Chairman: I Leslie
General Manager: Dr J I Cromarty

SHETLAND
28 Burgh Road
Lerwick ZE1 0QP
Telephone: 0595-5678
Chairman: Mrs F Grains
General Manager: B J Atherton

TAYSIDE
PO Box 75, Vernonholme
Riverside Drive
Dundee DD1 9NL
Telephone: 0382-645151
Chairman: J C Macfarlane
General Manager: Dr R C Graham

WESTERN ISLES
Health Board Offices
37 South Beach Street
Stornoway
Telephone: 0851-702997
Chairman: Mrs M A MacMillan
General Manager: J J Glover

GENERAL REGISTER OF BIRTHS, DEATHS AND MARRIAGES (SCOTLAND)

New Register House
Edinburgh EH1 3YT
Telephone: 031-334 0380
Registrar General: Dr C M Glennie

CONVENTION OF SCOTTISH LOCAL AUTHORITIES
Rosebery House
9 Haymarket Terrace
Edinburgh EH12 5XZ
Telephone: 031-346 1222
Secretary General: Roy MacIver

COMMISSION FOR LOCAL ADMINISTRATION IN SCOTLAND
23 Walker Street
Edinburgh EH3 7HX
Telephone: 031-225 5300
Commissioner: Robert Peggie
Secretary: Janice Renton

COMMISSION FOR LOCAL AUTHORITY ACCOUNTS IN SCOTLAND
18 George Street
Edinburgh EH2 2QU
Telephone: 031-226 7346
Chairman: Professor Ian Percy

NON-DEPARTMENTAL PUBLIC BODIES UNDER THE SCOTTISH OFFICE

NEW TOWNS

CUMBERNAULD DEVELOPMENT CORPORATION
Corporation Office
Cumbernauld House
Cumbernauld
Glasgow G67 3JH
Telephone: 0236-721155
Chief Executive: D Millan

EAST KILBRIDE DEVELOPMENT CORPORATION
Atholl House
East Kilbride
Glasgow G74 1LU
Telephone: 0355-241111
Managing Director: J C Shaw

GLENROTHES DEVELOPMENT CORPORATION
Balgonie Road
Markinch, Glenrothes
Fife KY7 6AH
Telephone: 0592-754343
Chief Executive: Martin Cracknell

IRVINE DEVELOPMENT CORPORATION
Perceton House
Irvine
Ayrshire KA11
Telephone: 0294-214100
Managing Director: R A Rickets

LIVINGSTON DEVELOPMENT CORPORATION
Livingston
West Lothian EH54 6QA
Telephone: 0506-414177
Chief Executive: J Pollock

CLYDE RIVER PURIFICATION BOARD
Function: To promote the cleanliness of rivers, estuaries, coastal waters and ground-water, and conserve water resources in the region.
Rivers House
Murray Road
East Kilbride G75 0LA
Telephone: 0355-238181
Chairman: A MacLean JP

CROFTERS COMMISSION
Function: Responsible for maintaining the register of crofts, letting and sub-letting of crofts, and the removal of land from crofting tenure.
4-6 Castle Wynd
Inverness IV2 3EQ
Telephone: 0463-237231
Chairman: H A M MacLean

EDINBURGH TOWN CONSERVATION COMMITTEE
Function: To administer conservation grants for properties within the Edinburgh Conservation area.
Chairman: Lord Cameron of Lochbroom
13A Dundas Street
Edinburgh EH3 6QG
Telephone: 031-557 5222

FORTH RIVER PURIFICATION BOARD
Function: To promote the cleanliness of rivers, estuaries, coastal waters, and ground-water, and conserve water resources in the area.
Clearwater House
Heriot Watt Research Park
Avenue North
Edinburgh EH14 4AP
Telephone: 031-449 7296
Chairman: Councillor R King

GENERAL TEACHING COUNCIL
Function: Responsible for the registration of professional teachers in Scotland.
5 Royal Terrace
Edinburgh EH7 5AF
Telephone: 031-556 0072
Council Convener: Miss MR Caden

HANNAH RESEARCH INSTITUTE
Function: To conduct research and development relevant to the production and use of milk.
Kirkhill, Ayr KA6 5HL
Telephone: 0292-76013
Chairman: Sir William Kerr Fraser

HIGHLAND RIVER PURIFICATION BOARD
Function: To promote the cleanliness of rivers, estuaries, coastal waters and ground-water, and to conserve water resources in the region.
Strathpeffer Road
Dingwall IV15 9QY
Telephone: 0349-62021
Chairman: N M Graesser

HIGHLANDS AND ISLANDS ENTERPRISE
Function: To promote the economic and social development of the Highlands and Islands. Like Scottish Enterprise, H&I Enterprise has oversight of the Local Enterprise Companies which are the Scottish parallel of the TECs in England.
Bridge House, 20 Bridge Street
Inverness IV1 1QR
Telephone: 0463-234171
Chairman: A F Morrison
Chief Executive: I A Robertson

MACAULAY LAND USE RESEARCH INSTITUTE
Function: To conduct research into land use in order to assess the environmental, economic and social impact of agriculture.
Craigiebutcher
Aberdeen AB9 2QJ
Telephone: 0224-318611
Chairman: Professor J M M Cunningham

MOREDUN DISEASE RESEARCH INSTITUTE
(Animal Disease Research Institute)
Function: To conduct research into animal diseases that undermine biological efficiency, impair welfare, and threaten public health.
408 Gilmerton Road
Edinburgh EH17 7SH
Telephone: 031-6643262
Chairman: J Stobo

NATIONAL BOARD FOR NURSING, MIDWIFERY AND HEALTH VISITING FOR SCOTLAND
Function: Responsible for approving courses leading to professional qualifications.
22 Queen Street
Edinburgh EH2 1JX
Telephone: 031-226 7371
Chairman: Miss C Asher

NATIONAL GALLERIES OF SCOTLAND
Function: To display, research and develop collections of works of fine art.
The Mound
Edinburgh EH2 2EL
Telephone: 031-556 8921
Chairman: A M M Grossart

NATIONAL LIBRARY OF SCOTLAND
Function: Scotland's legal book depository, housing more than six million books, maps, music, manuscripts and periodicals.
George IV Bridge
Edinburgh EH1 1EW
Telephone: 031-226 4531
Chairman: Rt Hon The Earl of Crawford and Balcarres

NATIONAL MUSEUMS OF SCOTLAND
Function: To provide Scotland with a national museum service of international standing.
Chambers Street
Edinburgh EH1 1JF
Telephone: 031-225 7534
Chairman: R H Smith

NORTH-EAST RIVER PURIFICATION BOARD
Function: To promote the cleanliness of rivers, estuaries, coastal waters and groundwater, and to conserve water resources in the region.
Greyhope House
Greyhope Road
Aberdeen AB1 3RD
Telephone: 0224-248338
Chairman: J B Gordon

POLICE EXAMINATIONS BOARD
Function: To oversee the qualifying examinations required for the recruitment and promotion of police officers in Scotland.
Chairman: Mrs L McKay

SCOTTISH OFFICE
HOME AND HEALTH DEPARTMENT
POLICE DIVISION
St Andrew's House
Edinburgh EH1 3DG
Telephone: 031-244 2152

RED DEER COMMISSION
Function: To conserve and control red and sika deer.
Knowsley, 82 Fairfield Road
Inverness IV3 5LH
Telephone: 0463-231751
Chairman: P Gordon-Duff-Pennington

RENT ASSESSMENT PANEL FOR SCOTLAND
Mulberry House
16 Picardy Place
Edinburgh EH1 3JT
Telephone: 031-557 0555
President: G F Robertson
Secretary: Mrs N Eagle

ROWETT RESEARCH INSTITUTE
Function: To advance understanding of the biochemical and physiological aspects of
mammalian nutrition.
Greenburn Road, Bucksburn
Aberdeen AB2 9SB
Telephone: 0224-712751
Chairman: J Provan

ROYAL COMMISSION ON THE ANCIENT AND HISTORICAL MONUMENTS
OF SCOTLAND
Function: Responsible for compiling the inventory of ancient and historical monuments,
and specifying those most worth preserving.
John Sinclair House
16 Bernard Terrace
Edinburgh EH8 9NX
Telephone: 031-662 1456
Chairman: Rt Hon The Earl of Crawford and Balcarres

SCOTTISH AGRICULTURAL WAGES BOARD
Function: Responsible for fixing minimum wages, holiday entitlement and other condi-
tions for agricultural workers.
Pentland House
47 Robb's Loan
Edinburgh EH14 1TY
Telephone: 031-244 6392
Chairman: RA Bennett

SCOTTISH ARTS COUNCIL
Function: To develop and improve knowledge and understanding of the arts.
Scottish Arts Council
12 Manor Place
Edinburgh EH3 7DD
Telephone: 031-226 6051
Chairman: Dr William Brown

SCOTTISH COMMUNITY EDUCATION COUNCIL
Function: To promote the development of community education in Scotland.
Roseberry House
9 Haymarket Terrace
Edinburgh EH12 5EZ
Telephone: 031-313 2488
Chairman: Mrs B Vaughan

SCOTTISH CONVEYANCING AND EXECUTRY SERVICES BOARD
Function: Suspended.
Room 229, St Andrew's House
Edinburgh EH1 3DG
Telephone: 031-244 2417
Chairman: Professor P Love

SCOTTISH COUNCIL FOR EDUCATIONAL TECHNOLOGY
Function: To promote the use of modern technologies in Schools, further and higher education, at work and at home.
74 Victoria Crescent Road
Glasgow G12 9JN
Telephone: 041-334 9314
Chairman: J Graham

SCOTTISH CROP RESEARCH COUNCIL
Function: To conduct research on agricultural, horticultural and industrial crops.
Mylnefield, Invergowrie
Dundee DD2 5DA
Telephone: 0382-562731
Chairman: J Millar

SCOTTISH ENTERPRISE
Function: To promote the development of Scotland's economy and competitiveness. This is the supervisory body for Scotland's Local Enterprise Companies, which parallel the Training and Enterprise Councils of England.
120 Bothwell Street
Glasgow G2 7JP
Telephone: 041-248 2700
Chairman: Professor D MacKay
Chief Executive: C Beveridge

SCOTTISH EXAMINATION BOARD
Function: To conduct examinations and award certificates for secondary education in Scotland.
Ironmills Road, Dalkeith
Midlothian EH22 1LE
Telephone: 031-663 6601
Chairman: I L Fraser

SCOTTISH FILM COUNCIL
Function: Responsible for the development and promotion of the film industry and culture in Scotland.
74 Victoria Crescent Road
Glasgow G12 9JN
Telephone: 041-334 4445
Chairman: A Shiach

SCOTTISH HIGHER EDUCATION FUNDING COUNCIL
Function: To promote the quality and encourage the expansion of teaching and research in Scottish higher educational institutions.
Donaldson House
97 Haymarket Terrace
Edinburgh EH12
Telephone: 031-313 6500
Chairman: Professor John Shaw

SCOTTISH HOMES
Function: Responsible for the promotion of owner occupied and rented housing.
Thistle House
91 Haymarket Terrace
Edinburgh EH12 5HE
Telephone: 031-313 0044
Chairman: Sir James Mellon

SCOTTISH HOSPITAL ENDOWMENTS RESEARCH TRUST
Function: To support clinical and biomedical research with the aim of encouraging young scientists and doctors.
16 Hope Street, Charlotte Square
Edinburgh EH2 4DD
Telephone: 031-226 2561
Chairman: Sir A Williams

SCOTTISH MEDICAL PRACTICES COMMITTEE
Function: Responsible for the distribution of GPs throughout Scotland.
Room A023, Trinity Park House
South Trinity Road
Edinburgh EH5 3SE
Telephone: 031-552 6255, extension 2055
Chairman: Dr D J Callander

SCOTTISH NATURAL HERITAGE
Function: Responsible for the conservation and enhancement of Scotland's national heritage.
12 Hope Terrace
Edinburgh EH9 2AS
Telephone: 031-447 4784
Chairman: Magnus Magnusson
Chief Executive: Roger Crofts

SCOTTISH SEED POTATO DEVELOPMENT COUNCIL
Function: To promote the domestic and foreign marketing of Scottish seed potatoes.
Haddington House
Sidegate, Haddington
East Lothian
Telephone: 0620-823488
Chairman: J Stobo

SCOTTISH SPORTS COUNCIL
Function: Responsible for the development of sport and physical recreation.
Caledonia House
South Gyle
Edinburgh EH12 9DQ
Telephone: 031-317 7200
Chairman: G M Simmers
Chief Executive: F A L Alstead

SCOTTISH TOURIST BOARD
Function: To maximise the economic benefit of tourism for Scotland.
23 Ravelston Terrace
Edinburgh EH4 3EU
Telephone: 031-332 2433
Chairman: Ian Grant

SCOTTISH VOCATIONAL EDUCATION COUNCIL
Function: Responsible for developing, accrediting and awarding vocational qualifications.
Hanover House
24 Douglas Street, Glasgow G2 7NQ
Telephone: 041-248 7900
Chairman: J D F Miller

SOLWAY RIVER PURIFICATION BOARD
Function: Responsible for the cleanliness of rivers, estuaries, coastal waters and ground-water, and the conservation of water resources in the region.
Rivers House, Irongray Road
Newbridge
Dumfries DG2 0JE
Telephone: 0387-720502
Chairman: J Nelson

TAY RIVER PURIFICATION BOARD
Function: Responsible for the cleanliness of rivers, estuaries, coastal waters and ground-water, and the conservation of water resources in the region.
1 South Street
Perth PH2 8NJ
Telephone: 0738-27989
Chairman: I Mitchell

TWEED RIVER PURIFICATION BOARD
Function: Responsible for the cleanliness of rivers, estuaries, coastal water and ground-water, and the conservation of water resources in the region.
Burnbrae
Mossilee Road
Galashiels TD1 1NF
Telephone: 0896-2425
Chairman: A J C Hewat

ADVISORY BODIES

ADVISORY COMMITTEE ON DENTAL ESTABLISHMENTS
ADVISORY COMMITTEE ON MEDICAL ESTABLISHMENTS
ADVISORY COMMITTEE ON SITES OF SPECIAL SCIENTIFIC INTEREST
ANCIENT MONUMENTS BOARD FOR SCOTLAND
BUILDING STANDARDS ADVISORY COMMITTEE
CENTRAL ADVISORY COMMITTEE ON JUSTICES OF THE PEACE
CHILDREN'S PANELS ADVISORY COMMITTEES
CONSULTATIVE COMMITTEE ON FRESHWATER FISHERIES
EXTRA PARLIAMENTARY PANEL
HILL FARMING ADVISORY COMMITTEE
HISTORIC BUILDINGS COUNCIL
    20 Brandon Street
    Edinburgh EH3 5RA
    Telephone: 031-244 2966
    Secretary: I G Dewar

JUSTICE OF THE PEACE ADVISORY COMMITTEES
LOCAL GOVERNMENT BOUNDARY COMMISSION
    Address c/o Scottish Office
    Telephone: 031-244 2196
    Chairman: the Hon Lord Osborne
    Secretary: L J D Boyd

LOCAL REVIEW COMMITTEES FOR HM PRISONS AND YOUNG OFFENDERS'
INSTITUTIONS
MENTAL WELFARE COMMISSION FOR SCOTLAND

25 Drumsheugh Gardens
Edinburgh EH3 7RB
Telephone: 031-225 7034

PARLIAMENTARY BOUNDARY COMMISSION
PAROLE BOARD
POLICE ADVISORY BOARD
POST OFFICE USERS' COUNCIL FOR SCOTLAND
43 Jeffrey St
Edinburgh EH1 1DN
Telephone: 031-244 5576
Secretary: R L L King

ROYAL FINE ART COMMISSION
SCOTTISH AGRICULTURAL CONSULTATIVE PANEL
SCOTTISH CENTRAL FIRE BRIGADES ADVISORY COUNCIL
SCOTTISH CONSUMER COUNCIL
314 St Vincent St
Glasgow G3 8XW
Telephone: 041-226 5261
Chairman: Deirdre Hutton
Director: Ann Foster

SCOTTISH CONSULTATIVE COUNCIL ON THE CURRICULUM
SCOTTISH CRIME PREVENTION COUNCIL
SCOTTISH ECONOMIC COUNCIL
SCOTTISH HEALTH SERVICE ADVISORY COUNCIL
SCOTTISH INDUSTRIAL DEVELOPMENT ADVISORY BOARD
SCOTTISH POLICE BOARD OF GOVERNORS
SCOTTISH RECORDS ADVISORY COUNCIL
STANDING COMMITTEE ON RESIDUAL VALUES OF FERTILISERS AND FEEDING STUFFS
SCOTTISH STUDENTSHIP SELECTION COMMITTEE
SCOTTISH VALUATION ADVISORY COUNCIL
ADVISORY COMMITTEE ON SCOTLAND'S TRAVELLING PEOPLE
ADVISORY PANEL OF ECONOMIC CONSULTANTS
SECRETARY OF STATE'S (ELECTRICITY) FISHERIES COMMITTEE
Telephone: 031-244 4999

SCOTTISH NATURAL HERITAGE
12 Hope Terrace
Edinburgh EH9 2AS
Telephone: 031-447 4784
Chairman: Magnus Magnusson
Chief Executive: Roger Crofts

LOCAL ENTERPRISE COMPANIES

ARGYLL AND THE ISLANDS ENTERPRISE
The Enterprise Centre
Kilmory
Lochgilphead
Argyll PA31 8SH
Telephone: 0546-602281/602563
AND
Hazelburn Business Park
Millknowe
Campbeltown PA28 6HA
Telephone: 0586-552338
AND
24 Argyll Street
Dunoon PA23 7HJ
Telephone: 0369-55114
AND
4 George Street
Oban PA34 5RX
AND
25 Victoria Street
Rothesay PA20 0EG
Telephone: 0700-504830
Chief Executive: David MacIntyre

CAITHNESS AND SUTHERLAND ENTERPRISE
Scapa House
Castlegreen Road
Thurso KW14 7LS
Telephone: 0847-66115
Chief Executive: Andrew Thin

DUMFRIES & GALLOWAY ENTERPRISE
Cairnsmore House
Bankend Road
Dumfries DG1 4TA
Telephone: 0387-54444
Chief Executive: Irene Walker

DUNBARTONSHIRE ENTERPRISE
Spectrum House
Clydebank Business Park
Clydebank G81 2DR
Telephone: 041-951 2121
Chief Executive: Donald MacInnes

ENTERPRISE AYRSHIRE
17-19 Hill Street
Kilmarnock KA3 1HA
Telephone: 0563-26623
Chief Executive: David McDonald

FIFE ENTERPRISE
Huntsman's House
33 Cadham Centre
Glenrothes KY7 6RU
Telephone: 0592-621000
Chief Executive: Robert MacKenzie

FORTH VALLEY ENTERPRISE
Laurel House
Laurelhill Business Park
Stirling FK7 9JQ
Telephone: 0786-451919
Chief Executive: Bill Morton

GLASGOW DEVELOPMENT AGENCY
Atrium Court, 50 Waterloo Street
Glasgow G2 6HQ
Telephone: 041-204 1111
Chief Executive: Stuart Gulliver

GRAMPIAN ENTERPRISE LIMITED
27 Albyn Place
Aberdeen AB1 1YL
Telephone: 0224-211500
Chief Executive: Lance Fullerton

INVERNESS AND NAIRN ENTERPRISE
Castle Wynd
Inverness IV2 3DW
Telephone: 0463-713504
Chief Executive: Fiona Lang

LANARKSHIRE DEVELOPMENT AGENCY
New Lanarkshire House, Willow Drive
Strathclyde Business Park
Bellshill ML4 3AD
Telephone: 0698-745454
Chief Executive: Archie Bethel

LOCHABAR LTD
St Mary's House, Gordon Square
Fort William PH33 6DY
Telephone: 0397-704326
Chief Executive: Douglas MacDiarmid

LOTHIAN AND EDINBURGH
ENTERPRISE LTD
Apex House
99 Haymarket Terrace
Edinburgh EH12 5HD
Telephone: 031-313 4000
Chief Executive: Dr Des Bonnar

MORAY BADENOCH AND
STRATHSPEY ENTERPRISE
Elgin Business Centre
Maisondieu Road
Elgin IV30 1RH
Telephone: 0343-550567
AND
The Square
Grantown on Spey
Moray PH26 3HF
Telephone: 0479-3288
AND
57 High Street
Forres IV36 0AE
Telephone: 0309-675520
Chief Executive: Dick Ruane

ORKNEY ENTERPRISE
14 Queen Street
Kirkwall KW15 1JE
Telephone: 0856-874638
Chief Executive: Ken Grant

RENFREWSHIRE ENTERPRISE
25-29 Causeyside Street
Paisley PA1 1UL
Chief Executive: Tony Cassidy
Telephone: 041-848 0101

SCOTTISH BORDERS ENTERPRISE
Bridge Street
Galashiels TD1 2SW
Telephone: 0896-58991
Chief Executive: David Douglas

SCOTTISH ENTERPRISE TAYSIDE
Enterprise House
45 North Lindsay Street
Dundee DD1 1NT
Telephone: 0382-23100
Chief Executive: Graham McKee

SHETLAND ENTERPRISE
Toll Clock Shopping Centre
26 North Road
Lerwick ZE1 0PE
Telephone: 0595-3177
Chief Executive: Bill Fraser

SKYE AND LOCHALSH ENTERPRISE
Kings House, The Green
Portree IV51 9BS
Telephone: 0478-612841
Chief Executive: Lorne Macleod

WESTERN ISLES ENTERPRISE
3 Harbour View
Cromwell Street Quay
Stornoway PA87 2DF
Telephone: 0851-703625/703905
AND
Balivanich
Benbecula PA88 5LA
Telephone: 0870-602646
Chief Executive: Donnie Macaulay

WALES

Welsh Office:
Gwydyr House
Whitehall
London SW1A 2ER
Telephone: 071-270 3000

Cathays Park
Cardiff CF1 3NQ
Telephone: 0222-825111

Until the 1960s Wales was part of the portfolio of the Home Secretary and many aspects of Welsh affairs were simply dealt with by the relevant mainstream department. Since then the Welsh Office has acquired some of the character of the Scottish Office, that is to say a more 'vice-regal' feel, and the status inside the Cabinet of the Welsh Secretary has been growing, especially since the Conservatives felt able to dispense with the tradition that the Welsh Secretary needed to be Welsh. (The Secretary of State for Scotland must, by contrast, be Scottish.) Regarded previously either as a backwater appointment or one necessarily reserved for elder Welsh statesmen it has become a stepping stone to higher things for rising men.

The Welsh Office has responsibility for health and social services, education, the Welsh language, arts and culture, local government, housing, agriculture and fisheries, roads, tourism and so on. It oversees the impact on Wales of the European Union, especially the operation of the European Regional Development Fund. It also has oversight responsibilities for economic affairs and regional planning.

Many of its senior officials are Welsh but, in contrast say to the Scottish Office, will typically have been educated outside the Principality and probably have extensive experience of public administration elsewhere.

Head of Department: Michael Scholar (Grade 1). Born: 1942. Educated: St Olave's Grammar, Bermondsey; St John's College, Cambridge. After pursuing an academic career joined HM Treasury in 1969, serving in Private Office five years later. After a secondment to Barclays Bank he was Private Secretary to Prime Minister Margaret Thatcher, becoming an Under-Secretary in HM Treasury in 1983.

Legal: Solicitor and Legal Adviser: David Lambert. Born: 1940. Educated: Barry Grammar; University College of Wales, Aberystwyth. Qualified as a solicitor, joining the Welsh Office in 1966 and becoming Assistant Legal Adviser eight years later.

Principal Establishments Officer: Clifford Stevens. Born: 1941. Educated: Stationers' Company School, London. Joined the Foreign Office, but moving to the Board of Trade and later the Civil Service Department, joining the Welsh Office in 1986.

Principal Finance Officer: Richard Wallace. Born: 1946. Educated: Clifton College; King's College, Cambridge. Joined the Ministry of Social Security in 1968, moving to Wales in 1986.

Economic Affairs (also agriculture, and training): John Craig (Grade 2). Born: 1943. Educated: Robert Richardson Grammar, Sunderland. Joined HM Customs and Excise in 1961 moving subsequently to the National Board for Prices and Incomes and, in 1970, to the Welsh Office where he served in Private Office in 1980.

Head of Agriculture Department: Owen Rees. Born: 1934. Educated: Llanelli Grammar; Manchester University. Joined the Board of Trade moving in 1969 to the Cabinet Office 1969 and to the Welsh Office two years later.

Director, Industry Department: Derek Jones.

Head of Economic Development and Training Group: Michael Cochlin.

Social Policy (including education, health, transport and local government): John Lloyd (Grade 2). Born: 1940. Educated: Swansea Grammar; Clifton College; Christ's College, Cambridge. Joined HM Treasury in 1962 becoming Under-Secretary at the Welsh Office twenty years later.

Head of Education Department: Stephen Martin. Born: 1952. Educated: Watford Grammar; Hull University. Joined the Welsh Office in 1974, serving in Private Office five years later and in 1980s taking responsibility for housing.

Head of Housing, Health and Social Services Policy Group: Roger Jarman. Born: 1935. Educated: Cathays High School, Cardiff; University of Birmingham. Worked at Vauxhall Motors before joining the Civil Service Department and, in 1972, the Welsh Office where he has worked on land use and transport.

Head of Transport, Planning and Environment Group: George Craig. Born: 1946. Educated: Brockley County Grammar; Nottingham University. Joined the Ministry of Transport in 1967 and the Welsh Office three years later, working in Private Office in 1978.

Director, Health Policy: Peter Gregory. Born: 1946. Educated: Sexeys Grammar, Blackford; University College, Swansea; Manchester University (PhD). Joined the Welsh Office in 1971, becoming an Assistant Secretary in 1982.

Head of Local Government Reorganisation Group: John Shortridge. Born: 1947. Educated: Chichester High School; St Edmund Hall, Oxford; Edinburgh University. Joined Ministry of Housing before working for Shropshire County Council. He joined the Welsh Office in 1984 serving in Private Office three years later.

EMPLOYMENT SERVICE
Companies House
Maindy, Cardiff CF4 3UZ
Telephone: 0222-380705
Director, Wales: Bernard Pearce

DEPARTMENT OF EMPLOYMENT
Training, Enterprise and Education Directorate, Welsh Office
Companies House
Maindy, Cardiff CF4 3UZ
Telephone: 0222-388588
Director: Colin Jones

WALES HEALTH

Welsh Office
Crown Offices
Cathays Park, Cardiff CF1 3NQ
Telephone: 0222-825111

Chief Medical Officer and Head of Health Professionals' Group: Dr Deirdre Hine. Born: 1937. Educated: Heathfield House, Cardiff; Welsh National School of Medicine. After service with Glamorgan County Council, taught at University of Wales College of Medicine before joining the Welsh Office as Deputy Chief Medical Officer, later becoming director of the Welsh Breast Cancer Screening Service.

Chief Nursing Officer: Miss M P Bull

WELSH HEALTH COMMON SERVICES AUTHORITY

Heron House
35/43 Newport Road
Cardiff CF2 1SB
Telephone: 0222-471234
Chief Executive: N Kirk
(A special health authority under the National Health Service Act 1977.)

WELSH HEALTH SERVICE COMMISSIONER FOR WALES

4th Floor
Pearl Assurance House
Greyfriars Road
Cardiff CF1 3AG
Telephone: 0222-394621
Unit Leader (Grade 7): S Pearson

THE COUNTRYSIDE COUNCIL FOR WALES

Plas Penrhos
Ffordd Penrhos
Bangor
Gwynedd LL57 2LQ
Telephone: 0248-370444
Chairman: E M W Griffith
Chief Executive: Ian Mercer

NATIONAL PARKS

BRECON BEACONS NATIONAL PARK
Established: 1957 (1,344 sq km, 519 sq miles)
Brecon Beacons National Park
7 Glamorgan Street
Brecon LD3 7DP
Telephone: 0874-624437
Officer: A M H Fitton

298

PEMBROKESHIRE COAST NATIONAL PARK

PEMBROKESHIRE COAST NATIONAL PARK
Established: 1952 (583 sq km, 225 sq miles)
Pembrokeshire Coast National Park
County Offices
Haverfordwest
Dyfed SA61 1QZ
Telephone: 0437-764591
N J Wheeler

SNOWDONIA NATIONAL PARK
Established: 1951 (2,170 sq km, 838 sq miles)
Snowdonia National Park
National Park Office
Penrhyndeudraeth
Gwynedd LL48 6LS
Telephone: 0766-770274
Alan Jones

TRAINING AND ENTERPRISE COUNCILS IN WALES

GWENT TEC
Glyndwr House, Unit B2
Cleppa Park
Newport
Gwent NP9 1YE
Telephone: 0633-817777
Chairman: Roger Jones
Chief Executive: David Evans

MID GLAMORGAN TEC
Unit 17-20 Centre Court
Main Avenue
Treforest Industrial Estate
Pontypridd
Mid Glamorgan CF37 5YL
Telephone: 0443-841594
Chairman: John Phillips
Chief Executive: Allen Williams

NORTH EAST WALES TEC
Wynnstay Block
Hightown Barracks
Kingsmill Road
Wrexham
Clwyd LL13 8BH
Telephone: 0978-290049
Chairman: John Troth
Chief Executive: Tim Harris

POWYS TEC
1st Floor
St David's House
Newtown
Powys SY16 1RB
Telephone: 0686-622494
Chairman: David Margetts
Chief Executive: James Wagstaffe

SOUTH GLAMORGAN TEC
3-7 Drakes Way
Waterfront 2000
Atlantic Wharf
Cardiff CF1 5AN
Telephone: 0222-451000
Chairman: Eric Crawford
Chief Executive: Paul Sheldon

TARGED NORTH WEST WALES TEC
Llys Britannia
Parc Menai, Bangor
Gwynedd LL57 4BN
Telephone: 0248-671444
Chairman: Geoff Drake
Chief Executive: Enid Rowlands

WEST WALES TEC
Orchard House
Orchard Street
Swansea SA1 5DJ
Telephone: 0792-460355
Chairman: Robert Hastie
Chief Executive: Chris Jones

EXECUTIVE AGENCIES IN WALES

CADW: WELSH HISTORIC MONUMENTS
(For details *see* Chapter Three.)

NON-DEPARTMENTAL PUBLIC BODIES UNDER THE WELSH OFFICE

EXECUTIVE BODIES

AGRICULTURAL WAGES COMMITTEES

CLWYD & GWYNEDD AWC
Caernarfon Divisional Office
Penrallt
Caernarfon
Gwynedd
Telephone: 0286-674144 ex 351
Chairman: Ivor Gillord Richards (Clwyd)
Trevor Morgan (Gwynedd)

DYFED AWC
Carmarthen Divisional Office
Picton Terrace
Carmarthen
Dyfed SA31 3BT
Telephone: 0267-234545 ex 213
Chairman: Eira Jenkins

GLAMORGAN, GWENT & POWYS AWCS
Llandrindod Wells Divisional Office
Government Buildings
Spa Road East
Llandrindod Wells
Powys LD1 5HA
Telephone: 0597-823777 extension 302
Chairman: Peter Leslie Gooderson (Glamorgan)
John Evans (Gwent)
WG Davies (Powys)

CARDIFF BAY DEVELOPMENT CORPORATION
Function: To establish Cardiff as an international maritime city, and to promote urban regeneration.
Baltic House
Mount Stuart Square
Cardiff CF1 6QP
Telephone: 0222-471576
Chairman: Sir Geoffrey David Inkin

COUNTRYSIDE COUNCIL FOR WALES
Function: To promote, conserve and enhance the natural beauty and amenity of Wales, and conserve its flora and fauna.
Plas Penrhos

Efordd Penrhos
Bangor
Gwynedd LL57 2LQ
Telephone: 0248-370444
Chairman: Edward Michael Wynne Griffith

CURRICULUM ASSESSMENT AUTHORITY FOR WALES
Function: Responsible for helping Schools implement the national curriculum.
Castle Buildings
Womanby Street
Cardiff CF1 9SX
Telephone: 0222-344946
Chairman: Rudi Plaut

DEVELOPMENT BOARD FOR RURAL WALES
Function: To create and promote a self-sustaining market-based rural economy.
Ladywell House
Newton
Powys SY15 1JB
Telephone: 0686-626965
Chairman: Edward Gyn Davies

HOUSING FOR WALES (TAI CYMRU)
Function: To increase the supply of well-managed good quality housing for people in need.
25-30 Lambourne Crescent
Llanishen
Cardiff CF4 5ZJ
Telephone: 0222-747979
Chairman: John Derek Allen

LAND AUTHORITY FOR WALES
Function: Responsible for assembling and marketing housing sites, social housing schemes, private developments and urban renewal.
Custom House
Custom House Street
Cardiff CF1 5AP
Telephone: 0222-223444
Chairman: Sir Geoffrey David Inkin

NATIONAL LIBRARY OF WALES
Function: The National Library is the Welsh legal depository library.
National Library of Wales
Aberystwyth
Dyfed SY23 5BD
Telephone: 0970-623816
Chairman: Professor Emeritus J Gwynn Williams

NATIONAL MUSEUM OF WALES
Function: The main physical repository of Welsh cultural heritage.
National Museum of Wales
Cathays Park
Cardiff CF1 3UP
Telephone: 0222-397951
President: C R T Edwards

ROYAL COMMISSION ON ANCIENT AND HISTORICAL MONUMENTS
Function: Responsible for the survey and recording of ancient and historical monuments and constructions.
Crown Buildings
Plas Crug
Aberystwyth
Dyfed SY3 2HP
Telephone: 0970-624381
Chairman: Professor Beverly Smith

SPORTS COUNCIL FOR WALES
Function: To promote sport and physical recreation.
Sophia Gardens
Cardiff CF1 9SW
Telephone: 0222-397571
Chairman: Ossie Wheatley
Director: L Tatham

WALES TOURIST BOARD
Function: To optimise the economic benefits of tourism for the people of Wales.
Brunel House
2 Fitzalan Road
Cardiff CF2 1UY
Telephone: 0222-499909
Chairman: Anthony Robert Lewis

WALES YOUTH AGENCY
Function: To promote, assist and support work with and the development of services for young people in Wales.
Leslie Court
Lon-Y-Lyn
Caerphilly
Mid Glamorgan CF8 1BQ
Telephone: 0222-880088
Chairman: Thomas Gerald Reames Davis

WELSH DEVELOPMENT AGENCY

Function: To assist the development of Wales by attracting inward investment, encouraging the development of the industrial property market, eliminating industrial dereliction, and improving the development of urban and rural areas.

Pearl House
Greyfriars Road
Cardiff CF1 3XX
Telephone: 0222-222666
Chairman: David Rowe-Beddoe

WELSH NATIONAL BOARD FOR NURSING, MIDWIFERY AND HEALTH VISITING

Function: Responsible for ensuring that professional standards for education are complied with.

13th Floor
Pearl Assurance House
Cardiff CF1 3XX
Telephone: 0222-395535
Chairman: Stanley Wyn Jones

THE WELSH ARTS COUNCIL

Holst House
9 Museum Place
Cardiff CF1 3NX
Telephone: 0222-394711
Director: Thomas Arfon Owen

ADVISORY BODIES

ADVISORY COMMITTEE FOR WALES (RIVERS)
AGRICULTURAL DWELLING HOUSE ADVISORY COMMITTEES
AGRICULTURE ADVISORY PANEL
ANCIENT MONUMENTS BOARD
WELSH SCHEME FOR THE DEVELOPMENT OF HEALTH AND SOCIAL RESEARCH
HILL-FARMING ADVISORY SUB-COMMITTEE
HISTORIC BUILDINGS COUNCIL
HOUSING MANAGEMENT ADVISORY PANEL
LIBRARY AND INFORMATION SERVICES COUNCIL
LOCAL GOVERNMENT BOUNDARY COMMISSION
MENTAL HANDICAP ADVISORY PANEL
PLACE NAMES ADVISORY COMMITTEE
POST OFFICE USERS' COUNCIL FOR WALES

Caradog House
St Andrews Place
Cardiff CF1 3BE
Telephone: 0222-374028
Secretary: G J Mackenzie

URBAN INVESTMENT GRANT APPRAISAL PANEL
WELSH COMMITTEE FOR POSTGRADUATE PHARMACEUTICAL EDUCATION
WELSH CONSUMER COUNCIL
Castle Buildings
Womanby St
Cardiff CF1 2BN
Telephone: 0222-396056
Chairman: Miss Beata Brookes
Director: Miss Katherine Hughes

WELSH COUNCIL FOR POSTGRADUATE MEDICAL AND DENTAL EDUCATION
WELSH DENTAL COMMITTEE
WELSH INDUSTRIAL DEVELOPMENT ADVISORY BOARD
WELSH LANGUAGE BOARD
WELSH MEDICAL COMMITTEE
WELSH NURSING AND MIDWIFERY COMMITTEE
WELSH OPTICAL COMMITTEE
WELSH PHARMACEUTICAL COMMITTEE
WELSH SCIENTIFIC ADVISORY COMMITTEE
Telephone: 0222-825111 extension 3785

TRIBUNALS

AGRICULTURAL LAND TRIBUNALS
MENTAL HEALTH REVIEW TRIBUNAL
RENT ASSESSMENT PANEL
VALUATION TRIBUNALS
Telephone: 0222-825111 extension 3785

OTHER BODIES

WELSH JOINT EDUCATION COMMITTEE
245 Western Avenue
Llandaff
Cardiff CF5 2YX
Telephone: 0222-561231
Secretary: G Lloyd Jones

WELSH ASSOCIATION OF COMMUNITY AND TOWN COUNCILS
Pen Roc, Rhodfa'r Mor
Aberystwyth SY23 2AZ
Telephone: 0970-612801
General Secretary: Mrs Mary Thomas

ASSEMBLY OF WELSH COUNTIES
County Hall, Cathays Park
Cardiff CF1 3NE
Telephone: 0222-780094
Hon Secretary: D Hugh Thomas

WELSH OFFICE OF THE ASSOCIATION OF DISTRICT COUNCILS
Units 10/11, Raleigh Walk
Atlantic Wharf
Cardiff CF1 5LN
Telephone: 0222-462722

NORTHERN IRELAND

Northern Ireland Office
London:
Whitehall
London SW1A 2AZ
Telephone: 071-210 3000

Belfast:
Stormont Castle
Belfast BT4 3ST
Telephone: 0232-520700

'Direct rule' of Northern Ireland was instituted in 1972. The Northern Ireland (Temporary Provisions) Act transferred to a newly created Secretaryship of State and the United Kingdom Parliament the legislative and executive powers that hitherto had been carried out by the Northern Ireland Parliament meeting at Stormont and the Ulster 'state'. For the new Secretary of State an Office was created to oversee – temporarily – the workings of an extensive Belfast bureaucracy which possesses its own gradings and Civil Service appurtenances.

Successive efforts have been made to make the Province's government look less exotic. The Northern Ireland Constitution Act of 1973 provided for a devolved Assembly to oversee the executive but local agreement was not found then or since. An Assembly was elected under the Northern Ireland Act 1982, in an effort to find agreement on proposals for a new legislature but it was dissolved four years later without result. In 1985 the British and Irish governments signed an agreement under which an Intergovernmental Conference was set up. In it the Irish Government is entitled to put forward views and propositions about certain Northern Irish affairs.

Northern Ireland lacks the structure of elected local authorities that exists elsewhere in the United Kingdom. Elected councils have few powers. The 'central state' in Ulster provides housing, education and exists, in many ways, as the employment backbone of the Province; without it, the economy would collapse. To protect officials, the Government publishes only lists of positions in the Northern Ireland Office and the Northern Ireland Civil Service.

Permanent Under-Secretary of State: John Chilcot (Grade 1). Born: 1939. Educated: Brighton College; Pembroke College, Cambridge. Joined the Home Office in 1963, serving in Private Office there both in 1966 and again in 1978. After a secondment to the Cabinet Office in 1984 and then to the City firm of Schroders he returned to the Home Office in 1987.

LONDON OFFICE
Deputy Secretary:
Under-Secretaries:
1 economic and social, security and international and constitutional and political divisions
2 principal establishment and finance officer

BELFAST OFFICE
Deputy Secretary:
Under-Secretaries:
1 law and order and forensic science
2 police and criminal justice
3 political affairs and information services
4 prison regimes, personnel, security and operations, industry, education and services
Controller of prisons

NORTHERN IRELAND CIVIL SERVICE
    Stormont Castle
    Belfast BT4 3TT
    Telephone: 0232-520700
Head of the Northern Ireland Civil Service: David Fell (Grade 1a). Born: 1943. Educated: Royal Belfast Academical Institution; The Queen's University, Belfast. Worked in commerce and taught before becoming a civil servant in 1969 in the Northern Ireland Office. He was Permanent Secretary of the Department of Economic Development (NI) in 1984.

DEPARTMENT OF AGRICULTURE FOR NORTHERN IRELAND
Grade 2 (NICS)
Grade 3

NORTHERN IRELAND COURT SERVICE
Director (Grade 3)

CROWN SOLICITOR'S OFFICE FOR NORTHERN IRELAND
    Royal Courts of Justice
    Chichester Street
    Belfast BT1 3JY
    Telephone: 0232-235111

DEPARTMENT OF ECONOMIC DEVELOPMENT
    Netherliegh
    Massey Avenue
    Belfast BT4 2JP
    Telephone: 0232-763244
Permanent Secretary:

INDUSTRIAL DEVELOPMENT BOARD
Telephone: 0232-233233

DEPARTMENT OF EDUCATION FOR NORTHERN IRELAND
Rathgael House
Balloo Road
Bangor
County Down BT19 7PR
Telephone: 0247-270077
Permanent Secretary:

DEPARTMENT OF THE ENVIRONMENT FOR NORTHERN IRELAND
Clarence Court
10-18 Adelaide Street
Belfast BT2 8GB
Telephone: 0232-540540
Permanent Secretary: (Grade 2)
Personnel, central management, finance, solicitors and central claims: Grade 3
Planning and urban affairs: Grade 3
Housing, local government, environment service: Grade 3
Water privatisation, land registry, transport, fire service, road safety education, airports: Grade 3

DEPARTMENT OF FINANCE AND PERSONNEL
Parliament Buildings
Stormont
Belfast BT4 3SW
Telephone: 0232-520400
Rosepark House
Upper Newtownards Road
Belfast BT4 3NR
Telephone: 0232-520400

DEPARTMENT OF HEALTH AND SOCIAL SERVICE NORTHERN IRELAND
Dundonald House
Upper Newtownards Road
Belfast BT4 3SF
Telephone: 0232-520500
Permanent Secretary: (Grade 2a)
Central Services: Grade 3
Health and Personal Social Service Management Executive, Chief Executive: (Grade 3)
Health and Personal Social Services, Policy and Strategy Command: Grade 3
Medical and Allied Services, Chief Medical Officer

DEPARTMENT OF THE DIRECTOR OF PUBLIC PROSECUTIONS FOR NORTHERN IRELAND
Royal Courts of Justice
Chichester Street
Belfast BT1 3NX
Telephone: 0232-234089
Director: A M Fraser QC

POLICE AUTHORITY FOR NORTHERN IRELAND
River House, 48 High Street
Belfast BT1 2DR
Telephone: 0232-230111
Secretary and Chief Executive: (Grade 3)

LANDS TRIBUNAL FOR NORTHERN IRELAND
Royal Courts of Justice
PO Box 410, Chichester Street
Belfast BT1 3JJ
Telephone: 0232-327703
Compensation, ground rent adjudication and tax appeals.

STANDING ADVISORY COMMITTEE ON HUMAN RIGHTS
55 Royal Avenue
Belfast BT1 1TA
Telephone: 0232-243987
Chairman: R Charles Hill QC
Commission advises the Secretary of State on adequacy of anti-discrimination law.

OFFICE OF THE NORTHERN IRELAND PARLIAMENTARY COMMISSIONER FOR ADMINISTRATION AND THE NORTHERN IRELAND COMMISSIONER FOR COMPLAINTS
33 Wellington Place
Belfast BT1 6HN
Telephone: 0232-233821
Commissioner: Mrs Jill McIvor
Senior Director: K McWilliams (Grade 5)

ELECTORAL REGISTRATION AND ELECTIONS – NORTHERN IRELAND
3rd Floor
65/67 Chichester Road
Belfast BT1 4JD
Telephone: 0232-245353
Chief Electoral Officer: P A Bradley

HEALTH

CENTRAL SERVICES AGENCY
27 Adelaide Street
Belfast BT2 8FH
Telephone: 0232-324431
General Manager: S J Hodkinson
The Health and Personal Social Services (NI) Order 1972 constitutes the agency, responsible for central payments, central supplies.

EASTERN HEALTH AND SOCIAL SERVICES BOARD
12-22 Linenhall Street
Belfast BT2 8BS
Telephone: 0232-321313
Chairman: N C D Ferguson
General Manager: P G Kinder

NORTHERN HEALTH AND SOCIAL SERVICES BOARD
County Hall
182 Galgorm Road
Ballymena BT42 1QB
Telephone: 0266-653333
Chairman: R J Hanna
General Manager: D D Smyth

SOUTHERN HEALTH AND SOCIAL SERVICES BOARD
20 Seagoe Industrial Area
Portadown
Craigavon
Co Armagh BT63 5QD
Telephone: 0762-336611
Chairman: J D Thompson
General Manager: J Lamb

WESTERN HEALTH AND SOCIAL SERVICES BOARD
15 Gransha Park
Clooney Road
Londonderry BT47 1TG
Telephone: 0504-860086
Chairman: R G Toland
Area General Manager: T J Frawley

EDUCATION AND LIBRARY BOARDS

Function: The five education and library boards are responsible for building and maintaining controlled Schools. They pay running costs and employ teachers.

BELFAST BOARD
40 Academy Street
Belfast BT1 2NQ
Telephone: 0232-329211
Chairman: Rev J McAllister

WESTERN BOARD
Campsie House
1 Hospital Road
Omagh
Co Tyrone BT79 0AW
Telephone: 0662-240240
Chairman: B McIvor

NORTH-EASTERN BOARD
County Hall
182 Galgorm Road
Ballymena
Co Antrim BT42 1HN
Telephone: 0266-653333
Chairman: Rev R F S Poots

SOUTH-EASTERN BOARD
18 Windsor Avenue
Belfast BT9 6EF
Telephone: 0232-381188
Chairman: H R Small

SOUTHERN BOARD
3 Charlemont Place
Armagh BT61 9AZ
Telephone: 0861-523811
Chairman: NRD Mulligan

EXECUTIVE AGENCIES OPERATING IN NORTHERN IRELAND

NORTHERN IRELAND CHILD SUPPORT AGENCY
ORDNANCE SURVEY OF NORTHERN IRELAND
RATE COLLECTION AGENCY
SOCIAL SECURITY AGENCY (NI)
TRAINING AND EMPLOYMENT AGENCY (NI)
VALUATION AND LANDS AGENCY
(For details *see* Chapter Three.)

OTHER NON-DEPARTMENTAL PUBLIC BODIES UNDER THE NORTHERN IRELAND OFFICE

AGRICULTURAL RESEARCH INSTITUTE
Function: To conduct research and development into crop and animal production, and to provide specialist advice on plant and animal husbandry.
Large Park
Hillsborough
Co Down BT26 6DR
Telephone: 0846-682484
Chairman: W G Smyth

AGRICULTURAL WAGES BOARD
Function: To fix the remuneration of agricultural workers.
Dundonald House
Belfast BT4 35B
Telephone: 0232-520100
Chairman: Kevin Murnaghan

ARTS COUNCIL FOR NORTHERN IRELAND
Function: To promote the arts in Northern Ireland and to advice the Government on policy for the arts.
185 Stranmillis Road
Belfast BT9 5DU
Telephone: 0232-381591
Chairman: D Deeny

COMMUNITY EMPLOYMENT (ENTERPRISE ULSTER)
Function: To provide community based work for the long-term unemployed.
Armagh House, Ormeau Avenue
Belfast BT2 8HB
Telephone: 0232-234393
Chairman: L O'Hagan

COUNCIL FOR CATHOLIC MAINTAINED SCHOOLS
Function: To promote standards, give advice, employ teachers, and plan and manage school provision for Catholic maintained schools.
160 High Street
Holywood, Co Down BT18 9HT
Telephone: 0232-426972
Director: D Flanagan

COUNCIL FOR POSTGRADUATE MEDICAL AND DENTAL EDUCATION (NI)
Function: To co-ordinate and develop postgraduate medical and dental education and training.
5 Annandale Avenue
Belfast BT7 3JH
Telephone: 0232-491731
Chairman: Derek Gordon

312

EQUAL OPPORTUNITIES COMMISSION (NI)
Function: To promote equality of opportunity between the sexes and enforce sex equality legislation.
Chamber of Commerce
22 Great Victoria Street
Belfast BT2 7BA
Telephone: 0232-242752
Chairman: Mrs R J Smyth

FAIR EMPLOYMENT COMMISSION
Function: To promote equality of opportunity and the elimination of discrimination on religious or political grounds.
2nd Floor
Andras House
60 Great Victoria Street
Belfast BT2 7BB
Telephone: 0232-240020
Chairman: Bob Cooper

FIRE AUTHORITY FOR NORTHERN IRELAND
1 Seymour Street
Lisburn BT27 4SX
Telephone: 0846-642219
Chief Fire Officer: K McNeill

FISHERIES CONSERVATION BOARD
Function: To represent the interests of rod anglers, commercial fishermen, commercial salmon and eel fishing companies, and sport and tourism.
1 Mahon Road
Portadown
Co Armagh BT62 3EE
Telephone: 0762-334666
Chairman: Jaspar Parsons

FOYLE FISHERIES COMMISSION
Function: Joint Northern Ireland-Republic of Ireland body responsible for the conservation, protection and improvement of fisheries in the Foyle region.
8 Victoria Road
Londonderry BT47 2AB
Telephone: 0504-42100
Chairman: John Anderson

GENERAL CONSUMER COUNCIL (NI)
Function: To promote and safeguard the interest of consumers with particular responsibility for transport, electricity and agriculture.
Elizabeth House
116 Holywood Road

Belfast BT4 1NY
Telephone: 0232-672488
Chairman: Lady Anne McCollum

HEALTH AND SAFETY AGENCY (NI)
Function: To promote health and safety at work.
Canada House
22 North Street
Belfast BT1 1HA
Telephone: 0232-243249
Chairman: Ann Shaw

INDEPENDENT COMMISSIONER FOR POLICE COMPLAINTS
Function: To provide an independent oversight of investigations into complaints against the police.
Chamber of Commerce House
22 Great Victoria Street
Belfast BT2 7LP
Telephone: 0232-244821
Chairman: James Grew

INDUSTRIAL TRAINING BOARD
Function: The eight ITBs, catering, clothing, construction, distribution, engineering, food and drink, textiles and road transport, are responsible for assessing and meeting the training needs of their respective industries.
Swinson House
Glenmount Road
Church Road
Newtownabbey BT36 7LH
Telephone: 0232-365171
Chairman: W F Gillespie

LABOUR RELATIONS AGENCY
Function: To promote the improvement of industrial relations through its advisory, conciliation and arbitration services.
Windsor House
Bedford Street
Belfast BT2 7NU
Telephone: 0232-221442
Chairman: F A Mackle

LIVESTOCK MARKETING COMMISSION
Function: To promote the Northern Ireland livestock and meat industry.
57 Malone Road
Belfast BT9 6SA
Telephone: 0232-381022
Chairman: John Millar

LOCAL ENTERPRISE DEVELOPMENT UNIT
Function: To assist small business to become established, grow and survive.
Upper Galwally
Belfast BT8 4TB
Telephone: 0232-491031
Chairman: Paul McWilliams

MENTAL HEALTH COMMISSION
Function: To keep under review the care and treatment of people who are mentally ill.
Elizabeth House
118 Holywood Road
Belfast BT4 1NY
Telephone: 0232-651157
Chairman: Henry Pierce

NATIONAL BOARD FOR NURSING, MIDWIFERY AND HEALTH VISITING (NI)
Function: Responsible for the colleges of nursing and for the provision of courses in nursing, midwifery and health visiting.
Directorate of Estate Services
Stoney Road
Dundonald
Belfast BT16 0US
Telephone: 0232-520025
Chairman: Elizabeth McNair

NORTHERN IRELAND COMMISSIONER FOR THE RIGHTS OF TRADE UNION MEMBERS
Function: To grant assistance to any union member seeking to take proceedings against their trade union in the High Court.
Canada House
22 North Street
Belfast BT1 1HA
Chairman: Margaret-Ann Dinsmore

NORTHERN IRELAND CURRICULUM COUNCIL
Function: To review all aspects of the curriculum for grant-aided schools.
Orchard Buildings
Stranmillis College
Stranmillis Road
Belfast BT9 6BY
Telephone: 0232-381414
Chairman: Professor D McCloy

NORTHERN IRELAND FISHERY HARBOUR AUTHORITY
Function: To improve, manage and maintain the three fishery harbours of Ardglass, Kilkeel and Portavogie.
22 English Street
Downpatrick

Co Down BT30 6AB
Telephone: 0396-613844
Chairman: Clinton Whitley

NORTHERN IRELAND HIGHER EDUCATION COUNCIL
Function: To advise on planning and funding universities and higher education in
Northern Ireland.
Rathgael House
Balloo Road
Bangor
Co Down BT19 7PR
Telephone: 0247-270077
Chairman: Sir Kenneth Bloomfield

NORTHERN IRELAND HOUSING EXECUTIVE
The Housing Centre
2 Adelaide Street
Belfast BT2 8PB
Telephone: 0232-240588
Chief Executive: W V Blease
(Formed in 1971 to take control of local authority housing stock; estimated at 165,000
units in 1993; 5000 staff. Majority of executive appointed by the Secretary of State.)

NORTHERN IRELAND SCHOOLS EXAMINATIONS AND ASSESSMENT COUNCIL
Function: To support education by providing quality GCE and GCSE examinations, and
develop assessment arrangements for 5 to 16-year-olds.
Beechill House
42 Beechill Road
Belfast BT8
Telephone: 0232-704666
Chairman: Professor D Rea

NORTHERN IRELAND TOURIST BOARD
Function: To encourage the Northern Ireland tourist industry.
River House
48 High Street
Belfast BT1 2DS
Telephone: 0232-231221
Chairman: Hon Hugh O'Neill

OFFICE OF ELECTRICITY REGULATION NORTHERN IRELAND
Brookmount Buildings
42 Fountain Street
Belfast BT1 5EE
Telephone: 0232-311575
Director General: G R Horton

PIG PRODUCTION DEVELOPMENT COMMITTEE
Function: To improve the quality of pig production in Northern Ireland.
c/o Pig Testing Station
14 Kirby's Lane
Antrim BT41 4PP
Telephone: 0849-64137
Chairman: Robert Overend

POLICE AUTHORITY FOR NORTHERN IRELAND
Function: To maintain an adequate and efficient police service, including the size of the Royal Ulster Constabulary, provide and maintain all buildings and equipment, appoint all chief constables, and act as the discipline authority.
River House
48 High Street
Belfast BT1 2DR
Telephone: 0232-230111
Chairman: Tom Rainey

PROBATION BOARD FOR NORTHERN IRELAND
Function: To supervise offenders placed on probation and other orders by the courts.
RAC House
79 Chister Street
Belfast BT1 4SP
Chairman: Sean Curran

PUBLIC SERVICE TRAINING COUNCIL
Function: To propose better standards of management and improved service delivery in the public sector.
Chamber of Commerce House
Great Victoria Street
Belfast
Telephone: 0232-230076

ROYAL ULSTER CONSTABULARY
Brooklyn
Knock Road, Belfast BT5 6LE
Telephone: 0232-650222
Chief Constable: Sir Hugh Annesley

SPORTS COUNCIL FOR NORTHERN IRELAND
Function: To propose sport and physical recreation in Northern Ireland.
House of Sport
Upper Malone Road
Belfast BT9 5LA
Telephone: 0232-381222
Chairman: D Allen
Director: J E Miller

317

STAFF COMMISSION FOR EDUCATION AND LIBRARY BOARDS
Function: To make recommendations to the Education and Library Boards on training, appointment and promotion procedures for their officers.
Lamont House
Purdys Lane
Belfast BT8 4TA
Telephone: 0232-692461
Chairman: M Moroney

ULSTER FOLK AND TRANSPORT MUSEUM
Function: To illustrate all aspects of Ulster folk life by displaying traditional buildings and modes of transport.
Cultra
Holywood
Co Down BT18 0EU
Telephone: 0232-428428
Chairman: Professor F D W Harkness

ULSTER MUSEUM
Function: To display the province's artefacts, antiquities, art, botany, zoology and local history.
Botanic Gardens
Belfast BT9 5AB
Telephone: 0232-381251
Chairman: M Solomon

ULSTER SHELTERED EMPLOYMENT
Function: To provide employment for severely disabled people including the blind.
Lawnbrook Avenue
Shankill Road
Belfast BT13 2QD
Telephone: 0232-322881
Chairman: J C Morton

VAUGHAN'S CHARITY
Function: A trust fund to help develop new or improved methods of farming, management and training in Fermanagh.
Enniskillen Agricultural College
Levaghey
Enniskillen
Co Fermanagh
Telephone: 0356-323101
Chairman: Mrs N Acheson

YOUTH COUNCIL FOR NORTHERN IRELAND
Function: To advise on the development of the Youth Service, and encourage cross-community activities and facilities for young people.
Lamont House
Purdys Lane
Belfast BT8 4TA
Telephone: 0232-643882
Chairman: J F Campbell

ADVISORY BODIES

ADVISORY COMMITTEE OF THE THERAPEUTIC PROFESSIONS ALLIED TO MEDICINE
BOUNDARY COMMISSION FOR NORTHERN IRELAND
CENTRAL DENTAL ADVISORY COMMITTEE
CENTRAL MEDICAL ADVISORY COMMITTEE
CENTRAL NURSING ADVISORY COMMITTEE
CENTRAL PERSONAL SOCIAL SERVICES ADVISORY COMMITTEE
CENTRAL PHARMACEUTICAL ADVISORY COMMITTEE
CHARITIES ADVISORY COMMITTEE
CLINICAL ENGINEERING AND MEDICAL PHYSICS SERVICES ADVISORY COMMITTEE
CLINICAL IMAGING SERVICES ADVISORY COMMITTEE
COMMITTEES FOR THE EMPLOYMENT OF DISABLED PEOPLE
DISABILITY LIVING ALLOWANCE ADVISORY BOARD NI
DISTINCTION AND MERITORIOUS SERVICE AWARDS COMMITTEE
DRAINAGE COUNCIL FOR NORTHERN IRELAND
INDUSTRIAL DEVELOPMENT BOARD FOR NI
INDUSTRIAL RESEARCH AND TECHNOLOGY BOARD
LABORATORY SERVICES ADVISORY COMMITTEE
LAW REFORM ADVISORY COMMITTEE
NORTHERN IRELAND CITIZEN'S CHARTER PANEL
NORTHERN IRELAND ECONOMIC COUNCIL
POISONS BOARD
POST OFFICE USERS' COUNCIL FOR NORTHERN IRELAND
STANDING ADVISORY COMMITTEE ON HUMAN RIGHTS
STATISTICS ADVISORY COMMITTEE
STATUTE LAW COMMITTEE FOR NORTHERN IRELAND
TRAINING AND EMPLOYMENT ADVISORY BOARD
    Telephone: 0232-529000

TRIBUNALS

DISABILITY APPEALS TRIBUNALS
FAIR EMPLOYMENT TRIBUNALS
MEDICAL APPEALS TRIBUNALS

NORTHERN IRELAND INDUSTRIAL COURT
REGISTERED HOMES TRIBUNAL
SCHEMES OF COMPENSATION FOR LOSS OF EMPLOYMENT THROUGH CIVIL
UNREST
SOCIAL SECURITY APPEALS TRIBUNALS

OTHER BODIES

ASSOCIATION OF LOCAL AUTHORITIES OF NORTHERN IRELAND
123 York Street
Belfast BT15 1AB
Telephone: 0232-249286
Secretary: R McKay

THE ISLE OF MAN

Chief Secretary: J F Kissack
Government Offices
Douglas IOM
Telephone: 0624-626262

Chief Financial Officer
The Treasury
Douglas IOM
Telephone: 0624-626262

CHANNEL ISLANDS

THE BAILIWICK OF GUERNSEY
States Supervisor: F N Le Cheminant
Sir Charles Frossard House
St Peter Port
Telephone: 0481-724411

Chief Executive Officer, Board of Administration: R T Kirkpatrick
Board of Administration
PO Box 43
Guernsey
Telephone: 0481-44104

ALDERNEY
Clerk of the States: D V Jenkins

SARK
Seneschal: L P de Carteret

HERM
Tenant Major: A G Wood

THE BAILIWICK OF JERSEY
Greffier of the States: R S Gray
States Offices
Telephone: 0534-73060

Treasurer, States: G Baird
States' Treasury
Cyril Le Marquand House
The Parade
St Helier
Telephone: 0534-79111

8
THE MISCELLANEOUS STATE

A map of the state has to include a variety of territories, small and large, which do not fit easily into the central land mass but are neither to be consigned to the outer regions. Without the collection of direct taxes undertaken by the Inland Revenue and of Value Added Tax, collected by HM Customs and Excise, the state could not function. Yet these are not fully fledged departments – they 'belong' to the Treasury, even if both enjoy a striking esprit de corps, extending to the wearing still of traditional uniforms and tricorn hats at Customs. A society that does not pay its taxes is not much of a society. 'To tax and to please, no more than to love and be wise, is not given to men', wrote Edmund Burke.

Important, in a different way, to the functioning of the state is the Metropolitan Police. Its constitution is idiosyncratic: its 'Authority' is the Home Secretary who appoints a Receiver and the Police Commissioner. But once in office he enjoys, with other chief constables, large operational autonomy and, uniquely, an opportunity to speak out not just on matters of criminal investigation and public order but urban affairs in general. The Metropolitan Police is home to the Special Branch, semi-autonomous in its operations, and which enjoys a special relationship with the Security Service, MI5.

But definitions are slippery. Is the Bank of England part of the state? The Chancellor of the Exchequer announced, to fanfare, that he was publishing minutes of his conversations with the Bank's governor – as if the latter were some sort of foreign potentate who could not be necessarily trusted to write up an accurate account for his people, the tribes of money dealers in the City. Is the Royal Household in and of the state? It subsists on the mixture of public money voted by Parliament and the private income of the monarch and her dependents, so the answer must be half and half.

And how do we classify the House of Commons and the other pieces of Parliament? The Houses of Parliament are the source of legislation and the controllers of the public purse. The have a small bureaucracy of their own. But do they not stand outside the executive state and monitor its activities? Members of

Parliament certainly ought to be the first if not the last port of call for all those anxious about what government is doing, yet they rarely are.

Here is an example. A new public-sector industry has grown up in recent years – regulation. As sectors have been sold off, as markets have been introduced into education, health and the social services, new regulators, watchdogs and auditing bodies have been created – to ensure that private interest is subordinate to public purpose. But what the Government has created is a jumble, a patchwork of sometimes overlapping regulatory responsibilities. There is no framework of accountability or co-ordination to control what the water regulator or the social housing regulator or the inspector of school standards or the auditors are doing. Who watches the watchdogs? Who regulates the regulators ?

Whitehall has no mechanism for collating the experience of, say, Ian Byatt, in charge of water prices and service with, say, Her Majesty's Chief Inspector of Schools, no way of comparing these different regulatory bodies or feeding back information to service providers, or the public. There exists no way in which the regulators can be checked or their performance compared one against another. Sir Bryan Carsberg, former director-general of the Office of Telecommunications, expressed his personal philosophy in saying 'As a regulator you have rather small resources compared to the industry you're regulating and in order to get a reasonable balance you have to be prepared to go out and take a rather energetic line.'

Above all, the question of who regulates the regulators remains unasked and unanswered. Professor Rudolf Klein of the University of Bath has argued for a National Regulatory Office – perhaps on the model of the National Audit Office – which might answer to a House of Commons Select Committee on Regulatory Regimes. Such a body – itself accountable to Parliament – could help solve the growing problem of regulating the regulators. But this solution requires Parliament, the House of Commons, to do two things it has found very difficult as the 20th century has progressed. One is to muster some real capacity to monitor, gather and analyse detailed information about government – in other words to professionalise itself by recruiting staff and expertise. The second, even more difficult, is for Members of Parliament occasionally to stand back from party allegiance and seek to put the higher interest (if there is one) of the nation and the public above sectional advantage.

The list of miscellaneous state bodies that follows is of course not exhaustive. It is intended to point only at functions which do not readily fall into the main categories. How do we delineate the tribe of Ombudspeople – its numbers recently augmented by the creation of Pensions Ombudsmen? Some of them can respond directly to the public's complaint. But with the main Ombudsman, the Parliamentary Commissioner for Administration, the public has to take a problem to an MP and thus approach the Ombudsman circuitously.

THE METROPOLITAN POLICE

New Scotland Yard
Broadway
London SW1H 0BG
Telephone: 071-230 1212

London has four-fifths of all terrorist offences, three-quarters of drugs offences. It is the site of most major fraud, has far more than its portion of murder and rape, suffers half the country's armed robberies. London is policed by one-fifth of the country's total number of police officers at an annual cost of £1.6 billion. Most is met by London councils, on which the Met makes a Home Office-approved precept; they then tack this on council tax bills. About 1 per cent of the Met's budget comes in the form of a special grant by the Home Office in recognition of the 'national' aspects of police work in London. In addition the Met provides a home for what is in effect a national police force, the Special Branch.

Commissioner: Sir Paul Condon. Educated: St Peter's College, Oxford. Joined the Metropolitan Police in 1967, rising to Inspector in 1975 and Superintendent at Bethnal Greeen in 1981. He was Chief Constable of the Kent Constabulary from 1989 to 1992.

Deputy Commissioner: Sir John Smith. Born: 1938. Educated: St Olav's and St Saviour's Grammar. Served in the Irish Guards and joined the Met in 1962. After heading the Scotland Yard Drugs Squad he moved to become Deputy Chief Constable of Surrey in 1981 and an Inspector of Constabulary in 1990.

Receiver: Graham Angel (Grade 2).

The Receiver is a relic from the days when an officer was needed to receive money from the parishes of London to pay for the force Sir Robert Peel established in 1829. Nowadays the Receiver is Scotland Yard's top civilian. The job combines several functions. It is the Receiver who supplies the Commissioner with buildings and equipment, on behalf of the Home Secretary. The Receiver carries Scotland Yard's annual bid for funds across the road to Queen Anne's Gate, where the Home Office is located. The Receiver has a right of access to the Home Secretary if he thinks financial propriety at the Yard is at stake.

THE INLAND REVENUE

Somerset House
London WC2R 1LB
Telephone: 071-438 6622

The Board of Inland Revenue collects and regulates income tax, together with such other direct taxes as stamp duty, petroleum revenue tax, capital gains and corporation tax. Its Valuation Agency is the principal source of property valuations, for example for the purpose of levying council tax. Unlike most other parts of the central state, Revenue inspectors are formally recognised to possess certain rights of independence. Although the Inland Revenue is technically a department of the Treasury answerable to the Chancellor, it enjoys operational autonomy and a distinct *esprit de corps*.

In 1992-3 the Revenue collected £76.1 billion in taxes and duties, the bulk of that in the form of Income Tax. Although National Insurance is a Department of Social Security responsibility, now delegated to an Executive Agency, most of the actual collection is done by the Inland Revenue. Corporation Tax, currently worth some £16 billion a year, is the other big money-spinner for the Revenue, and one of the most cost-effective in terms of how much it costs to collect each pound.

Some £4.6 billion resulted in 1992-3 from Revenue work on compliance – checking and chasing, equivalent to the yield from an increase of nearly three pence in the basic rate of income tax. In recent years great changes have been occurring in the Revenue's organisation, as it has sought to unify functions in single offices and prepare for more simplified ways of assessing tax obligations. Inland Revenue has set itself the target of producing 10,000 staff savings by the turn of the century. A new structure will underpin the introduction of Simplified Assessment for taxpayers from 1996-7.

Chairman of the Board of Inland Revenue: Sir Anthony Battishill (Grade 1). Born: 1937. Educated: Taunton School; Helen's School, Exeter; London School of Economics. Joined the Inland Revenue in 1960, moving to HM Treasury in 1963. After a secondment to the Central Policy Review Staff he moved from the Treasury to the Revenue to become first deputy then, in 1986, chairman of the Board.

SUBJECT DIVISIONS, STATISTICS AND ECONOMICS

Deputy Chairman of the Board: Clive Corlett (Grade 2). Born: 1938. Educated: Birkenhead School; Brasenose College, Oxford. Joined the Inland Revenue in 1960. Seconded to HM Treasury in 1972 and 1979 becoming Director, Inland Revenue in 1985.

Director, Personal Tax Division: Eugene McGivern. Born: 1938. Educated: St Mary's Grammar, Belfast. Joined Revenue 1955. He became Under-Secretary, Business Taxation Division in 1986.

Director, Capital and Valuation and Financial Institutions Division: Michael Cayley. Born: 1950. Educated: Brighton College; St John's College, Oxford. Joined Inland Revenue in 1973 becoming an Under-Secretary in 1991.

Director Statistics and Economic Office: Reginald Ward. Born: 1942. Educated: Leicester, Aberdeen and Oxford Universities. Joined the Inland Revenue in 1994 after a career embracing the private sector (NCL, ICL) and the state (Treasury, DTI) as an economist and statistician.

Director Savings and Investment Division: Brian Mace. Born: 1948. Educated: Maidstone Grammar; Caius College, Cambridge. Joined the Revenue 1973 becoming an Under-Secretary in 1990.

Principal Assistant Solicitor (legislation, charities, etc.): Douglas Johnston. Born: 1935. Educated: Manchester Grammar; Jesus College, Cambridge. Called to Bar 1963 and joined Revenue in 1968.

Principal Assistant Solicitor (personal, oil, etc.): Geoffrey Butt. Born: 1943; Educated: Royal Masonic School, Bushey; University of Reading. Qualified as a solicitor in 1970 then joining HM Customs. Moved to the Revenue in 1993.

Principal Assistant Solicitor (capital gains, avoidance): Algie Bates. Born: 1936. Educated: Kettering Grammar; St Catharine's College, Cambridge. After being called to the Bar joined the Inland Revenue in 1966.

Director, Quality Development: Keith Deacon. Born: 1935. Educated: Sutton County Grammar; Bristol University. Joined Revenue in 1962 later chairing the Civil Service Selection Board and becoming Director of Operations for the Revenue in 1991.

Director, Business Operations Division (BOD): Michael Johns. Born: 1946. Educated: Judd School, Tonbridge; Queens College, Cambridge. Joined the Revenue in 1967, becoming Director, Central Division in 1992.

Director-General, Principal Establishment Officer: Geoffrey Bush (Grade 2). Born: 1942. Educated: Cotham Grammar, Bristol. Joined Revenue 1973, becoming Director of Information Technology in 1990.

Director of Management Services Division (project director, Nottingham relocation): Neil Munro. Born: 1947. Educated: Wallasey Grammar; St John's College, Oxford. Joined Revenue 1970 becoming Deputy Director of Personnel in 1991.

Director, Company Tax Division: Peter Lewis. Born: 1937. Educated: Ealing Grammar; St Peter's Hall, Oxford. Inspector of Taxes 1960. Director, Personal Tax Division 1986.

Director, International Division: Ian Spence. Born: 1938. Educated: Dulwich College; Jesus College, Cambridge. Joined the Revenue in 1962; was seconded to the Department of Economic Affairs in 1966. He became an Assistant Secretary at the Revenue in 1975.

Director, Business Profits Division: John Gribbon. Born: 1943. Educated: Coleraine Academical Institution; University of London. Qualified as a Chartered Accountant, becoming an Inspector of Taxes in 1966 and Deputy Director of Operations (compliance) in 1989.

MANAGEMENT AND INFORMATION TECHNOLOGY: PERSONNEL ETC.

Deputy Chairman: Steve Matheson (Grade 2). Born: 1939. Educated: Aberdeen Grammar; Aberdeen University. Joined as HM Inspector of Taxes in 1961, serving in Private Office in 1976. He later became project manager for the computerisation of PAYE and director of information technology in 1984.

Director of Information Technology Office: John Yard. Born: 1944. Educated: St Marylebone Grammar. Joined the Revenue in 1963 becoming an Inspector in 1971. He became head of the Change Management Group in 1992.

Director of Personnel: John Gant. Born: 1944. Educated: University of Newcastle upon Tyne. Joined the Inland Revenue as an Inspector in 1966 becoming Deputy Director, Operations in 1990.

CENTRAL SUPPORT DIVISION: CHANGE MANAGEMENT ETC.

Director General: Geoffrey Bush (Grade 2). Joined as a Tax Officer in 1959, became an Inspector of Taxes in 1968 and thereafter worked as a District Inspector, Technical Specialist and Tax Policy Adviser. As an Under Secretary he first headed a central secretariat supporting the Board, then became Director of Information Technology. From January 1993 he led the team responsible for developing an IT Strategic Partnership.

Director, Change Management: Douglas Smith. Born: 1947. Educated: Leeds Central High School. Joined the Revenue in 1963 subsequently becoming Assistant Director, Information Technology and Change Management.

Principal Finance Officer: R Martin.

Solicitor of the Inland Revenue: Brian Cleave (Grade 2). Born: 1939. Educated: Exeter University. Joined the Revenue in 1967 becoming Principal Assistant Solicitor in 1986 and Solicitor four years later.

OFFICE OF POPULATION CENSUSES AND SURVEYS
St Catherine's House
10 Kingsway
London WC2B 6JP
Telephone: 071-242 0262

The Office of Population Censuses and Surveys is, for all its small size, a great office of state. The phrase 'Victorian values' has been prostituted in recent years as code for individualist private enterprise; some of the greatest monuments to the Victorian age are still with us, in the shape of habits of collective government intervention in the most intimate aspects of our lives – like births, deaths and marriages. OPCS enters the 1990s, gearing up for the 1991 Census and a large-scale reform of births, deaths and marriages registration, with its essential trustworthiness unimpaired. OPCS remains the centre of gravity of social statistics in the United Kingdom, its methods are state-of-the-art and its people well respected in academe and internationally. OPCS continues to supply interpretation and commentary on its figures. And that is no inconsiderable achievement at the end of decade of financial and political pressure. That OPCS escaped after it was surveyed critically in the early 1980s by a Rayner scrutiny team earned it the reputation in Whitehall as the 'one that got away'. As we write, discussions are going on about merging OPCS and the Central Statistical Office.

The office of Registrar-General, which doubles up with that of director of OPCS, is likewise a great office, symbolic – in the way the tax inspectorate is – of the legitimacy of the state's demands on British citizens and subjects.

Director and Registrar-General for England and Wales: Peter Wormald (Grade 2). Born: 1936. Educated: Doncaster Grammar; The Queen's College, Oxford. Ministry of Health 1958; HM Treasury 1965; Under-Secretary DHSS 1978.

Deputy-Director and Chief Medical Statistician: Dr John Fox. Born: 1946. Educated: Dauntsey's School; University College, London; Imperial College PhD. Statistician Employment Medical Advisory Service 1970; professor City University 1980.

Deputy Director and Director of Statistics: Eric Thompson. Born: 1934. Educated: Beverley Grammar; London School of Economics. Shell International; General Register Office; Greater London Council. Director of statistics, Department of Transport

---

HM CUSTOMS AND EXCISE
New King's Beam House
22 Upper Ground
London SE1 9PJ
Telephone: 071-620 1313

HM Customs and Excise exists to collect and administer certain indirect taxes, customs and Value Added Tax, which was introduced when Britain joined the European Community. Customs seeks to prevent the importation in the UK of a range of goods. It is responsible for the compilation of the overseas trade figures. A recent emphasis in its work has been accommodating new freedoms to trade and travel within the

327

EC's Single Market. In 1994-5 the estimated running costs of Customs and Excise were £762 million, of which £545 million went on staff pay. Customs was recently named Public Sector Employer of the Year by the Working Mothers Association.

In 1992-3, Customs raised £37.2 billion in VAT, just over £6 billion from tobacco duties and just over £5 billion for duties on alcoholic drink. Taxes on hydrocarbon oils raised over £11 billion. Customs' total take was nearly £63.5 billion.

Chairman: Valerie Strachan (Grade 1). Born: 1940. Educated: Newland High, Hull; Manchester University. Customs 1961; Department of Economic Affairs; Home Office. Customs Principal 1966; Head Joint Management Unit, Cabinet Office/HM Treasury 1985.

Deputy Chairman: Sandy Russell (Grade 2). Born: 1938. Educated: Royal High School, Edinburgh; Edinburgh University; Scottish Development Department, Scottish Office; Private Office; Civil Service Department 1976; Director, Organisation, Customs 1985.

CENTRAL DIRECTORATE (BUDGET AND PLANNING, STATISTICS, EU)

Commissioner and Director: Michael Eland. Born: 1952. Educated: Worksop College; Trinity College, Oxford. Called to Bar. HM Customs 1975; Cabinet Office 1982; Private Secretary to Lord President of Council 1987.

VAT CONTROL DIRECTORATE (REGISTRATION, RETURNS)

Commissioner and Director: Elisabeth Woods. Born: 1940. Educated: South Hampstead High School; Girton College, Cambridge. Ministry of Pensions; DHSS; HM Treasury 1980; Head of Finance at DSS in 1988.

CUSTOMS DIRECTORATE

Commissioner and Director: Martin Brown. Born: 1949. Educated: Bolton School; New College, Oxford. Customs 1971; Treasury Private Office; Barbados Government 1984.

Principal Establishments and Finance Officer (Deputy Chairman of the Board): Peter Jefferson Smith (Grade 2). Born: 1939. Educated: Trinity College, Cambridge. Joined Customs 1960.

PERSONNEL DIRECTORATE

Commissioner and Director: Dennis Battle. Born: 1942. Educated: Bedford Modern School. Customs 1962; became an Assistant Secretary in 1985.

ORGANISATION DIRECTORATE

Commissioner and Director: Richard Allen. Born: 1949. Educated: Loughborough Grammar; Merton College, Oxford. Joined Customs 1970; Private Office; Director Internal Taxes 1990.

OUTFIELD DIRECTORATE

Commissioner and Director: Anthony Sawyer. Born: 1939. Educated: Surrey. Insurance industry. Customs 1964; Collector, Edinburgh 1984

Solicitor: David Nissen (Grade 2). Born: 1942. Educated: King's School, Chester; University College, London. Solicitor; West Midlands Gas Board; Sussex Police; Customs 1973; legal adviser to Department of Energy.

Deputy Solicitor: R D S Wylie

Deputy Solicitor: G Fotherby

THE BANK OF ENGLAND
Threadneedle Street
London EC2R 8AH
Telephone: 071-601 4444

The Bank of England's former role as informal regulator of the banking system has shrunk. It retains some power as the note-issuer for the state and the regulator of credit – under the watchful eye of the Treasury.

The Bank is something like an executive agency of the Treasury, though its dignity and traditions would prevent that thought ever being expressed formally. In recent years, both Governors and Chancellors have been tempted by the idea of making the Bank formally independent, and giving it an explicit task: cutting inflation or maintaining price stability by controlling the supply of money and credit. The former Governor, Robin Leigh Pemberton, was not abashed at the principle of committing himself to cut inflation, and being appraised accordingly. Nor his successor Eddie George. But there is a large proviso. The Bank would need the operational and political freedom granted to central banks by both the New Zealand and American systems. That would mean the Treasury losing an instrument of control. But is independence for the Bank any different from, say, the way the Treasury says it is treating the Central Statistical Office in order to foster public confidence in its figures?

When Chancellor Nigel Lawson mooted the idea of cutting the Bank free, the then Prime Minister – Margaret Thatcher – used a telling phrase. Letting the Bank get on with monetary policy, she said, would involve 'abdicating responsibility'. So far her successor seems to agree and the Bank, though operationally autonomous, remains fixed under the skirts of the Treasury.

Governor: Eddie George. Born: 1938. Educated: Dulwich College; Emmanuel College, Cambridge. Joined the Bank in 1962 and has risen up the ranks. He has been seconded to the IMF and to the Bank for International Settlements. He became Deputy Chief Cashier in 1977 and Executive Director of the Bank in 1982.

Deputy Governor: Rupert Pennant-Rea. Born: 1948. Educated: Peterhouse, Zimbabwe; Trinity College, Dublin; Manchester University. Worked for a trade union then the Bank of England before joining *The Economist* newspaper in 1977 and later becoming its editor.

THE NATIONAL AUDIT OFFICE
157-197 Buckingham Palace Road
Victoria
London SW1W 9SP
Telephone: 071-798 7000

One of the most striking aspects of the National Audit Office is physical: for a department concerned with rooting out waste and extravagance it occupies oddly grandiloquent headquarters, in the former British Airways terminal in Victoria. The Comptroller-General's is an old office. He answers to the Members of the House of Commons appointed to the Public Accounts Committee on the economy, efficiency and effectiveness of public spending and in turn the PAC can call the custodians of public money – for example permanent secretaries in Whitehall departments – to account. The NAO provides him with reports and analysis on the accounts of government departments. In principle the NAO's budget is the responsibility of another Parliamentary body, the National Accounts Commission, though the Treasury takes a close interest in what NAO staff are paid and how many there are.

The NAO is supposed to chase every penny allocated by Parliament in public expenditure. In practice it shares auditing tasks with the Audit Commission and a variety of other public auditors. Not all NAO reports are followed up by the MPs on the PAC; not all are published and some are the subject of fierce internal debates before they are. Running the NAO during 1994-5 is estimated to cost £36.5 million.

Comptroller and Auditor General: Sir John Bourn. Born: 1934. Educated: Southgate County Grammar; London School of Economics PhD. Air Ministry. HM Treasury. Civil Service College, Ministry of Defence. Northern Ireland Office. Deputy Under-Secretary of State MoD (defence procurement).

Deputy Controller and Auditor General: Robert Le Marechal. Born: 1939. Educated: Tauntons School, Southampton; Exchequer and Audit Department 1957. Director of Audit, E&AD.

Assistant Auditor General (corporate, personnel, information technology): M Pfleger.

Assistant Auditor General (agriculture, home affairs, transport, revenue, etc.): David Dewar. Born: 1934. Educated: Leith Academy. Exchequer and Audit Department, 1953; Director of Audit 1977.

Assistant Auditor General (health, social security etc): J Marshall.

Assistant Auditor General (estates management, overseas, Scotland): John Higgins. Born: 1940. Educated: Hendon County School; Hastings Grammar; Exchequer and Audit Department 1958; chief auditor 1977; Canadian Government 1983.

Assistant Auditor General (defence, education, trade): Lewis Hughes. Born: 1945. Educated: Devonport High School for Boys; City of London College; Exchequer and Audit Dept 1963.

OMBUDSMEN
PARLIAMENTARY COMMISSIONER FOR ADMINISTRATION
Church House
Great Smith Street
London SW1P 3BW
Telephone: 071-276 3000
(**enquiries Telephone**: 071-276 2130)

The PCA was an invention of the 1960s, when the Scandinavian term was borrowed. In fact the Commissioner has no direct relationship with the public; complaints have to be referred to him by Members of Parliament. His remit is maladministration by government departments and certain public bodies. Many of the institutions of the 'New State' are not covered.

Under recent government plans to open up more official information, the Ombudsman will deal with appeals by members of the public who feel they have been refused access in contravention of the Code of Practice on Government Information.

Commissioner (Ombudsman): William Reid (Grade 1). Born: 1931. Educated: Robert Gordon's College; University of Edinburgh; Trinity College, Cambridge. Ministry of Education 1956; Cabinet Office 1964; Accountant General, Department of Education and Science; Deputy Secretary Scottish Office 1978.

Deputy Commissioner: John Avery. Born: 1940. Educated: Plymouth College, Leeds University. Called to Bar; Board of Trade; Office of Fair Trading.

HEALTH SERVICE COMMISSIONERS
Church House
Great Smith Street
London SW1P 3BW
Telephone: 071-276 3000
(**enquiries Telephone:** 071-276 2130)

The HSC is responsible for investigating complaints lodged directly by members of the public against NHS authorities that are not dealt with by them to the satisfaction of the complainant.

Commissioner: William Reid.

Deputy Commissioner: Richard Oswald. Born: 1941. Educated: The Leys School, Cambridge. National Health Service administration. District Administrator Leeds West 1977.

PENSIONS OMBUDSMAN
11 Belgrave Road
London SW1V 1RB
Telephone: 071-834 9144

This office was created under the Social Security Act 1990 to deal with complaints against employers and other providers of occupational and providers of personal pensions. No fee is charged by the Ombudsman who aspires to act as an impartial adjudicator.

Ombudsman: Dr Julian Farrand

PRISON OMBUDSMAN
(address to be confirmed)

This new post is intended to provide a source of recommendations and advice to the Prison Service and Home Secretary on the basis of his experience investigating prisoners' grievances – with the exception of complaints about prison medical staff's clinical judgements and the Home Secretary's discretion over release dates.

Prison Ombudsman: Sir Peter Woodhead. Born: 1939. Educated: Leeds Grammar; Royal Naval College, Dartmouth; pilot, aircraft carriers; director Naval Ops 1985.

REVENUE ADJUDICATOR
3rd Floor
Haymarket House
Haymarket
London SW1Y 4SP
Telephone: 071-930 2292

The Adjudicator responds to complaints about the way the Inland Revenue treats tax-payers' affairs and makes recommendations to the Inland Revenue about settlements.

Revenue Adjudicator: Elizabeth Filkin. Born: 1940. Educated: Birmingham University. Lecturer National Institute for Social Work; Chief Executive National Association of Citizens' Advice Bureaux. Director of Community Services, London Docklands Development Corporation.

OFFICE OF THE SOCIAL SECURITY AND CHILD SUPPORT COMMISSIONERS
Harp House
83 Farringdon Street
London EC4A 4DH
Telephone: 071-353 5145

The Commissioner is the final point of appeal to decide claims and complaints to do with social security, child benefit, child support, industrial injury benefits.

Chief Commissioner: His Honour Judge Machin QC. Born: 1936. Educated: St Albans School. Called to the Bar. Crown Court Recorder 1979.

COMMISSION FOR LOCAL ADMINISTRATION IN ENGLAND
21 Queen Anne's Gate
London SW1H 9BU
Telephone: 071-915 3210

Under the Local Government Act 1974 the Commissioner investigates complaints from members of the public about injustice caused by maladministration in local government.

Secretary: Gordon Adams.

Commissioners: (Chairman) Edward Osmotherley. Born: 1942. Educated: East Ham Grammar; Fitzwilliam College, Cambridge. Ministry of Housing. Harkness Fellow; Assistant Secretary, Department of the Environment; Head of machinery of government division, Civil Service Department 1980; Deputy Secretary Department of Transport.

Patricia Thomas. Born: 1940. Educated: King's College, London. Head of School of Law Lancashire Polytechnic 1973.

(The appointment of a third commissioner is pending.)

THE QUEEN'S HOUSEHOLD
Buckingham Palace
London SW1A 1AA
Telephone: 071-930 4832
Private Secretary: Sir Robert Fellowes. Born: 1941. Educated: Eton. Served Scots Guards. Director, Allen Harvey and Ross Ltd. Assistant Private Secretary to the Queen, 1977.

THE HOUSE OF LORDS
Parliament Office
House of Lords
Westminster
London SW1A 0PW
Telephone: 071-219 3000
Chairman of Committees: The Lord Ampthill
Secretary (Grade 4): B P Keith

THE HOUSE OF COMMONS
Westminster
London SW1A 0AA
Telephone: 071-219 3000
Clerk of the House of Commons (Grade 1): Sir Clifford Boulton. Born: 1930. Educated: Newcastle under Lyme High School; St John's College, Oxford. House of Commons Clerk 1953.

THE CHURCH OF ENGLAND
Church House
Great Smith Street
London SW1P 3NZ
Telephone: 071-222 9011

THE GENERAL SYNOD OF THE CHURCH OF ENGLAND
Church House
Great Smith Street
London SW1P 3NZ
Telephone: 071-222 9011

The General Synod consists of a House of Bishops, a House of Clergy and a House of Laity. It meets twice a year and legislates for the Church's internal affairs – but under rules laid down in statute law, for example the Church of England Assembly (Powers) Act 1919.

Secretary General: Philip Mawer. Born: 1947. Educated: Hull Grammar; Edinburgh University. Joined Home Office 1971, served in Private Office 1987; moved to Cabinet Office as Under-Secretary 1989 becoming Secretary General in 1990.

Presidents: The Archbishop of Canterbury, Rt Rev George Carey. Address: Lambeth Palace London SE1 7JU and The Old Palace, Canterbury, Kent CT1 2EE. Born: 1935. Educated Bifrons Secondary Modern; London University; London College of Divinity. Lecturer; later vicar in Durham; principal of theological college; Bishop of Bath and Wells 1987.

The Archbishop of York, The Most Rev and Rt Hon John Habgood. Address: Bishopthorpe Palace, Bishopthorpe, York YO2 1QE. Born: 1927. Educated Eton; King's College, Cambridge; Cuddesdon Theological College. Was vice-principal Westcot House Theological College, Rector in Jedburgh; Bishop of Durham 1973.

THE CHURCH COMMISSIONERS
1 Millbank
London SW1P 3JZ
Telephone: 071-222 7010
Secretary: Patrick Locke
Chairman: The Archbishop of Canterbury

9
CONCLUSION

Is the British state healthy? The answer depends on whether the patient is taken to be the public, serviced and regulated by the state, or the state's servants, whether elected or appointed. So far as the first of these groups is concerned – the public – interest in, let alone knowledge of, the systems by which it is ruled is slight at best. For most people – tax payers, benefit receivers, voters – the extent to which the state is judged healthy is determined simply by the efficiency by which the state delivers its services. The management regime which regulates these services is of marginal interest at most. The creation of Next Steps Agencies, to take just one obvious example, has barely broken the skin of public awareness

And yet perhaps there is some evidence of anxiety that as the state devolves more and more of its role to outside bodies, so this new government at arm's length, because necessarily less responsive to the traditional processes of democratic control, is becoming necessarily less accountable. However appealing the theory of the state adapting itself to the rigours of the market may seem, few would suggest that the state should – indeed could – become, for example, no more than Marks and Spencer under a different name.

William Waldegrave, then Minister for Public Services, made a speech in late 1993 in which he tried to feel his way round these questions. Is there a 'democratic deficit' in the public sector, he asked? He listed the arguments of those who contend there is:

(a) that the government's reforms have transferred power to appointed and unaccountable trusts and quangos;

(b) that far from increasing the control of individuals over public services, the reforms have reduced it;

(c) that in the Civil Service, the creation of Next Steps Agencies has undermined ministerial responsibility and affected the capacity of Parliament to hold public officials to account.

The solution to this 'crisis' is usually given as two-fold:

(a) power should be given to local authorities;

(b) a wide range of legally binding rights, responsibilities and constitutions should be established.

But this analysis, said the minister, was wrong. Accountability has not been lost but gained: executive agencies are not independent organisations, they are fully accountable to Parliament through ministers. Once appointed, chief executives in agencies are civil servants, with a clearly defined independence in operational matters which, by simplifying and making more explicit the division between policy and executive, provides MPs with a faster and more complete service.

The amount of information available to Parliament has accordingly been increased. In education, for example, the creation of grant-maintained schools must be taken in tandem with the implementation of a National Curriculum enabling parents to see more clearly how teachers and schools are performing. As a result, more information is available to parents, allowing them to make better-informed decisions about their children's education. In parallel, says the Government, the NHS reforms have retained the Secretary of State's ultimate responsibility to Parliament for the service as a whole, but when there are problems in an individual hospital it is the chairman or chief executive of the trust board who must solve them.

The key point according to the Government is not whether those who run public services are elected, but whether they are producer- or consumer-responsive. Services cannot necessarily be made more responsive to the public simply by giving citizens a democratic voice in their make-up. It is this that underpins Prime Minister John Major's initiative to offer the public a set of charters – written documents containing statements of how services are to be provided without spelling out how much should be provided or at what cost.

So is the argument that consumer consciousness can somehow replace civic spirit? Who, for example, is to decide how much is spent on a service – the consumer who receives it or the taxpayer who funds it ? The Benefits Agency may have refurbished its local offices and started treating its claimants in a much more civilised fashion but the big political question remains: how much are the citizenry at large willing to see transferred to the poor and to pensioners by way of income support? Are there not real limits, too, to applying the idea of 'consumption' to many public services? Take crime. The public's main consumerist demand of the police is that they stop or clear up crime. But experts, including the police, consistently resist measures to calibrate their effectiveness: crime, it is said, answers to too great a variety of other factors. Consumerism applied to the police means policemen treating the public with consideration and politeness. Such behaviour may go some way towards reassuring the public but it remains essentially cosmetic and does little or nothing to reduce anxiety, whether or not it is deserved, about increasing crime rates.

Consumers rarely worry about who the chairman of Marks and Spencer is. But someone has to appoint the Chairman of the Health Authority or the members of a Training and Enterprise Council. Those appointments are made by ministers or officials who, in theory, are answerable to voters in the political system. And is there anything wrong with a politically driven public service? Behind the new managerial emphases in the public service, some people have detected a contempt for the messiness, the untidiness, the compromising nature of politics. They have seen something corporatist, perhaps even authoritarian, behind much of the new managerialist thinking.

Moreover, consumerism has shown itself ineffective in controlling public bodies. Recent years have witnessed the rise of what some have called an 'audit' culture – the creation and expansion of organisations providing a checking mechanism, especially of money. One unresolved tension in the creation of the 'new state' has been how far the centre can allow the periphery to go its own way when the centre, above all the Treasury, wants control not just of financial aggregates but of the actual disbursement in wages and salaries, capital spending and so on.

But can auditors substitute for the public in calling spenders of public money to account? Auditors tend to be called in only once the horse has bolted. What point is there in their locking the stable door, however expertly? Is there not anyway a contradiction between giving managers more head room while simultaneously tightening the accounting shackles around their ankles?

Alongside the increasing use of auditors has come substantial spending on another breed of professional: management consultants. Since the 1980s the belief has grown that if private firms of management consultants have the key to success in the private sector that key could be turned to equal effect in public locks, too. It is a view that is spreading fast. In 1992 and 1993, the Department of Education, for example, employed consultants to advise on the preparation of colleges for independence; data collection; the finances of the Royal Academy of Dramatic Art; and pensions payments options for teachers. The cost? £2.39 million. In similar initiatives in 1993 and 1994, the Cabinet Office employed Andersen Consulting to assess the Mark Charter, Coopers and Lybrand were commissioned to study the management of supercomputing and Ernst and Young to report on the future of the Government Telecommunications Network. These are merely a handful of examples among many. But how necessary were these operations? Were they value for money? Has the Government simply been seduced by what many claim is the surface lure of management consultancy, a lucrative but ultimately unmeasurable activity whose principal effect is no more than to make those employing the consultants feel good? Why should the state need to turn to such highly paid advisers? Convincing answers have yet to be provided. During 1994 the auditors began to stir themselves to look at the amounts spent on consultants. In a report the Audit Commission noted that much of the £120 million a year being spent on management consultancy by local and health authorities was imperfectly accounted for: too many contracts were let without tenders; there was insufficient follow-up and scant evaluation of how much value consultants added.

The Efficiency Unit reported that up to £65 million a year was being spent unnecessarily by Whitehall and central government agencies on consultants. It recommended that, perhaps in the Department of Trade, a central brokerage be set up to monitor contracts let to consultants and – where necessary – pass on critical judgements of their performance.

How much further have the changes in the organisation of the state recorded in this book to run? At least some Conservative ministers are prepared to admit privately that the government sector is at best bloated, at worst that large areas of it are entirely unnecessary. Though even the most doctrinaire concedes that there is an irreducible core to the state, they argue none the less that further privatisation is essential before a new equilibrium between public and private sectors can be struck. Yet such a development remains tantalisingly out of reach. Even as one arm of the state is amputated, another grows. As the state evolves, so it assumes ever more responsibilities. New functions are found, new organisations created. Take the Millenium Fund, the nine-strong commission chaired by the Secretary for National Heritage, and which will receive around 20 per cent of the proceeds of the National Lottery. Neither the Fund, the Secretary of National Heritage nor the Lottery were even dreamed of five years ago.

The position is complicated further by the distance between citizen and government. True, the Government has made moves to 'bring the public back in' by recruiting ordinary people into public service, generally part-time. A recent example was the announcement by the Lord Chancellor that the public is to be invited to play some new role in the supervision of judicial appointments. Similarly, in October 1991 Prime Minister Margaret Thatcher asked her Cabinet colleagues to take a close look at the record of their departments in the appointment of women and members of ethnic minorities to public bodies. But although nomination forms are available from the Public Appointments Unit in the Cabinet Office there is little sign that the lay service of state is really being extended. The Public Appointments Unit oversees some 42,000 appointments to public bodies. Yet its database of members of the public at the end of 1993 numbered only 5,000. Of these 38 per cent had nominated themselves, 32 per cent had come via Government departments, and the rest from personal recommendations from professional organisations or MPs and ministers.

There is an unfinished agenda right at the centre of the state, too. Why is the central machinery apparently so inept at delivering co-ordinated policy initiatives which span the departments? Since the abolition of the Central Policy Review Staff, the core of the state possesses no formal means of thinking for itself. The mechanism of Cabinet Committees, co-ordinated through the Cabinet Office, often seems singularly ineffective in delivering 'difficult' policies. Again, crime provides a case in point. The causes and prevention of crime along with the detection and punishment of criminals are questions which involve several departments and which need to be addressed in detail and over time. There are other social issues of this kind – for example, the obligations of fathers and the responsibility of parents. To touch them, the state needs sophisticated policy tools which more than one department must wield and which will work only with patience and a willingness to take the long view. Yet this fundamental capacity seems lacking. One of the great questions of the decade thus becomes what the state, however it is organised, can do to affect, let alone to redirect, social trends.

Meanwhile if lower down the tree civil servants can transform themselves into more effective managers, more responsive to consumer pressures, more 'market-orientated',

338

shouldn't similar reflexes be built in among the higher branches? Why is it, some people ask, no proper job description exists for the Permanent Secretaries? Who are their 'clients'? What criteria should be brought to bear to measure their performance? And as the state changes, is there not a danger that continuity at the centre is lost, that civil servants lose their sense of a wider public interest? As the Scott Inquiry into the supply of defence equipment to Iraq was unfolding in 1993 and 1994, questions were asked about the public-service ethic. Is it any more than one of obedience to the departmental line or the wishes of ministers? Some have broadened the question to ask what public service amounts to in modern Britain. No one asks the executives of Marks and Spencer to do more than seek to maximise their earnings by delivering a commercial service. What more should be asked of public-sector executives? Do they need a conscience, or a special morality that might, for example, empower them occasionally to say to the ministers or appointed chairmen they serve that there is a higher interest and that they will not carry out their commands?

This question has been posed most starkly in terms of telling the whole truth and nothing but the truth to Parliament. If, as the Conservative government has argued, Parliament is the main, indeed the only, locus of accountability then it is surely necessary that Parliament knows all. But during the Scott affair, it became clear just how little Parliament does know of the workings of the executive state and thus how incapable Members of Parliament are as the ultimate 'managers' of the public sector.

But here again there are countervailing trends. The old doctrine of Official Secrecy has been rescinded. The security and intelligence services are much more open than they were. Even MI5 now considers it has need of the services of a public relations officer. Under the Code of Practice promulgated by William Waldegrave in 1994 in his capacity as Minister for Open Government, swathes of information about what (domestic) departments of state are doing should become more easily accessible, though it may take a sustained campaign and some precedent-setting appeals to the Ombudsman (whom the Government wants to adjudicate if departments withhold information) actually to see the new material in the bright light of day. An important step in opening up hidden decision-making was taken by Chancellor of the Exchequer Kenneth Clarke with his decision to publish minutes of key meetings between the Treasury and the Bank of England on monetary policy. His argument was functional: greater openess could only help financial markets and thus smooth fluctuations.

And yet it is often not so much material contained in a file that needs to be exposed to scrutiny as the processes by which the state holds itself together. How is the chairman of a health agency appointed? Who decides – and how – how much a grant-maintained school is to receive by way of recurrent grant or permission to spend on capital works? Why was this man rather than that one preferred as the new Permanent Secretary of the Department of the Environment? What was the basis of the decision? Who attended the committee meeting (the Senior Appointments Selection Committee) where it was taken? Various people can seek to ask the questions – in the press, in Parliament – but ultimately it will be perhaps only public dissatisfaction with the products of the system which will guarantee they get answered.

Is a new ethic needed for the public service in Britain as it moves towards the 21st century? 'I for one', said Stephen Dorrell, now Secretary for the National Heritage, 'would be wholly opposed to any change which undermined the enviable reputation of British civil servants for integrity and political independence.' But that reputation might need to be sacrificed in order to accommodate the new state and its managerial ethos. How is it possible to retain some higher idealism for public-sector work while suggesting, subtly or otherwise, that in most cases the private market works better to secure the happiness and well-being of mankind – and thus by implication that the public sector is at best a residual or marginal category? What price ethics then?

The big question remains unanswered. Can the idealism of public service be reinvigorated or has it been tainted beyond hope of recovery by the irresistible combination of the last decade's management changes and the inevitable arrogance bequeathed by 15 years of unbroken rule? It is hard to avoid the feeling that the answer is no. Everywhere one turns, in central as much as in local government, in the appointed bodies and quasi-government, it is difficult to escape the sense that something has been lost. How do we recover a sense of identity and purpose? Where is the irreducible core?

There are two problems. One is what, at heart, a renewed philosophy of public service should aim to achieve. The other is who is best placed to attempt to voice the new synthesis – for who would deny that some of what has happened since the 1980s by way of changes in managerial styles and organisational purposes should not be retained?

It would be idle to pretend it is going to be easy to sum up what public service amounts to in the 1990s. There is, for example, the vexed problem of 'the people'. We need to go back to Walter Lippmann or even James Bryce and think again about the shibboleths of democracy. The Conservative government has made much of the public's right to choose. But who is to be allowed to assert, for example, that if the public says it wants the ends it has none the less failed to will the means; or, as the Local Government Commission has found, that the public's ostensible choices are incoherent and contradictory?

How far is it up to public managers in health, Whitehall or local government at least occasionally to stand up and say to their masters the politicians – and through them the people – that there is a public interest that goes wider than a specific vote in a specific election – and wider still than the doctrine that ministers or councillors or appointed chairmen and women are always right, whatever idiocy they are preaching?

INDEX

341

359